American Foreign Policy
Since World War II

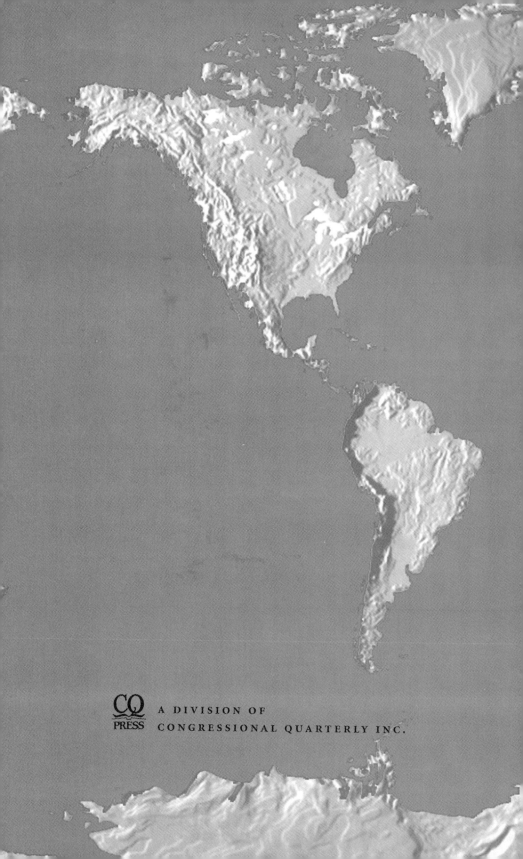

CQ A DIVISION OF
PRESS CONGRESSIONAL QUARTERLY INC.

American Foreign Policy Since World War II

THIRTEENTH EDITION

JOHN SPANIER
University of Florida

STEVEN W. HOOK
University of Missouri

Book and cover design: Kachergis Book Design, Pittsboro, North Carolina

Cover photo credits, clockwise from top right: National Archives, UPI/Bettmann, *Washington Post,* Reagan Presidential Library, Reuters, Bush Presidential Materials Project, R. Michael Jenkins, Library of Congress. *Interior photo credits:* 1 Kennedy Presidential Library, 21 National Archives, 47 Library of Congress, 74 UPI/Bettmann, 101 World Bank, 129 AP/Wide World Photos, 150 UPI/Bettmann, 174 *Washington Post,* 197 Reagan Presidential Library, 226 Reuters/Bettmann, 254 Reuters, 291 Alex S. MacLean.

Library of Congress Cataloging-in-Publication Data
Spanier, John
      American foreign policy since World War II / John Spanier, Steven W. Hook. -- 13th ed.
          p.   cm.
      Includes bibliographical references and index.
      ISBN 0-87187-819-4
      1. United States--Foreign relations--1945-1989.   2. United States--Foreign relations--1989-   I. Hook, Steven W., 1959-   .
      II. Title.
      E744.S8   1995
      327.73'009'045--dc20

95-6691
CIP

To Suzy and Debra-Lynn

Contents

Maps

Preface

It is said that the United States is good at winning wars and losing the peace that follows. This aphorism, the product of American setbacks after the Spanish-American War and the two world wars, may apply to the Cold War as well. America emerged as the world's preeminent power after its struggle against the Soviet Union, yet widespread expectations of a peaceful international order were quickly swept away by a succession of regional crises. The United States has been thrust into many of these crises, often taking a leadership role in seeking their resolution. But its leaders, shorn of their Cold War mission, have been unable to articulate a new, overriding basis for the country's foreign policy. In its absence, U.S. actions have been tentative, spasmodic, and internally divisive.

The search for a new guiding principle for America's role in world politics is the context for the thirteenth edition of *American Foreign Policy since World War II*, which first appeared at the peak of the Cold War. This edition marks a departure from the previous twelve in several respects. While its central themes remain intact, its scope has widened from the Cold War to the war's turbulent aftermath in the mid-1990s. In keeping with this edition's broader objective, the description and analysis of the Cold War years have been condensed, and the treatment of these sections has been modified to consider the issues, problems, and patterns of American foreign policy behavior since the Soviet Union's abrupt collapse. The book features a new design, updated maps, and an expanded bibliography to complement the revised text. Finally, this volume marks the arrival of Steven W. Hook, the first coauthor in the book's long history.

After the Soviet implosion in late 1991, no immediate and overwhelming security threat confronted the United States; its most pressing problem was its relative economic decline and loss of competitiveness in the expanding world economy. Under these circumstances, was it indeed time for the country to withdraw from the world and concentrate on reviving the economy and solving the many domestic problems that had accumulated during the Cold War years? Or should the United States, as the sole remaining superpower, stay active and truly make the world "safe for democracy" now that it was no longer constrained by any countervailing power? Indeed, given its enormous strength, did the United States not have some moral obligation to end the spreading civil wars and regional crises? As foreign policy analyst Leslie Gelb observed in *Foreign Affairs* in late 1994,

> If we fail to ameliorate and check this scourge, both the victims and the unpunished killers will undo much of what we value and undermine efforts to mold a just and stable international order. Without such an order, there can be little hope to tend the planet, nurture more tolerant societies, sustain economic progress, or contain the perilous spread of military and nuclear power. . . . The failure to deal with such strife, and to do something about mass murder and genocide, corrodes the essence of a democratic society.[1]

Critics of this view believed that the United States should ignore this alleged moral imperative, intervening only where its strategic and material interests were at stake. In fact, a large body of public opinion favored this response, which found expression in the midterm elections of November 1994 that placed the Republican Party in control of both houses of Congress for the first time since 1952. The failure in the 1990s of humanitarian interventions in Somalia and Bosnia strengthened the case of many traditional realists that foreign policy divorced from national interest was irrational, and that military action that relied on the shared interests and coordinated responses of many great powers was doomed to failure. Adherents of this view favored increased military spending in the 1990s but insisted that the better-equipped U.S. armed forces respond only to clear threats to the country's national security.

This debate between the so-called moralists and realists is not new. It has its roots in America's "national style," which is influenced by its geographic position, historic experience, economic system, and political values. In fact, every nation-state has its particular way of seeing the world and defining its own role in it. In America's case, its national style has led the country to sway between isolationism in peacetime and moral crusading in wartime. From 1812 until World War I the United States remained detached from great-power politics, which meant the diplomacy of the "Old World" in Western Europe. Not until after World War II, when it was confronted by the Soviet Union's formidable threat, did the United States accept an ongoing role as a great power in peacetime as well as at war. But unlike in the world wars, a protracted, low-intensity global struggle characterized America's policy of communist containment.

America's conduct during this period is examined in this book for two reasons. First, it reveals important lessons about the nation's foreign policy style and how it is influenced by long-standing cultural values, by the perceptions of its leaders and their definition of the enemy, and by the inescapable

---

1. Leslie Gelb, "Quelling the Teacup Wars," *Foreign Affairs* (November/December 1994): 2.

demands posed by the volatile international system. In short, a careful examination of this period reveals how America behaves as a superpower. And it presents an opportunity to contrast its behavior during the Cold War with that of the distant past—and with the rhetoric and declared intentions of its leaders.

The second reason is that many international problems in the mid-1990s are legacies of the Cold War. U.S. foreign policy continues to bear its imprint in many important respects, including the structure and global deployment of its armed forces, the scope of its alliances, the ongoing tensions in many former "theaters" of superpower conflict, and the recurring disputes between the White House and Congress over war powers, intelligence gathering, and defense spending. Strong anti-American sentiment lingers in many parts of the world, finding expression in terrorist bombings, the spread of weapons of mass destruction, and the continuation of civil wars that once were often inflamed by both Cold War combatants.

In this respect many events that took place in the wake of the Cold War, including the Gulf War against Iraq, probably would not have occurred had the Cold War continued. Iraq, as a Soviet client state, would have been restrained from invading Kuwait in 1990 because of the danger of a clash between the United States and the Soviet Union. The collapse of the Soviet Union, however, freed regionally ambitious leaders like Saddam Hussein to pursue their expansionist goals. Ironically, if the Gulf War was a direct result of the Cold War's end, the U.S.-led victory in that war was a direct result as well. Unlike in Korea or Vietnam, where the United States was restrained by the fear of escalation of a "limited war," in the Gulf War, Washington did not have to be concerned about the possibility of Soviet intervention on the side of Iraq. A quick victory instead of protracted hostilities was the outcome.

In the late 1990s and into the next century, the fate of Russia and Eastern Europe will undoubtedly affect the United States, as will the search for a new collective security system in Western Europe, the former Soviet Union, and East Asia. The rationale for the North Atlantic Treaty Organization (NATO) was predictably blurred after the collapse of the adversary for which it was created. Cracks in the alliance were further widened by NATO's failure to intervene effectively in the Balkan conflict and its efforts to expand the alliance to include such Eastern European states as Poland and Hungary, which ruptured relations between the NATO states and Russia, producing a "Cold Peace," in the words of Russian president Boris Yeltsin.[2] The United Nations, meanwhile, has proven to be only as effective as the collective interests of the

2. For a related analysis, see Zbigniew Brzezinski, "A Plan for Europe," *Foreign Affairs* (January/February 1995): 26–42.

states contributing troops to its peace-keeping missions. In the cases of Bosnia and Somalia these collective interests have proven to be elusive.

Although America's current ambivalence toward foreign affairs is not unique to this period, its global stature is. The U.S. military has largely retained its global deployments, and its arsenal of conventional and nuclear weapons is by far the world's largest. The U.S. economy, having withstood a resurgence of foreign competition, still produces nearly twice the volume of goods and services of those of its closest rivals. And, despite constant domestic upheavals, America's political values and institutions, as well as its outlets of cultural expression, are widely emulated overseas. Thus in terms of both conventional power resources and the increasingly important areas of "soft power" (to use Joseph Nye's phrase[3]), the United States maintains a level of global predominance that has few historical precedents.

But global predominance aside, American leaders face a wide range of problems—ethnic revanchism, economic dislocation, the crisis of "failed states"—in the final years of the twentieth century. Under the faltering Clinton administration these leaders have become increasingly divided, and the Republican-led Congress has become increasingly assertive. How can students of U.S. foreign policy get a better grip on these problems? That will require understanding the central themes of American foreign policy and America's global experience since World War II. Better equipped, they can then fully participate in the revived debate on America's current and future role in the rapidly changing international system.

We wish to extend our continuing gratitude to CQ Press. Special thanks are also due to two individuals who have made extraordinary contributions to this edition: Brenda Carter, who has been consistently enthusiastic and supportive of this enterprise, and Sabra Bissette Ledent, whose meticulous attention to detail, skillful editing, mastery of prose, and diplomatic talent in managing two coauthors with sometimes differing views contributed enormously to the organization, substance, and readability of this edition. Responsibility for the interpretation of the dilemmas confronting contemporary American foreign policy and the perspective through which they should be seen rests, of course, with the authors.

3. Joseph S. Nye, Jr., *Bound to Lead* (New York: Basic Books, 1990), chap. 6.

In his historic speech in 1963 in West Berlin, President John Kennedy re-affirmed the close relationship between the United States and its European allies.

CHAPTER ONE

The American Approach to Foreign Policy

The end of the Cold War was supposed to usher in a new era of peace and harmony. With the collapse of communism in the Soviet Union, the disintegration of the Soviet Union's Warsaw Pact alliance, and the fragmentation of the Soviet Union itself into many republics, the wave of the future appeared to be Western democracy. And since democracies reputedly were peaceful in their behavior toward other democracies, peace appeared to be secure.

This spread of peace would be reinforced by the growing economic inter-dependence among nations, a sign of the emerging global economy. Since every nation's prosperity now depended on everyone else's, a nation that sought to isolate itself from the growing webs of interdependence would harm itself economically. More important, in a world in which a nation's economic welfare depended on maintaining good economic relations with other nations, no nation could pursue a course of political aggressiveness and expansion, let alone use force, without hurting itself. Political restraint, moderation in foreign policy, prudence, and conciliation would be the advisable policies for any nation. And, not to be forgotten, just as the fear of a nuclear holocaust had kept the Cold War cold, so the danger of a military clash igniting a nuclear conflagration would keep the new world peaceful, at least among the great powers, which had started and fought two world wars and conducted the forty-five-year-long Cold War.

But these expectations have hardly been met. The Soviet Union and the United States had barely declared the Cold War over when Iraq's ruler, Saddam Hussein, invaded neighboring Kuwait and threatened the other oil kingdoms of the Persian Gulf. In January 1991 the United States and several other countries went to war in the Persian Gulf to force the Iraqis out of Kuwait and protect the oil wells on which their industries depended so heavily. A few months later the Soviet Union disappeared from the map as the Baltic republics regained the independence they had lost in 1940 and the other twelve republics that had formerly constituted the Soviet Union declared their independence and sovereignty as they all sought to shake off Moscow's long dictatorial dominance. As the Soviet grip on Eastern Europe loosened, the ethnic rivalries that had for so long been suppressed by Soviet occupation and hegemony resurfaced. In the months that followed, Czechoslovakia peacefully broke up into the Czech and the Slovak republics. Yugoslavia was not so fortunate. Its breakup was cataclysmic as the dominant Serbs, who had helped to start World War I with the assassination of the visiting Austrian Archduke Franz Ferdinand, renewed their quest for a Greater Serbia. The world stood by in horror, but nevertheless passively, as the Serbs proceeded with the "ethnic cleansing" of the former Yugoslavia, especially in Bosnia-Herzegovina with its majority population of Muslims.

In the African state of Somalia the government vanished with the end of the Cold War, leading to a violent struggle for power among different clans, exposing the population to mass starvation, and provoking a United Nations-sponsored humanitarian intervention in late 1992. This effort initially succeeded in feeding Somalia's people, but it turned into a nightmare after foreign troops became involved in the civil war and were withdrawn after some (including many Americans) were killed in the fighting. This not only reinforced the reluctance of outsiders to intervene militarily in Bosnia but also made any large-scale intervention in Rwanda, another African state which descended into chaos in 1994, impossible.

In the United States in 1992, many people sought a return of the days when domestic concerns were paramount. To them, such "foreign entanglements" seemed remote from U.S. national interests and thus unworthy of its involvement. Despite these public sentiments, and contrary to the mandate of a new president who had vowed to make domestic prosperity his top priority, foreign affairs continued to preoccupy the American government. Saddam Hussein, who only recently had shattered the post-Cold War euphoria, precipitated a second U.S. mobilization late in 1994 when he again massed his elite Republican Guards along the Kuwaiti border. An assertive U.S. response forced the Iraqi to back down, but his ability to disrupt the region at the time and place of his choosing was clearly demonstrated. The second and more controversial U.S. intervention was in Haiti, the poorest state in Latin America. In response to a reign of terror across the island nation and a mass exodus of refugees to the Florida coast, the United States occupied Haiti and began the same process of "state building" that had proven impossible in Somalia. Many in the United States opposed this effort, questioning the threat to U.S. interests and the prospects that the occupation would indeed "restore" democracy to a country that had had little experience with it.

The United States also took the lead role in defusing a crisis in North Korea, whose communist government had purportedly begun manufacturing nuclear weapons in violation of the Nuclear Non-proliferation Treaty, signed by most of the world's nations, including North Korea. Although American negotiators secured pledges from Pyongyang to dismantle its weapons program, their reluctance to press the case more aggressively left the agreement ambiguous—and, very likely, North Korea with a small number of functional nuclear bombs. Thus as in the case of Iraq and Haiti, U.S. involvement in North Korea had not fully resolved matters and left open the probability of new crises in the years to come.

LEARNING FROM EXPERIENCE

This study begins at the end of World War II and the outbreak of the Cold War—but why? Of what possible relevance is the Cold War to the vastly different contemporary system? Is it really necessary to first grasp why the Cold War erupted and how it was conducted in order to understand the events that followed? A hint: if the Cold War were still on, there probably would not have been a war in the Persian Gulf in 1991, nor would there have been an exchange of recognition in 1993 between the Israeli government and the Palestinian Liberation Organization, two bitter enemies who have long used violence against one another. The Middle East peace process, initiated by the

3

United States after the defeat of Iraq, would in all likelihood have remained barren, instead of realizing the beginnings of a Palestinian state and the normalization of Israeli-Jordanian relations in 1994. And certainly it is dubious whether Czechoslovakia would have fragmented into two separate republics, or whether Yugoslavia would have dissolved into a vicious and bloody civil war. Nor is it likely that the United States would have had to intervene in Somalia to feed its people or in Haiti to restore its elected leader who had been overthrown by a military junta.

Above all, the United States would not have had to undergo the difficult and sometimes agonizing search for a new role in the world: Should it stay largely aloof from the persistent problems of the world and focus on its many domestic problems, including rebuilding its economic base in an increasingly competitive world? Or, as the world's sole remaining superpower, should it continue to play an assertive role? If so, what specific commitments would that role entail?

In effect, then, without understanding the Cold War—why it broke out and how it was conducted—one cannot really understand the events that have occurred since the collapse of the Soviet Union. Nor is it possible to understand why the post-Cold War world, which had been expected to bring a new era of peace, has in fact been so troublesome, violent, and unstable, and has not afforded the United States and the American people the relief and ability to focus on internal matters. This is so even though in the contemporary world, military power—in which the United States remains preeminent—may be taking a backseat to economic power, indeed so much so that some observers have talked of an era of "geoeconomics" whose principal actors would be trading states such as Japan.[1]

The beginning of any understanding of the problems and dilemmas confronting the United States, first during the forty-five years of the Cold War and then into the twenty-first century, starts with the proposition that America, like all nations, has a distinctive perspective on world politics. How nations act in the international arena depends in large measure on their geography, resources, and historical backgrounds, as well as the environment in which they coexist with other states. These national styles may vary considerably, but all states quickly learn the rules of the game, or what they must do to ensure their survival and to achieve a measure of security. They ignore these rules at their peril.

Because for most of its existence the United States had isolated itself from the European state system, its national style was molded far more than that of

---

1. Richard Rosecrance, *The Rise of the Trading State: Commerce and Conquest in the Modern World* (New York: Basic Books, 1986). See also Edward Luttwak, "From Geopolitics to Geoeconomics," *National Interest* (Summer 1990): 17-23.

other states by its domestic experiences and democratic values and outlook. Not schooled by continual involvement in international politics like the Europeans, Americans approached foreign policy in a way that was not only peculiarly theirs, but also significantly different from that of other great powers. The contrast in approaches to foreign policy was particularly strong between the United States and the Soviet Union, which emerged after World War II as the United States's chief adversary. Perhaps one reason was that the United States felt secure in the Western Hemisphere, but czarist Russia (later Soviet Russia) could never feel secure because of its proximity to other great powers which, over the centuries, had their own problems and ambitions.[2] Even so, the United States learned to play the international game with increasing skill, although during the decades of conflict with the Soviet Union its distinctive national style exerted a strong influence over most of its foreign dealings.

This book will explore how that style specifically influenced the conduct of America's Cold War policies, whether it contributed to the victory over the Soviet Union, and, if so, how. Moreover, did the United States occasionally aggravate the Soviet-American struggle, exposing the world to the dangers of nuclear war, and, more fundamentally, did it prolong a struggle that could otherwise have been settled much earlier? Indeed, in the post-Cold War period the question has even been raised about whether America's policy of "containment" was in fact a necessary prerequisite for the Soviet defeat. Whatever the answers, this look at American foreign policy after World War II will ponder these and other questions and, more important, will reveal a broader perspective for analyzing and comprehending the foreign policy issues that the United States is confronting in a much different and rapidly changing world.

THE VOLATILE STATE SYSTEM

American foreign policy from World War II to the present is basically the story of the interaction and tension between the state system and the American style of dealing with other countries. In the state system each member—especially the great powers, its principal actors—tends to feel a high degree of insecurity. In the absence of a world government that could safeguard it, each state knows that it can depend only on itself for its preservation and safety; self-protection is the sole protection in an essentially anarchical system. Understandably, then, states tend to regard one another as potential adversaries, threats to each other's territorial integrity and political independence. In

2. John Spanier, *Games Nations Play*, 7th ed. (Washington, D.C.: CQ Press, 1990), especially 92-117.

short, the very nature of the state system breeds feelings of insecurity, distrust, suspicion, and fear. This atmosphere produces a constant competition for power in which each state, to reduce its insecurity, seeks to enhance its power relative to that of a possible foe. If a state perceives its neighbor as a potential enemy, it tries to deter an attack or political coercion by becoming a little stronger than its neighbor, or at least as strong. The neighbor, in turn, also fears attack or political intimidation. It understands that its best interests lie in increasing its strength to forestall either contingency or, if necessary, in winning a war, should matters go that far.

It is not the alleged aggressive instinct of humans as "naked apes" or their presumed desire for acquiring ever greater power that accounts for what is popularly called *power politics*. Rather, power politics stems from each state's ongoing concern with its security, which is the prerequisite for the enjoyment of its particular way of life. Because the external environment is seen as menacing to their security, states react fearfully against what they believe to be threats. In such a context it does not take much for one state to arouse another's apprehensions and to stimulate reciprocal images of hostility that each finds easy to substantiate by its opponent's behavior. Indeed, in most instances this enmity is maintained despite contradictory evidence and even avowedly friendly acts. Conciliatory behavior is often seen as an indicator of weakness and may invite exploitation. Or it may be regarded as a trick to persuade a state to relax its guard.

It is easy to understand why in these circumstances a balance of power is required to keep the state system from breaking down. A balance or equilibrium makes victory in a war less probable and more costly. In the absence of a world government to keep that peace, such a balance is presumed to be that distribution of power most likely to deter an attack. By contrast, the possession of disproportionate power might tempt a state to undertake aggression because the cost of gaining a predominant position and imposing its will on other states would be far less than that incurred in a balance of power. In other words, the fundamental assumption underlying the state system is that its members cannot be trusted with power because they will be tempted to abuse it. Unrestrained power in the system constitutes a threat to all states; power is, therefore, the best antidote to power. As one close observer of international politics, Arnold Wolfers, has noted:

Under these conditions [of anarchy] the expectation of violence and even of annihilation is ever-present. To forget this and thus fail in the concern for enhanced power spells the doom of a state. This does not mean open constant warfare; expansion of power at the expense of others will not take place if there is enough counterpower to deter or to stop states from undertaking it. Although no state is interested in a mere balance of power, the efforts of all states to maximize power may lead to equilibrium. If and when that happens, there is "peace" or, more exactly, a condition of stalemate or truce. Under the conditions described here, this balancing of power process is the only available "peace" strategy.[3]

Power thus elicits countervailing power—that is, when the balance of power is disturbed, equilibrium tends to be restored by the emergence of counterpower. The basic rule of the "international game," then, is that all states should resist attempts by any state to expand and seek a predominant position in the international system. As history has shown, states that ignore the rule do so at their own peril.

THE BALANCE OF POWER AND THE END OF U.S. ISOLATIONISM

What all this means is that any state's behavior can be explained to a very significant degree in terms of the ever-changing distribution of power. As that distribution changes, so does a state's behavior or foreign policy.

During most of the nineteenth and early twentieth centuries, the United States was able to preserve its isolation from power politics and enjoy an unprecedented degree of security because the balance of power on the European continent was maintained by Britain. But Germany's unification in 1870 and its subsequent rapid industrialization eventually forced the United States to end its isolation. Germany's growing strength coincided with and hastened the relative decline of British power. Indeed, the early years of World War I showed clearly that even when British power was thrown in on the side of France and Russia, the three allies could barely contain Germany. With the collapse of czarist Russia in 1915 and the transfer of almost 2 million German soldiers from the Russian front to the western front, a German victory became a distinct possibility. The United States would then have faced a Germany astride an entire continent, dominating European Russia and, in alliance with Austria-Hungary and perhaps the Ottoman Empire, extending German influence into the Balkans and the Middle East as far as the Persian Gulf. It was at that point that Germany's unrestricted submarine warfare, which included attacks on American shipping, led to a U.S. declaration of war. With America's entry into the war, the Allies were then able to contain the German spring offensive of 1918, leading to Germany's defeat.

After its victory the United States retreated into its customary isolationism. But American bankers, with the tacit approval of the government, maintained ties to Europe, playing an important role in its economic recovery and stabilization during the 1920s. Their primary motive, however, was to recover money loaned to the European allies during World War I. Although the U.S. economy rivaled that of all of Europe and the United States exercised some

---

3. Arnold Wolfers, *Discord and Collaboration* (Baltimore: Johns Hopkins University Press, 1965), 83.

economic influence, it refused to define for itself a political and military role consistent with its economic power. U.S. military power had been decisive in Germany's defeat, but the United States wanted nothing to do with great-power politics. It began to play a political role again only when the balance of European power was upset once more by the eruption of World War II in 1939 and the defeat of France in 1940. The United States faced the possibility of Britain's defeat and the control of Eurasia by Germany, Italy, and Japan—all antidemocratic states. To prevent this, President Franklin Roosevelt undertook a number of measures to help Britain withstand any Nazi assault. He sent fifty old destroyers to defend the English Channel, and he set up the lend-lease program to provide munitions, food, and other material support. This commitment to Britain was necessary even though such actions increased the risk of war with Germany. In fact, by the time of the bombing of Pearl Harbor in December 1941, the United States was already engaged in an undeclared naval war with Germany in the Atlantic, and full-scale war was merely a matter of time.

THE U.S. DEFINITION OF SECURITY

Two points deserve emphasis. First, the defense of U.S. security has always involved more than physical security. The German threat during World War I was not the likelihood of an immediate invasion, nor was invasion the main threat even after the defeat of France early in World War II. Then why did the United States twice forsake its isolationism? Surely the width of the Atlantic and Pacific Oceans would protect the United States.

American security was threatened because any state, especially a state that was undemocratic as well as antidemocratic, that controlled all the resources—human, natural, and industrial—of Eurasia, the Middle East, and Africa, and that organized these resources and transformed them into military power, might some day be able to attack North America. This would be particularly true if Britain were defeated and the British navy no longer guarded the sea highway to the Western Hemisphere. Even if Britain sank its navy rather than see it joined with the fleets of Germany and its allies (Italy in World War II) and defeated nations, the German navy might come to dominate the Atlantic approaches to the Western Hemisphere. This certainly would be true if Germany absorbed the British fleet. Such circumstances would require the United States to mobilize its resources fully and be on constant alert for a possible attack by an opponent with more people and superior resources. Most probably the only way the United States could match this dominant Eurasian power would be by transforming itself into a "garrison state," a disciplined, militarized society, which, in the name of security, would have to sacrifice democracy and individual liberty in the name of self-defense.

The more immediate reason for U.S. intervention was that the security of a democratic America was inextricably interwoven with the survival of other democracies, especially France and Britain. After France collapsed in 1940, Roosevelt explained to the American public why the United States had to assist Britain: the United States could not survive as a lone democratic island surrounded by totalitarian seas. Democracy in America could not flourish unless democratic values prospered in other societies. There might be no physical threat to the nation, but the aim of American foreign policy had never been just the security of the United States as a piece of real estate; the purpose had been to defend the security of a democratic America, which had required that democratic values flourish internationally.

The other point to be emphasized is that, despite the U.S. concern with security in Europe, the timing of the interventions in 1917 and 1941 was not in each case a rational decision made by Washington. It was Berlin's decision in 1917 to launch unrestricted submarine warfare against all shipping to England that brought the United States into the war, and it was Tokyo's decision to sink the U.S. fleet at anchor in Hawaii that led to the American declaration of war against Japan. But for Hitler's reckless declaration of war against the United States—a country he held in great contempt—U.S. power would have been directed only against Japan, and Germany, the far stronger power, would have faced only Britain and Russia, both already reeling from German blows. But for German and Japanese mistakes, the United States might *not* have entered the two world wars. At the very least, the timing would have been different. The decisions to go to war were not made by the United States even though the balances of power in Europe and Asia were imperiled and American security was at stake. The United States was saved from itself by its enemies.

Great powers usually do not leave decisions about their security to their adversaries. The strategy of the major states in the state system is—or should be—to oppose any state that seeks predominance because this constitutes a grave threat to their own security. The failure of the United States twice to act according to the logic dictated by the balance of power largely stemmed from its particular national style.

THE AMERICAN NATIONAL STYLE

The style reflected in the American response to war in Europe and later to the Cold War was the product of domestic experience. By giving priority to internal political and economic tasks, a characteristic of the United States since its founding, the nation had successfully isolated itself from European power politics. With nonthreatening neighbors to the north and south and open seas to the east and west, the United States could take security for granted. Free from external threats, it could focus on its development as a democratic society.

THE AMERICAN SENSE OF DESTINY

The ability of the United States to live in isolation during the nineteenth century and the first decade of the twentieth century cannot be attributed *only* to the nation's distance from Europe, or to Europe's preoccupation with industrialization and class conflict at home and colonialism abroad, or to the strength of the Royal Navy. The nature of democracy also must be considered. The United States saw itself as more than just the world's first "new nation"; it also was the world's first democracy and, as such, the first country in history with the desire to improve the lot of ordinary people, to grant them the opportunity to enrich and ennoble their lives. ("Give me your tired, your poor, your huddled masses yearning to breathe free," reads the inscription on the Statue of Liberty.) The more perfect union was to be an egalitarian society. European concepts of social hierarchy, nobility and titles, and bitter class struggles were not to be planted in its democratic soil.

From the very beginning of their national life, Americans professed a strong belief in what they considered their destiny—to spread, *by example,* freedom and social justice to all and to lead humankind away from its wicked ways to the New Jerusalem on earth. The massive immigration of the late nineteenth century was to reinforce this sense of destiny. "Repudiation of Europe," American novelist John Dos Passos once said, "is, after all, America's main excuse for being." Europe stood for war, poverty, and exploitation; America, for peace, opportunity, and democracy. But the United States was not merely to be a beacon of a superior democratic domestic way of life. It also was to be an example of a morally superior democratic pattern of international behavior. The United States, then, would voluntarily reject power politics as unfit for its foreign policy. Democratic theory posits that people are potentially rational and moral and that their differences can be settled by rational deliberation and moral exhortation. Indeed, assuming this to be true, the only differences that could arise would simply be misunderstandings, and, since people are endowed with reason and a moral sense, what quarrels could not be settled given the necessary goodwill? Peace—the result of harmony among people—was considered the natural or normal state.

Conversely, conflict was considered a deviation caused primarily by wicked leaders whose morality and reason had been corrupted by their exercise of uncontrolled authority. Power politics was an instrument of selfish and autocratic rulers—that is, leaders unrestrained by democratic public opinion—who enjoyed wielding it for personal advantage. To them, war was a grand game. They could remain in their palatial homes, continuing to eat well and to enjoy the luxuries of life, and suffer none of the hardships of war. These fell upon the ordinary people, who had to leave their families to fight, to endure the higher taxes to pay for the war, and possibly to see their homes and families destroyed. The conclusion was clear: undemocratic states were inherently warlike and evil; democratic nations, in which the people controlled and regularly changed their leaders, were peaceful and moral.

The American experience seemed to support this conclusion: the United States was a democracy, and it was at peace. Furthermore, peace seemed to be the normal state of affairs. It was logical, then, that democracy and peaceful behavior and intentions should be thought of as synonymous. Americans never asked themselves whether democracy was responsible for the peace they enjoyed, or whether peace was the product of other forces. The frequent wars of Europe appeared to provide the answer: European politics was power politics, reflecting the undemocratic nature of European regimes. Americans had cut themselves off from Europe and its class conflicts and power politics after the Revolutionary War—America had to guard its democratic purity and abstain from any involvement in the affairs of Europe lest it be soiled and corrupted. Nonalignment or isolationism, therefore, was the morally correct policy, for it allowed the United States to quarantine itself from Europe's hierarchical social structures and immoral international habits.

By confusing the results of geography and Europe's focus on Asia, the Middle East, and Africa with the virtues of American democracy, Americans could smugly enjoy their self-conferred moral superiority as the world's first democracy. It was the Monroe Doctrine, proclaimed in 1823, that first stressed, officially and explicitly, this ideological difference between the New World and the Old World. It declared specifically that the American political system was "essentially different" from that of Europe, whose nations engaged frequently in warfare. The implication was very clear: democratic government equals peace, and aristocratic government—which was identified with despotism—means war. It also allowed the United States to engage in a bit of hypocrisy by acting like other nations in its continental expansion but disguising the motives in the noblest of terms such as "manifest destiny." By drawing the distinction between the New and Old Worlds and warning the Europeans to keep their "hands off" this hemisphere, Americans were, in effect, opening the way for the establishment of U.S. preeminence and dominance. It would not be the last time that the United States would invoke the double standard, proclaiming a loftier moral position than that of other great powers—all the while acting pretty much as they did.

THE DEPRECIATION OF POWER IN INTERNATIONAL POLITICS

But this association of peace with democracy was not the only reason for the American depreciation of power politics in the eighteenth and nineteenth centuries. Another was that the United States was largely a one-class society, in which most shared a belief in a common set of middle-class, capitalistic, and democratic values. America was unique among nations in this respect. The European countries were, by contrast, three-class societies. In addition to the middle class, they contained in their bodies politic an aristocratic class, whose energies were devoted either to keeping itself in power or to recapturing power and returning to the glorious days of a feudal past. Moreover, European urbanization and industrialization during the nineteenth century had given birth to a proletariat, which, because it felt it did not receive a fair share of the national income, became a revolutionary class. The nations of the Old World were a composite of these three elements: a reactionary aristocracy, a democratic middle class, and a revolutionary proletariat. These nations had, in an intellectual as well as a political sense, a right, a center, and a left.

The United States had only a center, both intellectually and politically. It had never experienced a feudal past and therefore possessed no large, powerful aristocratic class on the right. Because it was by and large an egalitarian society, it also lacked a genuine left-wing movement of protest, such as socialism and communism. America was, as French political observer Alexis de Tocqueville said, "born free" as a middle-class, individualist, capitalistic, democratic society. It was not divided by the kinds of deep ideological conflicts that in France, for example, set one class of people against another. No one class was ever so afraid of another that it preferred national defeat to domestic revolution—as in France in the late 1930s, when the *haute bourgeoisie* was so apprehensive of a proletarian upheaval that its slogan became "Better Hitler than Blum" (Leon Blum, the French Socialist leader).

This overwhelming agreement on the fundamental values of American society and Europe's intense class struggles reinforced the American misunderstanding of the nature and functions of power on the international scene. Dissatisfied groups never developed a revolutionary ideology because the growing prosperity spread to them before they could translate their grievances against the capitalist system into political action. (Black Americans were an important exception because they never shared this wealth or political power.) Aside from the Civil War, then, America—politically secure, socially cohesive, and economically prosperous—was able to resolve most of its differences peacefully. Thus, by living in isolation, the United States could believe in an evolutionary, democratic, economically prosperous historical process; revolution and radicalism were condemned from this perspective. In sharp contrast, because of their internal class struggles and external conflicts among themselves, the nations of Europe fully appreciated that social conflict is natural and that power plays a crucial role in resolving conflict.

In the past, in fact, Americans have been so in accord on basic values that whenever the nation has been threatened externally it also has become fearful of internal disloyalty. It is one of the great ironies of American society that, while Americans possess this unity of shared beliefs to a greater degree than most other people, their apprehension of external danger has repeatedly led them, first, to insist on a general and somewhat dogmatic reaffirmation of loyalty to the "American way of life" and then to hunt for internal groups that might betray this way of life. Disagreement has often become equated with disloyalty; people have been accused of "un-American" thinking and behavior and labeled "loyalty or security risks." Perhaps only a society so overwhelmingly committed to one set of values could be so sensitive to internal subversion and so fearful of internal betrayal. In contrast, perhaps only a society in which two or more ideologies have long since learned to live together can genuinely tolerate diverse opinions: Who has ever heard of "un-British" or "un-French" activities? The United States has often been called a "melting pot" because of the many different nationality groups it includes, but, before each generation of immigrants has been fully accepted into American society, it has had to be "Americanized." Few Americans have ever accepted diversity as a value. American society has, in fact, taken great pride in destroying diversity through assimilation.

Politics did not, in any event, seem very important to Americans during the nineteenth century, when, in an era of laissez-faire capitalism, the basic assumption was that people were economically motivated. Self-interest governed behavior. Individuals, seeking to maximize their profits, produced what the consumers wanted. The laws of supply and demand and the free market therefore transformed each person's economic selfishness into socially beneficial results—"the greatest good for the greatest number." Politics mattered little in this self-adjusting economic system based on entrepreneurs whose combined efforts resulted in the general welfare. The best government was the government that governed least. Arbitrary political interference with the economic laws of the market only upset the results these laws were intended to produce. Private property, profit, and the free market were the keys to ensuring the happiness of people by providing them with abundance. Capitalism, in short, reflected the materialism of the age of industrialization.

To state the issue even more bluntly: economics was good and politics was bad. This simple dichotomy came naturally to the capitalist middle class. For them, the benefits of economic freedom were as "self-evident" as the truths stated in the Declaration of Independence. And had this economic freedom not been gained only through a long and bitter struggle of the European middle class to cut down the authority of the powerful monarchical state and, finally, to overthrow it by revolution in France? The middle class, as it had grown more prosperous and numerous, had become increasingly resentful of paying taxes from which the aristocracy was usually exempt, of the restrictions placed on trade and industry, of the absence of institutions in which middle-class economic and political interests were represented, of the class barriers to the social status that came with careers in the army and in the bureaucracy, and of the general lack of freedom of thought and expression. Because the middle class identified the power of the state with its own lack of freedom, its aim was to restrict this power. Only by placing restraints on the authority of the state could it gain the individual liberty as well as the right to private enterprise it sought. Democratic philosophy stated these claims in terms of the individual's "natural rights." The exercise of political authority was equated with the abuse of that authority and the suppression of personal freedoms. The power of the state had to be restricted to the minimum to ensure the individual's maximum political and economic liberties.

It was with this purpose in mind that the U.S. Constitution divided authority between the states and the federal government, and, within the latter, among the executive, legislative, and judicial branches. Federalism and the separation of powers were deliberately designed to keep all governments—and especially the national government—weak. Secular problems would be resolved, not by the state's political actions, but by the individual's own economic actions in society in peacetime.

The American experience reflected this philosophy; millions of people came to the United States from other lands to seek a better way of life. America, a virgin land, was the earthly paradise where everyone could earn a respectable living. There was the western frontier with its rich soil, and, later, during the Industrial Revolution, the country's bountiful natural resources. The environment, technology, individual enterprise, and helpful governmental policies enabled the American people to become the "people of plenty." A good income was sought for two reasons: economically, to attain a comfortable standard of living and, psychologically, to gain social status and to earn the respect of one's fellow citizens.

It followed logically that if people in an egalitarian society were judged primarily by their economic achievements, they would concentrate on getting ahead. It was not surprising, therefore, that money came closer to being the common standard of value in the United States than in any other country. Money was the symbol of power, prestige, and success, just as failure to earn enough money was a token of personal failure.

It was hardly surprising that in these circumstances the solution to international problems in America's first century was considered a matter of economics rather than politics. Economics was identified with social harmony and the welfare of all peoples; politics was equated with conflict, war, and death. Just as the "good society" was to be the product of free competition, so the peaceful international society would be created by free trade. An international laissez-faire policy would benefit all states, just as a national laissez-faire policy benefited each person within these states. Consequently, people all over the world had a vested interest in peace in order to carry on their economic relations; trade and war were incompatible. Trade depended on mutual prosperity. War, on the other hand, impoverished and destroyed and created ill will among nations. Commerce benefited all the participating states; the more trade, the greater the number of individual interests involved. Commerce created a vested interest in peace; war was economically unprofitable and therefore obsolete. Free trade and peace, in short, were one and the same cause.

THE PENCHANT FOR CRUSADING

One result of this American depreciation of power politics was that the United States began to draw a clear-cut distinction between war and peace in its approach to foreign policy. Peace, on the one hand, was characterized by a state of harmony among nations; conflict, on the other hand, was considered abnormal and war a crime. In peacetime one needed to pay little or no attention to foreign problems; indeed, to do so would divert people from their individual materialistic concerns and upset the whole scale of social values. The effect of this attitude was clear: Americans turned their attention toward the outside world with reluctance and usually only when provoked—that is, when a foreign menace had become so clear that it could no longer be ignored. Or, to state it somewhat differently, the United States rarely initiated policy; the stimuli responsible for the formulation of American foreign policy came from beyond America's borders.

But once Americans were provoked and the United States had to resort to force, the employment of this force was justified in terms of the moral principles with which the United States, as a democratic country, identified itself. War could be justified only by presuming noble purposes and completely destroying the immoral enemy who threatened the integrity, if not the existence, of these principles. American power, then, had to be "righteous" power; only its full exercise could ensure salvation or the absolution of sin. A second result of the depreciation of power politics, therefore, was that the national aversion to violence became transformed on occasion into a national glorification of violence, and wars became ideological crusades to destroy the enemy state and then send its people to democratic reform school. Making the world "safe for democracy"—the stated objective during World War I—was to be achieved by democratizing the populace of the offending nation, making its new rulers responsible to the people they governed, and thereby converting the formerly authoritarian or totalitarian state into a peaceful democratic state and banishing power politics for all time. Once that aim had been achieved, the United States could again withdraw into itself, secure in the knowledge that American works had again proved to be "good works."

This was the pattern of American foreign policy: a pendulum-like swing from isolationism to interventionism, from withdrawal to crusading, and back again. As a self-proclaimed morally and politically superior country, the United States could remain uncontaminated only by abstaining from involvement in a corrupt world or, if the world would not leave it alone, destroying the source of evil by applying maximum force and fighting a total war. In short, both the isolationist and the crusading impulses sprang from the same moralism. These swings tended, moreover, to be accompanied by radical shifts of mood: from one of optimism, which sprang from the belief that America was going to reform the world, to one of disillusionment as the grandiose objectives the United States had set for itself proved beyond its capacity to reach. Feeling too good for this world, which clearly did not want to be reformed but preferred its old corrupt habits, the nation retreated into isolationism to perfect and protect its way of life. Having expected too much from the use of its power, the United States then also tended to feel guilty and ashamed about having used its power at all.

The third result of the depreciation of power politics was that Americans divorced force from diplomacy. In peacetime, diplomacy unsupported by force was supposed to preserve the harmony among states. But in time of war political considerations were subordinated to force. Once the diplomats had failed to keep the peace with appeals to morality and reason, military considerations became primary, and the soldier was placed in charge.

The United States, then, rejected the concept of war as a political instrument and Carl von Clausewitz's definition of war as the continuation of politics by other means.[4] Instead, it regarded war as a politically neutral operation that should be guided by its own professional rules and imperatives. The military officer was a nonpolitical man who conducted his campaign in a strictly military, technically efficient manner. And war was a purely military instrument whose sole aim was the destruction of the enemy's forces and despotic regime. Policy and strategy were unrelated; strategy began where policy ended. After the Japanese attack on Pearl Harbor, the secretary of state turned to the secretary of war and said the situation was now out of his hands; it was all up to the War Department. As the war in Europe was coming to a close, the British asked Gen. George C. Marshall, architect of the Western allies' victory, to send U.S. forces to liberate Prague and as much of Czechoslovakia as possi-

---

4. This phrase sums up the essence of Clausewitz's famous book, *On War*. First published in 1832, it remains the most outstanding effort in Western history to understand war's international dynamics and its relationship to political policy and goals. The best modern translation and editing are by Michael Howard and Peter Paret, *On War* (Princeton: Princeton University Press, 1976).

ble before the Soviet army arrived. Marshall responded that he would not risk American lives for "purely political purposes"—a commendable sentiment, but what is war about if not the achievement of political purposes?

For Americans, then, war was a means employed to abolish power politics; war was conducted to end all wars. This same moralistic attitude, which was responsible for the Americans' all-or-nothing approach to war, also militated against the use of diplomacy in its classical sense: to compromise interests, to conciliate differences, and to moderate and isolate conflicts. Although Americans regarded diplomacy as a rational process for straightening out misunderstandings between nations, they also were extremely suspicious of it. If the United States was by definition moral, it obviously could not compromise, for a nation endowed with a moral mission could hardly violate its own principles; that constituted appeasement and national humiliation. The nation's principles would be transgressed, the nation's interests improperly defended, the national honor stained. To compromise with the immoral enemy was to be contaminated with evil. Moreover, to reach a settlement with enemies rather than wiping them out in order to safeguard those principles would be to acknowledge American weakness. This attitude toward diplomacy, which, in effect, made its use as an instrument of compromise difficult, reinforced the predilection for violence as a means of settling international problems. War allowed the nation to destroy its evil opponent but permitted it to keep its moral mission intact and unsullied by compromise.

THE CONTRAST BETWEEN THE UNITED STATES AND THE TRADITIONAL GREAT POWERS

On the eve of the Cold War, then, the American approach to foreign policy contrasted sharply in a number of important respects with the conduct of states long immersed in international politics. Unlike much of the rest of the state system, the United States was a highly secure state; it needed neither a large army nor navy to protect it. Moreover, the military and its values were basically despised because they were believed to be contrary to those of a democracy, and it was the building of democracy that the nation considered its first task. The result was the pattern just described: a swing from an isolationist position in which the country served as an example of social justice on earth to a posture of massive and violent intervention. Consistent, continual participation in the international system was not the norm.

Furthermore, the American perception of an international harmony of interests contrasted sharply with the state system's emphasis on the inevitability of conflict and differences of interests among states. Americans regarded conflict as an abnormal condition; the rest of the state system perceived harmony to be an illusion. The United States, long isolated from Europe and therefore not socialized by the state system, did not accept the reality and permanence of conflicts among its members. Indeed, differences between states were considered unnatural. But when they did occur, such differences should not be deep or long-lasting. Rather, they were attributed to wicked leaders (who could be eliminated), authoritarian political systems (which could be reformed), or misunderstandings (which could be straightened out if the adversaries approached each other with sincerity and empathy). Once these obstacles had been removed, peace, harmony, and goodwill would reign supreme.

Because the United States considered itself a morally and politically superior society, its attitude toward the use of power internationally was dominated by the belief that the struggle could be avoided by isolating the country from it or could be eliminated by crusading against those countries indulging in power politics. Moralism in foreign policy proscribed the use of power in peacetime; power could be employed only in confrontations with unambiguous aggression, transformed then into an obligation to fight on behalf of righteous causes. In short, power could be legitimated only by democratic purposes; otherwise, its exercise would be evil and would necessarily arouse guilt feelings.

The great American compulsion to feel moral about the nation's behavior reinforced the cyclical swings from isolationism to crusading and back again. The perception of power as simply the raw material of international politics—its use as an instrument of compromise, conciliation, and moderation in interstate politics, its discriminating application toward achievement of specific and less-than-total objectives—was clearly antithetical to the American understanding of power. The term *power politics* was itself an anathema, a reminder of a way of doing things that the New World hoped it had left behind, and a potential threat to its virtue if the nation were to indulge in that kind of immoral Old World behavior.

One of the most telling characteristics of America's national style in conducting foreign policy has been that after every major war the reasons for the country's participation in struggle and bloodshed have been reinterpreted. These revisionist histories have had certain common themes: the conflicts in which the nation became entangled did not in fact threaten its security interests; it became involved because the politicians saw a menace where none existed, and this illusion was promoted by propagandists who aroused and manipulated public opinion, by soldiers with bureaucratic motives, and, above all else, by bankers and industrialists—the "merchants of death" of the 1930s, the "military-industrial complex" of the 1960s—whose economic interests benefited from the struggle. America's engagements in the two world wars of this century (as in the Cold War later) were mistakes; they were really unnecessary or immoral, if not both. The enemy identified yesterday as the aggressor and *provocateur* actually did not represent a threat to American security at all; to the contrary, the threat came from within. But for certain domestic forces the United States could have continued to isolate itself from international politics. Note also that these internal groups propelling the nation into war were said, in characteristic American fashion, to be motivated by profit.

The fundamental revisionist assumption, then, was that the nation had a choice between employing or not employing power politics. Conversely, revisionism rejected the idea that the distribution of power in the state system left the United States—or any other country, for that matter—with a choice only of whether or not it would help to maintain the balance of power. Power was equated in this instance with its abuse. Abstention from its use and the creation of a truly just society at home were considered wiser and more moral policies. Crusading, allegedly for the reform of the world, risked corrupting America's very soul because it diverted attention and resources from reform at home to military preparation and war. Revisionism, then, was essentially an argument for continued isolation from power politics.

But if one could not avoid power politics or abolish it, there was yet another solution: to flee the divisive world of power into the more united world of economics. The belief that political conflict among states could be transformed into cooperation among nations when they focused on what was truly important—the improvement of humanity's material and social life—was another major characteristic of American style. If power politics and concern for security led to conflict and war, economics with its concern for raising everyone's standard of living bound all people together, regardless of nationality or race. They had to cooperate for their common good. The revulsion against the concept of maintaining the balance of power, the renewed emphasis on "interdependence" that followed the Vietnam War, and the Clinton administration's emphasis on foreign economic policy, are hardly novel. Even while the Republic was still young there were already those who felt that

the [national political] barriers that existed seemed artificial and ephemeral in comparison with the fine net by which the merchants tied the individuals of the different nations together like "threads of silk.". . . [T]he merchants—whether they are English, Dutch, Russian, or Chinese—do not serve a single nation; they serve everyone and are citizens of the whole world. Commerce was believed to bind the nations together and to create not only a community of interests but also a distribution of labor among them—a new comprehensive principle placing the isolated sovereign nations in a higher political unit. In the eighteenth century, writers were likely to say that the various nations belonged to "one society"; it was stated that all states together formed "a family of nations" and the whole globe a "general and unbreakable confederation." [5]

5. Felix Gilbert, *To the Farewell Address: Ideas of Early American Foreign Policy* (Princeton: Princeton University Press, 1961), 57.

| The
American
Approach
to Foreign
Policy | The United States after World War II, therefore, faced the world with attitudes and behavior patterns formed by its long period of isolationism from Europe. More specifically, the nation confronted the Soviet Union, formerly czarist Russia, a state with long experience in international politics. The Soviet-American rivalry would dominate world politics for nearly half a century, with profound implications for the domestic and foreign policies of nearly every nation-state. And it would leave a legacy in the 1990s that continues to be felt worldwide. |

Franklin Roosevelt confers with Winston Churchill and Joseph Stalin at Yalta in February 1945 about military strategy and the structure of the postwar world.

CHAPTER TWO

From World War to Cold War

The United States emerged from World War II as the dominant political, economic, and military power in the world. The land mass from France to Russia lay in ruin, Japan and its short-lived East Asian empire were devastated, and China remained in a state of protracted civil war. The United States, however, was relatively unscathed by the war and emboldened by its victory over fascism in Europe and Asia. For the second time in three decades the United States had been drawn into world war and had triumphed.

But its moment of glory, its attainment of primacy after a steady evolution from continental to regional to global power, did not last long. Even before the embers of World War II had cooled, the sparks of a new conflict illuminated the future of American foreign policy, and the elation over military victory was quickly overtaken by new problems, responsibilities, and challenges to regional and global stability. Americans would face the equally daunting task of winning the peace.

Signs of the coming schism were not apparent as the final battles of World War II were waged in central Europe and East Asia. Before one of the wartime conferences between Prime Minister Winston Churchill and President Franklin Roosevelt, a U.S. War Department memorandum forecasting the Soviet Union's postwar position concluded that it would be the dominant power in Eurasia for the foreseeable future:

> With Germany crushed, there is no power in Europe to oppose her tremendous military forces. . . . The conclusions from the foregoing are obvious. Since Russia is the decisive factor in the war, she must be given every assistance, and every effort must be made to obtain her friendship. Likewise, since without question she will dominate Europe on the defeat of the Axis, it is even more essential to develop and maintain the most friendly relations with Russia.[1]

The importance of this assessment lies less in its prediction of the Soviet Union's postwar position, which was fairly obvious, than in its statement of American expectations about future Soviet-American relations. Military leaders apparently accepted without any major misgivings the prospect of the Soviet Union as the new dominant power in Europe; they did not imagine that it might replace Nazi Germany as a grave threat to the European and global balance of power. Although twice in the twentieth century the United States had been propelled into Europe's wars at exactly those moments when Germany became so powerful that it almost destroyed this balance, the lessons of history—specifically, the impact on American security of any nation's domination of Europe—had not yet been absorbed. Roosevelt and the American government did not attempt to reestablish a balance of power in Europe to safeguard the United States; they expected this security to stem from mutual Soviet-American goodwill, unsupported by considerations of power. This reliance on goodwill and mutual esteem was to prove foolish at best—and at worst potentially fatal.

AMERICAN WARTIME ILLUSIONS

Postwar expectations of an "era of good feeling" between the Soviet Union and the United States exemplified the quixotic nature of American foreign affairs, which perceived war as a disruption of the normal harmony among nations, military force as an instrument to be used only to punish the aggressors or war criminals, and those who cooperated in its ideological crusade as equally moral and peace-loving. Once the war was finished, this thinking presumed, the natural harmony would be restored and the struggle for power would end.

1. Quoted in Robert E. Sherwood, *Roosevelt and Hopkins*, vol. 2 (New York: Bantam Books, 1950), 363-364.

The implication was clear: the United States need take no precautionary steps against its noble wartime allies in anticipation of a possible disintegration of the alliance and potential hostility among its partners. Instead, it was hoped that the friendly relations and mutual respect that American leaders believed had matured during the war would preserve the common outlook and goals and guarantee an enduring peace. This rosy scenario pertained to the Soviet Union itself, despite its alien ideology and the tyrannical conduct of its leader, Joseph Stalin.

In Washington, members of the foreign policy elite generally reflected this idealism. They hailed the globalization of America's moral vision and its rejection of old-style power politics. As World War II wound down, Secretary of State Cordell Hull anticipated the day in which "there will no longer be need for spheres of influence, for alliances, for balance of power, or any other of the special arrangements through which, in the unhappy past, the nations strove to safeguard their security or to promote their interests." [2] He was joined in this view not only by President Roosevelt but also by most of his foreign affairs team, including Sumner Welles, Charles Bohlen, and Averell Harriman, ambassador to the Soviet Union.

These optimistic expectations of future Soviet-American relations made it necessary to explain away continuing signs of Soviet distrust. This was particularly true during World War II when the West delayed opening up a second front against Germany. When the front was postponed from 1942 to 1943 to 1944, Stalin became very bitter. He brusquely rejected Allied explanations that they were not yet properly equipped for such an enormous undertaking, and he especially denounced Churchill for declaring that there would be no invasion until the Germans were so weakened that Allied forces would not have to suffer forbiddingly high losses. To Stalin, this was a weak explanation because the Soviets accepted massive casualties as a matter of course. "When we come to a mine field," Marshal G. K. Zhukov explained to Gen. Dwight Eisenhower after the war, "our infantry attacks exactly as if it were not there. The losses we get from personnel mines we consider only equal to those we would have gotten from machine guns and artillery if the Germans had chosen to defend that particular area with strong bodies of troops instead of with mine fields." [3] It was no wonder, then, that the Soviets dismissed Allied explanations and fastened instead on what was for them a more reasonable interpretation of American and British behavior. From the Marxist viewpoint the Allies were doing exactly what they should be doing—postponing the second front until the Soviet Union and Germany had exhausted each other. Then the United States and Britain could land in France, march into Germany

2. Quoted in Herbert Feis, *Churchill, Roosevelt, Stalin: The War They Waged and the Peace They Sought* (Princeton, N.J.: Princeton University Press, 1957), 238.
3. Quoted in Dwight Eisenhower, *Crusade in Europe* (New York: Doubleday, 1948), 514.

without heavy losses, and dictate the peace to Germany and the Soviet Union. The Western delay was seen as a deliberate attempt by the world's leading capitalist powers to destroy their two major ideological opponents at one and the same time. Throughout the war the Russians displayed again and again this fear of hostile Western intentions.

Meanwhile, after the war the United States and Soviet Union confronted the awkward process of dividing the liberated territories in central Europe, a process that foreshadowed the geopolitical wrangling of the Cold War. After American and British forces forced the unconditional surrender of Italy in July 1943, they resisted sharing control of that country with their Russian allies. Soviet leaders were equally wary about ceding dominion over the Balkan states, and later Poland, to their allies to the west. Western calls for self-determination throughout the region were interpreted by Soviet leaders as challenges to a Soviet role in the postwar architecture. On a personal level, ill will between Stalin and Western leaders Franklin Roosevelt, Harry Truman, Averell Harriman, and Winston Churchill steadily intensified throughout this process.

American leaders found a ready explanation for the repeated indications of Soviet suspicion. They thought of Soviet foreign policy not in terms of the internal dynamics of the regime and its ideological enmity toward all non-communist nations, but solely in terms of Soviet reactions to Western policies. New to great-power politics, they had little knowledge of Russian history and, therefore, of Russia's historical goals under czarist and Soviet rule. The few experts in the State Department were ignored; in fact, Roosevelt never took the secretary of state along to any of the wartime conferences with Churchill and Stalin.

Soviet distrust of the West was viewed by the president against the pattern of the West's prewar anti-Soviet acts: the Allied intervention in Russia at the end of World War I aimed at overthrowing the Soviet regime and, after the failure of that attempt, the establishment of the *cordon sanitaire* in eastern Europe to keep Soviet influence from spreading; the West's rejection of Soviet offers in the mid- to late 1930s to build an alliance against Hitler; and, especially, the Munich agreement of 1938, which, by destroying Czechoslovakia, opened Hitler's gateway to the East. Western efforts to weaken and ultimately destroy the Soviet Union, as well as attempts to turn Hitler's threat away from the West and toward Russia, were considered the primary reasons for Soviet hostility.

To overcome this attitude, American leaders thought they had only to demonstrate good intentions. The question was not whether Soviet cooperation could be won for the postwar world, but how it would be gained. And if these efforts bore fruit and created goodwill, what conflicts of interest could not be settled peacefully in the future? Various Soviet policies and acts during the war—the disbanding of the Comintern (the vehicle for international communism), the toning down of communist ideology and the new emphasis on Soviet nationalism, the relaxation of restrictions on the church, and, above all, the statement of Soviet war aims in the same language of peace, democracy, and freedom used by the West—seemed to prove that if the Western powers demonstrated their *bona fides* (good faith) they could convert the Soviets into allies.

Roosevelt's efforts to gain this cooperation focused on Stalin. In that respect Roosevelt's instincts were correct: if he could gain Stalin's trust, postwar Soviet-American cooperation would be possible. But in another respect his instincts were poor. Roosevelt's political experience was in the domestic arena. He had dealt successfully with all sorts of politicians and had managed to resolve differences by finding compromise solutions. As a result, he had great confidence in his ability to win Stalin's favor. He would talk to Stalin as "one politician to another." In short, Roosevelt saw Stalin as a Russian version of himself, who, as a fellow politician, could be won over by a mixture of concessions and goodwill. It did not occur to Roosevelt that all of his considerable skills and charm might not suffice. At home these qualities were enough because he and his opponents agreed on goals; differences were over the means. But between the United States and the Soviet Union the differences were over the ends, the kind of world each expected to see when the war was over.

In February 1945 at the Yalta Conference of the Big Three—Roosevelt, Stalin, and Churchill—Roosevelt and his advisers believed they had firmly established amicable and lasting relations with the Soviet Union. Stalin had made concessions on a number of vital issues and had promised cooperation in the future. He had accepted the establishment of the United Nations on the basis of the American formula that the veto in the Security Council would be applied only to enforcement action, not to peaceful attempts at the settlement of disputes. Moreover, in the Declaration of Liberated Europe he had promised to support self-government and allow free elections in Eastern Europe. He also had responded to the wishes of the American military and promised to enter the war against Japan. Finally, he had repeatedly expressed his hope for fifty years of peace and great-power cooperation.

The new era of goodwill was to be embodied in the United Nations, where the peoples of the world could exercise vigilance over their national leaders. The United Nations was regarded as democracy working on an international scale. Just as citizens within democratic states could constantly watch their representatives and prevent them from effecting compromises injurious to their interests, so the people of all countries would now be able to keep an eye on their leaders, making it impossible for them to strike secret deals that would betray the people's interests and threaten the peace of the world. International public opinion, expressing its pacific ideals across national boundaries, would maintain a constant guard over the diplomats and hold them accountable. Power politics would be replaced by reliance on sound universal principles and good faith. Upon his return from Yalta, Roosevelt told Congress and the American people that his recent conference with Stalin and Churchill "ought to spell the end of the system of unilateral action, the exclusive alliances, the spheres of influence, the balances of power, and all the other expedients that have been tried for centuries—and have always failed." Instead, "We propose to substitute for all these, a universal organization in which all peace-loving nations will fully have a chance to join." [4]

The State Department had been even more emphatic about the subordination of power politics to universal moral principles. Its Subcommittee on Territorial Problems stated that "the vital interests of the United States lay in following a 'diplomacy of principle'—of moral disinterestedness instead of power politics." [5] No comment could have summed up more aptly the American habit of viewing international politics in terms of abstract moral principles instead of clashes of interest and power, and no institution could have embodied more fully the immediate postwar hope for a return to "normalcy."

THE RUSSO-SOVIET APPROACH TO FOREIGN POLICY

In Chapter 1 it was argued that before World War II American foreign policy was to a large degree driven by a cultural tradition that reflected the nation's detachment from Europe and its pursuit of a democratic alternative in the New World. This approach to foreign affairs produced numerous contradictions and more than a few crises along the way, and the U.S. adaptation to the Cold War challenged many deeply held convictions about the dangers of "foreign entanglements" to external security and internal liberty.

Such cultural influences affect the foreign policies of *every* nation-state, in ways that are as numerous as the cultures themselves. As a result, it is useful to consider this dimension of foreign policy in any interstate conflict, and it is especially useful to contrast the American tradition with that of its Cold War rival, the Soviet Union. Soviet leaders also inherited a distinct cultural style of foreign policy, the product of centuries of fractious coexistence with a diverse and often-menacing external environment. They then integrated the lessons of Russian history with the maxims of Marxist-Leninist ideology to fashion an aggressive approach to postwar foreign affairs. But how were these historic

4. Quoted in James MacGregor Burns, *Roosevelt, The Soldier of Freedom* (New York: Harcourt, Brace, Jovanovich, 1970), 582.
5. Quoted in Feis, *Churchill, Roosevelt, Stalin,* 207.

Russian roots rendered compatible with communist ideology under the banner of the Soviet Union?

THE RUSSIAN BACKGROUND

As in the American case, the source of the Russo-Soviet "style" of foreign policy is revealed simply by analyzing a globe. Unlike the United States and other maritime powers, Russia was not blessed by geography. Unprotected by natural barriers such as oceans or mountains, its people were vulnerable to invasions from several directions. And the enormous size of its territory rendered internal cohesion, communication, and transportation very difficult, especially given the polyglot demographics of the Russian people.

During the thirteenth and fourteenth centuries, Russia was ruled by the Mongols from the East. By the 1460s Mongol domination had been repelled and Muscovy emerged as the capital of a Russian superstate. In more modern times, Napoleon Bonaparte's armies invaded and captured Moscow in 1812; British and French armies landed in the Crimea in 1854-1856; Japan attacked and claimed territories in eastern Russia in 1904-1905. Germany invaded Russia twice during the twentieth century, defeating it in 1917, which led to the collapse of the monarchy and the ascension of the Bolsheviks to power. Germany almost defeated Russia again within a few months of its attack in June 1941. Between 1917 and 1941 the Western allies supported the anti-Bolshevik side, and in 1920 the Poles almost defeated a Russia exhausted by civil war.

Historically, therefore, Russia could not take its security for granted or give priority to domestic affairs. In these circumstances political power became centralized in the state, which, under both the czars and communist leaders, firmly held the far-flung regions together. Such efforts, however, required large standing military forces, and much of the Russian population was mobilized in their service. Indeed, the Russian armed forces were consistently larger than those of the other European great powers, a fact not lost on leaders in Warsaw, Budapest, Paris, and London.

This militarization of Russian society, purportedly for defensive purposes, carried with it the potential for outward aggression as well. Historian Richard Pipes has remarked that Russia no more became the world's largest territorial state by repelling repeated invasions than a man becomes rich by being robbed.[6] The same lack of natural frontiers that failed to protect Russia from invasion also allowed its power to extend outward from its frontiers. Indeed, sustained territorial expansion has been called the "Russian way." According to President Jimmy Carter's national security adviser, Zbigniew Brzezinski,

6. Richard Pipes, as quoted by Zbigniew Brzezinski, *Game Plan* (Boston: Atlantic Monthly Press, 1986), 19-20.

any list of aggressions against Russia in the last two centuries would be dwarfed by Russian expansionist moves against its neighbors.[7]

Whether Russian motives were defensive or offensive, the result was a pattern of expansion. To the degree that Russian rulers feared attacks, they pushed outward to keep the enemy as far away as possible. Territorial extension became a partial substitute for the lack of wide rivers or mountains that might have afforded a degree of natural protection. Individual rulers' ambitions, such as Peter the Great's determination to have access to the sea, also resulted in territorial conquest and defeat of the power blocking that aim (in this instance, Sweden). Even before the Bolsheviks seized power, authoritarianism, militarism, and expansionism characterized the Russian state; being a good neighbor was an alien concept. The basic "rules" of the state system—the emphasis on national interests, distrust of other states, expectation of conflict, self-reliance, and the possession of enough power, especially military power—were deeply ingrained in Russia's leaders.

THE SOVIET INGREDIENT

These attitudes were modified and strengthened by the outlook of the new regime after 1917. Russian political culture was fused with Marxist ideology, as adapted to Russian circumstances by Vladimir Lenin, to create an all-encompassing *weltanschauung* (world view). The new leaders' ideological outlook did not dictate action in specific foreign policy situations, but it did provide them with a broad framework for perceiving and understanding the world.

To these new leaders history centered around the class struggle between, on the one hand, the rich and privileged who owned the means of production, and, on the other hand, the greater numbers of propertyless citizens who worked for them. Why were most human beings poor, illiterate, and unhealthy? Why did states fight wars? The answer was that a small minority of capitalists, monopolizing the industrialized world's wealth and power, exploited those who worked in their factories to maximize profits. To keep wages down, they kept food prices low so that agricultural labor also lived in destitution. Domestically as well as internationally, wars were one result of the ongoing search by these capitalists for profits.

Another result was the conflict waged over dividing up the non-European colonial world. For Lenin, global imperialism represented the highest stage of capitalism. He viewed World War I as a climactic showdown among capitalist empires, a fight for the spoils of the developing world now that their own frontiers were closed. If human beings were ever to live in freedom and enjoy

7. Zbigniew Brzezinski, "The Soviet Union: The Aims, Problems, and Challenges to the West," in *The Conduct of East-West Relations in the 1980s*, Adelphi Paper No. 189, Part I (London: International Institute for Strategic Studies, 1984).

a decent standard of living in peace and fraternity with other countries, capitalism would have to be replaced by communism.

As Lenin was aware, the application of Marxism to Russia suffered from one glaring deficiency. In Karl Marx's dialectic view, communism stemmed directly from the failures of capitalism. Thus a communist society must first experience industrialization, urbanization, and the enlistment of its working classes into an organized "proletariat." This, of course, did not pertain to the largely agrarian Russia whose population was barely emerging from its feudal traditions. So Lenin attempted to resolve this problem by centralizing power in a "vanguard" of enlightened Marxists, who would bring communism to the Russian people without first exposing them to the contradictions and inequalities of capitalism. Once firmly in place within the Kremlin, this vanguard would then disseminate Lenin's ideological vision through a pervasive propaganda campaign.

Ideology was more than a way of viewing the world; it also gave the Soviet leaders a mission. For them, capitalism was the chief obstacle to humanity's liberation. Thus Soviet leaders considered the American and West European governments to be enemies because of what they were—capitalist. Moreover, unlike the thinking of states in the traditional state system who had no permanent friends and enemies and who changed allies as the distribution of power changed, Soviet ideology clearly discriminated friend from foe on a permanent basis. Because the Soviet Union defined capitalist states as foes, and because the Soviet mission internationally was to export its revolution and create a new postcapitalist international order, the relationship between it and the capitalist states would be marked by conflict until the victory of Soviet ideology. Its leaders, moreover, took it for granted that the capitalist states were equally hostile and determined to eliminate communism and the Soviet Union, if only to avoid their own demise.

The effect of this pattern was to perpetuate historic Russian suspicions of foreigners and feelings of insecurity. Soviet leaders believed the state system, composed of capitalist states, was a very hostile environment. They rejected the latter's professions of goodwill and peaceful intentions and committed their country to the "inevitable and irreconcilable struggle" against these states. They fostered a strong emphasis on self-reliance and an equally intense concern with the Soviet Union's relative power. Tactically, they were convinced that when an enemy made concessions in negotiations or became more accommodating, it was not because the enemy wanted a friendlier relationship but because it was *compelled* to do so by the Soviet Union's growing strength, a viewpoint that obviously led to a self-sustaining rationale for ever more military power.

Russian history stood as a warning to Soviet leaders that peace was but a preparation for the next war. Their ideological perceptions strengthened the view that peace was but the continuation of the last war by other means. The Soviet world view, in short, reinforced the historically repetitious cycles that had previously and consistently resulted in a further expansion of their power. Even if it were granted that insecurity drove this expansion rather than any historical mission, the result for neighboring states remained the same—they were vulnerable. They were perceived as inherent threats to Soviet interests and they represented possible additions to the Soviet Union's own frontiers. Such a drive to achieve absolute security in a system in which no state could achieve that aim short of total domination left other states insecure and contributed to the volatility of the international system.

The contrast between American culture and national style, which emphasized peace as normal and conflict as abnormal, and that of the Soviet Union, which stressed the pervasiveness of war, could not have been more striking. Both societies felt a sense of historical mission, yet their principles, goals, and tactics were worlds apart. When these clashing cultural traditions intersected with the scrambled international system after World War II, the seeds of the Cold War were sown in fertile soil.

SOVIET RETRENCHMENT IN EASTERN EUROPE

The Cold War did not follow neatly on the heels of World War II as described in most history books. To the contrary, both struggles overlapped in time and space as the advances of the Allied armies of World War II determined who would control which territories. It was control over the central European "heartland" that was, of course, critical, although Soviet and American interests also clashed from Teheran to Tokyo.

The American dream of postwar peace and great-power cooperation was shattered as the Red Army, having finally halted the Nazi armies and decisively defeated the Germans at Stalingrad in late 1942, began slowly to drive the enemy out of the Soviet Union and then to relentlessly pursue the retreating Germans to Berlin. Stalin, who in 1940 had annexed the three Baltic states (Latvia, Lithuania, and Estonia) after signing the Nazi-Soviet pact, thus expanded into Eastern Europe and began to impose Soviet control on Poland, Hungary, Bulgaria, Romania, and Albania. (Yugoslavia was by then under the communist control of Marshal Tito, the Yugoslav partisan leader who had fought bravely against the German occupation, and Czechoslovakia was under the threat of the Red Army.)

In each nation of Eastern Europe occupied by their troops, the Soviets established pro-Soviet governments. The key posts in these regimes—the ministries of the interior, which usually controlled the police, and defense, which controlled the army—were in the hands of the communists. With this decisive lever of power in their grasp, it was an easy matter to extend their domination and subvert the independence of these countries. As the war drew to a close, it became clear that the words of the Yalta Declaration, in which the Soviets had committed themselves to free elections and democratic governments in Eastern Europe, meant quite different things to the Soviets and to the Americans.

For the Soviet Union, control of Eastern Europe, and especially Poland, was essential. "The question of Poland is not only a question of honor but also a question of security," Stalin observed. "Throughout history, Poland has been the corridor through which the enemy has passed into Russia. Twice in the last thirty years our enemies, the Germans, have passed through this corridor. . . . Poland is not only a question of honor but of life or death for the Soviet Union." [8] It was thus inevitable that the Soviet Union would try to establish supportive regimes throughout the area. To the Soviets, democratic governments meant communist regimes and free elections meant elections from which parties not favorable to the communists were barred. The peace treaties with the former German satellite states, which were painfully negotiated by the victors in a series of foreign ministers' conferences during 1945 and 1946, could not loosen the tightening Soviet grip on what were by now Soviet satellite states.

Winston Churchill, concerned about Stalin's behavior in Eastern Europe, urged the United States to send forces to capture the symbolically important German capital of Berlin instead of rounding up the remnants of Germany's defeated army; to advance the U.S. armies as far east as possible, including farther into Czechoslovakia; to not pull U.S. forces back to their agreed-upon occupation zones in Germany until Stalin had observed his agreements in Eastern Europe; and, until then, to not shift the bulk of American military power from Europe to the Far East for the final offensive against Japan. Washington declined all these suggestions. Roosevelt had promised that all American troops would be withdrawn within two years after the war. Why then should Stalin worry about American opposition to his efforts to control Eastern Europe? Stalin exercised caution when he encountered opposition, but he ignored diplomatic notes of protest. Carefully waiting to see what the United States would do, Stalin allowed free elections in Czechoslovakia and Hungary, the two states nearest to American power. But continued U.S. and British verbal protests, unsupported by action, did not impress Stalin.

Consequently, Hungary's freedom was soon destroyed by the Soviets. Finally in 1948 even the Czech government, in which the Communist Party had the largest plurality, was overthrown by the Soviets in a coup d'état. Contrary to Roosevelt's earlier expectations, not even a communist-controlled coalition government was acceptable to Stalin. Indeed, as the Soviet satellization of

8. Joseph Stalin, as quoted by Winston Churchill, *The Second World War,* vol. 5, *Triumph and Tragedy* (Cambridge, Mass.: Houghton Mifflin, 1953), 369.

Eastern Europe was to show, the failure of the United States was not the failure of efforts to accommodate Soviet interests in Eastern Europe; it was the failure to resist Stalin earlier. Because Stalin apparently saw no limits to Soviet expansion and his conception of Soviet security left little, if any, security for his neighbors, that limit had to be defined by the Soviets' Western adversaries.

Given the demands from and circumstances within the state system, this Soviet behavior was understandable. Each state had to act as its own guardian against potential adversaries in a system characterized by conflict among states and a sense of insecurity and fear on the part of its members. As the alliance against the common enemy came to an end, the Soviet Union predictably would strengthen itself against the power most likely to be its new opponent. As czarist Russia, with a long history of invasions from the East and West, it had learned the basic rules of the international game through bitter experience. As Soviet Russia, its sense of peril and mistrust had been intensified by an ideology that posited capitalist states as implacable enemies.

But the growing conflicts about the future of Eastern Europe underscored the profound differences between the United States and Soviet Union. Roosevelt acted precisely on the assumption that noncommunist did not have to mean anti-Soviet. During the war he had been all too aware of the consequences of a possible Soviet-American clash in the wake of Germany's defeat. He therefore single-mindedly pursued a policy of friendship toward the Soviet Union. Roosevelt, however, did not view free elections in that area in terms of the creation of a new anti-Soviet belt. For him, free elections, noncommunist coalition governments in which communists might participate if they gained a sizable vote, and amicable relations between East and West were quite compatible.

The model he had in mind was Czechoslovakia. As the only democracy in that area, Czechoslovakia had maintained close ties with the West since its birth after World War I. But because France and Britain had failed to defend Czechoslovakia at Munich in 1938, and betrayed it by appeasing Hitler, it also had become friendly with the Soviet Union. After 1945 Czechoslovakia, like the other East European states, knew that it lay in the Soviet sphere of influence and that its security depended on getting along with, not irritating, its powerful neighbor. Czech leaders adopted friendly relations with the Soviet Union and signed a security treaty with it. In one of the rare free elections the Soviets allowed in Eastern Europe, the Communist Party received the largest vote of any party and therefore the key posts in the government. To share power in a coalition government, however, was to share power with class enemies. Soviet security therefore required ideological homogeneity in Eastern Europe.

During World War II the heroic Soviet war effort and sacrifices had created an enormous reservoir of goodwill in the West. Had the Soviets acted with greater restraint after the war and accepted states that, regardless of their governments' composition, would have adjusted to their Soviet neighbor, Stalin could have had the security he was seeking. But Stalin did not trust Roosevelt. No matter how personable the president was, no matter how sincere his statements of postwar friendship, Stalin saw him as the leader of a capitalist nation. As a "tool of Wall Street," Roosevelt could not be sincere in his peaceful professions.

SOVIET EXPANSION BEYOND EUROPE

Western resolve to balance Soviet power intensified steadily during the 1940s, precipitated by Stalin's attempt to extend Soviet influence beyond Eastern Europe. The United States had accommodated itself to Soviet control of Eastern Europe, especially Poland, the corridor through which Germany had attacked Russia twice in a quarter century. Moscow's security interests were understandable, and Washington, despite its disappointment over the Soviet failure to fulfill its Yalta obligations in Poland, quickly recognized the new Polish government as well as the other Soviet-installed regimes in Eastern Europe.

But then the Soviets began moving toward the Persian Gulf and into the Mediterranean. Iran, Turkey, and Greece were the first to feel pressure. If Soviet behavior in Eastern Europe could be explained in defensive terms, this was less true for the area south of the Soviet Union, the line that runs from Turkey to India. Long before Stalin, the czars had sought access to the Mediterranean via the Dardanelles Straits. Simultaneously they had tried to expand to the south to bring Soviet power closer to the Middle East and the Persian Gulf. Pressure on Iran began in 1946, when the Soviets refused to withdraw their troops from that country. These troops had been there since late 1941, when the Soviet Union and Britain had invaded Iran to forestall increased Nazi influence and to use Iran as a corridor through which the West could ship military aid to the Soviet Union.

During this period the Soviet Union also sought influence in Turkey. Indeed, the Soviets had begun to do this as early as June 1945 when they made several demands: the cession of several Turkish districts lying on the Turkish-Soviet frontier, the revision of the Montreux Convention governing the Dardanelles Straits in favor of a joint Soviet-Turkish administration, the severance of Turkey's ties with Britain and the conclusion of a treaty with the Soviet Union similar to those that the Soviet Union had concluded with its Balkan satellites, and finally, the leasing to the Soviet Union of bases for naval and land forces in the Dardanelles for its "joint defense."

In Greece communist pressure was exerted on the government through

Legend

- – – – Soviet border 1939
- —— Soviet border 1947–1991
- Soviet gains in western territory, 1939–1947
- States under Soviet control by 1948
- Independent communist state

SOVIET EXPANSION IN EUROPE, 1939–1948

widespread guerrilla warfare, which began in the fall of 1946. Civil war in Greece was nothing new. During the war communist and anticommunist guerrillas had spent much of their energy battling each other instead of the Germans. When the British landed in Greece and the Germans withdrew, the communists attempted to take over Athens. Only after several weeks of bitter street fighting and the landing of British reinforcements was the communist control of Athens dislodged; a truce was signed in January 1945. Just over a year later the Greeks held a general election in which right-wing forces captured the majority of votes. In August 1946 the communist forces renewed the war in the north, where the Soviet satellites in Eastern Europe could keep the guerrillas well supplied.

In all these situations the American government was once more confronted with the need to support Great Britain, the traditional guardian of this area. In the case of Iran the United States and Britain delivered firm statements that strongly implied that they would use force to defend Iran and took the issue to the United Nations for a public airing. The Soviet response in March 1946 was that the Red Army would be withdrawn during the next five to six weeks. In the case of Turkey the United States sent a naval task force into the Mediterranean immediately after the Soviets made their demand over the Dardanelles. Twelve days later the United States formally replied to the Soviets by rejecting their demand to share responsibility for the defense of the straits with Turkey. Britain sent a similar reply.

This geopolitical posturing was repeated in many other regions as World War II gave way to the Cold War. Control over Japan and the Western Pacific region was an additional bone of contention. The United States had long sought Soviet assistance in its struggle against Japan's Emperor Hirohito, just as the Soviets had repeatedly sought active U.S. intervention in Western Europe. Neither side had been especially receptive to the other's concerns, however, which helped to contaminate the atmosphere between the leaders. After the Potsdam Conference in July 1945, President Harry Truman became especially determined not to allow the Soviets to play any role in the control of Japan. Gen. Douglas MacArthur, Truman decided, would be given complete control in Japan after the war.

Although his efforts in specific areas were largely effective, President Truman's actions were merely swift reactions to immediate crises. They were not the product of an overall American strategy. Such a coherent strategy came only after a reassessment of Soviet foreign policy.

TOWARD THE STRATEGY OF CONTAINMENT

Eighteen months passed before the United States undertook that review, from the surrender of Japan on September 2, 1945, until the announcement of the Truman Doctrine on March 12, 1947. Perhaps such a reevaluation could not have been made any more quickly. Public opinion in a democratic country does not normally shift drastically overnight. It would have been too much to expect the American public to suddenly relinquish their attitude of friendliness toward the Soviet Union, inspired largely by the images of Soviet wartime bravery and endurance and by hopes for peaceful postwar cooperation. Moreover, citizens of the United States wished to be left alone to occupy themselves once more with domestic affairs.

In May 1945, at the end of the war with Germany, the United States had an army of 3.5 million organized into 68 divisions in Europe, supported by 149 air groups. By March 1946, only ten months later, the United States had only 400,000 troops left. Overall, the army had been reduced from 8 million to 1 million, the navy from 3.5 million to 1 million, and the air force from more than 200 to less than 50 combat groups. Thus the "most rapid demobilization in the history of the world" had largely been completed.[9]

This reduction of military strength no doubt encouraged the Soviet Union's intransigence in Europe and attempts to extend its influence. But the U.S. government would make no further concessions to lend the appearance of cooperation with the Soviet Union. It had tried to gain Soviet amity through cooperation and unilateral defense cutbacks; it was now up to Soviet leaders to demonstrate a constructive approach toward the United States as well. Paper agreements, written in such general terms that they hid divergent purposes, were regarded as having little value. Something more was needed: Soviet words would have to be matched by deeds.

The American secretary of state, James Byrnes, called this the "policy of firmness and patience": the United States would take a firm position in response to Soviet expansion, and it would not compromise simply to reach a quick agreement. American steadfastness presumably would wear the Soviets down and moderate their conduct. But there was no suggestion in this call for a tactical shift in how to negotiate with Moscow that the United States needed to organize international opposition to the Soviet Union. The new American position, as one political analysis concluded, "meant to most of its exponents that the Soviet Union had to be induced by firmness to play the game in the American way. There was no consistent official suggestion that the United States should begin to play a different game."[10] The prerequisite for such a suggestion was that American policy makers recognize that the Soviet Union was no longer just a difficult ally but an enemy.

9. Stephen E. Ambrose, *Rise to Globalism* (New York: Penguin, 1988), 79.
10. William Reitzel, Morton A. Kaplan, and Constance G. Coblenz, *United States Foreign Policy, 1945-1955* (Washington, D.C.: Brookings, 1956), 89.

George Kennan, the U.S. Foreign Service's foremost expert on the Soviet Union, presented in 1946 the basis of what was to be a new American policy that recognized the hostile character of the Soviet regime. In a detailed telegram sent from the U.S. embassy in Moscow, Kennan analyzed the communist outlook on world affairs.[11] In the minds of the Soviet leaders, he said, the Soviet Union had no community of interest with the capitalist states; to the contrary, they saw their relationship with the Western powers as one of an innate antagonism. Moreover, communist ideology had taught them that it was their duty to eventually overthrow the political forces in the outside hostile world, and in this feeling they were sustained by "the powerful hands of Russian history and tradition." After some time, observed Kennan, "their own aggressive intransigence with respect to the outside world began to find its own reaction. . . . It is an undeniable privilege for every man to prove himself right in the thesis that the world is his enemy; for if he reiterates it frequently enough and makes it the background for his conduct, he is bound to be right." [12] According to Kennan, this Soviet hostility would continue until the capitalist world had been destroyed. From this antagonism flowed many of the elements the West found "disturbing in the Kremlin's conduct of foreign policy: the secretiveness, the lack of frankness, the duplicity, the war suspiciousness, and the basic unfriendliness of purpose." He went on to point out that "these characteristics of the Soviet policy, like the postulates from which they flow, are basic to the *internal* nature of Soviet power, and will be with us . . . until the nature of Soviet power is changed." [13] Until that moment, he said, Soviet strategy and objectives would remain the same.

The American-Soviet struggle would thus be a long one, but Kennan stressed that Soviet hostility did not mean that the Soviets would embark on a do-or-die program to overthrow capitalism by a fixed date. Given their sense of historic inevitability, they had no timetable for conquest. In a brilliant passage, Kennan outlined the Soviet concept of the struggle:

The Kremlin is under no ideological compulsion to accomplish its purposes in a hurry. Like the Church, it is dealing in ideological concepts which are of a long-term validity, and it can afford to be patient. It has no right to risk the existing achievements of the revolution for the sake of vain baubles of the future. The very teachings of Lenin himself require great caution and flexibility in the pursuit of communist purposes. Again, these precepts are fortified by the lessons of Russian history: of centuries of obscure battles between nomadic forces over the stretches of a vast unfortified plain. Here caution, circumspection, flexibility, and deception are the valuable

11. This "long telegram" was later reprinted in the famous "X article" in the July 1947 issue of *Foreign Affairs*, entitled "The Sources of Soviet Conduct." Also reproduced in George F. Kennan, *American Diplomacy, 1900-1950*, (Chicago: University of Chicago Press, 1951), 107-128.
   12. Ibid., 111-112.
   13. Ibid., 115 (italics added).

qualities; and their value finds natural appreciation in the Russian, or the Oriental mind. Thus the Kremlin has no compunction about retreating in the face of superior force. And being under the compulsion of no timetable, it does not get panicky under the necessity of such a retreat. Its political action is a fluid stream which moves constantly, wherever it is permitted to move, toward a given goal. . . . The main thing is that there should always be pressure, increasing constant pressure, toward the desired goal. There is no trace of any feeling in Soviet psychology that the goal must be reached at any given time.[14]

How could the United States counter such a policy? Kennan's answer was that American policy would have to be one of "long-term, patient, but firm and vigilant containment." He viewed containment as a test of American democracy to conduct an intelligent, long-range foreign policy *and* simultaneously contribute to changes within the Soviet Union that ultimately would bring about a moderation of its revolutionary aims. The United States, he emphasized in a passage that was to take on great meaning forty years later,

has it in its power to increase enormously the strains under which Soviet policy must operate, to force upon the Kremlin a far greater degree of moderation and circumspection than it has had to observe in recent years, and in this way to promote tendencies which must eventually find their outlet in either the breakup or the gradual mellowing of Soviet power. For no mystical, messianic movement—and particularly not that of the Kremlin—can face frustration indefinitely without eventually adjusting itself in one way or another to the logic of that state of affairs.[15]

And why was the United States so favorably positioned for a long-term struggle with the Soviet Union? The reason, Kennan argued, was that industry was the key ingredient of power and the United States controlled most of the centers of industry. There were five such centers in the world: the United States, Britain, West Germany, Japan, and the Soviet Union. The United States and its future allies constituted four of these centers, the Soviet Union just one. Containment meant confining the Soviet Union to that one. The question, Kennan said, was not whether the United States had sufficient power to contain the Soviet Union but whether it had the patience and wisdom to do so.

ALTERNATIVES TO CONTAINMENT

Kennan's containment strategy was generally well received in Washington, whose leaders then embarked on the complex task of translating its generalities into specific initiatives. These would entail new strategies for the military services, a greater emphasis on economic statecraft and foreign assistance, and an ongoing effort to enlist foreign countries into bilateral and multilateral alliance networks. But in adopting containment, it must be em-

14. Ibid., 118.
15. Ibid., 127-128.

phasized that the Truman administration implicitly rejected two other courses of action that had substantial support.

The first was a retreat into the traditional pattern of U.S. isolation from European diplomacy. This alternative was rejected when, on the afternoon of February 21, 1947, the first secretary of the British embassy in Washington visited the State Department and handed American officials two notes from His Majesty's government. One concerned Greece, the other Turkey, but, in effect, they said the same thing: Britain could no longer meet its traditional responsibilities to those two countries. Because both were on the verge of collapse, the meaning of the British notes was clear: a Soviet breakthrough could be prevented only by an American commitment.

February 21 was a turning point for the West. Great Britain, the only remaining power in Western Europe, was acknowledging its exhaustion. It had fought Philip II of Spain, Louis XIV and Napoleon Bonaparte of France, Kaiser Wilhelm II and Adolf Hitler of Germany. It had preserved the balance of power that had protected the United States for so long that it seemed almost natural for it to continue to do so. But its ability to protect that balance had steadily declined in the twentieth century. Twice it had needed American help. Each time, however, Britain had fought the longer battle; the United States had entered the wars when it was clear that Germany and its allies were too strong for Great Britain and that America would have to help safeguard its own security.

The second course rejected in the adoption of the strategy of containment was a preventive war. The United States had an atomic monopoly until late 1949. In 1950 the United States had fifty bombs plus the means to deliver them, while the Soviet Union had only tested an atomic device. For a short time, then, the United States possessed the opportunity to establish a *Pax Americana,* or world empire. But exploitation of this atomic monopoly was never seriously considered. Quite apart from the relatively small size of the stockpile, the launch of an atomic Pearl Harbor on the Soviet Union was contrary to American tradition and universal standards of morality. Indeed, after Hiroshima the conviction grew that atomic weapons were too horrible to use and that in a future war there would be no winners. The bomb signaled a significant change: historically the principal task of the military had been to win wars; from now on its main purpose would be to *prevent* them. Atomic weapons could have no other rationale. By the mid-1950s, after both superpowers had tested nuclear devices and had confronted one another in a number of crises, and after the range of destruction had taken a quantum leap from kilotons (thousands of tons of TNT) to megatons (millions of tons of TNT), this conviction grew to absolute certainty. Such weapons could not defend a nation; rather, their use would destroy it.

The consequences of the potentially suicidal nature of nuclear warfare were profound: the United States was committed to a long struggle, and this struggle was to be carried on in a new way. Conflicts between great powers—between Athens and Sparta for the control of ancient Greece, between Rome and Carthage for control of the Mediterranean, or, in more modern times, between Germany and England for control of Europe—had been settled on the battlefield. Such a solution was no longer feasible. Thus the United States had to conduct a *protracted conflict* alien to its style. The term frequently given to this conflict—Cold War—was apt indeed. *War* signified that the U.S.-Soviet rivalry was serious; *Cold* referred to the fact that nuclear weapons were so utterly destructive that war could not be waged with "hot" (nuclear) weapons, but only with "cold" weapons (which included the use of limited conventional force but not nuclear force). But for the existence of nuclear weapons the superpower conflict at some point might well have escalated into a shooting war, as had already happened twice in the twentieth century.

The Cold War that followed therefore was a relationship characterized by long-term hostility and by a mutual determination to avoid a cataclysmic military showdown. As it took over Britain's role as the keeper of the balance of power, the United States had to learn power politics. But in protecting itself, it also had to learn how to manage a protracted conflict in peacetime, a new experience and one at odds with its historic ways of dealing with an enemy state and the international system.

THE CHANGING OF THE GUARD: SEA POWER VERSUS LAND POWER

Historically the U.S. role was similar to Britain's: primarily a naval power, it was to contain the outward thrust of a land power from the Eurasian "heartland." After World War I a British geographer, Halford MacKinder, interested in the relationship of geographic position to international politics (referred to as *geopolitics*), stated the axiom "Who rules East Europe commands the Heartland [Eurasia]; Who rules the Heartland commands the World-Island [Eurasia and Africa, which, on the map, look like a centrally located island]; Who rules the World-Island commands the World." [16] Some years later an American geopolitician, Nicholas Spykman, coined a reply to MacKinder: "Who controls the Rimland [the peripheral areas around Eurasia] controls Eurasia; who rules Eurasia controls the destinies of the world." Although these axioms may be considered too simplistic—and there is some danger in accepting geography as too deterministic a factor in explaining the behavior of states—they explain rather well the essence of the British-German and the U.S.-Soviet conflicts. As the heartland power sought domina-

16. Sir Halford J. MacKinder, *Democratic Ideals and Reality* (New York: Henry Holt, 1919), 150.

tion over Eurasia, if not the "World-Island," which would have made it the dominant global power, the "offshore" naval power sought control of the Eurasian rimlands in order to deny that domination to the heartland power and thereby contain it.

Indeed, before World War I, before the German threat received Britain's primary attention, *czarist* Russia—then incorporating Finland, the three Baltic states, and Poland—had been London's concern. Russian power was spreading eastward to the Pacific, southward from Siberia into Manchuria and into northern China, southward from the Caucasus to Turkey and into Iran toward the Persian Gulf, and southeastward toward the frontier of British India, the area of today's Afghanistan and Pakistan. British power along the rim running from Turkey to India guarded the perimeter around Russia. When Russia pushed into Korea toward Japan, Japan attacked and defeated Russia, thereby also limiting the spread of Russian influence in northern China. After that, Russia focused on the Balkans, where it came into conflict with Austria-Hungary, the ally of Germany, which had become the Continent's most powerful country. Germany became the great threat to British interests, and Britain twice went to war with Germany which, in each conflict, invaded Russia. A victorious Germany would have controlled the heartland—indeed, in World War II victory would have given Germany control from the Atlantic to the Pacific—plus the Middle East, the area linking Europe, Asia, and Africa.

After Germany's second defeat in 1945 the Russian threat reemerged. Already the heartland power, Soviet Russia extended its arm into the center of Europe, reclaimed its dominant position in northern China, and sought to exploit weaknesses along its southern border from Turkey to Pakistan. Thus one reason for the postwar conflict was *geopolitical:* Russian land power expanded but was halted by the countervailing power exerted by a maritime nation. These clashes occurred along the perimeter from Turkey to Iran and then in Western Europe.

It is important to understand the location of the initial conflicts because revisionists argue that whatever the Soviet Union's intentions were, its lack of a large fleet and intercontinental air power meant that it represented no threat to the United States. They point out, moreover, that the United States held an atomic monopoly. Thus the demobilization from a military force of 12.1 million to 1.6 million and the reduction from a budget of more than $80 billion to approximately $13 billion counted for little. In fact, the United States was a hegemon—that is, it was the dominant power in the system and there really was no Soviet threat. Only one part of this argument is correct, however: the Soviet Union did not represent a direct threat to the security of the United States in the Western Hemisphere. But the Soviet army, even after substantial demobilization, remained a formidable force of 175 divisions and certainly one that was able to pressure Soviet neighbors to the south, threaten the western rimlands of Eurasia, and hold America's friends and potential allies hostage. That is why the governments of Iran, Turkey, Greece, and Western Europe feared a revival of American isolationism and sought U.S. countervailing support. To be sure, the small U.S. atomic arsenal could have wreaked great damage on Russian cities, but it could not have stopped the Soviet army from overrunning Western Europe.

In the balance that emerged after World War II, the United States greatly benefited from its productive economy, which had not been damaged by the war; its atomic monopoly, although the number of bombs and bombers available to deliver them remained small in the first years after the war; and the appeal of its democratic political system. The Soviet Union was advantaged by its powerful conventional forces; its geographical position at the center of Eurasia; and, at a time when democracy was still widely identified with the failed capitalism of the 1930s and the Soviet Union with its heroic resistance to the Nazis, its communist ideology. That ideology appealed to the working classes in such nations as France and Italy, as well as political movements that were seeking power in such countries as China. Thus American political leaders after 1945 did not conclude that the United States was a hegemonic power. To the contrary, they were anxious about a balance of power that to them appeared very precarious.[17]

THE U.S. DECLARATION OF (COLD) WAR

On March 12, 1947, President Harry Truman went before a joint session of Congress to deliver one of the most important speeches in American history. After outlining the situation in Greece, he spelled out what was to become known as the Truman Doctrine. The United States, he said, could survive only in a world in which freedom flourished. And it would not realize this objective unless it was

willing to help free peoples to maintain their institutions and their national integrity against aggressive movements that seek to impose upon them totalitarian regimes. *This is no more than a frank recognition that totalitarian regimes imposed on free peoples, by direct or indirect aggression, undermine the foundations of international peace and hence the security of the United States. . . .*

At the present moment in world history nearly every nation must choose between alternative ways of life. The choice is often not a free one. . . .

I believe that we must assist free peoples to work out their own destinies in their own way.[18]

17. Joseph S. Nye, Jr., *Bound to Lead* (New York: Basic Books, 1990), 70-72.
18. Italics added. The drama of this period and Truman's speech to Congress are still best captured in Joseph M. Jones, *The Fifteen Weeks* (New York: Viking Press, 1955), 17-23.

The president asked Congress to appropriate $400 million for economic aid and military supplies for Greece and Turkey and to authorize the dispatch of American personnel to assist with reconstruction and to provide their armies with appropriate instruction and training. And he implicitly offered U.S. assistance to other states with his open-ended appeal to "free peoples." One of his most critical tactical victories in winning approval for these measures was that over Michigan senator Arthur Vandenberg, a prominent Republican isolationist and chairman of the Senate Foreign Relations Committee. With Vandenberg's endorsement, the spirit and financial requirements of the Truman Doctrine were embraced by Congress.

The United States thus initiated the policy of containment. The emerging clash between the postwar superpowers, anticipated by the Truman administration in the late 1940s, was made increasingly evident by hostile actions on both sides. To many, the crucial step was taken on July 2, 1947, when the Russian delegation walked out of a meeting in Paris among Americans and other Western leaders to discuss the distribution of Marshall Plan aid (see Chapter 3). Henceforth the two antagonists would not even put forward the appearance of great-power cooperation or *rapprochement.*

As for the Truman Doctrine itself, a closer look is required because of its universal nature and call for a new anticommunist crusade. In five respects the initiatives launched by President Truman served as the embodiment of America's acceptance of global responsibility.

First, Soviet expansion left the United States with little choice but to adopt a countervailing policy. With the war over, the United States would have much preferred to concentrate on domestic affairs, as the massive postwar demobilization clearly demonstrated. Americans were about to unleash their pent-up demands for consumer goods as U.S. industry converted from wartime to peacetime production. The change from isolationism to internationalism was the product of the postwar bipolar distribution of power and its attending demands for a strong American role. As in the past, the United States was reluctantly drawn into great-power conflict because of an impending imbalance in the nation-state system.

Second, anticommunism was not the major ingredient of American policy during and immediately after World War II. During the war the United States had sought to overcome the Kremlin's suspicions of the West to lay the foundation for postwar cooperation. At the end of the war, the principal concern of American policy makers was not to eliminate the self-proclaimed bastion of world revolution and enemy of Western capitalism, or to push the Soviet Union out of Eastern Europe; it was to prevent a complete return to the historic position of oceanic isolation. Containment was launched after further attempts to reconcile differences with Moscow failed and after continued Soviet pressure, denunciations, and vilification. Hostile Soviet behavior and words were the reasons for the gradual shift of American policy and public opinion from amity to enmity.

Third, the role of anticommunism in American policy was essentially to mobilize congressional and public support for the policy once it had been decided on. A nation that had historically condemned power politics as immoral needed a moral basis for its new use of power. For a people who were weary after four years of war, who identified the termination of war with the end of power politics, who were used to isolation from Europe's wicked affairs, anticommunism was like the cavalry's bugle call to charge. It fit neatly into the traditional American dichotomy of seeing the world as either good or evil, thereby arousing the nation for yet another foreign policy mission. President Truman was conscious of the public's desire to retreat into isolationism after a war, and he was unsure it was ready to commit itself to a potential conflict. He recognized the need to "sell" the public on the United States's new role in foreign policy by exaggerating the threat the nation faced. Indeed, until the Vietnam War undermined this anticommunist consensus, it served the policy makers' purposes; the policy of containment received widespread public and congressional support from both Democrats and Republicans. (As revealed later, Asian policy was to be the major exception to this rule.)

Fourth, despite the universalism of the Truman Doctrine, its application was intended to be specific and limited, not global. American policy makers were well aware that the United States, although a great power, was not omnipotent; national priorities had to be decided carefully and power applied discriminately. American responses, then, would depend both on where the external challenges occurred and on how Washington defined the relation of such challenges to the nation's security. Containment was to be implemented only where the Soviet state appeared to be expanding its power. The priority given to balance-of-power considerations was evident from the very beginning. Despite the democratic purposes stated by the Truman Doctrine, its first application was to Greece and Turkey, neither of which was democratic. Their strategic location was considered more important than the character of their government.

In Western Europe, of course, America's strategic and power considerations were compatible with its democratic values. The containment of the Soviet Union could be equated with the defense of democracy. But outside of Western Europe, strategy and values were often incompatible. The United States confronted a classic dilemma: protecting strategically located but undemocratic nations, such as Iran, Turkey, and Greece, might make the containment of Soviet power possible, but it also risked America's reputation and weakened the credibility of its policy. Yet alignment only with democratic states, of which there were all too few, might make U.S. implementation of its containment policy impossible. The purity of the cause might be preserved, but the security of democracy would be weakened. This dilemma was to plague U.S. policy throughout the Cold War.

The fifth point, and perhaps the most important, is the contrasting nature of American and Soviet expansion. The Soviet Union, which already had annexed the Baltic states, imposed communist regimes on its neighbors and stationed Soviet forces there to ensure the loyalty of these states. None of these governments could have survived without the presence of Soviet troops. By contrast, Iran, Turkey, and Greece invited American assistance because they feared Soviet pressure and intimidation. Soviet expansion meant their loss of independence; America's expansion was designed to preserve it. If ever there were a defensively motivated expansion, it was the U.S. commitment in the eastern Mediterranean, which was followed by an even larger commitment to first revive and then defend the nations of Western Europe. All shared the U.S. perception of the Soviet Union as a threat to their political independence and territorial integrity and urged Washington to redress the post-1945 imbalance. Their concern was not U.S. expansion but a return to U.S. isolation.

While containing communism became the central preoccupation of U.S. foreign policy makers for a generation, it was not without its critics. Some felt it did not go far enough, that it failed to exploit U.S. military and economic supremacy and provided the Soviets with the initiative. Others felt it went too far. By codifying the Soviet-American conflict, it cemented a pervasive U.S. role in Europe and beyond and ensured a prolonged and dangerous global competition. Located as it was between these two extremes, the containment alternative attracted broad support among moderates both in the United States and abroad. While later leaders would modify the strategy, they adhered to its broader objectives with unusual consistency. It thus heralded an auspicious new era in U.S. foreign policy, perhaps best reflected in the title of Secretary of State Dean Acheson's memoir, *Present at the Creation*. To Acheson, the late 1940s

saw the entry of our nation, already one of the superpowers, into the near chaos of a war-torn and disintegrating world society. To the responsibilities and needs of that time the nation summoned an imaginative effort unique in history and even greater than that made in the preceding years of fighting. All who served in those years had an opportunity to give more than a sample of their best.[19]

As Acheson suggested, the early containment period was perhaps the most imaginative of U.S. postwar policy. After more than a century of isolationism, the collapse of the great powers of Western Europe and the ascension of the Soviet Union led the United States to accepts its role as the fulcrum of a new

19. Dean Acheson, *Present at the Creation* (New York: Norton, 1969), 725.

global balance of power. The Truman administration reconstructed a prosperous and democratic Western Europe and edged its nations away from past rivalries toward cooperation and unity. Through the military and economic integration of the United States and its Western allies, the volatile postwar system was stabilized and an elaborate framework for East-West competition was established. With the structure of the new order having been built, and with the West's tactical approach widely apprehended, responsibility shifted toward the equally demanding task of translating the new policy into practice.

Harry Truman and Gen. Douglas MacArthur often clashed over military matters during the Korean War. MacArthur was dismissed before the war ended.

CHAPTER THREE

Containment: From Theory to Practice

Twenty-one years separated the two world wars of the early twentieth century, providing their combatants with time to recover from their losses, restore some semblance of domestic order, redefine their national interests, and prepare for future challenges. But that was not the case after World War II, which, by contrast, led directly into the Cold War. Even before the war was over both the Soviet Union and the Western allies were posturing for spheres of influence in central Europe. And it was only six months after the Japanese surrender that Winston Churchill gloomily proclaimed that an "iron curtain" was descending across central Europe, drawing the battle lines of the next global confrontation. If there was an "interwar" period in this case, it was hardly perceptible.

Fortunately for the United States, the late 1940s was among the most imaginative years in U.S. diplomatic history. President Harry Truman—with an unusually cohesive team that included George Marshall, Dean Acheson, and George Kennan—transformed U.S. foreign policy so the United States could compete indefinitely as a political, economic, and military superpower. Although they would eventually succumb to partisan attacks, these "wise men" were credited with establishing the basis of Western strategy, which ultimately prevailed in the Cold War.[1]

In Western Europe the Truman administration not only reestablished democratic political order; it also established a transatlantic security system and a viable West Germany. All of this was underwritten by a U.S.-created economic order, the Bretton Woods system, which was based on open markets and the coordination of global monetary, trade, and development policy. Bretton Woods provided the economic growth and prosperity that allowed the members of the anti-Soviet coalition to carry out Truman's containment strategy for nearly three decades. Even after the Bretton Woods system faltered in the 1970s, its key institutions (the International Monetary Fund, World Bank, and General Agreement on Tariffs and Trade) remained intact through the century.

Europe's total collapse after World War II raised anew a fundamental question that had bedeviled U.S. leaders for years: Was Europe vital to U.S. security? America's interventions in the two world wars suggested that the answer was obvious. But both times the United States had been drawn into the conflicts only after prolonged periods of hesitation and by threats of German hegemony across the continent and beyond. The public had not understood the relationship between U.S. security and European affairs under other circumstances. At the end of each conflict the United States had tried to regain its detachment from Europe, the almost pathological instinct of Americans dating back more than two centuries. After the Second World War, however, the United States was forced, for the first time, to establish an *ongoing*, multifaceted relationship with Western Europe because in the precarious postwar order it alone had the resources to take the initiative.

Europe's vital importance became especially clear in the emerging bipolar world. It ranked second only to the United States in its collective economic power—in industry, productivity, and skilled workers, scientists, and engineers. Moreover, European-American trading and cultural ties were long-standing and strong. And, not least, as the Cold War intensified, Western Europe critically represented the buffer zone between the two superpowers. Given its enormous potential and its geographic position, Europe's security was indeed inseparable from U.S. security, and by the late 1940s this reality finally overcame national ambivalence toward the region.

1. Walter Isaacson and Evan Thomas, *The Wise Men* (New York: Simon and Schuster, 1986).

As the United States undertook efforts to revive Western Europe, however, it became clear that containing communism would require U.S. involvement in other parts of the world. In the late 1940s and early 1950s the Asian perimeter of the Soviet Union and China became another focus of U.S. containment, attracting both U.S. economic resources and combat forces.

In contrast to Western Europe, many Asian states had only recently emerged from colonialism and their nationalistic and anti-Western feelings were very strong. Nationalist China's collapse and the establishment of a communist government on the mainland in late 1949 further weakened the U.S. position in Asia. Thus the United States no longer confronted only the Soviet Union; it faced the combined strength of two large, heavily populated, militarily powerful communist states. Whereas pressure on Europe united the Western powers, however, pressure on Asia divided them by producing a split over the character and nature of the new Chinese regime and the degree to which it threatened Western interests.

In Washington, developments in Asia inspired a prolonged and heated debate between "Asia firsters" and those seeking to limit U.S. containment efforts to Western Europe. Events would propel the United States into action on both fronts.

REBUILDING WESTERN EUROPE

The war in Europe devastated the economies of all the countries, winners and losers alike. Their economic distress produced social and political turmoil that threatened to undermine efforts to create a shield against Soviet influence in the region. Although the Soviet Union also was decimated by the war and faced a prolonged period of recovery, its enhanced control over Eastern Europe provided Stalin and his successors with opportunities to exploit instability across the iron curtain.

Britain's state of near collapse was symptomatic of the situation throughout Europe. Britain's crisis was largely economic. An island nation, it traditionally depended on international trade for its livelihood. But the war had crippled its merchant marine, liquidated most of its investments, and destroyed many of its factories. With the means of financing its imports all but gone, Britain had to increase its exports; just to maintain the 1939 standard of living it had to raise its exports by 75 percent. By December 1946 Britain had reached only its prewar level of production. The future looked bleak and ominous: millions of Britons were unemployed, cold, and hungry—worn out by the long years of war and the determined postwar efforts to recover.

Postwar conditions in Germany also were dreadful. The war had been carried into the heart of that nation, and few cities or towns had escaped Allied bombing, street fighting, or willful destruction by the Nazis as they retreated.

To make matters worse, 10 million additional Germans came into these ruins from former German territory annexed by Poland. Millions of people were without food, shelter, or work. There was only one word to describe Germany in 1945—chaos. Three-quarters of the factories still standing in the American and British zones of occupation were closed. In January 1947 production fell to 31 percent of the 1936 level, Germany's best year; by February it had declined to 29 percent.

Allied policy was not designed to alleviate this situation. The Allies were primarily engaged with Germany's disarmament and demilitarization and with the elimination of all industries whose output could be used for military production. The United States and Britain were not particularly eager to rebuild Germany's industrial power; after all, it had taken the combined efforts of three world powers to bring the Nazi war machine to a halt and defeat it. Nor were the Allies especially concerned with the lot of the German people during the immediate postwar days. After six years of brutal warfare, such concern hardly could have been expected. The revelations of Nazi atrocities and crimes, of wanton destruction, and of millions of innocent people slaughtered in concentration camps were too recent to be dismissed.

The French, above all others, were not likely to forget the Nazis. Although the French economy had been badly damaged during the war, by late 1946 it had begun to recover. But iron and steel production had reached only half the prewar total. Coal was the key factor because the iron and steel industries were dependent on imported coal. But European coal production was still well below the pre-1939 annual average. France's industry was therefore unable to produce sufficient goods for its sizable farm population to buy. Farmers withdrew fields from crop cultivation, keeping more food for their families and feeding more grain to their livestock. Meanwhile, the urban population was short of food, and the government had to spend scarce resources to buy food from abroad. The harsh winter of 1946-1947 only intensified these problems.

This situation was made to order for the large, well-organized French Communist Party. One-quarter of France's electorate—practically the entire working class—voted for the communists. (In Italy, the figure was one-third of the electorate.) The reason for this was simple: French and Italian capitalism had alienated these voters. The workers were, in effect, internal émigrés who voted communist to protest a system they felt had long mistreated them; unlike workers in Britain and the United States, they had suffered all the hardships of capitalism while enjoying few of its benefits, such as good wages and social opportunities. As a result, the Communist Party in France enjoyed a powerful position in politics and trade unions.

These difficult conditions forced Western leaders to respond immediately. It was obvious that their actions could not be limited to a single area such as economic development, military defense, or political reform. Their response must be comprehensive, including all these areas, and, more important, take the form of an overriding dedication to preserving Europe as the front line of Cold War defense.

ECONOMIC RECONSTRUCTION AND
THE MARSHALL PLAN

With Europe on the verge of not only economic ruin but also a complete political and social breakdown, everything seemed to force it into dependence on the United States. Most of the items needed for reconstruction—wheat, cotton, sulphur, sugar, machinery, trucks, and coal—could be obtained in sufficient quantities only from the United States. But short of food and fuel, with its cities and factories destroyed, Europe could not earn the dollars to pay for the commodities required for its recovery. Moreover, the United States was so well supplied with everything that it did not have to buy much from abroad. The result was the ominous *dollar gap*—a term that frightened the Europeans because it denoted Europe's economic collapse and its complete dependence on the United States to recover economically and politically.

Because the United States could not permit the Soviet Union to extend its influence beyond the iron curtain, U.S. policy makers had to find a way to help Western Europe recover. The prescribed cure was a massive injection of dollars. Only a tremendous program of economic aid could restore Europe's economy, enabling it to surpass its prewar agricultural and industrial production. American aid was made conditional, however, on economic cooperation among the European states. In this respect, the United States clearly held itself up as a model. The Economic Cooperation Act of 1948 called specifically for European economic integration. America, it stated, was "mindful of the advantage which the United States has enjoyed through the existence of a large-scale domestic market with no internal trade barriers and [believed] that similar advantages can accrue to the countries of Europe." In official American opinion, integration became the prerequisite for Europe's recovery and the necessary basis for long-range prosperity.

President Truman's secretary of state, George Marshall, for whom the European Recovery Program was named, first stressed the economic cooperation required by the United States. He called on the European states to devise a plan for their *common* needs and *common* recovery. The United States would furnish the funds, but the Europeans had to assume the initiative and do the planning. The result was the Organization for European Economic Cooperation (OEEC), which estimated the cost of Europe's recovery over a four-year period to be $33 billion. The president asked for $17 billion, which Congress cut to $13 billion. The amount actually used by the Economic Cooperation Administration (ECA) between 1948 and the end of 1951, when the program ended, was just over $12 billion. Britain, France, and West Germany together received more than half of this amount.

The original invitation by the United States to the nations of Europe to plan their joint recovery was deliberately extended to *all* European countries, including the Soviet Union and the nations of Eastern Europe. If the United States had invited only the nations of Western Europe, it would have placed itself in a politically disadvantageous position in which it would have been blamed for the division of Europe and the intensification of the Cold War. Actually, had the Soviets participated, Congress probably would not have supported the Marshall Plan for two reasons: first, the costs would have risen astronomically as a result of the very heavy damage suffered by the Soviet Union during the war, and, second, anti-Soviet feeling was growing. The risk had to be accepted, however; it had to be the Soviets, who, by their rejection of Marshall Plan aid, would be responsible for the division of Europe.

Was the Marshall Plan a success? The results tell their own story. By 1950, when the Korean War broke out, Europe already was exceeding its prewar production by 25 percent; two years later this figure was 200 percent higher. British exports were doing well, French inflation was slowing, and German production had reached its 1936 level. The dollar gap had been reduced from $12 billion to $2 billion. In human terms, Europe's cities were being rebuilt and its factories were busy, its stores restocked, and its farmers productive. The Marshall Plan was a huge success, and at a cost that represented only a tiny fraction of the U.S. national income over the same four-year period. These were the State Department's best years as it took the lead in organizing U.S. foreign policy, which reflected some of the best characteristics of the country: its self-confidence and generosity, energy and imagination. These were years of excitement as the United States emerged as a great power and as young men and women from government, business, finance, and academia flocked to Washington and Western Europe to ensure the success of the Marshall Plan. Winston Churchill called it "the most unsordid act in history."

MILITARY REARMAMENT AND THE NATO ALLIANCE

Soon after the Marshall Plan was launched, however, it became clear that the plan by itself would not suffice. In February 1948 the Soviets engineered a coup d'état in Prague, and—ten years after the Munich agreement and Adolf Hitler's subsequent seizure of that betrayed nation—Czechoslovakia disappeared behind the iron curtain. A few months later, in June, the Soviets imposed a blockade on Berlin in an effort to dislodge the Western powers. It is not surprising that the Western Europeans felt jittery at these overt signs of Soviet hostility and aggressive intent. It suddenly became crystal clear that a prerequisite for Europe's recovery was military security.

The Europeans already had made some moves in this direction. In March 1947 France and Britain had signed the Treaty of Dunkirk to provide for their mutual defense against a threat to their security. Exactly a year later, Great Britain, France, the Netherlands, Belgium, and Luxembourg signed the Brussels Pact of collective self-defense. The pact members expected the system of collective defense, officially proclaimed the Western European Union, to attract American military support. They were not disappointed. In April 1949 Belgium, Canada, Denmark, France, Great Britain, Iceland, Italy, Luxembourg, the Netherlands, Norway, Portugal, and the United States created the North Atlantic Treaty Organization (NATO). The NATO treaty called for "continuous and effective self-help and mutual aid" among its signatories; an invasion of one "shall be considered an attack against them all." Former isolationist Arthur Vandenberg, chairman of the Senate Foreign Relations Committee, hailed the agreement as "the most important step in American foreign policy since the promulgation of the Monroe Doctrine."

For the United States, NATO set a precedent. For the first time in its history the country had committed itself to an alliance in peacetime. Instead of again allowing the balance of power to be upset and once more becoming drawn into a war after it had started, the United States now expected to prevent this by committing itself to the preservation of the European balance on a permanent basis. Collective security under NATO would be combined with economic development efforts to seal the long-term cooperation of the United States and its allies in Western Europe. Conversely, the formation of NATO would propel the integration of states in Eastern Europe under the Warsaw Pact and solidify the division of the continent.[2]

A central assumption underlying U.S. strategy was that Soviet fears of meeting NATO resistance and the promise of all-out war would *deter* aggression. The policy of deterrence relied almost exclusively on American nuclear power—that is, on the ability of the Strategic Air Command (SAC) to inflict such heavy damage that an enemy would, in effect, be committing suicide if it launched an attack. The United States would rely on this strategy of nuclear deterrence throughout the Cold War, continually expanding and modernizing its atomic arsenals so that its promise of apocalypse would be guaranteed.

But the explosion of the first Soviet atomic bomb in late 1949 foreshadowed a time when the Soviet Union, too, would possess a stockpile of nuclear weapons and the means to deliver them. Indeed, just as the NATO alliance was being organized, deterrence became a double-edged sword that would complicate the strategies and inhibit the actions of both sides. Under these conditions of emerging *mutual* deterrence, Western

2. The Warsaw Treaty Organization (WTO), established in May 1955, comprised the Soviet Union and seven satellite states in Eastern Europe. The WTO was modeled on the order of NATO, although the Soviet satellites played a relatively minor role in managing the alliance.

leaders pursued both strategic (nuclear) defense and conventional rearmament. The latter was aimed at shoring up NATO forces along the "tripwire" between East and West. The critical zone of collective security would, once again, be found in Germany at the intra-German border between East and West.

THE GERMAN PROBLEM AND THE 'FORWARD STRATEGY'

The need for ample forces presented the European states with a painful dilemma. They were still in the midst of economic recovery and were not able to devote a large share of their national budgets to rearmament. The American answer was the rearmament of Germany. If France and Britain could not supply the necessary troops along the iron curtain tripwire, Germany would have to. This decision seemed eminently correct because this "forward strategy" required that NATO would try to hold West Germany. In turn, of course, German rearmament reinforced the need for a forward strategy. The West Germans could hardly be persuaded to rearm if they could not be assured that West Germany would not be turned into a battlefield and that German troops would not be used merely for the defense of France and Britain. Thus the question of Germany arose once more. It was not a new question, but this time it received new answers.

Germany had held the key to the European balance of power since at least 1870 when Prussia defeated France, Europe's preeminent land power, and established a united Germany. This was true of Germany even in defeat in 1945. Almost from the cessation of hostilities, the Soviet Union and the United States began their contest over Germany. East Germany was in Soviet hands; the Western powers occupied West Germany. Actually, the Allies were fortunate, for West Germany contained the great majority of Germany's population and the heart of its industrial power. East Germany possessed far fewer resources, and what little of value it retained after World War II was hauled away in boxcars to the Soviet Union.

During the war Joseph Stalin, Winston Churchill, and Franklin Roosevelt established a four-power Allied Control Commission (with France as the fourth power) that would administer West Germany as a single economic unit. But in practice this task proved impossible. Shortly after the surrender of Nazi Germany, the Allied powers pursued separate goals in a divided Germany. The Soviet Union violated key aspects of the occupation plan, propelling Western distrust and ensuring the long-term division of Germany. Furthermore, as Europe's economic collapse became clearer and the Cold War began, it became necessary to lift Germany out of its economic stagnation and make its industry contribute to the general economic recovery of Europe. In July 1946 the United States offered to merge its zone with those of Britain and France; West Germany was to be integrated to speed up its industrial recovery. The French, fearing Germany's reviving strength, at first refused to participate but later joined.

The Soviets reacted to this event by blockading West Berlin in 1948. Berlin, like Germany, was supposed to be administered by the four occupying powers, but the growing Cold War divided the city just as it did Germany. Lying deep in East German territory, surrounded by Soviet divisions, the Western half of the city was an easy and vulnerable spot for the Soviets to apply pressure on the Western powers. But the issue at stake was more than the Western presence in Berlin: it was Germany itself. Berlin, as the old capital of Germany, was the symbol of the ongoing conflict between the Soviet Union and Germany, two countries that had fought two cataclysmic wars in forty years. Germany had beaten Russia the first time and almost defeated it the second. The Soviets did not want to see West Germany become a partner of the West.

The Soviet Union's fear of Germany, however, was not completely responsible for its actions in Berlin. If Soviet fear of Germany had been so deep, the Soviets would have accepted an American proposal, offered by Secretary of State James Byrnes, of an alliance of twenty-five or even forty years to neutralize Germany. Moreover, although the Soviet Union had been much weaker than Germany before World War II, it emerged from that conflict far stronger—a superpower, in fact—while Germany, in spite of its potential strength, was now only a second-class power. The Soviet-German balance of power had shifted decisively in the Soviet Union's favor, and another German attack on the Soviet Union was unlikely. In fact, in any war, whether it acted unilaterally or as an ally of the United States, Germany would be the battlefield and therefore the first country to be destroyed. Germany's fear of this consequence was a sufficient deterrent.

Playing it safe, however, the Soviets resorted to a test of strength to forestall West Germany's revival: a blockade of West Berlin. If the Allies could be forced out of Berlin, German confidence in the United States would be undermined. The Germans would not attach themselves to a friend too weak or too fearful to protect them. Indeed, if American willpower crumbled under Soviet pressure, France and Britain also would lose confidence in the United States. Thus had it not been met, the Berlin crisis would have destroyed the evolving U.S. commitment in Europe (NATO was still in the future) and nullified U.S. efforts to rebuild Western Europe as a partner in the struggle against the Soviet Union. In short, the Soviet goal was to drive the United States out of Western Europe, leaving the United States with little choice but to defend its position in West Berlin because the consequences for failure were so enormous. To that end, the United States launched a continuous airlift of supplies to Berlin instead of attempting to puncture the blockade on the ground, which might have sparked armed conflict between superpower regiments.

The Soviets waited to see if the Western powers could take care of West Berlin's 2.5 million citizens indefinitely. It would take a minimum of 4,000 tons of food and fuel daily—an enormous amount of tonnage to ship in by air. But after 324 days the Soviets were convinced that the Americans and the British were more than equal to the task. Although the total supplies did not immediately reach the 4,000-ton target, Western planes eventually flew in as much as 13,000 tons daily. Planes landing at three-minute intervals flew in 60 percent more than the 8,000 tons that had previously been sent each day by ground transport. Faced with this colossal Allied achievement, the Soviets called off the blockade in May 1949.

The U.S. determination to hold Western Europe and not to allow further Soviet expansion had been demonstrated. The West Germans clearly saw that they could count on America to protect them. Just as NATO had been the prerequisite for Europe's economic recovery, the Berlin airlift was the final American act that led to Germany's resurgence. The United States had laid the basis for Germany's economic recovery through Marshall Plan funds; in NATO it would give Germany the sense of military security without which its economic reconstruction could not have been completed. For the time being, the Soviet efforts to "decouple" Western Europe from the United States ended.

THE DRIVE FOR WESTERN EUROPEAN INTEGRATION

Ironically it was renewed fear of Germany's rising strength that stimulated further efforts toward European integration. The specter of a fully revived Germany struck fear into most of Germany's neighbors. The French, with their memories of 1870, 1914, and 1940, were particularly alarmed. Germany's recovery, stimulated by America's response to the Cold War, posed a serious problem for Germany's partners: How could they hold Germany in check when it was potentially the strongest nation in Europe outside of the Soviet Union? Ever since Germany's unification, France had dealt with the inherently greater strength of its aggressive and militaristic neighbor by forming alliances that could balance Germany's power. Because Britain usually preferred to retain a free hand, and because British interests were at times opposed to those of France, the French had relied primarily on Continental allies. Before World War I they had discovered such an ally in Russia, and between the two wars they had found partners in Poland, Czechoslovakia, Romania, and Yugoslavia. None of these alliances had saved France, however. In both world wars British and American power (aided by the Soviets in World War II) had been the decisive factor in defeating Germany. After the Second World War and despite the extension of Soviet power into the heart of Europe, France still saw Germany as the enemy, and in December 1944 the French signed a mutual assistance treaty with the Soviets, making an alliance they considered necessary for their security. Soviet hostility soon disillusioned the French and deprived the treaty of any meaning, however. In fact, this hostility made it necessary to add Germany's power to that of the West.

The failure of this traditional balance-of-power technique, in which an inferior power sought to balance a stronger nation, led France to seek a new way to exert some control over Germany's growing power. French leaders found an imaginative means in European integration. Through the creation of a supranational community, to which Germany could transfer certain sovereign rights, German power could be controlled. Instead of serving national purposes, German power would serve Europe's collective purposes.

ECONOMIC INTEGRATION IN EUROPE

France made its first move in the direction of a united Europe in May 1950, when Foreign Minister Robert Schuman proposed the formation of the European Coal and Steel Community (ECSC) composed of "Little Europe" (France, Germany, Italy, and the Benelux countries of Belgium, the Netherlands, and Luxembourg). The aim of the Schuman Plan, as it also was known, was to interweave German and French heavy industry to such an extent that it would be impossible ever to separate them. Germany never again would be able to use its coal and steel industries for nationalistic and militaristic purposes. War between Germany and France would become not only unthinkable but also impossible.

The new French technique of restraining Germany was more than an incorporation of Germany's superior strength, thereby subjecting Germany to a degree of French control. "Europeanization" also was a means for France to achieve a balance with Germany. The combination of the French and German coal industries would strengthen French heavy industry and create a Franco-German equilibrium within the ECSC. Economic integration would allow France to overcome its inferior industrial strength, caused primarily by its lack of energy sources such as the coal needed to heat the furnaces; Europe's largest coal deposits lay in the German-controlled Ruhr and Saar regions.

The French plan, however, was not devised only to control Germany's resurgent power or to give France greater strength relative to Germany. It had a third and more ambitious goal in mind: a united Europe under French leadership. France alone was too weak to pursue an active role in a world dominated by two superpowers. Even in the Western coalition the most influential European nation was not France but Britain. With Germany's recovery, it was very likely that Bonn's voice and opinions also would outweigh those of

Paris in Washington. By itself France would remain dependent on its American protector, powerless to affect major Western policy decisions. A united Europe, with Franco-German unity at its core, was therefore France's alternative to remaining subservient to the United States and without major influence either in NATO or on the world stage. Through a united Europe France could gain an equal voice with what Charles de Gaulle was later to call the "Anglo-Saxons" in NATO, and possibly even exert independent pressure on the Soviet Union.

These, then, were the benefits the French expected to gain from the Schuman Plan. They saw clearly that the nucleus of a united Europe would have to be a Franco-German union. But first the antagonism between these two states, born of their traditional enmity, would have to be healed. Moreover, the French recognized that a united Europe had to be built on a solid foundation—not simply on dreams or sentiment. They knew they would have to tie together the interests of politically powerful and economically important groups in the countries of Europe *across* national boundaries. The removal of all trade barriers in the coal and steel sector would encourage the modernization of mines and plants. Once producers had adjusted to the wider market and witnessed its opportunities, they would want to remove national barriers in other areas.

The French showed great political astuteness in their selection of heavy industry as the first sector to be integrated because coal and steel formed the basis of the entire industrial structure and represented a sector that could not possibly be separated from the overall economy. The French expected that, as the benefits of the pooling of heavy industry became clear, other sectors of the economy would follow suit, eventually leading to the creation of a "United States of Europe" with a huge market and a mass-production system. In brief, this "functionalist" approach stressed supranational cooperation and institutions within a limited sphere and the creation of common interests within that particular area of activity before extending it to other fields.

EUROPEAN MILITARY INTEGRATION

The ECSC institutions, the embryo of a united Europe, were soon applied to a new area: the military forces of the different countries. The French originated this idea as well in response to American insistence on German rearmament. To the French, the rearmament of their old enemy was distasteful and dangerous but unavoidable because France could not supply more troops. The French remained determined, however, that the world would never see another *German* army, *German* general staff, *German* war ministry, or *German* ministry of armaments. Thus the French proposed the formation of a European Defense Community (EDC). A European army, composed of army corps in which no more than two divisions could be of one nationality, would be an instrument for checking Germany's rising military power while using it for Europe's defense. The EDC treaty was signed in May 1952. NATO, however, remained the supreme command and maintained a formal link to the EDC. Because all EDC members except Germany were members of NATO, this link ensured that Germany would be obligated to come to NATO's defense and vice versa. It also made it clear that NATO had a double purpose: contain Soviet power as well as control German power.

For West Germany, entry into the EDC was another step toward regaining full equality with the other Western powers and asserting its political prestige. Most important, in return for providing the EDC with 500,000 men organized into twelve divisions, Germany recovered its sovereignty, as the Federal Republic of Germany (FRG), with certain limitations. The Allies reserved their authority to protect the security of their forces in the FRG (not only against external aggression but also against possible attempts by the extreme left or right to subvert West Germany from within), to govern Berlin, and to preserve their exclusive right to negotiate with the Soviet Union on the question of German reunification.

The likelihood of German reunification, however, was small because Western proposals to unite Germany always included terms that the Soviet Union could not possibly accept such as reunification via free elections in both halves of Germany and the freedom for a reunified Germany to conduct its own foreign policy. Thus the Allied terms in effect ensured the continuation of a divided Germany, which was precisely what the Western Europeans, especially France, wanted. The division of Germany solved the German problem for Moscow as well because it brought Soviet power to West Germany's doorstep, reminding it of the dangers of any further military adventures, and legitimated the presence of the Soviet army in Eastern Europe. In short, the division of Germany served both adversaries' purposes and—except for a short but dangerous period in the late 1950s and early 1960s when the Soviets tested the status quo—served as the basis for the longest peace Europe has known in the twentieth century. A divided Germany might not have been just according to the principle of national self-determination, but it was part of a clearly split Europe in which both Moscow and Washington knew where the lines were between their respective spheres of influence and what the danger was of crossing these lines at any point.

Thus American foreign policy in Western Europe had been a success. The Truman Doctrine had inhibited Soviet opportunism in the Middle East, the Mediterranean, and the Persian Gulf. The Marshall Plan and Bretton Woods accords had set Europe on the path to economic recovery, democracy, and social stability. The United States had transformed a position of great weakness and vulnerability into one of relative strength. It had drawn a clear line between the American and Soviet spheres of influence and demonstrated, in

Turkey, Greece, and Berlin, that it was in Europe to stay. (The Greek crisis had passed when Yugoslavia was ejected from the Soviet bloc in 1948; the Yugoslavs no longer provided aid to the Greek guerrillas.) What all this meant was that Europe was no longer a profitable field for guerrilla warfare, coups d'état, subversive attempts, or military intimidation. Instead, it had become a barrier to the extension of Soviet influence.

In the American defense strategy of the early Cold War years, then, Europe held strategic priority; Asia was of secondary interest, as it always had been. Europe, in fact, was seen as so vital to American security that any Soviet move in Western Europe would be met with an all-out clash with the United States and NATO (a promise delivered explicitly to Soviet leaders throughout this period). In contrast, no single area in Asia was thought to be worth the cost of total war. The region was too distant, its economies too peripheral to Western interests, its political and social systems too distinct from those in the West.

In Europe the rapid recovery effectively restrained both the domestic appeal of communism and Soviet opportunism in the region. Thousands of miles away, however, the impending collapse of Nationalist China created a geopolitical vacuum and turned Soviet attention toward its Asian frontiers. This shift was consistent with Kennan's predictions of Russo-Soviet strategy, of its propensity to redirect its expansionist efforts toward whichever region along its massive periphery appeared vulnerable. It was in Asia, therefore, that the most violent conflicts of the Cold War would occur over the next two decades.

CONFRONTING REVOLUTION IN ASIA

The collapse in 1949 of Nationalist China, on whom the United States was counting in the emerging Cold War, led to the establishment of the People's Republic of China (PRC) under the leadership of communist Mao Zedong. The communists' victory was followed in 1950 by the PRC's takeover of Tibet, the invasion of South Korea by communist North Korea, and the expansion of Western containment efforts into the Far East.

The invasion of South Korea in June 1950 provoked a military response by the United States, under the aegis of the United Nations, and represented the first test of Kennan's containment policy. As the Korean War dragged on without resolution, however, President Truman and his administration lost popularity. Charges of conspiracy and betrayal and of "losing" China and being "soft" on communists at home and abroad were made by Truman's political opponents, creating a central campaign issue in the 1952 presidential election. However distorted the charges were, they limited the Truman administration's diplomatic freedom, pressured it into a policy of global anticommunism, and resulted in more than twenty years of confrontation with China.

The U.S. failure to establish normal relations with China was a strategic error of the first order. It helped to provoke Chinese intervention in the Korean War, prevented Washington from exploiting Sino-Soviet differences when they first surfaced, and was a major cause of the later tragic U.S. intervention in Indochina. Indeed, the events in Asia in the late 1940s and early 1950s were to have a profound impact on American foreign policy throughout the Cold War.

THE CHINESE REVOLUTION AND U.S. RESPONSE

During World War II the United States had a twofold purpose in the Pacific: to defeat Japan and to help to create a powerful and friendly China that would play a leading role in protecting the postwar peace in the Far East. At Cairo in 1943 the United States and Great Britain had promised to return "all the territories Japan had stolen from the Chinese, such as Manchuria, Formosa, and the Pescadores." It also awarded China one of the five permanent seats on the United Nations Security Council. Thus China was granted equal status with the Soviet Union, Great Britain, France, and the United States.

In typically American fashion, President Franklin Roosevelt and his advisers thought that the mere pronouncement that China was a great power could actually convert it into one: one need only believe strongly enough in the desirability of an event for it to happen. Perhaps American policy makers also hoped that if China were considered a great power, it would behave like one. But American faith without a viable Chinese government was not enough to accomplish the task. In their quixotic desire to create stability in East Asia based on such a Sino-American alliance, the Roosevelt and Truman administrations ignored the depth of hostilities between domestic factions in China and the unlikelihood of a negotiated settlement on terms favorable to the United States.

The primary obstacle to establishing an ally in China was resolving the ongoing civil war. Quite apart from the Japanese occupation of large areas of the country during the war, there were two Chinas: a Nationalist China and a communist China. The communists were not scattered throughout the whole population, as they were in Europe. Already in control of large segments of northwest China before the war, the communists had extended their sphere during the war by expanding into north-central China. As this protracted struggle continued, it became clear that a negotiated settlement was impossible. Both sides sought a monopoly of power, and each believed that it could defeat its opponent; compromise was thought to be unnecessary.

China's pro-American Nationalist government, however, was losing popular support and disintegrating. Perhaps the Nationalists were the victims of fate. Except for the two years from 1929 to 1931, the government had had to fight for its very survival—against the Japanese, who attacked Manchuria in 1931 and China in 1932 (Shanghai) and 1937, as well as the communists. Faced with both external and internal dangers, Nationalist leader Chiang Kai-shek had neither the time nor the resources to formulate and implement the political, social, and economic reforms China needed. His principal concerns were military: to stem the Japanese advance and maintain himself in power. The modernization of China—above all, the problem of meeting peasant aspirations—was strictly secondary.

Indeed, Chiang's failure to appease the peasants, the vast majority of China's population, as well as unchecked inflation and rampant corruption among government officials, would prove fatal to his efforts to gain control of the country. A government whose principal social and economic support came from the landlords was unlikely to carry out reforms the peasants sought. These same peasants provided most of the conscripts for the Nationalist army, whereas the eligible sons of the rich were likely to avoid military service because their families bribed corrupt officials. In the same way, the rich tended to avoid paying taxes. Thus Chiang's Nationalist government, far from attracting the peasants, seemed to be doing its best to alienate them. Indeed, as the government continued to lose popularity, it began to resort to force to hold its position. The resulting police and military measures further alienated the people, ensuring a communist victory in the civil war.

The blame for these events often has been attributed to President Franklin Roosevelt and the Yalta "betrayal." It was charged that concessions made to Stalin by Roosevelt to expedite the end of World War II against Japan by having the Soviet army attack Japanese troops in Manchuria undermined America's major ally, Nationalist China. But this was not true. To take the charge of betrayal seriously, one has to deny certain clear facts of wartime military strategy: namely, that the American military was unsure the atomic bomb would be a success; that they believed an invasion of Japan would be necessary to bring about Japan's surrender; that they expected to suffer large numbers of casualties and feared even more if the Japanese reinforced the home-island garrison with troops from Manchuria and northern China; and that, therefore, they wanted the Red Army to tackle these mainland forces before the U.S. invasion. The American government was willing to reward the Soviets if this would help save the lives of American soldiers.

Ultimately, it was the military struggle in China that played the key role in determining the outcome of the civil war there and the communist victory. Gen. David Barr, head of the American military mission in China, summed up the situation succinctly: "No battle has been lost since my arrival due to lack of ammunition or equipment. Their [the Nationalists'] military debacle, in my opinion, can all be attributed to the world's worst leadership and many other morale-destroying factors that led to a complete loss of the will to fight." [3] Nowhere was this more clearly demonstrated than in Chiang's failure, after his loss of northern China, even to attempt a defense of south China by making a stand along the Yangtze River. Chiang withdrew to Taiwan (in those days also called Formosa), an island lying 100 miles off China's coast. In the fall of 1949 Mao proclaimed the communist victory and establishment of the People's Republic of China.

One question about Nationalist China's defeat remains: Could the United States have prevented it? The answer is "perhaps"—*if* American officers had taken over the command of the Nationalist armies, *if* the United States had been willing to commit large-scale land, air, and sea forces, and *if* the United States had been willing to commit even greater financial aid than the approximately $2 billion already it had given since V-J Day. But these conditions could not have been met. America's rapid demobilization left it with too few forces either to supply the officers for the direction of the Nationalist forces or to intervene in China; the United States had only a small standing army at home. Nor were the American people in any mood to rearm and remobilize in 1947-1948. There was little enough sentiment in favor of "rescuing" Eastern Europe from Soviet hegemony—and far less for fighting a war in China.

Nor could more economic aid have saved Chiang. His corrupt, inefficient, and reactionary government did not provide a politically effective instrument through which to carry out the social and economic reforms China needed. In contrast, U.S. economic aid to Europe, the area considered most vital to American security, had a good chance of achieving its objective of the political and economic recovery of Britain and the Continent. It would have been unwise in these circumstances to divert a large slice of the government's not unlimited funds to attempt to restore a government that had lost the confidence of its own people. The power and wealth of the United States was, after all, not infinite; it had to be applied selectively. Areas of vital interest were to be the prime focus. Thus in Europe aid helped to build a wall of containment, but Nationalist China was a sieve. As Dean Acheson stated it:

Nothing that this country did or could have done within the reasonable limits of its capabilities could have changed that result; nothing that was left undone by this country has contributed to it. It was the product of internal Chinese forces, forces which this country tried to influence but could not. A decision was arrived at within China, if only a decision by default. [4]

Despite Chiang Kai-shek's debacle and the disintegration of his Nationalist government, the U.S. government took an optimistic view of develop-

---

3. U.S. Department of State, *United States Relations with China* (Washington, D.C.: Government Printing Office, 1949), 358.
4. Ibid., xvi.

ments. Shortly after the Nationalist collapse Acheson expressed his belief that, despite the common ideological points of view of the Chinese and Soviet regimes, they would eventually clash. Acheson predicted that Russia's appetite for a sphere of influence in Manchuria and northern China would arouse Chinese nationalism. The implications of this point of view were clear. If the Chinese communists were genuinely concerned with the preservation of China's national interest, they would resist Soviet penetration. Mao might be an independent communist leader like Yugoslavia's Marshal Tito. If Mao proved subservient to the Soviet Union, however, he would lose the support of the Chinese people. His regime would be identified with foreign rule because he would appear to serve the interests of another power, not of China. Whichever of these two developments occurred, the United States could only gain from the contradictions between communism and Chinese nationalism.

This analysis of Sino-Soviet relations indicated that the United States first had to disentangle itself from Chiang. Without this disassociation, the Chinese would link the United States with the government they had rejected. Moreover, a continued connection would foster the growth of anti-American sentiment in China, which was just what the administration hoped to prevent. The attention of the Chinese people must remain on the Soviet Union's actions. Under no circumstances, Acheson emphasized, must America "seize the unenviable position which the Russians have carved out for themselves. We must not undertake to deflect from the Russians to ourselves the righteous anger, and the wrath, and the hatred of the Chinese population which must develop." [5] Only by disengaging itself from Chiang Kai-shek could the United States exploit the anticipated clash of interests between China and the Soviet Union.

In short, the Truman administration wanted to do in 1950 what Richard Nixon finally did in 1972—reconcile its ideological differences with communist China and drive a wedge between it and the Soviet Union. But before this could happen, war broke out in another area in the region, Korea, with the unfortunate result of a bitter gulf, lasting twenty-two years, between the United States and the new China.

KOREA: THE LIMITED WAR BEFORE VIETNAM

Korea had been a divided nation since the end of World War II. Under the terms of the postwar settlement, the Soviets would disarm the Japanese above the thirty-eighth parallel and the United States below, thereby dividing the country temporarily. With the beginning of the Cold War, however, this divi-

5. "Crisis in Asia—An Examination of United States Policy," *Department of State Bulletin,* January 23, 1950, 115.

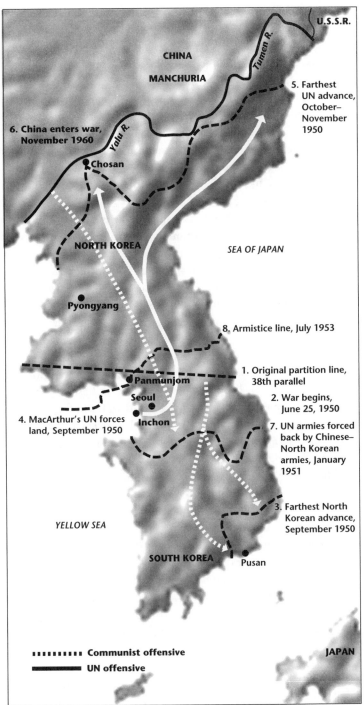

THE KOREAN WAR, 1950–1953

sion became permanent. All American attempts to negotiate an end to the division and establish a democratic and united Korea failed.

The United States had taken the problem to the United Nations in 1947, calling on that organization to sponsor free elections throughout the Korean peninsula. The Soviets, however, refused to allow the elections in North Korea, which had been transformed into a dictatorship, and the election was thus limited to South Korea. After the election the United States recognized South Korea as the official republic and the government of Syngman Rhee as its legitimate representative. It also extended economic, technical, and military aid to bolster his noncommunist government. Although South Korea was not an ally of the United States, there could be little doubt that the young republic was America's protégé.

Both the South and North Korean governments regarded themselves as the legitimate representatives of Korean nationalism, and each was dedicated to the reunification of the peninsula under its control. In that sense, the war that broke out when North Korea attacked South Korea on June 25, 1950—after protracted border fighting—was a civil war between two regimes determined to eliminate each other. But it also was an international war because events in Korea since 1945 had largely reflected the Cold War rivalry and conflict between the Soviet Union and the United States. North Korea's invasion of the south could not have occurred without Stalin's acquiescence, if not approval (which, according to one of Stalin's successors, was given in March 1949), and considerable Soviet military aid. In contrast, the Americans had worried that Rhee might go north and thus withheld the type of military equipment, such as heavy tanks, that would be needed for such a thrust. The South Korean army was not, therefore, sufficiently armed to resist an invasion.

The Americans, in any event, were taken by surprise by the North Korean attack. U.S. policy makers had been preoccupied with total war. In that context Korea had been left outside the American Pacific defense perimeter, which ran from the Aleutians to Japan, through the Ryukyus (Okinawa) to the Philippines. Indeed, in an all-out war the Korean peninsula itself would be neutralized by American air and sea power. American troops, in fact, had been withdrawn from Korea because in a major war they would probably be trapped by Soviet land forces. Thus the absence of a clear American commitment, as NATO served in Europe, had turned South Korea into a vacuum for communist expansion. Not expecting the United States to intervene in these circumstances, Stalin assented to the North Korean army attack.

Nevertheless, the survival of South Korea became immediately identified with the security interests of the United States. North Korea's aggression, which in Washington's opinion could not have been launched without Soviet encouragement and support, altered the basis on which Korea's strategic significance had been calculated. Korea's value could no longer be assessed in terms of its relative unimportance during a total war. The Cold War focused attention on the wider political and military implications for the containment policy of a North Korean military victory. For example, if the principal purpose of containment was to prevent further Soviet expansion, American inaction in the face of Soviet aggression would only encourage future aggressive acts. And if containment was possible only through an alignment of U.S. power with that of its allies, then failure to respond to South Korea's pleas for help would ensure the isolation of the United States. And, finally, if the United States stood by while South Korea fell, it would demonstrate to the world that the United States was either afraid of Soviet power or unconcerned with the safety of its friends or allies. American guarantees to help to preserve other nations' political independence would be regarded as valueless, leaving them with no alternative but to turn to neutralism for protection and to seek some form of accommodation with the Soviet Union.

In Asia this reasoning applied especially to Japan, a potential ally after Nationalist China's collapse and a nation that had long regarded South Korea as critical to its security. In Europe, NATO members recalled the U.S. retreat to isolationism after World War I. If the United States failed to come to the defense of South Korea, they would believe that, despite its recent NATO pledge of protection, the United States could not be counted on to keep its word. The stakes in Korea were therefore enormous: Japan would remain unaligned and Western Europe would be neutralized. Inaction would shift the Eurasian balance toward the Soviet Union and the PRC, leaving the United States strategically isolated. Consequently, Washington believed it had no choice but to oppose force with force.

At first the United States tried to stem the North Korean advance using air and sea forces alone. But after a few days Gen. Douglas MacArthur, the commander in chief in the Far East, reported that Korea would be lost unless ground forces were employed to halt the advancing enemy army. Thus the United States sent its occupation divisions from Japan to Korea under the aegis of the United Nations. This was done for two reasons. First, by virtue of the free election it had sponsored in South Korea, the United Nations had been intimately concerned with the birth of the young state. Second, one of the aims of American foreign policy was to associate its Cold War policies with the symbolic, humanitarian values of the United Nations. Although nations traditionally had justified their policies in moral terms, the United States had shown a marked propensity for doing so. American power had to be "righteous" power used not for purposes of power politics and selfish national advantage, but for the peace and welfare of all people. In fact, the war was an American effort, not controlled by the United Nations.

After initial setbacks the war went well for a while. In a daring operation on September 15, MacArthur, now UN supreme commander, landed an army at the west coast port of Inchon, 150 miles behind the North Korean lines. These forces then drove northward, trapping more than half the enemy army. The rest of the shattered communist army was in flight. On September 30 the UN forces reached the thirty-eighth parallel. The question confronting the United States was whether to cross it. The political aims of the war were compatible with the restoration of South Korea; they did not require a total war and the elimination of the North Korean government or the unconditional surrender of its troops. But the military situation favored the fulfillment of an American goal of several years' standing: the unification of the whole of Korea. Thus the U.S. government shifted its emphasis from containing the expansion of Soviet power to the forceful elimination of a Soviet satellite. The experience was to teach the United States the foolishness of changing limited political goals in the middle of a war in response to battlefield successes.

What was astounding was that the U.S. government believed it was politically safe to cross the thirty-eighth parallel and unify Korea. The administration did not think the Chinese communist leaders would consider the UN advance a threat to their security because they were Chinese first and communists second. Mao and his colleagues already were thought to be so involved in their struggle with the Soviet Union over the detachment of northern China, Manchuria, and Sinkiang that their eyes were fixed on their own northern provinces rather than on North Korea. There was therefore nothing to fear. The new objective of a militarily united Korea was sanctioned by a UN resolution on October 7.

But American policy makers miscalculated. The Chinese indeed viewed the American march to their border as threatening, just as Washington had perceived the North Korean march southward toward Japan as threatening. So Beijing sent its armies into North Korea under the guise of "volunteers," and in late November it launched a major offensive that drove the UN forces back below the thirty-eighth parallel. Throughout December 1950 and early January 1951, there was no certainty that UN troops could hold the peninsula, but they rallied and turned back the Chinese offensives. By March they had once more advanced to the thirty-eighth parallel. The administration was again faced with the decision of whether to seek a militarily unified Korea or accept a divided Korea.

There was no doubt about what MacArthur, articulating the traditional American approach to war, wanted to do. War, he said, indicated that "you have exhausted all other potentialities of bringing the disagreements to an end," and, once engaged, "there is no alternative than to apply every available means to bring it to a swift end. War's very objective is victory—not prolonged indecision. In war there is no substitute for victory." MacArthur went on to observe that the very phrase *resisting aggression* indicated "that you can destroy the potentialities of the aggressor to continually hit you" and not "go on indefinitely, neither to win or lose." One cannot fight a half war, he contended, although the administration's policy was based on the assumption, said MacArthur, that "when you use force, you can limit that force." This introduced a "new concept into military operations—appeasement." [6] MacArthur recommended a naval blockade of the Chinese coast; air bombardment of China's industrial complex, communications network, supply depots, and troop assembly points; reinforcement of his forces with Chinese Nationalist troops; and "diversionary action possibly leading to counter-invasion" by Chiang against the mainland.

The Truman administration rejected MacArthur's proposals as too risky. It feared that bombing China and defeating the Soviet Union's principal ally would lead to another global war. The Sino-Soviet treaty of February 1950 bound the Soviet Union to come to the aid of China if it were attacked by Japan "or any other state which should unite with Japan" (an obvious reference to the United States). Soviet self-interest in the Far East and the need to maintain Soviet prestige in the communist sphere would make it difficult for the Soviet Union to ignore a direct attack on the Chinese mainland.

Inherent in the administration's rejection of MacArthur's recommendations—and his dismissal from his post when he continued to push them—was the abandonment of the total war objective of a unified Korea and the elimination of its government. Instead, the original limited aim of the war, the defense of South Korea, was reasserted. This goal also was compatible with the other principal political reasons for which the United States had gone to war: the defense of Japan and the preservation of the NATO alliance. Indeed, by the time the war ended in 1953, Japan had become a U.S. ally, and NATO had been not only preserved but also strengthened by its own rearmament and the stationing of four American divisions in Europe. The wisest course therefore was to end the war where it had begun.

FROM ANTI-SOVIETISM TO ANTICOMMUNISM

The fall of Nationalist China and the Korean War transformed U.S. foreign policy less than a decade after it was formulated in the wake of World War II. Whereas the earlier focus of U.S. policy had been limited to containing Soviet power in Western Europe and the Eastern Mediterranean, it now spilled over into a broader anticommunist crusade. It was the alleged "loss" of China that had initiated this change. Americans had regarded China as their special ward since just before the turn of the century. The original inter-

---

6. Quoted in John Spanier, *The Truman-MacArthur Controversy and the Korean War* (Cambridge, Mass.: Belknap, 1959), 222.

est in China was not political but commercial—China was seen as a potentially huge market for American products. To that end, the United States had long regarded itself as the protector of China from foreign exploitation and invasion. Through the 1899 Open Door policy—aimed at preventing Great Britain, France, Russia, Germany, and Japan from shutting American commerce out of China and at obtaining an equal opportunity to sell on the Chinese market—the United States had become politically committed to preserving the territorial integrity and political independence of China.

Because the American people had never been prepared to fight for this objective, however, the United States had failed to protect China from external pressures and invasions. The Russians had established a sphere of influence in Manchuria by 1900, and the Japanese had replaced them after the Russo-Japanese War. During and after World War I, Japan had expanded its influence and control over China and in 1931 had begun another war to further its ambition to turn China into a Japanese vassal or colony. The Open Door policy, then, had been largely verbal. Indeed, the United States had never been prepared to support this policy militarily; it was one in which diplomacy was divorced from force. The result was the illusion that the United States had long been China's friend, extending to the Chinese people the bountiful benefits of Western civilization and coming to their rescue during World War II.

Americans were therefore shocked by the collapse in 1949 of Chiang Kai-shek, who during World War II had been lauded as a Chinese George Washington, and the establishment of communist control of the Chinese mainland. Certainly, they were totally unprepared for, and deeply resentful of, the propaganda emanating from Beijing accusing the United States of being "the Chinese people's implacable enemy . . . a corrupt imperialistic nation, the world center of reaction and decadence . . . a paper tiger and entirely vulnerable to defeat." They had expected that a "loyal" and fundamentally democratic China, grateful to America for protection and help, would emerge from World War II as a strong friend and powerful and reliable ally. The failure of these expectations in late 1949 came as a blow. Suddenly the relative security achieved by the containment policies in Europe—the Truman Doctrine, the Marshall Plan, the Berlin airlift, and NATO—seemed to have disintegrated. It appeared that the United States had stemmed the communist menace in Europe only to allow it to achieve a breakthrough in Asia.

The resulting insecurity and anxiety were further heightened by two other events. The first was the explosion in 1949 of the Soviet Union's first atomic bomb, which shattered the American monopoly on the weapon widely regarded as the principal deterrent against a Soviet attack. The second was the conviction in early 1950 of Alger Hiss, a high ranking U.S. government official during World War II, for perjury in connection with charges that he had delivered classified U.S. documents to the Soviet government in the 1930s. The

Hiss case was followed shortly by the confession of British scientist Klaus Fuchs that he had passed atomic secrets to the Soviets, apparently pointing to Soviet espionage in high places. The outbreak of the Korean War and communist China's subsequent intervention compounded America's sense of betrayal and anxiety.

PARTISANSHIP IN ASIAN POLICY

At the time all this was occurring, bipartisan support for U.S. policy was ending. The congressionally dominant conservative wing of the Republican Party had long been restless. The party, led by liberal Republicans, had lost the presidential elections of 1940, 1944, and 1948. They wanted to win with a conservative leader in 1952, but they could not win the presidency on the Republican record on domestic issues. The Republicans were the party of President Herbert Hoover and the Great Depression. The Democrats, who had won every presidential election since 1932, were the party of Roosevelt and the New Deal. Conservative Republicans therefore needed a foreign policy issue with which to beat the Democrats, even though liberal and moderate Republicans, led by Sen. Arthur Vandenberg, a former isolationist, had supported the internationalist policy of the Truman administration. But Vandenberg was dying, and, after China fell to the communists, bipartisanship on the Far East began to erode. Foreign policy became a partisan issue as the Republicans decided to exploit the public's frustrations with the perceived failures under Democratic administrations.

In the past, the Republicans recognized, whenever the United States had been drawn into the international arena its actions had met with quick success. It had beaten the British, the Mexicans, the Spanish, the Germans, and the Japanese. America had never been invaded, defeated, or occupied, as most other nations had been; it had, to be sure, made mistakes, but with its great power it had always been able to rectify them. America's history had witnessed only victories; its unbroken string of successes seemed evidence of national omnipotence.

It was this unquestioned assumption that suggested to the Republicans the reason for America's failures: treason within its own government. If America was all-powerful, its setbacks must have been the result of its own policies. Ostensibly the reason China fell was that the "pro-communist" administrations of Franklin Roosevelt and Harry Truman either deliberately or unwittingly had "sold China down the river." This conspiracy charge, articulated by Republican senator Joseph McCarthy and supported by fellow Republican senators Robert Taft and Richard Nixon, was simplicity itself: America's China policy had ended in communist control of the mainland; the administration leaders and the State Department were responsible for the formulation and execution of foreign policy; therefore, the government must be filled with communists and communist sympathizers who "tailored" American policy to advance the global aims of the Soviet Union. Low morale among the Chinese Nationalists, administrative and military ineptness, and repressive policies that had alienated mass support had nothing to do with it, nor did the superior communist organization, direction, morale, and ability to identify with popular aspirations.

The State Department bore the brunt of this rhetorical onslaught, with incessant attacks on its Foreign Service officers, regional directors, and on Secretary of State Acheson himself. But the accusations, usually carried in the press, were not directed only toward the State Department or government officials. Academics and others also were charged as being security risks or were accused of being "un-American." Many such individuals were fired, and others—especially stage actors and Hollywood figures—were blacklisted. The political atmosphere during the 1950s, in short, often bordered on national hysteria.

The most significant result was a shift in U.S. foreign policy from a limited anti-Soviet orientation to a broader anticommunist crusade. To be sure, actions by the United States in the Eastern Mediterranean and in Western Europe had been carried out in the name of anticommunism, but operationally these actions had been limited to countering Soviet moves. Washington had not hesitated to support communist Yugoslavia after its break with Moscow, and for a brief moment it had even predicted the likelihood of conflict between communist China and the Soviet Union. But the Republican attacks on the Democrats and the charges of appeasement, of being soft on communism, of losing China, and of treason placed the Democrats in a vulnerable position.

The aim of U.S. policy now became the prevention of any expansion by any member of the Sino-Soviet bloc. All communist states were considered enemies, regardless of whether they were large or small, strategically located or not, tied to Moscow as satellites or nationalist communist states, which, like Yugoslavia and communist China, were likely to pursue their own interests, even in conflict with the Soviet Union. Distinctions between America's vital and secondary interests, the importance of concentrating on the main adversary and not getting bogged down and wasting resources in conflicts with secondary enemies, and the ability to distinguish communist regimes that represented a threat to American interests and those that did not—all were lost in the crusading spirit. And how did all this affect the presidential election of 1952? The Republican charges hurt the Democrats so much that they lost that presidential election and were kept out of power for eight years. Moreover, future Democratic administrations, trying to avoid Republican accusations of being soft on communism, were particularly disposed to anticommunist interventions.

Anticommunism also intensified the deep rift between the United States and China. In 1950 Beijing observed that the United States not only did not recognize the communist government but also continued its support for the rival Nationalist regime in Formosa; that the United States was increasingly assisting the French fighting in Indochina; that it was strengthening its alliance with Japan, China's enemy; and that U.S. troops were marching to China's border with North Korea, despite Chinese warnings not to do so. Fearing that U.S. forces might cross the border, the Chinese government intervened in Korea, thereby turning the friendly relationship the United States once thought it had with China into armed conflict. That the United States had once been China's protector and benefactor may have been an illusion, but it was widely held, and the betrayal of friendship, alleged or real, always leaves a sense of frustration and anger. The Sino-American relationship had had an emotional intensity that did not characterize the relationship between the United States and the Soviet Union.

One can only speculate how events might have turned out during the Korean War if the United States had recognized the new Chinese government and had had diplomatic representatives in Beijing. Diplomats might have alerted Washington that the Chinese were alarmed at the U.S. advance in North Korea and that the repeated warnings to stop American forces short of China's frontier ought to be taken seriously. The American government received similar warnings from the Indian ambassador but, believing the ambassador to be pro-Chinese, the United States rejected the warnings. It would have had less reason to be suspicious of its own representatives and therefore might not have later blundered up to China's border.

The United States paid a heavy price for the breakdown of bipartisanship, for McCarthy's charges of treason, and for the crusading style that Nationalist China's collapse unleashed. But the even greater folly may have been that U.S. policy, now applying containment to the Sino-Soviet bloc, no longer seriously considered the possibility that Mao Zedong might become a second Tito because Mao, like Tito, drew his power from control of his party and military, not from Soviet troops in his country. Nor, therefore, did Washington any longer entertain the possibility that communist China might be used to contain Soviet power. Instead, for more than two decades the United States and China were bitter enemies as the United States felt compelled to contain both Soviet and Chinese power.

Secretary of State John Foster Dulles reports to Dwight Eisenhower on his mission to initiate a Korean political conference.

CHAPTER FOUR

Defining Spheres of Influence

When the Republicans won the presidential election of 1952, it was their first in twenty-four years. They won because they exploited public weariness with a containment policy that they charged had no end in sight. Whatever its successes in Europe, the policy had ended in the collapse of Nationalist China and the Korean War, a limited war contrary to the American tradition of all-out war and a clear victory on the battlefield. That war too appeared to have no end in sight, and after communist China's intervention it became—until Vietnam—the most unpopular war in American history. Led by World War II hero Dwight Eisenhower, the architect of the victory in Europe, the Republicans promised that they would be better stewards of the American national interest.

In preparing the nation for the long-term competition with the Sino-Soviet bloc, as it was then perceived, the Republicans promised a strategy that would avoid bankrupting the nation and placing too heavy a tax burden on the American people, as well as fighting more limited wars. To this end, they proposed three measures. The first was to halt the Korean War, which allowed the administration to cut the size of the army and avoid the cost of maintaining large standing ground forces. The second was to draw a clear line of containment, or "frontier," around the entire Sino-Soviet bloc. The Democrats already had drawn such a frontier from Norway to Turkey; the Republicans expected to strengthen and extend this frontier to the Middle East and the Far East. The third measure was to preserve this global boundary around the communist world with the deterrent power of the Strategic Air Command (SAC). The fear of total war with the United States was expected to deter the Soviets and Chinese from crossing the line. Moscow had only a minimum capability to reach the United States; Beijing had none. By contrast, SAC's bomber force was to reach 2,000 in the 1950s.

The reliance on strategic air power also was expected to appeal to the American public. "Massive retaliation" sounded more dynamic than containment and made possible a reduction in overall military expenditures. But, above all, massive retaliation was consistent with America's style in foreign policy, a style that has been based traditionally on a world view of mutually exclusive conditions: war or peace, force or diplomacy, aggressors or peace-loving states. Peace was normal; war was abnormal. Force was not necessary in the absence of conflict and hostilities; it was to be used only in wartime to destroy the source of war itself. Massive retaliation, then, fit this American approach completely. It was an all-or-nothing strategy that could not be used short of a Soviet attack on the United States or Western Europe. At the same time, American presidents consistently rejected preventive war, both at the time of the nation's atomic monopoly and later, during the 1950s and 1960s, the period of gradually declining strategic superiority. Deterrence was the American goal; the nuclear strategy was to retaliate after the opponent had struck first. If the United States were attacked, however, it would use massive retaliation, as in the two world wars, to punish and destroy the enemy in ways not conceivable until 1945.

Massive retaliation, by reducing the enemy's population centers and industries to rubble and radioactive dust, carried the American approach to war to its logical conclusion. Although some bombs were targeted on the small Soviet air force, the rapidly growing U.S. stockpile was to be used against all targets, both military and economic, in one huge war-winning blow. The hydrogen bomb's megaton explosive power, as opposed to that of the atomic bomb's kiloton power, made that possible. In the words of a navy captain attending an air force briefing on SAC's strategy at the time, the Soviet Union was to be left "a smoking, radiating ruin at the end of two hours."

In one sense, then, atomic weapons and the more destructive hydrogen weapons enabled the United States to pursue an old American dream in a new and gruesome way. By making nuclear war too destructive to fight, by making the distinction between victor and loser in such a conflict increasingly meaningless, the deterrent strategy aimed at eliminating war itself. This old goal had been sought through the "war to end all wars" crusade, or through international organization and cooperation, or through free trade and economic interdependence among nations. The goal could now be realized because war had become, in the popular phrase, "unthinkable."

But however traditional the philosophical basis of massive retaliation and whatever the benefits of economic and military retrenchment, Dwight Eisenhower's policy was not really that different from Harry Truman's: it sought to contain communism but to extend containment beyond Europe by drawing a frontier around the Sino-Soviet periphery and supporting that frontier with nuclear air power. Only in one essential aspect was the new administration's policy quite different—and this difference was critical. Truman and his secretary of state Dean Acheson had relied on atomic striking power to deter an attack on either the United States or America's "first line of defense" in Europe. But in Asia, when the communists had faced them with a limited aggression, the Truman administration had met this challenge with ground troops. The Eisenhower administration also expected to deter an all-out war with the threat of massive retaliation but declared that it would not fight local ground wars. Presumably this meant that it planned to deter any future limited attacks by threatening to retaliate against the Soviet Union or China.

This basic policy decision reflected Secretary of State John Foster Dulles's strong conviction that the only effective means of stopping a prospective aggressor was to give fair warning of what constituted aggression and to make clear that the punishment for an attack would far outweigh any possible military gains. Dulles believed that Korea would never have been invaded had the communists known that their attack would be met with retaliatory air strikes on Moscow. It was the absence of such a warning that had led the communists to act. The Eisenhower administration did not intend to repeat this mistake. It meant to draw the line so clearly that the enemy could be left in no doubt of the consequences of crossing the line. The expectation was that by going to the "brink of war," the United States would be able to deter future Koreas. This policy, which later became known as "brinkmanship," was to be applied first in an attempt to bring about a cease-fire in Korea.

SUPERPOWER TENSIONS AT THE BRINK

The idea, then, was to use the threat of a nuclear war to avoid having to fight one. At the same time the West also used this threat to preserve its wall of containment around the Sino-Soviet bloc. But how credible was this threat? Indeed, might it provoke the very war it sought to avoid? In the years to follow, these questions would be answered as the superpowers postured for advantage in several regional conflicts, testing the Eisenhower-Dulles formula and the more general strategy of communist containment.

ENDING THE KOREAN WAR

The truce talks that had begun in Korea in the summer of 1951 dragged on fruitlessly until they reached a deadlock. The war was a drain on the United States; it had to be ended. When the Eisenhower administration took office in January 1953, it decided that if its efforts to gain an armistice failed, it would bomb Chinese bases and supply sources in Manchuria and China, blockade the mainland coast, and possibly use atomic weapons. Later it claimed that its willingness to use force and not confine hostilities to the Korean peninsula were conveyed to the Chinese via the government of India.

In early June the deadlocked negotiations resumed, and in late July the armistice was signed. It is doubtful that the administration's threats were primarily responsible for the Chinese communists' willingness to conclude the war; there's no evidence that threats were made publicly or privately, or passed on to the Chinese directly or indirectly. Other factors appeared more critical. Chief among these was Joseph Stalin's death in March 1953. His successors proclaimed their belief in "peaceful coexistence" and tried hard to convince the noncommunist world that they wanted to relax international tensions. Agreement on an armistice and an end to the war would provide evidence of their earnestness. More important, they could not afford to risk increased international tensions and an enlarged war, which the Americans might launch if diplomacy failed to end this conflict, at a time when they were engaged in a struggle among themselves to succeed the late dictator.

The Korean War ended just where it had begun—at the thirty-eighth parallel—on basically the same terms the Truman administration had been unable to sign and after considerably more casualties. This line now became part of the global dividing line between the communist bloc and the noncommunist bloc. In August 1953 the United States signed a mutual security pact with South Korea designed to deter another attack from the north.

CONFLICT IN THE TAIWAN STRAITS

The line of containment also was drawn in the Taiwan Straits, where Sino-American relations had turned increasingly bitter and confrontational after the United States intervened in the Chinese civil war and China intervened in Korea. Soon after the Korean War ended, the People's Republic of China (PRC) sought to eliminate its rival on Taiwan. During the summer of 1954 the PRC began shelling the Nationalist-held offshore islands.

The United States and the Nationalists had signed a treaty of mutual defense in 1953 under which the United States guaranteed the security of Taiwan. In turn, the Nationalists pledged not to attack the mainland or to reinforce their offshore garrisons without the consent of the United States. While the offshore islands were not specifically included under the terms of the treaty, the president requested and received from Congress the authority to employ American armed forces to protect Taiwan and "such related positions and territories" as the president judged necessary. Although this did not specifically clarify whether the United States would defend Quemoy and Matsu, the communists certainly thought that it might, and they abstained from any invasion attempts of these islands, which were within artillery range of the mainland. When in August 1958 the communists resumed shelling the offshore islands, the United States again supported the Nationalists.

Thus the line remained where it had been before the two Taiwan crises—a few miles off the PRC's coast. Some months later Dulles reaffirmed this line when he firmly rejected Nationalist leader Chiang Kai-shek's calls to take back the mainland. American policy in the straits was committed to the preservation of the status quo. Each side should keep what it had and refrain from attacking the other. The Eisenhower administration thereby recognized what neither it nor its predecessor had been willing to admit publicly before: that the Nationalist expectation of recapturing the mainland was a myth. At the same time it tacitly acknowledged the Chinese communist government as continental China's *de facto* government. It had reconciled itself to the communist conquest of the mainland.

In the straits the administration was able to support its position with air and sea power; yet the possible use of nuclear weapons had been mentioned—if it became necessary to defend the status quo. But during this period the nuclear threat, which had not been invoked to end the Korean war, was shown to be a bluff. For all of his talk of American readiness to use nuclear weapons in defense, Eisenhower had no intention of using them in China. As a military man he knew that there were no appropriate targets, and as president he knew that the use of nuclear weapons was not politically feasible. To drop a bomb once again on Asians would lead to outrage and condemnation from the whole world, including America's allies in the North Atlantic Treaty Organization (NATO). America's declared policy of massive retaliation was in fact one of self-deterrence.

THE FIRST INDOCHINA WAR

After World War II, colonies that had long been ruled by European powers renewed their demands for independence. The British complied in India, Burma, and Ceylon, but the French in Indochina did not. Returning to Vietnam after its years of Japanese occupation, the French refused to grant any meaningful concessions to the government, which, under Ho Chi Minh, had proclaimed Vietnam's independence. Determined to reestablish sovereignty over their colony, the French recognized Ho's "Democratic Republic of Vietnam" as a free state within the French Union. As a part of the agreement the French would be allowed to maintain garrisons in Vietnam for five years. But within less than a year the Vietminh (as the Revolutionary League for the Independence of Vietnam was known) accused the French of violating the agreement. The Vietminh had been organized by Ho during World War II to convert Vietnam from a feudal society to a classless communist society. After the war it emphasized nationalism rather than communism to win independence for Vietnam. As a result, open conflict developed in 1946 between France and the communists and nationalists and soon escalated into the first Indochina war, which lasted eight years.

When France established an "independent" state of Vietnam in 1949 under Emperor Bao Dai, the Vietminh became, in effect, "rebels," but with the important difference that they were rebels identified as fighting for the independence of Vietnam. By contrast, Bao Dai, who spent much of his time on the French Riviera, was seen as a French puppet; in fact, he could not have survived one day in office without the support of French arms. Like Mao Zedong in China, Ho conducted guerrilla warfare and met with considerable success. The French, who generally held the cities, were at a disadvantage from the beginning, for, in the absence of genuine independence, the Vietnamese identified themselves with the Vietminh and saw the French as colonial rulers. In the long run France paid a high price for the war in lost lives, matériel, and prestige.

During the first years of the war, American public opinion was unsympathetic to France's attempt to reestablish its colonial control over Indochina. But three events led to U.S. involvement in this conflict. The first, in China, was the defeat of Chiang Kai-shek in 1949. This was seen as a blow to France because it meant that the new People's Republic of China could now provide assistance to the Vietminh. The second event was the outbreak of the Korean War, with the resulting shift of containment to Asia. And the third was the change in the political climate in the United States to anticommunism. The French, who earlier were seen as trying to hold onto the vestiges of their colonial empire, now were regarded as fighters in the common struggle against communism.

In 1950 the United States began to provide France with economic and military aid, and by 1954 the United States was paying about 75 percent of the costs of the war. The French position continued to deteriorate, however, especially once the Korean armistice was signed. Despite American warnings, communist China shifted its pressure from Korea to Indochina and increased its assistance to the Vietminh. On March 13, 1954, Vietminh forces launched an assault on the French fortress at Dienbienphu. The French position in northern Vietnam seemed close to collapse. It became painfully clear that the French could not hold on without American intervention. What was the United States to do?

Dienbienphu was the moment of decision for the administration. Eisenhower and Dulles had declared Indochina to be of strategic importance to American security and had cautioned China against direct or indirect intervention. The Chinese ignored these warnings, and the U.S. government had to "put up or shut up." It shut up; its threats turned out to be only bluffs.

THE REFUSAL TO INTERVENE

The reason for this inaction was fairly clear: American public opinion might have been strongly anticommunist, but it also indicated that the nation was tired of war. For that reason Eisenhower had withdrawn from Korea, and now he was unwilling to involve the United States in another such war. Furthermore, the administration already was cutting the size of the army in order to build U.S. nuclear forces for a policy of massive retaliation, and the army chief of staff counseled against intervention because of a lack of available troops. The administration, then, considered two courses of action. The first was to rescue the French by attacking the communist positions around Dienbienphu with air power alone, but this was rejected because air strikes by themselves could not halt the communist ground advance. Air power had failed to stop the North Korean army during the opening days of that war, and this failure had necessitated the commitment of U.S. troops.

The alternative course of action was to attack China with nuclear weapons. That would have been consistent with the administration's announced policy of massive retaliation. But the administration did not follow its policy. The reason was simple: it is one thing to deliver a threat of massive retaliation to an opponent and quite another to have the opponent believe it. The Soviets had not believed it before Korea, nor did the Chinese in Indochina. Thus the possible use of nuclear weapons was discussed—and rejected—by the president and his advisers. Both communist powers correctly guessed that the United States would not risk a total war for anything less than an attack on the United States or Europe. In any event, Eisenhower, as well as Truman before him, believed that an attack on China would risk Soviet intervention and a Soviet-American war.

Truman's experience with Korea had shown clearly that containment could not be successful without the willingness and capability to fight a limited war. Reliance on strategic air power was not a credible strategy for deterring or winning "Koreas." Ground forces were absolutely necessary if the United States was to escape either defeat or involvement in a total conflict. In their absence, U.S. nuclear threats were not really credible.

The result of the second demonstration of U.S. self-deterrence was the French government's decision to make the best of the situation by negotiating with the communists directly for an end to the war. The French people were as weary of Indochina as the American public had been of Korea. When the negotiations were over, the first Indochina war ended with the division of Vietnam at the seventeenth parallel. The communists retained control of northern Indochina, but it seemed only a matter of time until they took the rest of the country because the collapse of the southern rump state seemed imminent. The United States, however, prevented such a takeover by supporting the new government of Ngo Dinh Diem, a staunch anticommunist nationalist appointed by Bao Dai after Dienbienphu (Diem later ousted Bao Dai). The Eisenhower administration gave Diem economic and military aid to stabilize the situation in Vietnam, and the danger of collapse temporarily receded.

SEATO'S FOUNDING

The seventeenth parallel, like the thirty-eighth parallel in Korea, became part of the international frontier separating the communist and noncommunist worlds. In September 1954, to protect this frontier, the United States, Britain, France, Australia, New Zealand, the Philippines, Pakistan, and Thailand signed a treaty forming the Southeast Asia Treaty Organization (SEATO) to defend the area of the South Pacific, with the exception of Hong Kong and Taiwan. A protocol to the treaty extended SEATO's protection to Vietnam, Laos, and Cambodia. It also provided for joint action to meet aggression; an attack on any of its members would be considered a threat to all, and each would then act to meet the common danger in accordance with its constitutional processes. In case of subversion, the parties agreed to consult one another immediately and to agree on common measures to meet this threat.

SEATO, unlike the NATO alliance, had no unified command or joint forces. Its principal force was American sea and air power. The crucial element—land power—would have to be supplied by the member nations if the occasion arose. Moreover—and again unlike NATO—SEATO did not include most of the nations in the areas it planned to protect. Having just emerged from Western colonialism, India, Burma, Sri Lanka, and Indonesia were unwilling to be tied again to the West through a military alliance. They preferred to remain neutral in the struggle between the Western powers and the Sino-Soviet bloc. The Philippines was willing to join only because of its traditional ties to the United States, and Pakistan because it wished to acquire a source for arms against India. Only Thailand was genuinely concerned about the PRC's expansion. Australia and New Zealand were not really Asian powers.

SEATO, therefore, was mainly a non-Asian alliance formed for the defense of an Asian area, a weakness that was to plague the alliance. The absence of regional concern about China's expansion ensured SEATO's eventual failure, and French and British membership did not prevent that result. France was unlikely to defend an area from which it had been forced to withdraw in humiliation. Britain, which had opposed U.S. intervention in Indochina, saw the alliance as a means of restraining the United States in the future. SEATO was, in reality, a U.S. guarantee for the defense of South Vietnam; it would provide a legal basis for a unilateral intervention to preserve the dividing line between the two Vietnams. Like West Germany and South Korea, South Vietnam had become part of the Free World—that is, the American sphere of influence.

Presumably this ended the Vietnam problem since the Soviet Union and China appeared to accept the division of Vietnam. But Ho Chi Minh did not, as the United States was to discover. As for President Eisenhower, he had kept the country out of war, but he also had, because of the strength of anticommunism in the country, especially in his own party, kept America in Vietnam. He, in fact, substituted an American presence for a French presence—a situation for which the country was to pay dearly later.

But for the moment, at least, the situation in the Far East had been partially stabilized. The frontier between the American and Soviet-Chinese spheres had been drawn at the thirty-eighth parallel in Korea, in the Taiwan Straits, and at the seventeenth parallel in Indochina. And although it would not be clear until years later, the United States had, by standing fast in the Taiwan Straits, also helped to bring Sino-Soviet differences close to the breaking point. For China, unification with Taiwan was a priority; for the Soviet Union, Taiwan was not worth the risk of a war with the United States. Consequently the tiny islands of Quemoy and Matsu were to play a profound long-term role in accentuating Sino-Soviet differences and in eventually splitting the alliance between the two largest communist powers.

THE SOVIET SHIFT BACK TO EUROPE

In Europe NATO already had drawn the defense line. The strength of this line on the ground, however, depended on supplementing NATO forces with West German troops, and the NATO allies had chosen the European Defense Community (EDC) to achieve this goal. But in August 1954 the French National Assembly rejected that role for the EDC by a decisive majority; fear of Germany remained too great, and French nationalists wished to maintain France's identity and honor. This decision was a real blow to the efforts toward creating a situation of strength in Europe. The whole basis of NATO strategy and European integration was suddenly imperiled. The British found

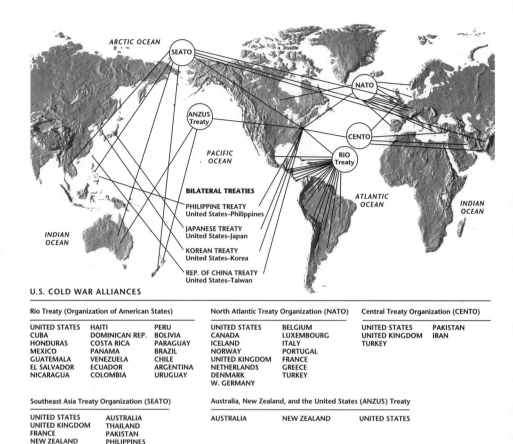

U.S. COLD WAR ALLIANCES

Rio Treaty (Organization of American States)			North Atlantic Treaty Organization (NATO)		Central Treaty Organization (CENTO)	
UNITED STATES	HAITI	PERU	UNITED STATES	BELGIUM	UNITED STATES	PAKISTAN
CUBA	DOMINICAN REP.	BOLIVIA	CANADA	LUXEMBOURG	UNITED KINGDOM	IRAN
HONDURAS	COSTA RICA	PARAGUAY	ICELAND	ITALY	TURKEY	
MEXICO	PANAMA	BRAZIL	NORWAY	PORTUGAL		
GUATEMALA	VENEZUELA	CHILE	UNITED KINGDOM	FRANCE		
EL SALVADOR	ECUADOR	ARGENTINA	NETHERLANDS	GREECE		
NICARAGUA	COLOMBIA	URUGUAY	DENMARK	TURKEY		
			W. GERMANY			

Southeast Asia Treaty Organization (SEATO)		Australia, New Zealand, and the United States (ANZUS) Treaty		
UNITED STATES	AUSTRALIA	AUSTRALIA	NEW ZEALAND	UNITED STATES
UNITED KINGDOM	THAILAND			
FRANCE	PAKISTAN			
NEW ZEALAND	PHILIPPINES			

a new solution, however, in the forgotten Brussels Treaty, which was revised to include Germany and Italy within a Western European Union (WEU). With the British commitment of four divisions to the continent, France dropped its reservations.

The Paris Pact, which established the WEU, came into force in May 1955. Thus ten years after Germany's defeat, its occupation came to an end, and the Federal Republic regained its sovereignty and entered NATO via the WEU. West Germany's military power could now be added to Western strength. Two important declarations were appended to these Paris agreements. In the first, the West German government subscribed to the principles of the United Nations and vowed never to use force to achieve the reunification of Germany or to modify its boundaries. In the second, the United States, Britain, and France declared that they recognized the Federal Republic as the only freely and legitimately constituted government entitled to speak for all of Germany, thereby indicating a policy of nonrecognition of the East German government. In addition, the allies would pursue German reunification by peaceful means, which in effect meant the preservation of a divided Germany. Finally, the Western powers stated that until "the conclusion of a peace settlement" they would continue to exercise their responsibilities with regard to the security of West Germany and West Berlin. NATO, like the European Coal and Steel Community (ECSC), was thus an instrument for uniting Western Europe and harnessing German power for its collective defense, as well as for controlling and restraining that power.

THE BIRTH OF THE COMMON MARKET

With Germany safely enrolled as a member of NATO, the continental European allies took a momentous step toward further economic and political integration: on June 1, 1958, France, West Germany, Italy, Belgium, the Netherlands, and Luxembourg established the European Economic Community (EEC), more commonly known as the Common Market, whose objective was to join them together into an economic union. Their plan was to achieve this in a twelve- to fifteen-year period, during which all six states would completely eliminate the tariffs and quota systems that hampered trade among them. They also would abolish restrictions on the intercountry movement of labor, capital, and services, with the exception of agriculture.

What were believed to be the chances for the development of this Common Market as it was being launched? The economic benefits were thought to guarantee it. As trade barriers were lowered and then eliminated, the increasing competition would result in the growth of efficient companies and the demise of the less efficient ones, unless they modernized or converted to new lines of production. All members were expected to gain. At its heart the Common Market was a bargain between French agriculture and West German industry. Both stood to benefit enormously from a continent-size market. Yet another factor was that the community would collectively receive advantages against third parties; it was strong enough to demand reciprocal lowering of tariffs. All these advantages outweighed the burdens each nation would suffer as a result of economic dislocation and hardships, which in fact would be minimized by being extended over a period of years and by being shared among all members.

The principal advantage of the Common Market, however, was seen to be political, not economic. A common market needs common policies; only one set of rules—not six—can govern its competitive behavior. In the long run the Common Market's success would lead to the adoption of common fiscal policies to control the ups and downs of the business cycle, a common currency, and a central bank. The economic "spillover"—

from the original common market in coal and steel into a common market for all sectors of the economy—was expected to stimulate political unification. Indeed, it was precisely the formation of a political union that had inspired the ECSC.

Initiated by France and strongly supported by West German chancellor Konrad Adenauer, the EEC was the culminating act of the movement to tie Germany so closely to a European community that it would never again be able to use its power for purely national ends. The formation of what came to be called the Inner Six was nothing less than the last link subjecting Germany to European restraints and responsibilities. Its success would make it impossible for Germany ever again to pursue a unilateral course.

Not surprisingly, the Soviet Union reacted quickly against the Common Market and attempted to break it up. A strong Europe, economically prosperous and politically stable, would not only prove a powerful barrier to Soviet expansionist ambitions, but also might threaten the Soviet status quo in Eastern Europe. The West European societies exercised a magnetic attraction for the satellite countries. West Berlin, alongside communist East Berlin, hampered Soviet control of East Germany. Hundreds of thousands of young, skilled and professional men and women left East Germany through West Berlin; it was an escape hatch that was depopulating the German Democratic Republic (GDR), as it called itself, of the very people it needed to run its society. Indeed, the real issue was the very survival of the GDR. Because it was an artificial creation, not recognized by most states that recognized West Germany as the true representative of German interests, the loss of the younger generation for whose welfare the GDR supposedly existed deprived it of a rationale for existence. And if East Germany were to collapse, would Poland and other East European states not follow? Thus if the existence of West Berlin and West Germany made the Soviet Union feel insecure about the status quo, Soviet apprehensions about a united Europe were even greater.

THE SECOND BERLIN CRISIS

From Moscow's vantage point the stability of the Soviet position in central and Eastern Europe depended basically on destroying the freedom of West Berlin. To achieve this objective the Soviet Union announced in November 1958 that at the end of six months it intended to end the four-power occupation. This ultimatum, then—the first Moscow had ever given the West—was clearly aimed at forcing the Allies to withdraw from West Berlin, thereby turning it into a "free city," but, in effect, incorporating West Berlin into East Germany. Once Western troops had left the city, West Berliners would feel isolated and unprotected, abandoned and completely helpless. The Soviet army and the East German army and police would surround them. In these circumstances what could the defenseless West Berliners do?

One way or another, then, the Soviets planned to remove a troublesome thorn from their side so that they would be in a better position to stabilize the status quo. Indeed, the destruction of West Berlin would have accomplished not only the Soviet Union's defensive aims but also its long-standing offensive purpose of weakening its opponents, perhaps fatally. If the Soviets could drive the Western powers out of Berlin, they also would be able to cut off the development of the Common Market before it gathered too much momentum and to shatter the NATO alliance. It was, above all, American power that guaranteed the freedom of the 2 million Germans living in West Berlin. If the United States were forced to abandon them, the Europeans would lose faith in America's ability to protect them. The Germans would be the first to read the lesson: because America could not guarantee their security, they would have to approach the Soviets independently.

Once approached, the Soviets would certainly demand that Germany abandon all its political, economic, or military ties to the West. But without Germany, there could be no Common Market because Germany provided much of the capital its partners needed for their economic development. And if Germany pulled out of the NATO alliance, the United States would have to send its troops home because it would be politically and strategically impossible to station them in France. Yet these troops were a symbol of the American commitment to defend Europe; they were psychologically and politically indispensable. No written guarantees could be substituted for this living embodiment of America's stake in Europe. Thus the central stake was the future of NATO and whether the Soviet Union could achieve a dominant position in Europe by neutralizing West Germany and driving the Americans back across the Atlantic Ocean.

THE SHIFTING BALANCE OF NUCLEAR FORCES

Berlin was the major test of postwar American policy, but it was not a repeat of the 1948 situation. At that time Stalin had acted on two assumptions: first, that the far larger Red Army contingents could deter an Allied attempt to break through to West Berlin on the ground, and, second, that the United States and Britain could not keep West Berlin alive. The first assumption proved to be correct, but the second was wrong. When Stalin realized this, he had to either call off the blockade or shoot down Allied planes and risk a war. America's atomic monopoly favored the first solution. But by 1957, a year before the Berlin ultimatum, the tide had turned technically for the Soviet Union. That year the Soviets tested the world's first intercontinental ballistic missile (ICBM), making America's determination to defend Berlin the following year riskier and costlier. Moreover, the ICBM test had followed a series of spectacular Soviet accomplishments in space. Soviet *Sputnik* satellites, which orbited the earth every ninety minutes, and the ICBM test were at the time considered impressive symbols of Soviet technological progress.

In turn, they raised serious questions in the United States about its historic technological leadership and the future of the balance of power. Soviet premier Nikita Khrushchev, in fact, immediately talked of mass-producing ICBMs and asserted that the balance of nuclear or strategic power was shifting toward the Soviet Union. In the United States widespread public concern and anxiety spread about a future "missile gap," which, because ICBMs were faster than bombers, meant that U.S. strategic forces would become more vulnerable to a surprise attack and might no longer be as effective as deterrent forces.

The Berlin crisis, in brief, was the most serious confrontation Washington had faced since 1948-1949. The Truman Doctrine, Marshall Plan, Berlin airlift, and NATO had made it very plain to Moscow that Western Europe was an area of vital American interest. Soviet domination over the western edge of the Eurasian continent was no more tolerable to the United States than German control. Presumably this knowledge had deterred the Soviets in the late 1940s, and it was the fear of war that had led them to direct their challenges to areas outside of Europe.

Now, however, ten years after the first Berlin crisis, the Soviets were once more challenging the West in Europe. Indeed, in reopening the Berlin issue the Soviets were seeking to convey a new sense of confidence in their ability to deal with the West. That confidence seemed to reflect the Soviet claim that the strategic balance was changing in their favor. Clearly Khrushchev was attempting to cash in on this claim, to undermine European confidence in the United States, and to drive a wedge between the European members of NATO, especially West Germany, and their transatlantic protector. This had been a Soviet goal since the early Cold War.

Given the limited nature of the Soviet challenge and the all-or-nothing nature of massive retaliation, what strategy could the United States devise to prevent the Soviet Union from slowly choking West Berlin to death? How could massive retaliation, a policy intended to deter an attack on the United States or invasion of Western Europe, be used to prevent the strangulation of West Berlin? Would Moscow be restrained by U.S. threats of massive retaliation in Berlin's defense when the United States had been self-deterred in Asia against far lesser threats to its interests?

EISENHOWER'S LEGACY TO KENNEDY

In the months of tension as the superpowers tested one another, it became increasingly clear that the United States was determined to stay in West Berlin, and that the Soviets were equally determined to push their adversary out of Berlin. In an effort to defuse the crisis, Eisenhower invited

Khrushchev to visit the United States in September 1959. His acceptance represented a tactical victory for the Soviets because Khrushchev knew that this summit conference could heighten the fears of the NATO allies that the United States and Soviet Union would negotiate a separate agreement at their expense.

This being said, Khrushchev's visit to the United States did have one positive result: the Soviets withdrew their threat to take unilateral action in Berlin in return for American willingness to negotiate on the problems of Berlin and Germany at a four-power summit meeting, which was scheduled for May 1960 in Paris. For American policy makers, this meant a postponement of the painful decision on whether Berlin was worth the cost of war. But if the administration believed that the crisis had ended, that from then on it could negotiate leisurely on Berlin and, if the Soviets did not accept its terms, preserve the status quo, it was quickly disabused of this notion. Khrushchev soon resumed his threats.

Shortly before the Paris summit, however, an event took place that shattered the conference after only one session and further postponed negotiations on Berlin. On May Day, 1,300 miles into Soviet territory, the Soviets downed an American "spy plane" loaded with photographic equipment for gathering intelligence data. The Eisenhower administration reacted to this unexpected and unhappy turn of events with considerable diplomatic ineptitude—first by lying about the U-2's mission and then, when the Soviets exposed the lie, in a move unprecedented in diplomatic history, by admitting that the American pilot had been taking aerial photographs of the Soviet Union and that the White House had lied in its previous announcement. The administration justified its actions by saying that Soviet secrecy necessitated this means of information-gathering to prevent a surprise attack; moreover, it asserted that it would continue this behavior.

For the Soviet premier to let this pass would be like acknowledging to the world, to his people, to his domestic enemies, and to his allies that he had surrendered to the United States the right to violate Soviet territory. Khrushchev could not survive such an admission. He therefore struck a belligerent pose in Paris, launched a blistering personal attack on Eisenhower, and demanded his apology for past U-2 flights and a promise that the flights would cease. These demands were rejected. Khrushchev thereupon suggested that the summit conference be postponed for six to eight months, and he bluntly told Eisenhower that he would not be welcome to visit the Soviet Union in June, as they already had planned. In short, Khrushchev said that he wanted nothing more to do with Eisenhower and that he would wait to negotiate the Berlin problem with the next administration. A new crisis had been put off for a little while longer.

It was inevitable, therefore, that the Soviets would raise the Berlin problem again once the new administration had taken over in January 1961. Khrushchev was still convinced that the global balance was shifting in his favor, and he remained confident that he was strong enough to acquire West Berlin. The new president, John Kennedy, fearing that Khrushchev might miscalculate, met the Soviet premier in Vienna to convey to him America's determination to defend West Berlin. Khrushchev discounted these warnings. His response was characteristic: a test of the president's resolution by reviving the original threat that the Berlin situation would have to be resolved within six months—that is, before the end of 1961. Thus the Vienna summit produced a result quite opposite of that sought: the very type of Soviet brinkmanship against which Kennedy had sought to caution the Soviet leader.

Kennedy, then, was quickly confronted with his Berlin crisis. Declaring his willingness to negotiate, he also stated that the United States was not willing to discuss merely how the West would withdraw from the beleaguered city, thereby leaving it for the communists to swallow. The West's right to be in the city stemmed from its victory over Nazi Germany. The Western presence in and access to the city and the freedom of West Berlin were not negotiable. Kennedy said, "We cannot negotiate with those who say: 'What's mine is mine, and what's yours is negotiable.' " More specifically, he asked, if the West refused to meet its clear-cut commitments in Berlin, where would it meet them?

On August 13, 1961, the communists built a wall that divided the city, thereby eliminating the escape hatch for East Germans. More than 200,000 East Germans already had escaped to the West in 1961 alone. They were to be added to the 2.5 million who had migrated westward from 1948 to 1960—20 percent of East Germany's entire population! The wall ended West Berlin's usefulness as a "showplace for Western capitalism" and violated the quadripartite status of Berlin. The West did not knock the wall down with bulldozers for fear of military conflict with communist—especially Soviet—forces. This passivity intensified Khrushchev's conviction that the United States would not fight and that he could, slowly but surely, increase the pressure on NATO and drive the West out of Berlin.

This possibility, and the American fear that the Soviet leader might miscalculate Western resolve and accidentally trigger a war, accounted for the difference between Kennedy's and his predecessor's reactions to the Berlin crisis. Unlike Eisenhower, Kennedy used the tensions over Berlin to build up American military power; the new president was determined to show Khrushchev that the United States was not bluffing when it declared its intentions to defend West Berlin. Kennedy moved in two directions; indeed, he had begun to do so almost immediately after assuming office. One aim was a "flexible re-sponse"; the United States needed more options than massive retaliation's suicide-or-surrender alternatives. This increased flexibility was to be achieved by building larger conventional forces. In Europe a conventional buildup would give NATO a more credible defense. Outside of Europe the United States also would have a capability to respond to limited challenges.

The other critical aim was to reduce SAC's vulnerability during the changeover from bombers to missiles. Bombers located at known sites were highly vulnerable to surprise attack. Even in a situation of mutual deterrence, the possibility that many of the enemy's bombers might be destroyed on the ground remained an incentive to attack. If they could be destroyed, the retal-iatory attack by a crippled remnant force might not be fatal to the attacking nation. In a crisis situation this possibility could tempt either side to launch a preemptive strike—even if the other side had no intention of striking. But long-range missiles, like the air force's Minuteman, could be widely dispersed and protected, or "hardened," in underground silos instead of being concen-trated on a few above-ground bases; missiles were not yet accurate enough to hit such silos. And the navy's Polaris missiles would be mobile underwater so that the enemy would at no time know where to strike them.

These concealment tactics deprived a surprise attack of its rationale. Obli-terating the enemy's cities would benefit the aggressor very little if the enemy still retained its retaliatory capacity. Surprise, therefore, no longer conferred any significant advantage to the side that struck first. Indeed, there was no longer any need to hit preemptively because enough missiles would survive the first strike to retaliate fully against the aggressor in a second strike. A first strike in these circumstances—which American policy makers generally con-ceded to the Soviets—would be completely irrational.

Invulnerable second-strike forces were believed to be the basis of *stable* mutual deterrence. Mutual deterrence, according to the arms control philos-ophy the Kennedy administration brought in, would not guarantee that war could be avoided. If the means of delivering nuclear bombs or warheads were vulnerable to attack, they might, particularly in crisis moments, tempt one side or the other to launch a first strike. Mutual deterrence in these condi-tions was unstable. Stabilizing the deterrent balance was therefore a priority for the new administration, which, over the next few years, deemphasized bombers and replaced them with hardened land-based and mobile sea-based missiles.

In the meantime, Kennedy, as cautious as Eisenhower, vacillated between his determination to stay in West Berlin and his equally strong determination to avoid conflict. Like Eisenhower, he was willing to negotiate with the Sovi-ets. The meager results of all bilateral American-Soviet negotiations, however, stemmed primarily from Soviet unwillingness to concede the right to any

Western presence in Berlin. Khrushchev was convinced that he had only to maintain Soviet pressure to evict the Western powers from the communist-surrounded and divided city. If, during this early period of the Kennedy administration, as during the late years of the Eisenhower era, the Soviets were unwilling to risk the final test, they had shown they would not hesitate to push the issue to a point of high tension by implying that they were willing to risk war and thereby exploit the West's fear of nuclear hostilities. This augured ill for the future if, first, the Soviet leaders could keep their challenges below the level of provocation that might arouse an American nuclear response, and, second, the Soviets could confine their challenges to the periphery of Western power, especially an isolated outpost such as West Berlin. As long as they followed these two fundamental precepts, they could continue to try to exploit the dilemmas of American strategy.

But it was the second rule that the Soviets failed to follow when they shifted the challenge to ninety miles from the American mainland—to Cuba—where the United States had little choice but to defend what it conceived to be its vital interests. Ironically, the Soviets placed missiles in Cuba because the Kennedy administration had concluded that no missile gap favoring Moscow existed, thus undermining the latter's claim of a changing strategic balance that should be reflected geographically in Europe. Cuba, then, was an effort to weaken U.S. strategic superiority and regain enough Soviet leverage to bring the Berlin crisis to a satisfactory conclusion.

SUPERPOWER CONFRONTATION IN CUBA

Cuba's revolutionary government dated from January 1, 1959, when its leaders overthrew the tyrannical dictatorship of Fulgencio Batista. During his struggle against Batista, Fidel Castro had identified himself with democratic government and social and economic justice and had gained widespread popularity among the Cuban people. This public support ensured the victory of his guerrilla army against the larger government forces. The Castro revolution was essentially a social revolution. Thus in the opening months of its rule, the new government moved to remedy the conditions of the people by instituting land reform and by building low-cost housing, schools, and clinics. But some features of this social revolution were bound to clash with the interests of the United States.

Although the United States had been instrumental in freeing Cuba from Spain in the Spanish-American War at the turn of the century, it had subsequently passed the Platt Amendment, which granted Americans the right to intervene at any time in Cuba for the preservation of Cuban independence, for the protection of life, property, and individual liberty, and for the discharge of Cuba's treaty obligations. By 1934, when the amendment was repealed, the United States had intervened militarily once in Cuba (1906-1909); it also had established a naval base at Guantánamo Bay. American capital controlled 80 percent of Cuba's utilities, 90 percent of its mines and cattle ranches, nearly all of its oil, and 40 percent of its sugar; approximately 25 percent of the American market was reserved for Cuban sugar. Despite this special commercial link, it was not surprising that the Cuban revolution directed its long pent-up nationalism and social resentment against the "Yankee imperialism" that dominated Cuba's economy. America's support of the Batista dictatorship until the moment of its collapse intensified anti-American sentiment. "Cuba, si! Yanqui, no!" became the Castro regime's rallying cry, the ceremonial burning of the American flag its ritual, and the confiscation of American property its reward. Yet Cuba in 1959 ranked fourth among Latin American nations in social and economic development (compared with the high teens today).

This anti-American nationalistic feeling, deliberately fostered by Castro to increase the popularity of his regime, led his government to become increasingly identified with communism. If he was going to break with the United States, which Castro assumed would oppose his reforms, then he had to look to Moscow, its rival. By doing so, Castro betrayed the revolution's original democratic promises, and Cuba became a dictatorship. All parties were abolished except for one—the Communist Party—upon whose organizational strength Castro had become increasingly dependent. Castro also linked Cuba closely to the communist bloc. The Soviet Union supplied Cuba with vast amounts of arms and accompanying military advisers. Cuban airmen were sent to Czechoslovakia to learn how to fly Soviet fighters, and a large number of Cuban technicians were trained in communist countries. Cuba's armed services soon ranked second only to America's as the largest in the Western Hemisphere. Diplomatic relations were established with all communist countries except East Germany, and economic agreements were signed with many of the same countries, including East Germany. Indeed, Cuba's economy became integrated into that of the communist bloc; 75 percent of the island's trade was with countries behind the iron curtain.

In January 1961 the United States cut off diplomatic relations with Cuba after a series of perceived provocations. If Castro at that point had attempted to seize the Guantánamo base, there would have been an excuse for open American intervention. Castro, though, was too shrewd to risk a seizure, but he also ruled out an accommodation with the United States. This dictator wanted to play a major role on the world stage—a role he could not achieve as the leader of either a pro-American or a neutral country of 10 million people on a small Caribbean island. He could do so only as a revolutionary leader who took on his giant neighbor as an enemy. But to stand up against the

United States he would need the support of the other giant, the Soviet Union. Thus Castro turned down all friendly overtures from the United States after he took power: a new, sympathetic American ambassador was kept waiting for weeks before being allowed to present his credentials and offers of foreign aid were rejected.

THE BAY OF PIGS

As Cuban-Soviet relations consolidated, the Eisenhower administration began to plan for Castro's overthrow. To this end, in April 1961 the new Kennedy administration launched an attempt by a small force of Cuban exiles— many of them former Castro associates who had become disillusioned by the premier's increasingly tyrannical rule, communist sympathies, and alignment with the Soviet Union—to land in Cuba and attempt to overthrow Castro. The U.S. Central Intelligence Agency (CIA), which had developed the plans for this operation and supervised their execution, assumed that, once the exiles had gained a beachhead in the Bay of Pigs, some units of Castro's army and much of Cuba's population would welcome the invaders as liberators. But the operation was a dramatic and appalling failure. The United States bungled it by basing a major foreign policy move involving American prestige on the glib assumption that a feeble beachhead operation would result in a mass uprising of Cubans against their government. The rumors and press reports, which conveyed the impression of a major invasion, made the failure appear even greater.

If nothing succeeds like success, it also can be said that nothing fails like failure. American prestige, already lowered by the Soviet Union's man-in-space achievement, sank to a new low. In his pointed comment in the *New York Times,* columnist Cyrus Sulzberger observed, "We looked like fools to our friends, rascals to our enemies, and incompetents to the rest." The administration had fallen victim to its own half-heartedness. The results of an unsuccessful invasion could have been predicted: an increase in Castro's domestic support, a revival of Latin American fears of "Yankee imperialism," a blunting of Kennedy's initially successful attempts to identify the United States with anticolonialism, and a loss of confidence in America's leadership by its allies.

Moreover, Kennedy was to set an unfortunate precedent for what was to become a pattern: to proclaim that a communist regime in the Caribbean-Central America area was a security threat to the United States, then use proxies in an effort to eliminate it, and finally to abandon those proxies when the going got tough because of fear of escalation and war or congressional and public opposition or alienation of Latin America's rising middle class. If vital interests really were at stake, this course was unworthy of a great power. In short, the United States attempted to counter the Soviet exploitation of the new nationalist and social revolution to its south by "partial measures and through proxies. It . . . sought solutions on the cheap." [1]

THE CUBAN MISSILE CRISIS

Thus Cuba survived as a communist base from which the Soviet Union could threaten the United States and subvert the security of other nations in the Western Hemisphere. The importance of this cannot be underestimated. The American position in the Western Hemisphere had been preeminent. The Monroe Doctrine had announced to the world that Latin America fell within the American sphere of influence and that Europe's colonial powers were to keep their hands off. In the decades that followed the United States had intervened repeatedly, especially in the Caribbean-Central American area. Although the motives for intervention varied, principal among them was the fear that a European power might establish its influence in an area that could be called America's "strategic rear," or, to use a Churchillian phrase, its "soft underbelly." During the early 1940s the concern had been with German power; after that, with Soviet power. A Marxist government had come to power in Guatemala in 1954. When it received arms from Czechoslovakia, the Eisenhower administration had intervened covertly to overthrow it, thereby setting a precedent for the Bay of Pigs. In short, the United States had never tolerated Latin American governments that leaned toward Germany or the Soviet Union—at least not in the smaller countries close to the Rio Grande and Florida.

With Fidel Castro's survival after the Bay of Pigs invasion, the United States no longer held a monopoly of power in the Caribbean and Central America. The Bay of Pigs disaster also incited Soviet intervention. In Moscow, where unfriendly regimes were not tolerated but crushed, Kennedy's prestige plummeted. According to the Soviet way of thinking, if it had been in the interest of the United States to eliminate Castro, then U.S. military intervention should have followed the bungled attempt by the CIA. A "serious" power does not tolerate its enemies so near and does not act squeamishly. It does what it has to do, regardless of international opinion. Moreover, if Castro's elimination was not important enough for the United States to risk criticism, then the intervention should not have been launched in the first place. But to do so and fail suggested weak nerves and a lack of foresight. Worse, it suggested fear of the Soviet Union. Why else would the United States not intervene with its own military forces in an area so close to it, as it had done many times in the past? Perhaps the Soviet Union should push a little further and see if Kennedy would tolerate a further extension of Soviet power.

1. Zbigniew Brzezinski, "America's New Geostrategy," *Foreign Affairs* 66 (spring 1988): 691.

And that is just what it did. Once the Soviets saw that the communist regime in Cuba was tolerated, they began to establish a missile base there. Washington had believed that the Soviet Union would not dare to do this in America's sphere of influence. In October 1962, however, a U-2 spy plane suddenly discovered, to the great surprise and consternation of American policy makers, that the Soviets were building launching sites for approximately seventy medium- and intermediate-range ballistic missiles (a number that could be increased later). That Khrushchev had dared to move his missiles so close to the United States and that he apparently expected no counteraction beyond ineffective diplomatic protests was a dangerous sign. He knew that war by miscalculation was the great danger; to prevent miscalculation was therefore an absolute necessity. But American vacillation at the Bay of Pigs and afterward had convinced the Soviet premier that the United States would not fight to protect its vital interests. Besides, Khrushchev thought Kennedy too young and inexperienced; Kennedy, Khrushchev told an American visitor, was "too liberal to fight."

Khrushchev had a great deal to gain. A failure to respond to his move would prove to America's NATO allies what they already feared: the United States had become vulnerable to attack and could no longer be relied on to protect Europe. Moreover, inaction in the face of Soviet missiles so close to the American coast would have validated Khrushchev's claim of a shift in the nuclear balance. The promised renewal of Soviet pressure on Berlin after the midterm U.S. congressional elections, together with the likelihood of an even more cautious American reaction than before, would have reinforced this impression. Only this time the Soviets could deliver an ultimatum to get out of Berlin or else, and they were in an increasingly favorable position to exert their will.

The threat in Cuba therefore had broad consequences. For the first time ever a large part of the North American continent would be vulnerable to Soviet missiles. The early warning systems against bombers and missiles were in the north because a Soviet attack had always been expected to come in over the Arctic. Moreover, American prestige was on the line, and not only in Europe. The sudden and unchallenged appearance of the opposing superpower in an area where the United States had long been paramount would have eroded America's authority and status and encouraged the spread of Castroism throughout Latin America. All anti-Castro forces, including the indispensable and all too few genuinely democratic reformers, would have been demoralized and perhaps paralyzed by Washington's inaction.

But for once Khrushchev overplayed his hand. He pressured the United States in the wrong place, and Washington could not avoid the test. If the stakes were high for the Soviet Union, they were even higher for the United States, and Kennedy felt that under no circumstances could he afford to lose.

Indeed, because he had warned the Soviet leader against placing offensive missiles in Cuba, Kennedy had to compel their withdrawal to preserve his credibility and America's. From the outset, however, the young president realized that the central issue was Soviet and allied perceptions of the balance of power.

Khrushchev's confidence, Kennedy realized, stemmed from a conviction that the United States no longer possessed the will to defend its interests. But such a notion was dangerous because, if left uncorrected, it would lead to a renewed and more determined challenge in Berlin—as Khrushchev already had announced. If the United States declared it would stand firm in Berlin but the Soviet leader did not believe it, a violent clash, possibly a nuclear war, might result. Characteristically, the Soviets had not committed themselves irrevocably in Cuba. They were willing to gamble for a big payoff, but they also were willing to suffer a serious setback to avoid a catastrophic clash. The Soviets were still seeking the limits of American tolerance in the Western Hemisphere.

To meet this crisis Kennedy placed a blockade around Cuba to prevent any further missile shipments, and he demanded the removal of the missiles already in place. American firmness and determination left Moscow little choice. For once the Soviets had to decide whether to fire the first shot—to break the American blockade of their missile-carrying ships—and risk a possible escalation of the conflict. Much to everyone's relief, the Kremlin backed down. It recognized that the United States had enormous conventional, especially naval, superiority in the Caribbean, and that it also could have mounted an invasion if it had been necessary. In the absence of sufficient conventional forces to support his ally so far away, Khrushchev was left with only one choice—risk nuclear war, which he was unwilling to do because he respected U.S. strategic superiority. America still had a huge bomber force, and Kennedy already had built up 200 ICBMs (of what a few years later was to be an ICBM force of 1,000). Khrushchev knew that his country had fewer than fifty first-generation missiles, exposed above the ground, and that it possessed no missile force to speak of despite its claims to the contrary. In fact, in 1961 U.S. satellites had learned the truth: there was indeed a missile gap, and it favored the United States. The shipment of Soviet missiles to Cuba was part of an attempt to reduce the nuclear imbalance that had resulted from Kennedy's rapid buildup, which had been stimulated by the years of Khrushchev's missile threats over Berlin and claims that he was mass-producing the new Soviet ICBMs. In any case, the resulting U.S. strategic strength set a clear upper limit to the pressure the Soviets could exercise on the United States. And the level of tension therefore rapidly declined as America's determination and willingness to use its power became clear. As Secretary of State Dean Rusk vividly described it, "We were eyeball to eyeball, and the other fellow just blinked."

Kennedy's critics had predicted that a Soviet humiliation in Cuba would compel Khrushchev to recoup his lost prestige by forcing the West out of Berlin. Khrushchev, however, called off both challenges, apparently believing that America's superior nuclear strength, as demonstrated in the Caribbean, also could be marshaled in Berlin. Local conventional superiority, which the Soviet Union possessed around Berlin, was not the decisive factor.

The missile crisis was therefore followed by years of détente (a relaxation of tensions). But there were two other outcomes as well. First, the United States had declared publicly that it would not invade Cuba. Thus although America had won a brilliant tactical victory, the Soviet Union had not suffered a strategic reversal; its base in the Caribbean remained intact. Second, Moscow decided it would never be humiliated again; it would build up its strategic nuclear power to U.S. levels, if not surpass them. The missile crisis had therefore been instructive to the Soviets—nuclear strength was politically usable.

AMERICAN STRATEGY AND FRONTIER DEFENSES

In the recurring crises over West Berlin from 1958 to 1962, as well as the Cuban missile crisis, the United States learned several lessons helpful to preserving the line around what was then still viewed as a cohesive Sino-Soviet bloc. The first lesson was that the threat of nuclear weapons could be used to deter the possibility of an all-out attack and contain limited challenges, but it could not prevent them. The advent of nuclear weapons, noted President Eisenhower, left no alternative to peace. However destructive, a conventional war (like World War II) distinguished winners from losers and, with time, both recovered from the human losses and the destruction of their cities and industries. But a nuclear war was likely to be suicidal; all participants were losers. The destruction would be on such a scale that no recovery would be possible. Total war, in short, had become irrational because the cost of war was completely disproportionate to any conceivable gains.

The United States, the Soviet Union, and communist China were all very aware of this historic change in the nature of warfare. World Wars I and II had been extremely costly; warfare now had become prohibitive. Thus policy makers in all major capitals, while on occasion talking tough and even threatening to go to war and use nuclear weapons, were in reality extremely careful in the conduct of policy to ensure that confrontations were resolved diplomatically, even if they involved public retreat and humiliation. This was better than escalation to armed clashes that might lead to a nuclear holocaust.

Thus despite massive retaliation and the talk of brinkmanship, the United States did not invoke the threat either in Korea in 1953 or in Indochina in 1954. And while nuclear war was certainly lurking in the background of the

Berlin crises, the possibility of its use came to the fore only during the Cuban missile crisis because of the likelihood of a U.S.-Soviet clash if the Soviet missiles were not withdrawn. The Soviet Union, while invoking the threat of war more menacingly and frequently to exploit Western fears of nuclear war, especially in Berlin, also remained extremely cautious even while its words were reckless. In the Taiwan Straits, in particular, this was dramatically demonstrated when it refused to back the PRC's efforts to reunify China, laying the Sino-Soviet schism open to public view while deepening it. And in Cuba it tried to install its missiles secretly before the United States could become aware of its move.

Nor was the PRC so eager to reunite with Taiwan or face the United States in Korea or Indochina that it would risk a confrontation, nuclear threat or not. Nuclear arms did not have to be invoked; they were just "there" and all the great powers knew it. Thus the nuclear powers were self-deterred from pushing any clash too far.

The second lesson was that mutual deterrence was not automatic. Indeed, advancing technology might upset the stability of the deterrent balance. And simply possessing the bomb was insufficient; the key to a *stable* deterrent balance was an invulnerable retaliatory force. If country A's force were vulnerable to attack by country B, A might be tempted to strike B preemptively rather than have its forces caught on the ground. Or A might lead B to strike first because B also feared a preemptive strike. In the late 1950s and early 1960s the Soviets claimed that they were mass-producing missiles that made American bombers vulnerable. If true this would have meant that the U.S. deterrent capacity would have declined as the Soviet first-strike capability grew. It affected, in any case, the psychology of the policy makers in Moscow and Washington, emboldening Khrushchev and making Eisenhower and Kennedy more cautious—until the latter was forced to the wall.

The Soviet Union's willingness to challenge the United States in Europe ten years after the first Berlin crisis was symptomatic of the effects of this perceived change in the balance. A Soviet claim of a shift in the nuclear balance led the Soviet Union to try to use "nuclear blackmail" or coercion to undermine the status quo. If Moscow could compel the United States to withdraw from West Berlin, NATO would collapse and the Soviet Union would become the hegemonic power in Europe. Only in Cuba in 1962, after it had become clear that Khrushchev had been bluffing and that he was not mass-producing ICBMs, did Washington regain its self-confidence and react vigorously.

Preserving deterrence, then, was a continuing, never-ending task, not because some change in the balance might have precipitated war, but because it might have affected the risks each side was willing to take as one side challenged the other. Neither side ultimately was willing to push "too far" diplo-

matically, lest it provoke nuclear war, but there was no question that the perception of the strategic balance did affect the degree of risks policy makers
were willing to accept in a specific situation: how far they calculated they
could push their opponent and how far they expected the latter to retreat and
comply with their demands. If Washington had still believed that U.S. strategic forces might have been vulnerable, would it have been willing to demand
that the Soviets withdraw their missiles from Cuba? If Moscow had really believed that the balance was changing in its favor, would it have complied or
continued to seek the West's exit from Berlin?

The third lesson was that unregulated arms competition was potentially
dangerous. In the rivalry between a democratic state and a totalitarian one,
the totalitarian state had a distinct advantage in the presatellite era. The Soviet
Union could easily gather information on U.S. arms, but because the Soviet
Union was a closed society, the United States could not accumulate information on the number and types of Soviet nuclear arms. After 1956, high-alti-
tude U-2 aircraft were the principal American means of collecting information. But because these aircraft could not survey Soviet territory daily,
Khrushchev could use his strategy of deception and claim that the Soviets had
weapons that they did not, in fact, possess and assert a capability to destroy
the U.S. deterrent bomber force—a capability they also did not have. The
United States could not be sure what was true. Earlier in the 1950s the Soviets
had flown the same few bombers around Moscow repeatedly to deceive
Western military observers. Only from 1961 on did Washington gain more reliable information from satellite observations and, for example, expose the
falsity of Soviet missile claims and the changing strategic balance.

But without the types of arms control arrangements that were to become
familiar after the 1950s, U.S. "worst case" assumptions about Soviet strength
were understandable. When hard information on Soviet nuclear strength was
lacking, the American reaction to Soviet claims was fear that bomber and
missile "gaps" existed and that they favored the Soviet Union. The United
States overreacted—for example, by increasing the number of missiles beyond those originally planned. Meanwhile, once Moscow knew that Washington knew that it had lied, the Soviets felt compelled to compensate for its
ICBM inferiority by placing in Cuba intermediate- and medium-range missiles, of which it had plenty. The subsequent missile crisis made leaders on
both sides more aware of the need for arms control to complement the unilateral acquisition of arms and the resulting action-reaction arms competition.

Finally, as Berlin and Cuba demonstrated, the chief function of military
power was to draw and protect "frontiers." These frontiers were clear: along
the inter-German border and through the middle of Berlin; at the thirty-
eighth parallel in Korea and the seventeenth parallel in Vietnam; along the

coast of China at Quemoy and Matsu; and at the "northern tier" of states from Turkey to Pakistan. Any attempt to cross these frontiers, either openly by direct attack or covertly by guerrilla warfare, risked hostilities. Admittedly, the lines drawn outside of Europe were extremely tenuous. The Central Treaty Organization (CENTO)—established in 1959 by the United States, Britain, Iran, Pakistan, and Turkey—and the Southeast Asia Treaty Organization (SEATO) were alliances in areas where nationalist forces opposed them. As a result, these alliances had little popular support in those regions, even in those states that were members, and the governments seeking to maintain this line were often unable, despite American help, to mobilize indigenous support, as was to become evident in Vietnam during the 1960s.

Indeed, the United States may have been better off had it not created what turned out to be poor replicas of NATO, which existed in a region where its people supported containment against a clearly perceived potential external aggression. The less successful alliances were organized in non-Western areas where containment was widely perceived as an attempt to preserve Western influence and reactionary regimes. America's containment strategy thus encountered greater difficulties as its geographic scope widened, a pattern which would become painfully evident within the developing world in the 1960s and 1970s.

In many developing countries economic growth has not kept pace with increasing population, political upheaval, and natural disasters.

CHAPTER FIVE

The Third World in the Crossfire

The Cold War that had started in Europe after World War II was extended to Asia in the 1950s with the fall of Nationalist China and the Korean War. Thus at the height of the Cold War political scientist Guy Pauker noted that four areas of the world were becoming major power centers: the United States, the Soviet Union, Western Europe, and the People's Republic of China. "In all four," he said,

productivity is on the increase, and the political system performs relatively well its integrating and decision-making functions. Despite major differences among them . . . these four areas are likely to be in a position to play major roles in political, economic, and cultural international affairs in the coming decade. In contrast, the Middle East, Southeast Asia, tropical Africa, and Latin America are apt to remain power vacuums during this period, owing to their lack of unity, political instability, economic stagnation, and cultural heterogeneity. It seems highly improbable that ten years from now any of the areas mentioned above will cease to be, respectively, a power center or a power vacuum.[1]

During the 1950s and 1960s the United States saw the unstable political and economic conditions in the developing countries, or Third World as it began to be known, as potentially dangerous. Moreover, the birth of so many new states, as Western colonialism collapsed after 1945, underlined the importance of this new Third World. The international system itself was no longer divided into the First World, or Western world of industrialized states, and the Second World, led by the Soviet Union. In 1946 the United Nations had 55 members. But by 1955 there were 76 members; by 1970, 127; by 1980, 160; and in the mid-1990s the figure was approaching 190. The vast majority of these member states were in developing regions. And in the UN General Assembly, with its principle of one country, one vote, these members could dominate the agenda.

But in the bipolar world of the Cold War, the "in-between" Third World was not an independent center of power but rather an object of seduction for the two superpowers, who were competing for the support, if not the allegiance, of the former colonial states. During their early years of independence, however, these states refused to align politically and militarily with either superpower. Among the first collective efforts of these new states was the establishment of a "nonaligned movement" and the assertion of their independence from the superpower rivals.

From its corner of the world, Moscow, and later Beijing, perceived the anticolonial revolt against the West as proof that the international capitalist order was disintegrating. Both Soviet and Chinese leaders saw an opportunity for taking the new states into a partnership to build an international communist order. From Washington's perspective, the challenge of Soviet and Chinese communism in the Third World stemmed not from conspiracy or military takeover but from the totalitarian model for modernization that communism offered the developing countries. The Soviet Union, discounting its rapid industrialization under Czar Nicholas II at the turn of the century, held itself up as a model of an underdeveloped country that had transformed itself into a modern industrial society in one generation. The developing countries' choice of which path to follow was seen as critical to American security and, more broadly, to an international environment safe for open societies and democratic values. As a leading U.S. scholar summed it up: "Whether most of these countries take a democratic or Communist or other totalitarian path in their development is likely to determine the course

1. Guy J. Pauker, "Southeast Asia as a Problem Area in the Next Decade," *World Politics* (April 1959): 325.

of civilization on our planet." [2] Perhaps with this in mind, the United States undertook the vital task of helping the new countries develop. For the United States, given the entrenched internal problems and the growing separation from the industrialized world of these countries, support for their development was more a matter of basic self-interest rather than of humanitarian concern for the poor.

THE REVOLUTION OF RISING EXPECTATIONS

Paradoxically, the disintegration of Western colonialism after World War II provided the most eloquent testimony to its success. The Western powers, including the United States in the Philippines, had justified their imperial domination in terms of bringing the "backward" peoples of the earth the benefits of Western democracy, medical science, and technology. It was the "white man's burden," or duty, to educate the people so that one day they could govern themselves.

The colonial powers apparently had taught their lesson well; they had ruled their colonies autocratically, while propagating the virtues of democracy. Ironically, the nationalist movements later used the same democratic ideals to challenge their rulers and ask them to practice what they preached. Indeed, educated in Europe or America, or in a Western school in their own country, the leaders of these nationalist movements fought the European powers by using the principles of democracy and national freedom they had learned. For them, these principles were incompatible with imperialism.

Once these countries became independent, however, they were left with a legacy of poverty, illiteracy, and disease. For example, in the 1950s annual per capita income in these nations rarely reached $100. To remedy the economic underdevelopment and to narrow the enormous gap between poor and rich nations, many developing countries turned to industrialization, which was to transform their traditional agrarian societies into modern, industrial, urban welfare states. Over the years this transformation would have great political significance as the citizens of developing countries were asked to transfer their allegiances from their local communities, which held their loyalty, to their new nations; the concept of national loyalty was new to them. For their part, the fledgling nations had to prove they could offer their people something not otherwise attainable. By achieving improved standards of living, nations would demonstrate that they deserved the popular support and allegiance they needed to survive and grow.

2. Eugene Stanley, *The Future of Underdeveloped Countries,* rev. ed. (New York: Praeger, 1961), 3.

In asking themselves in the 1950s whether they could develop themselves economically, the new countries realized that to a large extent the answer depended on whether their economic progress was faster than their population growth, or whether their "population explosions" would eat up any increase in national income. In 1830 the world population was 1 billion; by 1930 it had doubled. The figure in 1960 was 3 billion and the fourth billion took only fifteen years. Just as the developing countries would represent a majority of nation-states by 1970, their population growth rates would far exceed those in industrialized countries. Indeed, according to the best estimates, the world's population will grow to almost 6 billion people by the year 2000, with 80 percent living in the developing countries.

The concern was that, despite a later slowing of the population growth rate, the developing countries might still face the problem described by the Reverend Thomas Malthus more than 150 years ago—the hunger and poverty that result when the population grows faster than the means of subsistence. Malthus, who also was an economist, predicted this fate for the Western world unless the population growth were limited by either "positive checks" such as wars or epidemics, which result in a high death rates, or by "preventive checks," which produce low birth rates.

In contrast to the developing countries, the West made impressive economic progress after the Industrial Revolution, despite a population increase. Improved harvesting techniques provided plentiful food, and industrial advances raised the standard of living to heights never before attained, thereby refuting Malthus's gloomy prediction. The conditions facing the developing countries, however, were quite unlike those found in Western countries. One chief difference was that the Western countries had far smaller populations when they began industrializing, and their population growth did not outdistance the economic improvement. But India, for example, began its modernization with a population of 350 million, which it expected to reach 1 billion by 2000. China, with a population of 547 million in 1950, was home to 1 billion people in the early 1980s. Incredibly, if after its War of Independence the United States had possessed a population density equivalent to that of Egypt, today it would have more than 2 billion people instead of just over 250 million. Under these circumstances the United States would not have become a "developed" nation.

The European nations also enjoyed an enormous benefit in the New World and in their colonial empires, which provided them with outlets to relieve their population pressures. Indeed, about 60 million Europeans emigrated during the nineteenth and early twentieth centuries. By the 1950s there were about 400 million people of European descent living outside Europe. The United States and Canada, rich in resources and fertile land, easily absorbed millions of immigrants and still increased their living standards. Australia, New Zealand, and South Africa also expanded their populations and economies, although on a smaller scale. By absorbing a population that might otherwise have led to overcrowding in Europe, the colonies added materially to the European nations' wealth. The developing countries, however, were not able to find such empty and rich spaces to absorb their surplus populations.

Also unlike in Europe, where new agricultural technologies increased food supplies and temperate climates were more favorable to food production than the tropical climates and monsoons prevalent in developing countries, the nonindustrialized nations found themselves still engaged in primitive agriculture. Many of the new countries' governments, because they equated development with industrialization, neglected to modernize agriculture. To their leaders, agriculture was the symbol of their former colonial status as producers of raw materials. Even so, some countries experimented with intensive farming techniques. Using high-yielding crop varieties, improved but costly chemical fertilizers, and more effective pesticides, the so-called Green Revolution increased food production enough to keep up with the population growth. By the 1980s some developing countries even exported food, although many still could not feed themselves.

In the West the birth rate declined after 1850; with industrialization and the growth of cities came the spread of literacy and artificial birth-control techniques. Indeed, as it turned out, Malthus was right even about the West because preventive checks were adopted, with many industrialized states achieving "zero population growth" by the late twentieth century. But the Third World, whose population increases were in large part the result of the introduction of Western medicine, which reduced infant mortality and raised life expectancy, had not yet reached a similar level of economic development, and knowledge of birth-control methods and the willingness to use them spread more slowly than many expected. The poorer the populations were in the Third World—in sub-Saharan Africa, for example—the higher were their rates of population growth.

OBSTACLES TO MODERNIZATION
IN THE THIRD WORLD

With the exception of a few emerging newly industrialized countries such as Taiwan and South Korea, most Third World states in the 1950s and 1960s failed to match their economic development to their fast-rising rates of population growth, much less surpass them. Many of these countries simply did not have enough capital. Sufficient internal savings could not be squeezed out of people living at a subsistence level—at least, not without authoritarian

controls. As for earning capital through trade—particularly exports of primary products or raw materials such as coffee, tea, rubber, and tin—the developing countries had discovered in the past that such exports limited their
earning capacity. Because upon independence their economies remained tied
to those of their former colonial masters, their exports rose or declined with
every fluctuation in Western prosperity. If a major Western recession reduced the demand and price levels of natural resources (even oil until 1973),
the resulting losses of income often exceeded the Western aid extended during the same period. Furthermore, markets would become glutted with certain items because of overproduction or substitution. A nation trying to raise
its income by increasing production found its competitors doing the same,
which lowered world prices further.

Another problem was that the Western industrial nations, whose ever-
increasing demand for raw materials was supposed to furnish the capital for
economic development, no longer needed them to the degree anticipated because of the development of synthetics (such as rubber) or changing consumer habits (such as sugar substitutes). Thus the lack of stable international
commodity prices, similar to the parity prices paid to American farmers, as
well as the inventiveness of modern technology (for extracting resources from
the ocean's seabeds, for example) limited the prospects of financing industrialization via earnings from raw materials.

Foreign investment was another source of capital for economic development. In the initial period after independence, however, private capital was in
short supply for the kind of long-range development that the developing nations needed. Private American investments outside the United States were
largely being made by a small group of oil companies to build refineries and
to discover and pump out oil fields in Latin America and the Middle East, but
most investment capital stayed home because of the boom the American
economy experienced for most of the Cold War period. This was true for Europe as well. European capital was concentrated on rebuilding, modernizing,
and expanding Europe's industrial base. American capital that did go abroad
often went to the Common Market, where it would return sizable and relatively speedy profits. Because many developing countries were anticapitalist,
associating capitalism with colonialism, their attitude toward private investment was politically inhospitable.

Modernization, then, was the new nations' principal task, but they soon
realized that it was not just an economic undertaking; it was a political, social,
and intellectual undertaking as well. Indeed, taken to its extremes, modernization was a revolutionary process frequently marked by political instability
and violence rather than evolutionary, peaceful change.

One reason for this instability was that most of the new nations lacked administrative and political cohesion. Generally their populations had no single

common culture or language; in fact, tribal and regional conflicts abounded.
Citizens had no natural loyalty to their state and no tradition of cooperation
except on the one overriding issue of eliminating the colonial ruler. But once
the struggle for independence ended, power tended to fragment. For example, India split violently into Hindu India and Muslim Pakistan after independence, and the latter dissolved further into Pakistan and Bangladesh. The
Congo (now Zaire) fell apart when the Belgians withdrew. Cyprus divided
into Turkish and Greek factions. And Biafra broke away from Nigeria, only to
lose the subsequent civil war.

Even where actual disintegration did not occur, religious, linguistic, and
racial differences and antagonisms tended to tear apart the fabric of those
states that lacked any history of nationhood. In 1972, for example, the Tutsi
tribes in Burundi reportedly slaughtered 120,000 Hutus; this tribal violence
recurred in 1988. In the late 1980s Sri Lanka, formerly Ceylon, a large island
lying just off the southeastern coast of India, was tearing itself apart between
Hindu Tamils and Buddhist Sinhalese. The lesson appeared obvious: before
the formal process of "state building" could occur, stable *nations* in which the
needs of disparate peoples were respected had to be created.

The absence of a strong sense of national consciousness was soon reflected
in the way many of the leaders of the new countries built themselves up as
symbols of nationhood. They did not find this difficult because, as leaders of
the movements for independence, their prestige was usually high. But the
task was an essential one. Just as Louis XIV had proclaimed, *"L'état, c'est
moi,"* they too *were* the state; without their presence as its symbol the nation
would not hold together as a unit. One-party rule or military governments
existed almost everywhere in the Third World. In Africa, for example, the
world's last continent to be freed from colonialism, three-fourths of its 345
million people lived under single-party or military rule by the late 1960s, ten
years after independence.

Such policies might have seemed undemocratic, but they were widely justified by native rulers and believed to be necessary. Most people in the new
nations felt less loyalty to the state than to ancestors, family, village, or tribe.
Wherever the opposition represented these centrifugal forces, an American-
style democracy would have led not just to a change of government but to the
disintegration of the state. The alternatives facing the leaders of these countries were often not democracy or dictatorship but statehood or disintegration.

The political and revolutionary context of modernization also was revealed in the nature of nationalist revolutions, which directed their opposition not only against the colonial ruler but also against the traditional governing elites if they remained in power after independence. Many of the
developing countries were split into three main groups when they gained in-

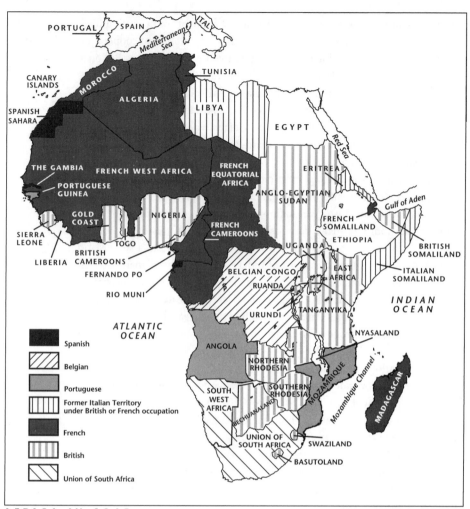

AFRICA IN 1945

Legend:
- Spanish
- Belgian
- Portuguese
- Former Italian Territory under British or French occupation
- French
- British
- Union of South Africa

dependence. The first was the ruling minority, usually composed of the land-owners or merchants, whose vested interest lay in the preservation of the status quo. Their wealth and power derived from continuing, as in the old colonial days, to send their nations' crops and natural resources to the West rather than industrializing themselves and becoming economically independent. The second group was peasants, villagers, small artisans, and shopkeepers (about 80 percent of the population in most developing countries)—those whose energies were spent largely on the day-to-day struggle for survival. This group, which had for centuries borne its hardships silently, awakened and demanded a better life. The third group, the urban intelligentsia, educated in Western ideas and committed to nationalism and modern-

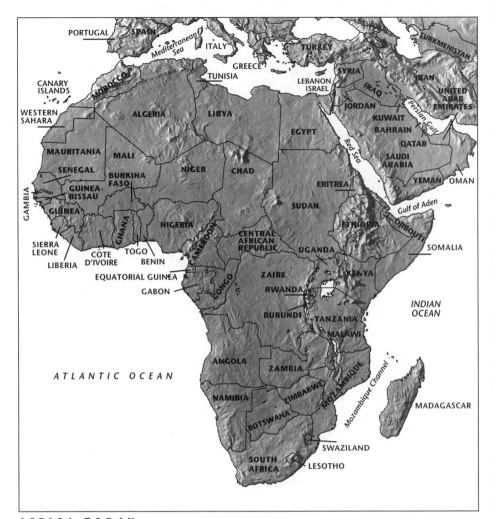

AFRICA TODAY

ization, voiced these resentments against the old way of life and articulated the new aspirations while it sought power to affect the political, social, and economic transformation of the country's societies. Without such social change—that is, the overthrow of the old ruling elites—modernization was inhibited. This was not a matter of "reform" but of revolution because the crucial issue was power. Who controlled the nation—the old ruling elite committed to the preservation of the traditional, preindustrial society or those who sought to democratize, modernize, and industrialize the nation? Only one thing was certain: few who rule yield their dominant political, social, and economic position without a struggle.

OTHER SEEDS OF DISCONTENT

Instability was able to take root even where economic development occurred, where national bonds did not disintegrate, and where the modernizing elite was in control. Such instability stemmed from a slowly rising standard of living that may not have created an increasingly satisfied—and therefore happy and peaceful—population. Capital for investment was accumulated only if it was not paid to the workers; low wages militated against mass consumption and allowed the reinvestment of capital into further economic expansion. Although living conditions may have improved, they did not satisfy the "revolution of rising expectations." Once the population realized that it no longer had to live in the poverty and filth of the past, that change was possible, that people could create a better life through their own efforts, they became dissatisfied. The gap between their expectations and achievements was particularly aggravating when the rulers lived well, even ostentatiously. Those living less well became frustrated. In turn, this spawned social discontent and an increasingly sullen, hostile, and more radical mood. In the 1960s and 1970s this pattern led the governments of many developing countries to be more assertive toward the United States, further aggravating North-South relations.

Social instability and turmoil were further promoted by the intellectual and cultural changes that accompanied the transformation of a traditional, static, rural society into a modern, dynamic, urban-industrial state. Many of the old customary and religious values that had helped people to accept their place in society and conduct themselves throughout life simply collapsed; people became disoriented, torn from their age-old moorings for which they had not yet found a substitute. Their ancestors had provided status and meaning for their lives; robbed of this, they became isolated and insecure atoms in a rapidly changing environment that they neither made nor comprehended. Secular values, emphasizing materialism and progress, replaced religious values that denied the importance of earthly existence and material possessions. A society in which individual effort was rewarded and people could rise socially according to merit replaced a society with a rigid social structure in which birth determined their place and religion often governed their mode of conduct.

Nationalism thus replaced local loyalty, and modern transportation and communication brought individuals to an awareness of the larger society in which they lived and worked. Impersonal ties to people far away in their country replaced former face-to-face relations with neighbors, and new skills and ways of thought had to be learned. In short, people had to forget many of their old ways and adapt to new conditions. In the best of circumstances these changes were difficult and agonizing. In other cases they produced social revolutions that often brought new regimes to power, which turned back modernization efforts. The Iranian people, for example, were undergoing this kind of upheaval in late 1978 and early 1979, when their religious leaders opposed the American-backed shah and his modernization, leading to his overthrow and the establishment of an Islamic theocracy. Precisely because modernization was associated with secular values, few in the West had taken seriously the possibility of the Ayatollah Ruhollah Khomeini's succession. The idea of an old man, a religious icon, coming to power was so at odds with contemporary ideas of modernization that the likelihood of its occurrence was dismissed as preposterous. Yet for the poor and the lowly in a rapidly changing society where tradition and customs were being eroded, often by forces alien to the indigenous population, religion retained a strong attraction and comfort.

DOMESTIC INSTABILITY AND
SUPERPOWER INVOLVEMENT

It was not surprising that during the 1960s and 1970s the domestic transformation of the developing countries had repercussions beyond their borders. The upheavals tended to disturb an international system largely defined by the frontiers drawn between the two superpowers' spheres of influence and by the Cold War rivalries. When the internal difficulties of the countries of the Third World spilled over into the external arena of international politics, or resulted in civil war or regional rivalries, they attracted the Soviet Union or the United States, leading to possible confrontation with the attendant danger of military conflict.

The two superpowers were attracted to Third World conflicts because such friction could either bring to power a group one superpower liked and the other disliked or result in regional expansion and influence that could be perceived as benefiting one and hurting the other. If one superpower was unwilling to tolerate what it considered to be, in terms of the overall balance of power, a local or regional setback, then it would intervene. Or, if it feared that if it did not intervene then its opponent might, the result might have been preventive intervention. In both cases it risked a similar move by its opponent. Looking to the future, Pauker observed, "Power vacuums are likely to disturb international relations increasingly. They are the natural targets for power centers wishing to extend their hegemony. They should be the object of anxious attention for those powers which want to strengthen the international balance." [3]

3. Pauker, "Southeast Asia," 325.

NATIONAL DISINTEGRATION AND CIVIL WAR:
THE CASE OF ZAIRE

If a new nation disintegrates into two or more parts, those who seek to re-unify their land or establish their new splinter states may appeal for help to sympathetic states that, for reasons of their own, may wish to see either a nation preserve its unity or a splinter state its independence. Such appeals were addressed especially to the Soviet Union or the United States in the early years of the Cold War.

One of the more dramatic examples of the way the survival of a new state involved the superpowers occurred in 1960 when the Belgian Congo became independent. Almost immediately the Congo fell into disorder. First, the rich mining province of Katanga, on whose copper and cobalt exports the Congo was largely dependent as a major source of revenue, split off into a separate state. Katanga's president had the support of the powerful Belgian mining interests, eager to protect their investments. Then the army began to revolt because it resented the continued presence of its Belgian officers and wanted them replaced with native leadership. In a wild spree Congolese soldiers began to attack white women (including nuns) and children, causing the Belgian settlers to flee, including the experts the Belgians had expected to leave behind to help the Congolese in their early period of self-government. All public services then collapsed because the Congo lacked an educated native elite. The Belgians had never trained one.

When the Belgians flew in paratroopers to protect their nationals, Congolese premier Patrice Lumumba saw the move as a Belgian attempt to restore colonial rule, and he appealed to the United Nations to send forces to help him. It was at this point that the Cold War was injected into the Congo. The UN troops, with no forces from the great powers, did not compel the Belgians to evacuate their paratroopers. UN Secretary-General Dag Hammarskjöld had ordered UN forces not to become involved in internal conflicts or in the contending political factions seeking to gain power over their rivals. This, however, had the effect of underwriting the divisions of the Congo. Lumumba turned against the United Nations, bitterly attacked the secretary-general, and accused Belgium and the Western powers, especially the United States, of conspiring against him. Lumumba's attacks grew increasingly racist. Finally, he asked the Soviet Union for help and received Soviet diplomatic backing, military supplies, and offers of troops, or "volunteers." Several neutrals, especially the United Arab Republic, Guinea, and Ghana, also extended their sympathy and support.

In early 1962, after all efforts to unify the Congo had failed, the United Nations reversed its original stand in order to preempt possible Soviet intervention. It finally adopted the policy of forcefully squashing the opposition. Although it took many months and cost lives, the country was "unified." Gen. Joseph D. Mobutu (he later changed his name to Mobutu Sese), who emerged as Zaire's leader for several decades, was supported by the United States for his anticommunist policies. Mobutu received vast amounts of American foreign aid, much of which he used to solidify his rule. Along the way he managed to expropriate much of the aid and the country's commercial wealth for his own purposes, to the point that by the 1990s he had become one of the world's richest men while his country slipped further into poverty and internal turmoil. His actions, and the case of Zaire in general, symbolized the disarray that resulted from the collision of Cold War politics and Third World development.

REGIONAL RIVALRIES: THE 1956 AND 1967 ARAB-ISRAELI WARS

Beyond the impoverished states of Africa, no area better exemplified how regional disputes became intertwined with the Cold War than the Middle East. Specifically, three sets of rivalries intersected: the Arab-Israeli enmity, intra-Arab rivalry, and the superpower competition. Each tended to reinforce the other. The Arabs, especially Egypt and Syria, received weapons and political support from the Soviet Union, while Israel received similar support from the United States. With all this help, then, the Arabs and Israelis were able to fight repeated wars.

While the victor, Israel, could never impose a settlement on its enemies because the Soviets would not allow their clients to be totally defeated, the Arabs never paid the penalty for losing and could always rearm and try to destroy Israel the next time. The superpowers supported their respective client states to expand their influence and weaken that of their Cold War adversary; simultaneously, they restrained their respective clients lest they be drawn into a direct confrontation. The larger Arab states tended to compete among themselves for leadership of the Arab world in terms of who would best defend Arab interests by the militancy of their anti-Israeli stance; even moderate and pro-Western Arab states (largely the oil producers) had to be anti-Israel.

It was the Eisenhower administration's effort to complete its wall of containment around the Sino-Soviet world that introduced the Cold War into the Middle East. In 1955 Britain, historically the preeminent Western power in the area, with American support established the Middle East Treaty Organization (METO), which included Turkey, Iraq, Iran, and Pakistan. Also known as the Baghdad Pact, METO extended the NATO line from Turkey to India. With the exception of Iraq, this "northern tier" was drawn along 3,000 miles of the Soviet Union's southern frontier and therefore drew a sharp reaction from that country. Although they had been rebuffed in Iran and Turkey, the Soviets had not surrendered their ambitions in the region. The Middle

East linked Europe, Africa, and Asia. For Britain, the area—and especially the Suez Canal—had long been the lifeline to India, the "Jewel in the Crown" of the old empire, and to its present Commonwealth. Of greater importance, Europe's economy was becoming increasingly dependent on the Middle East for oil (America was still self-sufficient). The power that could deny Europe oil would be able to dictate its future. In short, for the Soviet Union the Middle East was the place to outflank and neutralize NATO. Its opportunity to attempt this came as a result of several situations: the bitter Arab-Israeli conflict, the Anglo-Egyptian quarrel, Egypt's expansionist ambitions, and the U.S. attempt to draw the line of containment just south of the Soviet Union's border.

THE BEGINNINGS OF THE ARAB-ISRAELI CONFLICT

Arab antagonism toward Israel stemmed from the Balfour Declaration of 1917, in which Britain had pledged the establishment of a "national home" for the Jewish people in Palestine while promising the Arabs that the civil and religious rights of non-Jews would not be prejudiced. Zionists took this pledge as a promise to convert Palestine into a Jewish state; they considered Palestine, which had become a British mandate after the disintegration of the Ottoman Empire during World War I, to be their ancient and traditional homeland. The Arabs, meanwhile, feared that the Jewish immigration would crowd them out of what they also regarded to be their rightful homeland.

In November 1947 the United Nations partitioned Palestine into two independent states, one Jewish and the other Arab. The Arabs refused to accept this solution. On May 10, 1948, as Britain ended its mandate, the Jews proclaimed the state of Israel, and the armies of the Arab League (Egypt, Jordan, Syria, Lebanon, and Saudi Arabia) invaded the new state. In the ensuing war the Israeli army defeated the larger Arab armies, and the state of Israel became a fact of political life.

The Arabs, however, refused to recognize it as such. But Egypt, the leading Arab power, needed arms before reconfronting Israel. In September 1955 Egypt stunned the West by concluding an arms deal with Czechoslovakia, acting for the Soviet Union. Under this arrangement Egypt received a large quantity of arms, including planes and tanks. Egypt now thought that it had the means to achieve a decisive military victory over Israel. In April 1956 Egypt tightened the ring around Israel by forming a joint command with Syria, Saudi Arabia, and Yemen. In October Egypt, Jordan, and Syria announced another joint command, "the principal concern of which is the war of destruction against Israel." As Egypt solidified the encirclement of Israel and began to absorb the Soviet arms, the Israelis decided to strike before it was too late.

THE ANGLO-EGYPTIAN QUARREL AND
NASSER'S AMBITIONS

The
Third World
in the
Crossfire

World War II had intensified Egyptian nationalism and heightened the demand for a withdrawal of British forces (Britain had had a presence in Egypt since 1882, and the country was even a British protectorate from 1914 to 1922). In late 1951 the Egyptian parliament abrogated the 1936 Anglo-Egyptian treaty, and in July 1952 the new military regime that took over the Egyptian government from King Farouk pressed with renewed vigor for the removal of British troops. The Eisenhower administration supported the Egyptian demand in the belief that Col. Gamal Abdel Nasser, the real power behind the military coup, and the United States were natural allies. The military was believed to be anticolonial, progressive, and committed to improving people's lives and providing Egypt with a degree of political stability. If the United States helped Nasser to evacuate British troops from their Suez Canal base, the Egyptians might in fact become allies. But once it ousted British colonial control, the new regime turned to its number-one goal: to avenge itself by destroying Israel.

The removal of British forces from Egypt did not eliminate British power from the region. Britain shifted from Egypt to Iraq, its longtime friend, whose royalist regime needed Western protection from Egypt's new military regime. Nasser did not see the Baghdad Pact as a means of containing the Soviet Union; he saw it as an instrument to preserve Western domination throughout the area and, because Iraq had always been Egypt's traditional rival for Arab leadership, he considered the pact a personal challenge as well. The pact completed Nasser's alienation from the West, for his ambitions reached beyond eliminating Israel and expelling the British. He saw himself as a modern Saladin, the champion of the Arab cause. He promoted Pan-Arabism as a way of expanding his influence and that of his country. As the former dominant influence throughout the region, the West became Nasser's target.

The Baghdad Pact was the instrument of its own destruction because it helped bind Egypt to the Soviet Union. Its failure testifies to the difficulties of containing Soviet expansion by drawing lines outside of Europe. In Western Europe the states all shared a common perception of the Soviet threat and stood united against it. Outside of Europe, U.S.-Soviet competition intersected with regional rivalries, undermining the U.S. goal of containment and providing the Soviet Union with an opportunity to expand its influence. It was in Moscow's interest to destroy this alliance along the Soviet Union's southern frontier; it was in Cairo's interest to gain a source of arms to destroy Israel and to put political pressure on the pro-Western regimes in the area. Thus Cairo received its arms, and Nasser became a hero for the Arab people. By strengthening Nasser, the Soviet Union became the Arabs' greatest friend.

The United States further upset the West's position in the Middle East in July 1956 when it retracted its offer to help finance Nasser's pet project, the Aswan High Dam. The dam on the upper Nile was intended to raise Egypt's low standard of living by irrigating new land and providing electricity for industrial development. The retraction was a heavy blow to Egypt because the American loan was a prerequisite for further aid from the World Bank and Britain, and these offers, too, were withdrawn. Nasser regarded these decisions as a personal slap and national humiliation. A few days later, on July 26, he announced he would nationalize the Suez Canal and use the revenues collected from it to finance the dam. Arab nationalists were ecstatic, and Nasser's stature, already great, reached new heights.

The British government reacted sharply to Nasser's seizure of the canal. Prime Minister Anthony Eden believed that if Nasser could face the West with such a major act of defiance and go unpunished, Western influence would be destroyed throughout the Middle East. Western prestige—especially British prestige because south of America's "northern tier" Britain was the leading Western power in the Middle East—had to be upheld. The British were determined to stand up to Nasser, and they insisted on some form of international control for the canal. All attempts to bridge Anglo-Egyptian differences failed.

THE SUEZ WAR
AND U.S. INTERVENTION

In October 1956 the Israeli army marched into Egypt, where it quickly defeated the Egyptian forces on the Sinai Peninsula. The British and the French (who sought Nasser's downfall because of his aid to rebels trying to free Algeria from French control) intervened on Israel's behalf. But instead of facing the United States with a *fait accompli,* the result of a quick and effective intervention, their action infuriated the Eisenhower administration, which condemned their concerted military offensive. The reason for this American response was that, despite its disapproval of Nasser and the pro-Soviet direction in which he was leading Egypt, the administration saw his foreign policy as purely a reaction against Israel and Western colonialism. It remained convinced that if Israel had not existed, and if the Arab states had not long been dominated by the Western powers, especially Britain, the Arabs would not be anti-Western and pro-Soviet. The administration saw the invasion of Egypt as a golden opportunity to win Arab friendship. By saving Nasser, the United States could align itself with Arab nationalism; supporting Britain, France, and Israel would leave the Soviet Union as the sole champion of Arab aspirations.

In short, American opposition to the invasion and British attempts to reassert control over the Suez Canal would identify the United States with the anticolonialism of the entire underdeveloped world, and particularly with the anti-Israel and nationalistic sentiments of the Arab world. Because continued evidence of British power in the Middle East only antagonized the Arabs, the removal of this power and its replacement by American influence would be in the interest not only of the United States but also of all the Western powers. In this way the West's strategic and economic interests could be more adequately safeguarded. At least that was the rationale for the United States humiliating its two main allies, thereby turning Nasser's military defeat into a political victory. The favorable global contrast—Washington opposing great-power intervention against a smaller state at a time when the Soviets were intervening in Hungary to suppress its aspiration for national self-determination—was a factor as well.

America's opposition to the Suez invasion was the decisive factor in stopping the fighting. Given opposition to the invasion within Britain, the Commonwealth (Canada, India, and Pakistan), and the United Nations, the British government accepted a cease-fire and later withdrew its forces; France and Israel had little choice but to follow suit.

THE EISENHOWER DOCTRINE

It is ironic in view of America's leading role in halting the attack on Egypt that the Soviet Union was to reap the benefits. After it had become clear that the United States would not support the British and French invasion, the Soviet Union threatened "to crush the aggressor." The Soviet Union risked nothing to deliver these threats, but it was the country that received most of the credit from the Arabs for saving Nasser by its threats to exterminate Israel and attack Britain and France.

Recognizing this development, Eisenhower urged Congress to support a new commitment to resist communism in the Middle East. A joint resolution of Congress, known as the Eisenhower Doctrine, declared in 1957 that the United States considered the preservation of the Middle Eastern nations vital to American security, and that it was prepared to use armed force to assist any state requesting U.S. help to counter military threats "from any country controlled by international Communism." Despite the fact that the Soviet Union did not border any Arab state, it was clear that this proclamation was aimed at Nasser, whose great political victory only increased his self-confidence. Supported by the Soviet Union, whose aim it was to weaken if not eliminate all Western power in the Middle East, Nasser continued his expansionist drive. The whole Western position in the Middle East seemed to be on the brink of disintegration. Having helped to eliminate British power in the hope of winning Egypt's friendship against Moscow, the administration now found itself filling in the vacuum left by British power to contain what it saw as the emerging Moscow-Cairo axis.

Using its new doctrine as a pretext, the Eisenhower administration in 1958 resorted to force. Lebanon had been plagued for some time with civil war between Muslims and Christians. The Muslims wanted close relations, if not union, with the United Arab Republic (which comprised Egypt and Syria), and the Christians favored a pro-Western policy and the continued independence of Lebanon. Men and arms for the pro-Nasser elements were smuggled in from Syria. In Jordan, too, the situation took a turn for the worse when King Hussein dismissed his pro-Nasser government, which led to a general strike, massive street demonstrations, and riots. In response to this turmoil, the United States sent 14,000 men into Lebanon, and the British sent 3,000 paratroopers into Jordan. The large size of the American contingent seems to have been a deliberate warning to Iraq, where nationalist officers had seized power and overthrown the pro-British monarchy, and might have been tempted to nationalize Western oil resources. But its leader quickly gave assurances that he had no such intention, and possible American intervention in Iraq was forestalled.

The Anglo-American action saved Lebanon and Jordan. But it also was intended to have another important effect: to show Nasser and the Arabs that there were limits to Soviet willingness to come to their aid. Before the intervention the Soviets again had threatened to send "volunteers" to oppose the Western "imperialists" and had carried out conspicuous military maneuvers in Soviet central Asia and Transcaucasia. The firmness of the American position and the failure of the Soviet Union to do more than denounce the intervention and call for a diplomatic settlement made it very clear that there were limits to Soviet willingness to bail out the Arabs. This had a dampening effect on Nasser's anti-Western drive. Jordan, Lebanon, and Saudi Arabia had remained independent; Libya and the Sudan had resisted his attempts to subvert them; and, ironically, Iraq's officers briefly challenged Nasser for leadership of the Arab world—until its own leading general was himself overthrown and killed.

Meanwhile, the United States had become almost a full-fledged member of the Baghdad Pact (renamed the Central Treaty Organization, or CENTO, after Iraq's defection). But south of CENTO's fragile line remained all the basic problems that had given rise to the turmoil after 1955: the conflicts among the Arab states, the Arab-Israeli dispute, the overshadowing competition between the United States and the Soviet Union, and, above all, the rise of Arab nationalism. The American attempt to draw another "frontier" in the sands of the Middle East had been unsuccessful. Ironically it was this attempt that had drawn the Soviet Union and Egypt together to destroy the "northern tier," permitting Moscow to jump over the line that was supposed to contain it. It was thus only a matter of time until the next war would erupt.

By 1967 intra-Arab rivalries, combined with domestic economic failure, led Nasser to reassert his leadership of Arab nationalism. The result was another war. The Syrians, who had joined Egypt in a United Arab Republic, only to quit it as a result of Nasser's effort to dominate the union, now sought to displace him as the leader of Pan-Arabism. They openly and repeatedly called for Israel's destruction and stepped up their terrorist raids into that country. After the Israelis retaliated, the Syrians claimed in May 1967 that the Israelis were assembling their forces for a full-scale invasion of Syria. Nasser, claiming to be the great hero of the Arab peoples, either felt compelled to act or saw in the invasion rumor his opportunity to regain his leadership of Arab nationalism. After eleven years of receiving Soviet training and arms, Nasser seemed confident that his forces could beat Israel, which this time would be fighting by itself, without the aid of France and Britain.

In preparation for the confrontation the Egyptian leader moved reinforcements into the Sinai Desert and then demanded and obtained the withdrawal of the UN peace-keeping forces. Egyptian and Israeli forces now confronted each other for the first time since 1956. In his most deliberate provocation of Israel, Nasser blockaded the Gulf of Aqaba, Israel's lifeline through which it received its oil and other goods. Nasser then signed an alliance with Jordan. This meant that Arab armies surrounded Israel: Syria to the north, Egypt to the south, and Jordan to the east, with its highly regarded army directed to cut Israel in two at its narrow waist. All these actions were accompanied by increasingly shrill calls for a holy "war of liberation" and the extermination of all of Israel's inhabitants.

In these circumstances war was inevitable, unless Israel were willing to accept a major political defeat, which was an unlikely prospect. The preservation of peace, which could be achieved primarily by Nasser's removal of the blockade, depended on the United States and the Soviet Union. Washington was caught in a dilemma. On the one hand, the United States had recognized Israel's right to send ships through the gulf after compelling Israel to withdraw following its 1956 victory. On the other hand, it was deeply involved in Vietnam and therefore reluctant to take on a second conflict. Furthermore, a key question for American policy makers was whether such a test would precipitate a clash with the Soviet Union, which had with great fanfare sent warships into the eastern Mediterranean, fully supported the Arabs in their aims, and continually denounced Israel as an aggressive tool of American imperialism.

For Moscow the Arab-Israeli conflict had global implications. If Western influence could be expelled from the Middle East and if the Soviet Union could establish itself as the dominant power over this oil-rich region, Europe would be weakened and perhaps even neutralized. Thus for Moscow the stakes in seeing Nasser achieve a political victory were enormous, and Soviet political support and the naval show of force undoubtedly contributed to Nasser's intransigence and helped to restore his reputation in the Arab world. Had the Gulf of Aqaba blockade been successful, the Soviet Union would have earned the Arabs' everlasting gratitude as the primary force behind Egypt's political victory. Moreover, an effective blockade would have demonstrated the Soviet Union's ability to inhibit the American navy and would have jeopardized future American commitments to Israel. The Soviet Union had an opportunity to replace the West as the region's leading power.

But Moscow's ambitions were quickly frustrated in the region. Because Washington was unable to arrange a diplomatic solution, the Israelis attacked to seize the initiative in what had become an unavoidable clash. Routing the air forces of their Arab opponents in a brilliantly coordinated set of air strikes during the first hours of hostilities, they defeated the Egyptian army and reached the Suez Canal in three days—two days ahead of the record they set in 1956. They routed the Jordanian army and captured half of Jerusalem and the western bank of the river Jordan. Finally, they turned on the Syrian army and eliminated the bases on the Golan Heights from which Syria launched the terrorist raids and shelled Israeli settlements. Nasser's dreams of an Arab empire, and the Soviet Union's hopes for regional hegemony, were quickly shattered.

A WORLD DIVIDED INTO
RICH AND POOR NATIONS

The rivalry, then, between the world's two superpowers did not explode in a head-on collision. Instead, the United States and the Soviet Union built up their strategic arsenals while allowing regional hostilities in the developing world to serve as "theaters" of military confrontation. This process had several unfortunate consequences for the developing countries, many of which had only recently gained independence and were facing the difficult task of establishing stable governments. By imposing their ideological rivalry throughout the Third World, the superpowers militarized the countries in that region, arming both the sovereign leaders and those seeking to overthrow them. Furthermore, they undermined the efforts of the United Nations and regional organizations to resolve the paralyzing economic problems of developing countries and promote long-term economic development. Consequently, political and military issues were grafted onto the debate over the economic perils in the Third World and the appropriate ways to solve them.

THE COMMUNIST AND CAPITALIST
MODELS OF DEVELOPMENT

The
Third World
in the
Crossfire

Confronting an amalgam of political, social, and cultural changes (not just economic development) and experiencing revolutionary transformations (not just evolutionary progress), developing countries in the 1960s had no guarantee that they would climb what Robert Heilbroner termed the "Great Ascent." [4] In this context, the Soviet Union and China were willing to present themselves as models of development. Soviet communists, who had rapidly industrialized their country amid world war and vast social dislocation, appealed to the leaders of developing countries as a model of noncapitalist development. And China's leaders claimed that their way of organizing the masses to seize power by means of guerrilla war, and then for economic growth, was the model for Asia and the Third World in general.

To people suffering from chronic hunger and poverty, it may not have mattered that the Soviet Union had achieved industrialization by setting up totalitarian governments that brutally squeezed the necessary sacrifices out of the people, or that Maoist China had modernized its system of agriculture at the cost of tens of millions of lives. "Command" economics would at least provide the organization and efficiency to extract the sacrifices from the masses and the discipline to hold the nations together, to speed up the pace of their cultural revolutions while controlling social tensions produced by the early stages of development, and to depose ruthlessly the traditional ruling classes blocking the path to modernization. In the developing world, where the human costs of Sino-Soviet "modernization" were largely unknown, communism was attractive because it promised a fairly rapid and disciplined way of bringing about political, social, economic, and cultural changes. The beneficiaries of this system were claimed to be, not the rulers, but the majority populations in developing countries, who had labored for centuries without receiving a significant share of the wealth they produced.

The United States and other capitalist states, conversely, saw that the best way to compete with communism was to alleviate the conditions—poverty, ignorance, hunger, and social injustice—that were thought to provide the breeding ground for communism. Curing these conditions and giving people hope for a better life were the means to defeat it. This would be achieved once the Third World's development had gained a self-sustaining momentum. Communism's appeal to potential adherents was strong during the initial phase of modernization. During those early days, in the words of W. W. Rostow, later President Lyndon Johnson's national security adviser during the

4. Robert L. Heilbroner, *The Great Ascent* (New York: Harper Torchbook, 1963).

Vietnam War, communists would act as "the scavengers of the modernization process. Communism is best understood as a disease of the transition to modernization." [5] If the West offered assistance, it was opti-
mistically believed, the developing countries would evolve through predictable "stages of growth" into modern, industrial, and democratic societies that
would naturally look westward.

It was because of the competition of models that the United States, other
Western states, and multilateral agencies such as the World Bank and the Organization for Economic Cooperation and Development (OECD) first offered the developing countries economic aid and technical assistance. Western aid was intended to close the gap between rich and poor states, to
modernize the new nations without compelling them to use totalitarian
methods, to satisfy their "revolutions of rising expectations," and thereby to
create politically and socially stable societies. This process, in turn, was expected to create democratic governments and a more peaceful world by giving developing countries a vested interest in the international order and
Western values.

Although the nature of the problem seemed clear to many policy makers,
the rationale for economic aid to assist the new nations' development never
attracted the degree of public support that the more easily understandable
military preparations against the Soviets did. What was probably required, as
many suggested, was a progressive international income tax by which all the
advanced Western nations would contribute 1-2 percent of their annual national income for development. The World Bank's Pearson Commission in
1969 endorsed the 1 percent figure. But by then no Western country was giving that much. Despite the rapid economic growth of the industrial states
during the 1960s, their foreign aid spending had declined. This was particularly true for American aid to Europe, which, at the time of the Marshall Plan,
had been 2.75 percent of the gross national product (GNP). Aid to the developing countries was always less than 1 percent of GNP. In short, at a time
when the American GNP had risen by hundreds of millions of dollars, the national effort was out of proportion with its increasing capacity to pay and
with the growing gap between the rich and poor nations.

Indeed, the term *economic aid* was something of a misnomer. After 1950
and the eruption of the Korean War, most economic aid was, in fact, military
aid. Moreover, after Western Europe's recovery most of this aid was chan-
neled to allied countries that were not among the world's poorest: Turkey,
Pakistan, South Vietnam, South Korea, and in the 1980s and 1990s, Israel and
Egypt. The final sum actually allocated to economic development also was

5. W. W. Rostow, "Guerrilla Warfare in Underdeveloped Areas," in *The Guerrilla—And
How to Fight Him*, ed. T. N. Greene (New York: Praeger, 1962), 56.

concentrated in relatively few countries. Most developing countries got next to nothing.

LIMITATIONS TO THE U.S. AID EFFORT

Apart from the lack of public support for foreign aid, U.S. policy toward the developing countries suffered from three other liabilities. The first was that American dollars were all too often offered with the explicit or implicit assumption that the recipients should associate themselves with U.S. Cold War policies. Even if they did not formally ally themselves with the United States, they should often thank it for its generosity, praise it for the morality of its anticommunist stand, and certainly refrain from criticizing it. The United States was reluctant to give dollars to nations that would not join its side. But in these countries the basic aspiration was to concentrate on internal matters, to raise the standard of living and strengthen their independence, and to minimize their involvement in the Cold War. Most, therefore, preferred to remain nonaligned in the struggle between the United States and Soviet Union.

In preferring a generally nonaligned position, the developing countries believed they were following America's example. After all, after the United States gained its independence, it too avoided "entangling alliances" and preoccupied itself with internal developments. As a developing country, the United States was aware that its newly realized independence meant little without economic and political strength. Moreover, the United States had just thrown off the shackles of colonialism; its citizens had no desire to be once more tied to European powers. But American policy makers, especially during the 1950s, forgot that it was the United States that had set this example.

The second liability that hampered U.S. policy toward the developing countries during the early Cold War was racial discrimination within the United States itself. The persistent segregationist practices and exploitation of blacks in both the South and the North were flagrant violations of the democratic principles of freedom and human dignity so often proclaimed by the United States. The peoples of the developing countries not only claimed equal status for their nations but also sought equality as human beings. Segregation in America reminded them of their colonial days when white rulers had treated them as inferiors because of the color of their skin. Conditions in the United States began to change, however, during the Kennedy and Johnson administrations. As blacks heard Martin Luther King, Jr., articulate their aspirations for a life of more dignity and fuller participation in American society, as the ghettos exploded after King's assassination, the government began to outlaw certain discriminatory practices against blacks and to provide greater opportunities in jobs and housing. But racial problems continued to haunt the United States on the foreign front. In Rhodesia (now Zimbabwe) and South Africa, minority white-controlled governments, determined to stay in power, used abhorrent methods such as apartheid and strict police surveillance. The United States, despite its often-expressed disapproval of these policies, did not follow through with action. It imported Rhodesian chrome for years despite a UN embargo. And American companies in South Africa, although they provided their black workers with better working conditions and pay than local companies, lent support to South Africa through investment. America, the world's first state to articulate that all men were created equal, seemed all too often to say to the world that there was a qualifying phrase: "except blacks."

Third and more fundamental, U.S. relations with the developing countries were hampered by the American lack of understanding of class struggle and social politics. America, "born free" as a bourgeois democratic society, had managed to avoid the kinds of domestic conflicts over basic values that the countries of Europe had experienced and that plagued many of the developing countries. The United States had not experienced a genuine social revolution at its birth, for a revolution is characterized by violence; it seeks to destroy the institutions and social fabric of the old society and create a new society with new institutional and social class arrangements. Despite its self-proclaimed revolutionary character, the United States has been, according to former senator William Fulbright, a nonrevolutionary, conservative country.[6] Not surprisingly, therefore, America was not particularly sympathetic to revolutions and tended to equate revolution, per se, with communism. Deviations from middle-class American values were likely to be condemned as "un-American" and sinful, to be rooted out so that the "American way of life" would remain pure and unadulterated.

Indeed, the principal challenges to these values had come not from within the system but from outside the U.S. borders, and the United States had reacted to foreign threats—German, Japanese, Soviet—in two ways. Internally the government had hunted subversives, a procedure that infringed on civil liberties and endangered the security of traditional freedoms. Externally, government policy, before the atomic bomb, was the total destruction of the hostile regime so that American principles could survive untainted.

Thus, as already noted, the real or imagined communist threat in the early 1950s led to McCarthyism, a search for heresy in which the goal of eliminating alleged un-American attitudes and behavior justified any means, including disregard for due process of law, the basic guarantee of all civil liberties. In foreign policy the reaction to the communist threat was to support almost any regime, no matter how repressive, if it claimed to be anticommunist. As a result, the United States often allied itself with governments whose days

6. J. William Fulbright, *The Arrogance of Power* (New York: Vintage Books, 1967), 72-73.

were numbered; Chiang Kai-shek in China, Bao Dai in Indochina, and Ferdinand Marcos in the Philippines are but three examples.

This attitude was typical of American absolutism and its inability to understand the deeper social struggles of the Third World. In its attempt to contain communism—that is, to preserve the global status quo—the United States became committed to the domestic, social, and political status quo in these regions. In trying to preserve freedom, the United States was paradoxically supporting ramshackle autocracies that were unrepresentative of their peoples' aspirations. But this internal contradiction within the U.S. alliance system eventually had to resolve itself. American support for traditional regimes only bottled up the social and political resentment and ferment even more, thereby adding to the explosive forces that someday would burst forth and upset regional balances of power.

THE EXAMPLE OF LATIN AMERICA

Events in Latin America illustrate how U.S. foreign policy became driven by Third World events. To American leaders, revolutions based on the Cuban experience in 1958 and 1959 created a foothold for communism in the Western Hemisphere and thus constituted a threat to the United States. In Latin America, Fidel Castro's success in Cuba—and that of other charismatic rebels elsewhere—was made a real possibility by such conditions as the resentment against a history of U.S. interventions in the Caribbean and Central America; large-scale, private U.S. capital investments in and economic control of many Latin American economies; persistent U.S. support for the privileged few who, usually closely linked to American capital, sought to preserve their position by ignoring social grievances and establishing right-wing military dictatorships; and finally, the misery, poverty, and illiteracy of the majority of the people, who, although they lived in the countryside, were landless.

Latin Americans shared two aspirations that were sweeping through the developing areas: a better life for the masses and the desire of countries to determine their national destinies. The United States had exercised its hemispheric domination indirectly, usually by alliance with the wealthy landowning governing class. Americans may have believed that they were free of Europe's taint of colonialism, but that is not what Latin Americans thought. The Monroe Doctrine had turned the entire Western Hemisphere into a U.S. sphere of influence; the United States did not have to resort to direct colonial rule. Invested American capital spoke louder than guns, and the U.S. government did not have to give political orders when a nation was a "banana republic."

In these conditions the success of Castroism was thought to depend on two elements. First, it would depend on how the Latin American governments reacted to Castroism—whether they would undertake large-scale social and economic reforms or cling to their privileges. Public pressure for

UNITED STATES

BAHAMA ISLANDS

MEXICO

CUBA

PUERTO RICO

CAYMAN ISLANDS

HAITI

DOMINICAN REPUBLIC

BELIZE
HONDURAS

JAMAICA

GUATEMALA

NICARAGUA

EL SALVADOR

VENEZUELA

CENTRAL AMERICA

COSTA RICA

PANAMA

COLOMBIA

TRINIDAD & TOBAGO

ATLANTIC OCEAN

VENEZUELA

GUYANA

SURINAME

FRENCH GUIANA

COLOMBIA

ECUADOR

PERU

BRAZIL

BOLIVIA

PACIFIC OCEAN

PARAGUAY

CHILE

ATLANTIC OCEAN

URUGUAY

ARGENTINA

FALKLAND ISLANDS

SOUTH AMERICA

Cape Horn

change was rising, but would this change be revolutionary or evolutionary? If the ruling classes remained as hostile to reform and as irresponsible toward public welfare as in the past, Castro might be able to export his revolution. Wherever there was social injustice, destruction of the *ancien régime* appeared to be the only way to have a piece of land, enough food, or a job. Revolution and a "radical solution" became the only hope for a better life.

Second, the success of Castroism would depend on the effectiveness of U.S. policy directed toward alleviating the conditions that fostered popular resentment in Latin America. Whether the United States had the will to guide this revolution, however, was another matter. This was a task that required American acceptance of noncommunist left-wing movements and the expropriation of American property, neither of which would be easy because of the identification of reform with revolution and revolution with communism. Moreover, the United States was expected to invest billions of dollars in the Latin American economies to foster a self-sustaining rate of economic growth, to develop conditions in which private capital would be attracted to projects other than the extraction of raw materials or growth of single exportable crops, and to aid in the transformation of less-developed societies into modern, industrialized nations. In addition, Latin America's projected rapid increase of population lent urgency to development.

To meet this challenge, President John Kennedy, soon after assuming office in 1961, established the Alliance for Progress. He pledged $20 billion of primarily public money over the next decade to Latin America, and, even more significant, he emphasized the need for social change. Through the Peace Corps and other innovations, Kennedy hoped to revitalize Franklin Roosevelt's aspiration to make the United States a "good neighbor" of Latin America. Kennedy realized that, in the absence of such an effort, the possibilities of economic development were slight and the prospects of additional communist insurgencies were strong.

Castro's influence was illustrated by the U.S. intervention in the Dominican Republic. The impetus for this event was the overthrow in 1961 of Rafael Trujillo, who had ruled as a dictator for thirty-one years. Following a brief period of political turmoil, Juan Bosch, a man of genuinely democratic convictions, was elected president. Seven months later, Bosch was overthrown by a military coup d'état whose leaders announced that they would reestablish a "rightist state." In April 1965 the pro-Bosch forces revolted against this right-wing military government. Communists were thought to be active in the movement against the junta, and Washington feared they would create a second Cuba in the hemisphere. But the rebels claimed their revolution was led by noncommunists who only sought a return to constitutional government. Before the evidence was clear that the revolution was in fact communist-controlled, President Lyndon Johnson ordered American armed intervention.

The Dominican intervention demonstrated how obsessed the Alliance for Progress was with Castro. Without him there likely would have been no large-scale efforts to seek the democratic development of Latin America. The overt U.S. intervention—the first in fifty years in Latin America—therefore undermined the Alliance for Progress, which had tried to persuade the region's ruling elites to undertake reforms if they wished to avoid revolutionary violence. Latin America's ruling classes could now relax because there was an alternative: American intervention would save them from the consequences of their own folly in holding onto an unjust way of life. American policy south of the U.S. border, as in other areas of the world, thus continued to be dictated by the bipolar global struggle.

In Latin America, as in Africa and the Middle East, the globalization of containment had profound consequences. As many critics of the policy feared, the United States was gradually immersed in civil wars and regional conflicts far from its shores. But American leaders, bound by the logic of containment and fearful of "losing" ground to the communists—whenever that was—stayed loyal to the policy. Their strategy would lead to the calamitous U.S. intervention in Vietnam, where the faltering consensus in the United States favoring global containment would be put to the ultimate test.

Slogging through an abandoned rice paddy, the U.S. military carries out a search-and-destroy mission against the guerrillas. Such operations rarely worked and the Viet Cong invariably returned after the Americans left.

CHAPTER SIX

Vietnam and the Cost of Containment

The wreckage of World War II yielded to a more stable international order in the late 1940s and 1950s—but one increasingly split between two rival blocs. In this bipolar world the United States and the Soviet Union, through their allies and proxies, confronted one another indirectly in almost every region of the world. In a series of actions and reactions they drew "frontiers" between their spheres of influence and extended their competition to remote areas of otherwise marginal concern.

By virtue of the zero-sum, all-or-nothing nature of bipolarity, both great powers were always alert to the slightest shifts in power lest such shifts upset the equilibrium to give the adversary superiority. A gain of power and security for one was perceived as a loss of power and security for the other, and the opponent's moves, even if alleged to be defensive, were interpreted to be deliberate and offensive. Similarly, developments in regions of otherwise marginal importance also were ranked as significant and countered because such regions were seen as symbolically vital, and because their allegiance might tip the scales in favor of one or the other superpower. The bipolar superpower competition thus consisted of defining the frontiers around the U.S. and Soviet spheres of influence and then guarding this territorial status quo against encroachment, subversion, or defection.

VIETNAM AS A 'FRONTIER WAR'

U.S. involvement in Vietnam stemmed from the belief of American leaders that the seventeenth parallel dividing North Vietnam from South Vietnam represented a frontier between the free world and the communist world. Just as these leaders had decided to defend South Korea when North Korea crossed the thirty-eighth parallel, so they now decided to come to the assistance of South Vietnam. Also like the war in Korea, the Vietnam War was fought at a great distance from the United States, in a place where the frontier was very accessible to the enemy.

But that was only one of the problems the United States encountered in Southeast Asia. Vietnam was a divided society: North against South; Buddhists against Catholics; lowlanders against montagnards; and peasants against urban dwellers. Moreover, loyalties were primarily local and hostility to the central government ran deep because, as in most developing countries, the government historically had been that of the colonial power, represented at the local level by the tax collector and recruiting sergeant. Transportation and communication were primitive and industrial development nonexistent. In addition, this new state had emerged from the 1954 Geneva conference that had ended the first Indochina war between France and the Vietminh forces. Thus South Vietnam had no established political institutions and a precarious economy. Because that same Geneva agreement called for a general election to be held in 1954, the communist rebels (the Vietminh, or Viet Cong) expected South Vietnam to collapse. Hanoi assumed that a majority of the 12 million South Vietnamese would vote for Ho Chi Minh, who had led the nationalist struggle against the French. When those votes were added to most of the North's 15 million votes, the country would be reunited under communist control.

But Ho's popularity was the reason that neither the United States nor the new government in the South favored the election. The United States wanted the seventeenth parallel to be accepted as the new frontier, and the president of South Vietnam, Ngo Dinh Diem, a fervent Catholic and anticommunist, wanted to stay in power. In fact, their opposition was so decisive—whether the unsigned Geneva declaration mandating the election was politically binding or not—that Hanoi's chances for a peaceful takeover of the South ended, and so did its stance of reasonableness and restraint. At the time of the Geneva settlement, approximately 5,000-6,000 local guerrillas, presumably the Vietminh's political and military elite, had gone underground and had begun to live like peasants. About 90,000 went north; many later infiltrated South Vietnam. In 1959 the North Vietnamese began the armed struggle in the South. The second Indochina war had started.

This war, in short, began quite differently from the Korean War. Korea had begun with a clear-cut, aggressive attack, which aroused the American public and united the principal Western allies against the common threat. It also was a conventional war in which regular communist forces were checked by regular South Korean, American, and United Nations troops. By contrast, the French defeat at Dienbienphu in 1954 was a decisive moment in contemporary history because it demonstrated that guerrilla warfare could win against a larger, stronger, conventionally equipped army of even a major power. An internal uprising of guerrillas, directed and organized by the North, was therefore a shrewder manner of "crossing" the seventeenth parallel. It would lend the resulting struggle the aura of a civil war, which would make it less likely that the United States would come to the assistance of South Vietnam because of American doubts about the morality and wisdom of military involvement in such a conflict. Diem's increasingly autocratic rule and his failure to enlist the support of his population, especially the peasantry, through political, social, and economic reforms helped to prepare the ground for a successful guerrilla campaign and lent support to the view of the conflict as a civil war. It certainly provided the Viet Cong with fertile ground to mobilize support.

Another reason for U.S. involvement in Vietnam was that the war was seen in Washington as a test of its will, and meeting the test was believed to be necessary to maintain all frontiers. Until the noncommunist states of the area became more economically developed and possessed stable political systems and military defenses, the Asian balance depended on the United States. Commitments—and the administrations of Dwight Eisenhower, John Kennedy, and Lyndon Johnson all considered the United States to be committed to the defense of South Vietnam—were interdependent. The United States could not choose to defend West Berlin and Quemoy but not Matsu and South Korea. Washington believed that it could no more forgo the defense of the frontier in South Vietnam than in Greece and Turkey, in Western Europe and Berlin, or in Korea and Cuba. If one country fell, it would, in its turn, knock down the next one and so on down the line like a row of dominoes; the political and psychological impact of an American pullout would be felt throughout the area, if not in other regions as well, and the series of losses would upset the balance of power. As all commitments were viewed as interdependent, being unfaithful to one risked the collapse of all. The memory of Munich and the appeasement of Nazi Germany, which had failed to avert

World War II, was a stark reminder that to fight on the periphery now would prevent a bigger war later.

The assumptions underlying this perception, of course, were that the world was still bipolar and that the enemy was the Sino-Soviet bloc, which the United States continued to perceive as united, despite increasing evidence to the contrary. Signs of differences between the Soviet Union and China were generally explained as tactical differences on how the "communist world" ought to wage its "war" against the United States, not as fundamental conflicts of national interests between the two powers. Even if these had been recognized, it probably would not have made much difference because "Red China," with its population approaching 1 billion and its revolutionary rhetoric denouncing "American imperialism," was viewed by Washington as far more militant and dangerous than Moscow. Ho Chi Minh and the Viet Cong were seen as puppets of China, applying Mao Zedong's guerrilla warfare tactics to destroy a noncommunist government in a country within the American sphere of influence. If they succeeded, Vietnam would be added to China's power and thus to the Sino-Soviet bloc's power; it also would be an example to other revolutionary forces in Asia and elsewhere that the United States, despite its nuclear weapons, could be defeated. As for the nature of the warfare itself, Washington saw the North's war against the South as aggression similar to North Korea's against South Korea, even if North Vietnamese forces had not flagrantly crossed the seventeenth parallel. To American military commanders the war in the South was just another variant of conventional warfare which they felt their well-trained forces could defeat.

There was a double irony to this pattern of thinking. First, if the United States had had diplomats in Beijing, they would have known that North Vietnam was not a puppet: historically China and Vietnam often had been enemies, and in the early 1960s China was in the midst of a domestic upheaval so that the last thing Mao wanted was to risk a confrontation with the United States. Thus as with China's earlier intervention in Korea, the United States again paid a high price for its refusal to recognize the mainland regime. Second, if the containment of China had been a key goal of the U.S. intervention, then the United States should have let South Vietnam fall. Ho was a nationalist, not just a communist, and a united communist and nationalistic Vietnam would have proven a stronger barrier to any possible Chinese ambitions of hegemony in Southeast Asia than a noncommunist South Vietnam governed by an unpopular regime.

In truth, then, the Vietnam War, undertaken in the name of containment, undermined containment. The beneficiary of this effort was the Soviet Union, America's primary enemy, which was able to focus its resources on first catching up with and then surpassing the United States in nuclear weapons. Because of the popular backlash to the war and to military spending, the

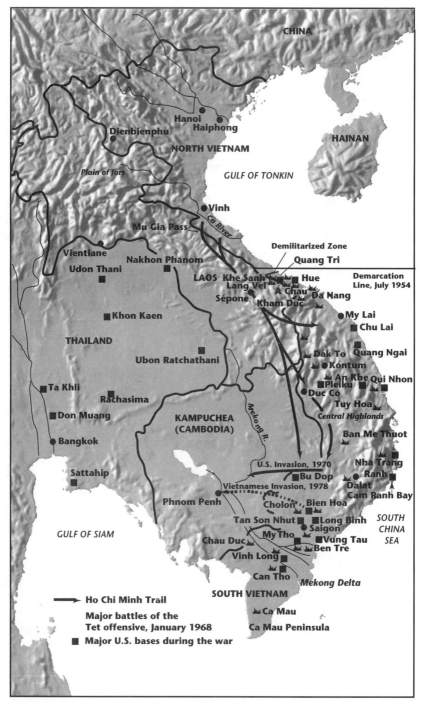

CHINA

Hanoi
Haiphong

NORTH VIETNAM

Dienbienphu

HAINAN

Plain of Jars

GULF OF TONKIN

●Vinh

Ca River

Mu Gia Pass

Demilitarized Zone

Vientiane
Nakhon Phanom

Quang Tri

Udon Thani

Demarcation
Line, July 1954

LAOS Khe Sanh ━ Hue
Lang Vei
Sépone A Chau Da Nang
Kham Duc

Khon Kaen

●My Lai
■Chu Lai

THAILAND

Ubon Ratchathani

Dak To Quang Ngai
●Kontum
An Khe Qui Nhon
Pleiku
Duc Co
Tuy Hoa
Central Highlands

Ta Khli

Rachasima

■Don Muang

KAMPUCHEA
(CAMBODIA)

Mekong R.

Ban Me Thuot

●Bangkok

Sattahip

U.S. Invasion, 1970

Nha Trang
■Bu Dop ●Ranh
Vietnamese Invasion, 1978
Dalat
Cam Ranh Bay

Phnom Penh

Cholon Bien Hoa

Tan Son Nhut ■ ■Long Binh
Saigon

GULF OF SIAM

My Tho
Chau Duc
Vung Tau
Ben Tre

SOUTH
CHINA
SEA

Vinh Long

Can Tho *Mekong Delta*

SOUTH VIETNAM

Ho Chi Minh Trail

Ca Mau

Major battles of the
Tet offensive, January 1968

Ca Mau Peninsula

■ Major U.S. bases during the war

VIETNAM

United States fell behind in the strategic buildup during the 1970s. Indeed, the key domino that fell was not South Vietnam but American public opinion.

DOMESTIC REASONS FOR THE INCREMENTAL INTERVENTION

Yet in a way the large-scale U.S. intervention in Vietnam by President Lyndon Johnson was by 1965 inevitable because, starting with the administration of Harry Truman, every president had deepened the involvement in Vietnam. Although Truman at first opposed France's postwar efforts to restore its colonial rule, he changed his position to overcome French resistance to the American plan for the revival of Germany, especially its rearmament. After the Korean War erupted, the French war in Indochina became part of the global struggle against communism. At the time of France's defeat at Dienbienphu in 1954, Eisenhower, though deciding not to intervene militarily, backed the new government in South Vietnam, organized after France's defeat and withdrawal, with economic assistance and military training for its armed forces. But this training was in orthodox warfare, not in the unorthodox or guerrilla warfare that already had been observed in Vietnam. The Southeast Asia Treaty Organization (SEATO) was supposed to be the new state's security guarantee. Kennedy escalated this commitment in the early 1960s by sending in 16,500 military advisers to help the South Vietnamese army. Beginning in the spring of 1965, Johnson transformed this commitment—and the conflict in general—by sending in 500,000 American troops.

Particularly significant during the years of piecemeal commitments was that at no point did policy makers in Washington resolve some basic questions about Vietnam: Was it vital to American security interests and, if so, how vital? If it had been vital earlier, was it still so in the early 1960s? Could the situation in South Vietnam be saved militarily given the nature of the Saigon government and its seeming lack of popular support? If American forces should be sent, then in what numbers? And how could they be used effectively in an unorthodox type of war? What cost, if any, was South Vietnam "worth" to the United States?

Because incremental U.S. commitments were made whenever conditions in South Vietnam appeared ominous, these questions were never really debated at the highest levels of the government. And if the reasons for American involvement were not clear to leaders, they were lost entirely on millions of citizens. But past American commitments foreclosed any meaningful debate except over how much force was needed to save South Vietnam.

During the Kennedy years, military advisers managed to prevent South Vietnam's total collapse, but by 1965 Johnson—who after Kennedy's assassination had concentrated on passing a major domestic reform program and getting reelected—could no longer operate on this basis and avoid the central question of what the United States ought to do. South Vietnam was about to be cut in two, and the Viet Cong would then be in a position to mop up first one part and then the other. In the face of this reality Johnson sent in 200,000 troops that year, extending U.S. involvement and turning an incremental policy into a long-term commitment. After years of neglect and procrastination and with the situation growing worse daily, Washington had neither the time nor the inclination to make a carefully calculated decision; when the crucial decision was made, it was made by Johnson, a new president, on the advice of the Kennedy staff and cabinet he had inherited. Long-range policy had become the prisoner of a number of earlier short-range decisions that had been made to tackle crises. Johnson's misfortune was that he could not procrastinate or make more piecemeal moves. He was stuck with the decision of whether to escalate to prevent the defeat of the South Vietnamese army or to become, as he phrased it, the first president in U.S. history "to lose a war." Each president had done just enough to prevent this defeat. Johnson's escalation was the logical culmination of his predecessors' decisions.

But perhaps even more important than foreign policy considerations was American domestic politics. Originally, in 1947, anticommunism often was used as a means of arousing the public and mobilizing popular support for Cold War policies while the nation in fact pursued more limited aims. But once an administration had justified its policy in terms of an anticommunist crusade and had aroused the public by promising to stop communism, it opened itself to attacks by the opposition party if setbacks were encountered, even if they occurred for reasons beyond America's ability to prevent them. The out-party could then exploit such foreign policy issues by accusing the in-party of appeasement, of having "lost" this or that country, and of being "soft on communism." This sort of accusation made it difficult to recognize the People's Republic of China, to build bridges to Eastern Europe, to negotiate with the Soviet Union or Cuba, and especially to discriminate between areas of vital and secondary importance to U.S. security.

Democratic administrations were more deeply affected by this political rhetoric than Republican administrations. The Democrats, who were in power when Nationalist China collapsed, were accused of "treason," of "selling out" China, and they lost the 1952 presidential election as a result. The desire to avoid accusations of being soft on communism had pushed Truman to advance northward across the thirty-eighth parallel before the 1950 midterm elections and made it impossible for him to negotiate any settlement of the war that would have left Korea divided. The wish to avoid similar accusations made it impossible for John Kennedy, who had campaigned on a tough anti-Castro platform, to reject the Eisenhower-initiated plan to invade Cuba, even though the new president had serious qualms about it. It led the Kennedy and Johnson administrations to make their piecemeal commitments in Vietnam, lest the Democrats be charged with the "loss" of Indochina as well as China, and it influenced Lyndon Johnson to bomb North Vietnam and to escalate the war by sending in the army. Even Eisenhower, a conservative Republican president and victorious general who had led the Allies to victory over Germany, a man who could hardly be accused of disloyalty, had felt threatened enough by the right wing of the Republican Party that in 1954 he did not pull the United States out of Vietnam. Instead, he kept America in Vietnam by supporting the new South Vietnamese government. Each president thought each step in the growing involvement in Indochina to be less costly than doing nothing and disengaging from Vietnam. In the context of U.S. politics, defeat was believed to be unacceptable. The costs of nonintervention in terms of loss of public and congressional support were calculated to be much higher than the costs of intervention.

These examples illustrate the high price the United States consistently paid for its penchant to crusade and to moralize power politics: overreaction, diplomatic rigidity, and overt or covert interventions that it otherwise might never have launched. National style was a principal cause of the long delay in recognizing China and the failure to exploit Sino-Soviet differences. Worse, it was the main reason for misunderstanding Asian communism, including the war in Vietnam. It was certainly a key reason, if not *the* reason, for the subsequent intervention. Because the domestic costs of losing a country to communism were so high, those in power felt compelled to intervene with the Central Intelligence Agency, marines, or army to avoid such losses. The desire to avoid accusations of appeasement, of betraying the nation's honor, and of weakening its security was keenly felt. This was especially true just before elections, and there was always an election coming up.

THE MISCONDUCT OF COUNTERGUERRILLA WARFARE

During its intervention in Southeast Asia, the United States virtually ignored the political structure of South Vietnam, which was the key to the successful use of American arms. For years the United States had supported Ngo Dinh Diem, a devout Catholic whose authoritarian rule and aloofness from the mainly Buddhist population had alienated most of it. By the time the military overthrew and murdered Diem in 1963, with Kennedy's knowledge and tacit blessing, the Viet Cong already controlled much of South Vietnam; the social, political, and economic reforms needed to win the war had been neglected too long. That the United States had acquiesced in the coup against Diem should have alerted future administrations; that Kennedy had said Diem had "gotten out of touch with the people" testified to the political bankruptcy in Saigon, as well as to the questionable wisdom of having begun the military intervention in the first place. Even with Diem gone, South Vietnam's governments were unable to rally popular support for a vigorous prosecution of the war against the Viet Cong.

But Saigon's succession of corrupt, reactionary, and repressive regimes apparently never reawakened thoughts in the minds of U.S. policy makers of Chiang Kai-shek and his Nationalist government in postwar China. At the time of China's fall, the Truman administration had decided China could not be saved, except perhaps—and it was only *perhaps*—by incurring enormous military and economic costs, which it felt the American public would not be willing to pay. In addition, these costs would have diverted the nation's resources and efforts from its area of primary interest in Europe where American security was at stake. In Dean Acheson's words, as noted before: "Nothing that this country did or could have done within the *reasonable* limits of its capabilities" could have changed the result in the conflict between Mao Zedong and Chiang Kai-shek.[1] In short, containment could not be achieved through a sieve. By attempting containment in South Vietnam, Truman's successors in Democratic administrations risked major domestic discontent. They also risked a public questioning the fundamental assumptions of the foreign policy that had led to the war.

Certainly the possibility of achieving a quick victory over the Viet Cong was remote, for a guerrilla war is totally different from traditional Western warfare. The militarily weaker side resorts to guerrilla tactics because it has no other options. The aim of a guerrilla war is to capture the government from within and to do so by eroding the morale of the army and by undermining popular confidence in the government, thus isolating it. To achieve this objective, guerrilla forces do not have to inflict a complete defeat on the government's forces or compel them to surrender unconditionally. Indeed, until the final stage of the war guerrillas do not even meet these forces openly, and then they do so only to apply the *coup de grâce*. Guerrilla war is therefore a protracted conflict in which the guerrillas use hit-and-run tactics—here, there, everywhere—and engage only those smaller and weaker government forces they can defeat. To cope with this strategy year in and year out, the government's troops must be dispersed to guard every town, every village, and every bridge against possible attack. Unable to come to real grips with the enemy and defeat it in battle, and suffering one small loss after another, the army becomes demoralized and its mood defensive.

Although such tactics gradually weaken the military strength of the army, the guerrillas' main effort is directed at the civilian population. As the weaker side of the conflict, the guerrillas aim to wrest the allegiance of the population

---

1. Department of State, *United States Relations with China* (Washington, D.C.: Government Printing Office, 1949), xvi (italics added).

away from the government so that, without popular support, the government simply collapses. The guerrillas do this in two ways. First, by increasing their control of the countryside, where most of the people live, and by winning battles with government forces, they demonstrate to the peasants that the government cannot protect them. The execution of the village chiefs, who are generally government representatives, proves this most vividly. Second, and even more important, the guerrillas exploit any existing popular grievances. Communist guerrillas do not pose as communists, and they do not usually receive support because they are communists. The populace supports them because it believes the guerrillas will oust the government with which it is dissatisfied and that a new government will meet its aspirations.

Indeed, according to Mao, guerrillas need the people "just as fish need water"; without popular support, the guerrillas would not receive recruits, food, shelter, and information on the government forces' disposition. The guerrillas gain the support of the peasantry by successfully representing themselves as the liberators from colonialism or foreign rule, native despotic governments, economic deprivation, or social injustice. In this way they isolate the government in its own country. Unlike conventional warfare in which each army seeks the destruction of the other's military forces, guerrillas base their strategy on mobilizing popular support. A government that has the allegiance of its population does not provide fertile soil for guerrillas; where social dissatisfaction exists, however, guerrillas find an opening.

Counterguerrilla warfare is therefore not purely military; it is also political. Although the government under attack must try to defeat the guerrillas in the field, its principal task is to tackle the political, social, and economic conditions that bred support for the guerrillas in the first place, to regain the "hearts and minds" of the populace. Counterguerrilla warfare, then, is an extremely difficult and sophisticated form of war to wage—far more so than the traditional clash of armies—because the war cannot be won without thoroughgoing reforms. Yet these reforms have to be carried out in the midst of a war, which is likely to last many years. Further complicating the situation, approximately fifteen counterguerrilla fighters are needed for every guerrilla— in short, a sizable army, and one trained in counterguerrilla tactics.

What all this means is that the United States finds such a war extremely difficult to fight. America likes its wars "strictly military." A war that is concerned primarily with social and political reforms runs completely counter to the American approach. The length of such a war also would cause great frustration because the U.S. government, under intense public pressure, likes to get its "boys home by Christmas." If this new kind of warfare did not yield swift and successful results, the American temptation would be either to pull out or to seek a shortcut to victory by purely military action.

During the war in Vietnam, American policy makers misplaced their confidence in the nation's military prowess and its ability to change the guerrillas' "rules of the game." In 1965 the illusion of American omnipotence had not yet died. After all, the United States had successfully confronted the Soviet Union in Cuba and compelled it to back down. Could there really be much doubt that its well-trained generals, in command of armies equipped with the newest and latest weapons from America's industry and under the leadership of that most efficient Pentagon manager, Secretary of Defense Robert McNamara, would be able to beat a few thousand "peasants in black pajamas"? With its sizable forces and its superior mobility and firepower, why should America have any problem finding the enemy's troops and destroying them, thereby compelling that enemy to desist from taking over South Vietnam? Characteristically, then, the emphasis was strictly military.

In Vietnam the kind of war being waged required forces to secure villages and to stay in them to root out the Viet Cong cells and show the villagers that Saigon did care about them. Instead, the military carried out massive search-and-destroy operations. And the guerrillas, even if driven away from the villages, returned after the helicopters had left and continued to control the countryside. Because such large-scale operations could not be launched without preparation at the base camp and were usually preceded by air strikes and artillery bombardments of the area in which the troops would land, the Viet Cong often disappeared and the whole operation ended in frustration.

American soldiers clearly did not understand the political nature of counterguerrilla war. They had been trained for conventional battle and to use maximum firepower to wear the enemy down in a war of attrition. The military was confident it could do this because its helicopters provided superior mobility and modern technology gave it the necessary firepower. The measure of success became the daily body count of communist dead.

When the war was extended by air to the North, the purpose of the bombing was clearly not military, although the United States claimed its goal was to stem the flow of men and supplies going south. (Guerrillas, however, can live off the land, and they capture many of their weapons from their enemies. In any case, the sustained American attacks on Chinese supply lines in North Korea during the Korean War had shown that air power alone was unable to stop the flow of supplies to the fighting zone.) The aim of the attacks was political—to persuade North Vietnam to stop the war. The gradual extension of these attacks was intended to stress that the United States meant to protect South Vietnam and would not withdraw, that the price Hanoi might have to pay for victory would be too costly, and therefore that it had better desist.

But the bombing did not weaken Hanoi's will to prosecute the war, nor did it cut the supplies sufficiently to hamper the fighting in the South or greatly reduce troop infiltration. Hanoi's persistence, in turn, led to increased military and political calls for more air strikes and new targets. Those who advocated increasing the air war did not acknowledge that air power could not by itself win the war; rather, they insisted that it could if it were used with maximum efficiency. Air power, in short, came to be seen by some as an efficient, effective way of fighting the guerrillas, throttling their supply lines, breaking their morale, and finally compelling them to end the conflict at little cost in lives to the defender.

This objective, however, remained unattainable. Even the more stable military regime of Nguyen Van Thieu and Nguyen Cao Ky, which sought to legitimate itself in the election of 1967, failed to implement a program of social and economic reform until 1970 when it adopted a major land reform program. It was particularly remiss in not earlier redistributing land from the usually absentee landlords to the peasants. Without such reforms the Viet Cong grew stronger. Militarily, every increase in American forces was met by increased infiltrations of both guerrillas and conventional troops from the North to the South. Nevertheless, the U.S. government issued optimistic battle reports and forecasts of victory on a regular basis.

The 1968 Tet (or Vietnamese New Year) offensive, launched on the last day of January, was the Johnson administration's Dienbienphu. Tet showed once and for all—and Americans could see it nightly on their television sets—that, despite the repeated optimistic predictions, the enemy had again been badly underestimated. It had launched a major countrywide offensive and attacked Saigon, Hué, and every other provincial capital; a Viet Cong squad had even penetrated the American embassy compound, thereby scoring a significant symbolic victory. The fighting that followed, however, was bloody and destructive of the Viet Cong. In fact, so many Viet Cong were killed that afterward the North Vietnamese army actually assumed the main burden of fighting the Americans. Nevertheless, the Viet Cong had clearly demonstrated that neither an American army of a half-million men nor the far larger South Vietnamese army could give the people living in the urban areas security—and the communists presumably already controlled much of the countryside.

THE POLITICAL BATTLEFIELD: THE UNITED STATES

In Vietnam, then, American power and its effectiveness in unorthodox warfare were shown to be greatly exaggerated. Tactically, American forces had seized and retained the offensive, claiming the destruction of large numbers of enemy soldiers. But strategically the Viet Cong had maintained the upper hand, and the Americans were on the defensive. For example, by using about 80 percent of their forces to find and destroy North Vietnamese troops in the relatively unpopulated central highlands and frontier regions, the

Americans were unable to secure and protect the 90 percent of the population living in the Mekong Delta and coastal plains. The pursuit of victory through physical attrition could not be transformed into military or political advantages. Indeed, in question was not just America's protective capacity but also its wisdom. Having left the cities unprotected, except for elements of the South Vietnamese army, allied forces had to fight their way back into the hearts of the various cities and towns the Viet Cong had infiltrated. Thus if after almost three years of American help South Vietnam was still that insecure and the enemy that strong, the wisdom of continuing the war, let alone sending further American reinforcements, was bound to be intensely debated.

As if this were not enough, many Americans perceived the war to be morally ambiguous, if not downright immoral. There had never been a clear-cut crossing of the seventeenth parallel dividing North Vietnam and South Vietnam, which made the accusation that Hanoi was an aggressor less believable. The undemocratic Saigon government and its apparent lack of popularity gave credence to the view of the war as a rebellion or civil war against Saigon's repression.[2] The massive, sometimes indiscriminate use of American firepower, which led to widespread destruction of civilian life; the creation of thousands of refugees; and, reportedly, the hostility of the peasants, whose support was vital for military success—these things and more had already pricked the consciences of many Americans concerned about their nation's historic image as compassionate and humane. The tanks rumbling into cities after Tet, the divebombing of apartment houses, the civilian suffering, and the personal tragedies left television viewers—who saw only one side of the war and not, for example, the Viet Cong's deliberate slaughter of thousands of professional people and bureaucrats in the city of Hué—asking themselves if there was any point in "destroying a country in order to defend it."

Within the United States the Tet offensive aroused antiwar feelings, which had been growing throughout 1967 as the war continued, seemingly without end. Johnson's initial support eroded on both the right and the left, with the right demanding an end to the war through escalation and the left seeking an end through deescalation, if not withdrawal. The articulate opposition to the conflict expressed by a number of liberal and moderate Republican and Democratic senators, especially the chairman of the Senate Foreign Relations Committee, J. William Fulbright, lent respectability to the opposition also vocalized by many politicians, professors, students, journalists, editorial writers, and television commentators. Indeed, after Tet Fulbright and his committee

2. Interestingly, in 1950 the South Korean government had a similar autocratic reputation, but the attack across the thirty-eighth parallel focused attention on North Korean ambitions and justified the American intervention. No one in the United States raised questions about defending a "corrupt dictatorship."

became an alternative source of interpretation and policy recommendations for the president.

Thus, although the Viet Cong were virtually destroyed during the Tet fighting, the United States suffered a political defeat. The guerrilla strategy of psychologically exhausting the opponent succeeded; the American strategy of physical attrition failed. The U.S. military won all the battles, including Tet, but lost the war as the public grew tired of it. Indeed, policy makers learned quickly that during such hostilities politics go on as usual, with most domestic interest groups pursuing their specific sets of interests and preferences; butter is not automatically subordinated to guns. But, as the costs of the conflict rise in terms of lives, inflation, and taxes, public disaffection also grows. So do antiwar demonstrations and parades, some of which in the 1960s spilled over into clashes with the police and supporters of the war.

The Vietnam War, then, involved two battlefields. The first, in Vietnam, was bloody but inconclusive militarily. The second, in the United States, was not bloody, but it was decisive politically. As the war dragged on, the nation's will to continue it declined, unlike in the two world wars (total wars), when the United States sensed that its security, if not its survival, was at stake, and thus all issues were subordinated to the prosecution of the war. In a limited war important issues may be at stake, but the security threat to the United States may not be apparent. How could the loss of South Korea or South Vietnam have diminished U.S. security? Neither North Korea nor North Vietnam could invade the United States.

The guerrillas were well aware of the two battlefields and of which one was more important. Gen. Vo Nguyen Giap, the North Vietnamese strategist who had overseen his country's victories against France and the United States, spoke of the impatience of democracies at war. He saw that a strategy in which the war never seemed to end, in which the minimum purpose was simply not to lose, would eventually erode the opponents' will to continue. As the war dragged on and as the casualties and costs mounted, the democracies would throw in the towel. It was their "home fronts" that were decisive, where the "real battle" would be won. For that reason, the Tet offensive was deliberately launched as the 1968 political primaries were about to begin in the United States, where opposition to the war had become widespread.

Disagreement over the war led two senators from the president's party, Eugene McCarthy and Robert Kennedy, to contest Johnson's renomination as the Democratic standard-bearer. Running as "peace candidates," they provided a rallying point for the growing numbers of Americans disenchanted with the war. Then in March 1968, at the end of the speech that laid the basis for the Paris peace talks, the president announced that he would not run for a second term. Lyndon Johnson's tragedy was that he had come into office seeking a "great society" in America; instead, the war destroyed him. The changing American mood was evident in the 1968 presidential campaign. Vice President Hubert Humphrey, nominated in Chicago after bloody clashes between police and antiwar students (many of them McCarthy supporters) and bitter disagreement among the delegates over the Vietnam platform, was mercilessly heckled during most of the campaign. As a member of the administration, he found it difficult to disavow the war; when he took his own "risk for peace," it was very late in the campaign.

In these circumstances of Democratic disunity, former vice president Richard Nixon, a career anticommunist, found it inexpedient to charge the Democrats with a "no-win" policy; instead he softened his views on the war. Indeed, in his speeches the menace abroad suddenly ran a poor second to the "moral decay" at home. Generally both candidates fell over themselves in their eagerness to abandon both anticommunist slogans and the war, offering instead hopes for an "honorable" peace in Vietnam and for "law and order" at home. Halting communist aggression was abandoned as an issue; stopping further costly foreign adventures—"no more Vietnams"—became the new issue. In Vietnam the only question was when to get out and on what terms. By not losing, the North Vietnamese had won; by not winning, the United States had indeed lost.

A NEW MOOD OF WITHDRAWAL

The year 1968 found the United States weary, disillusioned, and ready to retreat from its imperial role in Southeast Asia. This mood manifested itself in an attempt to curb presidential power in foreign policy, especially the power of the commander in chief to commit American forces to battle. Under the Constitution the president is chiefly responsible for the conduct of foreign policy, which made the office the target of those opposed to certain such policies. During the 1950s the conservatives had wished to limit presidential authority because the president was, in their minds, not anticommunist enough, and he might, acting on the advice of the "pro-communists" in the State Department, sell the country down the river. Beginning in the late 1960s the liberals too sought to restrain the president's authority, but for a different reason: in their opinion, the president, the "military-industrial complex," and the CIA supporting him were *too* anticommunist and were intent on involving the country in too many costly adventures abroad.

Conservative or liberal, the remedy for the "imperial presidency's" alleged abuse of its authority and its virtually solo determination of foreign policy was identical: to reassert the control of Congress in the formulation of external policy and to restore the constitutional balance that purportedly had been upset. The president presumably would be restrained so that, for conservatives, he would no longer be able to appease America's enemies or, for liberals, be able to act in an interventionist, warlike manner. The abuse of power by Nixon, a conservative president who resigned his office rather than be impeached, reinforced the liberal sentiment to curb presidential powers and compel a more restrained and moderate policy.

Additional evidence of the new mood was the widespread belief that priority should be given to the nation's domestic problems. These problems became apparent in the 1960s when the "affluent society," as it was called in the 1950s, began to reveal its seamier and more violent sides, such as urban slums, air and water pollution, and the dissatisfaction of the poor and disenfranchised, who were primarily blacks, Puerto Ricans, native Americans, Mexican Americans, and Asians. Critics of the war wanted to spend money to improve the quality of life for all American citizens. Instead of crusading for democracy abroad, they argued, the United States should start crusading to make *America* safe for democracy. Liberal critics of the war in Vietnam quoted Edmund Burke to the effect that "example is the school of mankind." The example should be one of a democratic society protecting the rights of its citizens as its paramount task.

But such freedom could not be fully enjoyed in a nation whose excessive preoccupation with foreign affairs drained its powers and resources, both human and material. An expansionist foreign policy, it was charged, was unlikely to bring with it any lasting greatness, prestige, and security. Rather, as the American Founders were quick to emphasize centuries earlier, the constant expenditure of energy in adventures abroad would ruin the country's domestic base. The Cold War preoccupation was corrupting of American society. Institutional imbalance was eroding constitutional processes, particularly when powerful and energetic presidents, in the name of national security, not only committed the nation to war but also sanctioned plots to assassinate foreign leaders such as Fidel Castro, lied to the American people and Congress about what they were doing or why they were doing it (intervention in Vietnam), acted covertly (bombing Laos and Cambodia), and in various ways violated the constitutional rights of American citizens. Moreover, the large-scale diversion of the country's resources to its external commitments meant a corresponding neglect of domestic needs.

Extensive involvement in the world, in short, was tainting the American promise and vision; the priority of foreign policy over domestic policy had to be ended. This idea always had been at the heart of the old isolationism: America could take care of its own needs, serve as an example for humankind, and remain pure in a morally wicked world only if it stayed out of or minimized its political involvement in it. The consequence of assuming an active role internationally was to endanger, not protect, American democracy.

Perhaps the most revealing evidence of America's reaction to Vietnam was the reassertion of the deep-seated attitude that viewed the exercise of power internationally as immoral and corrupting. Once power politics could no longer be justified in moral terms of democracy versus dictatorship, as in the two world wars, the sense of guilt over using power returned. To many, the Vietnam War represented a moral turning point in American foreign policy. Not surprisingly, sensitive people deeply committed to human values—and watching each day in history's first televised war the exercise of power in the form of violence—repented their former support of containment-through-power as if in giving that support they had been unwitting sinners. Fulbright, who had been a leading advocate of equating postwar foreign policy with moral mission, now attacked America's global role as evidence of an "arrogance of power." [3] He did not merely assert that the United States had over-extended itself and that its commitments needed to be cut down to its capacities. Nor did he say that Vietnam had been an unwise commitment, although the basic policy of containment had been correct. He stated something far more fundamental: that all great powers seemed to have a need to demonstrate that they were bigger, better, and stronger than other nations and that it was this arrogance of power, from which the United States then suffered, that was the real cause of international conflict and war.

In brief, it was the exercise of power per se that, regardless of a nation's intentions, made it arrogant. Power itself was corrupting; even if justified in moral terms, its use was immoral except in clear, unambiguous cases of self-defense. No idea could have been more characteristically American. Power was evil and its exercise tantamount to the abuse of power; abstention from power politics, providing an example to the world of a truly just and democratic society, was a more moral policy. America should be loved for its principles and for practicing what it professed, rather than be feared for its might. Democracy and power politics were simply incompatible.

DISENGAGEMENT FROM VIETNAM

Before the relationships among the United States, the Soviet Union, and China could be reshaped, the United States had to unburden itself of the Vietnam War. Vietnam was a drain on U.S. resources and a political albatross around the Nixon administration's neck. But in their thinking about acceptable terms for withdrawal, Nixon and his national security adviser Henry Kissinger were heavily influenced by their perceptions of great-power relationships. One course open to Nixon, which would have brought him popular acclaim, was to pull out all American forces immediately on the grounds that the United States had fulfilled long enough its obligations to defend Saigon.

3. J. William Fulbright, *The Arrogance of Power* (New York: Vintage Books, 1967).

But in the president's view the central issue was not when to get out of Vietnam but *how* to get out.

The Nixon administration was determined that it would neither just withdraw nor accept any settlement that was tantamount to a defeat—namely, a coalition government in Saigon controlled by the communists. Nixon believed that it would not be feasible to establish a relaxation of tensions or détente with the Soviet Union and China if America's prestige—reputation for power—were tattered. Why should the Soviet Union, which was rapidly building up its strategic power, settle for parity and mutually acceptable peaceful coexistence if it sensed that America was weak and could be pushed around? Why should China tone down its revolutionary rhetoric and conduct a more traditional state-to-state diplomacy, and indeed move closer to the United States, if it could not count on American strength and determination to resist what it saw as Soviet attempts at hegemony in Asia? In short, Nixon calculated that the country had to "hang tough" in Vietnam to normalize relations with the Soviet Union and China.

Nixon and Kissinger therefore devised a twofold strategy. First, American ground troops were to be withdrawn gradually to reduce the costs of the war and make further hostilities tolerable for the "silent majority," which Nixon felt was loyal, although fatigued, and would support him in an "honorable" ending of the war. But Nixon hoped the continued involvement of some U.S. forces, especially in the air, would provide an incentive for Hanoi to negotiate an end to the war. This incentive would presumably be all the stronger if the president's strategy worked at home—that is, if it removed Vietnam as a principal issue in the next election and facilitated Nixon's reelection. Hanoi, then confronted with the prospect that the war could last longer than four more years, would have a reason to settle the war diplomatically.

The second part of the president's policy was the "Vietnamization" of the war. As American troops were withdrawn, South Vietnam's forces would receive better training and modern arms so that they could take over the ground fighting. This would counter the criticisms and pressures that had multiplied in Congress, on campuses, and elsewhere for faster U.S. troop withdrawals and for the abandonment of Saigon. But the danger inherent in the president's strategy was that the North Vietnamese would attack after American troops were withdrawn but before the South Vietnamese were ready to meet the enemy in battle.

In March 1970 Cambodia's Prince Norodom Sihanouk, who had long tolerated the communist troops and supply lines in his country, was overthrown by an anti-Vietnamese military regime that wanted communist troops out of Cambodia. When the communists moved toward the Cambodian capital to unseat the new government, Nixon decided to intervene and, without public knowledge, ordered air strikes deep into Cambodia. Once this became known, it reignited domestic dissension. After four protesters at Kent State University were shot to death on May 4 by Ohio National Guardsmen, many campuses erupted, and a number of colleges and universities were completely shut down. Protesters once again turned out for peaceful mass demonstrations in Washington and in other cities. The reaction to U.S. policy in Cambodia made it clear that it would be foolhardy for the president to repeat such an action.

Unfortunately, South Vietnam's decrepit army remained the key to the success of the president's strategy. In the spring of 1972, with the U.S. Army withdrawn from the battlefield, North Vietnam launched an unexpected large-scale attack across the demilitarized zone between North Vietnam and South Vietnam. The South Vietnamese army performed poorly and only American air support staved off even worse losses.

Nixon was therefore in a quandary on the eve of a summit conference in Moscow to advance détente. The Soviet Union had supplied Hanoi with modern arms, and, whether or not it knew the date of the North Vietnamese offensive, Nixon thought the Soviet Union should have restrained its ally. As a great power, it must have known that a major South Vietnamese defeat would be humiliating to its adversary on the eve of vital negotiations from which Moscow had as much to gain as Washington. The president was unwilling to negotiate under the shadow of defeat.

With Vietnamization in danger, Nixon "re-Americanized" the war by ordering extensive bombing of the North and a blockade of North Vietnam's ports with mines. The aim was to stop the flow of Soviet and Chinese supplies. Simultaneously Nixon offered Hanoi the complete withdrawal of all American forces from Vietnam within four months if all prisoners of war were returned and an internationally supervised cease-fire were established. The communists could keep their forces in the South—a significant concession previously offered only in secret talks. Equally important, the president did not insist on the survival of Nguyen Van Thieu's government. He instead expressed hope that the U.S. withdrawal "would allow negotiations and a political settlement between the Vietnamese themselves." This new set of proposals provided a concrete and serious basis for negotiations. But Hanoi rejected the offer. It appeared to want the president to do the one thing he refused to do: guarantee communist control in Saigon. His proposal, in fact, had seemed to suggest that the North Vietnamese should do this job for themselves, if they could.

The North Vietnamese also faced a dilemma. Despite the heavy U.S. bombing and blockade, the Soviet Union had gone ahead with the summit meeting. And China no longer opposed a negotiated settlement of the war. Moscow and Beijing both gave priority to their relationships with Washington, leaving Hanoi politically isolated. Yet the North Vietnamese leaders had sought their goal of a unified Vietnam for so long, paid such a high price for it, and been so often cheated out of the fulfillment of their dream by their adversaries that they were suspicious of Nixon's offer and resentful of the declining Soviet and Chinese support.

But a month before the 1972 U.S. presidential election, Hanoi, probably fearing that Nixon's reelection might make him less accommodating, signaled its willingness to accept something less than a total victory. By late October Hanoi had negotiated a tentative Indochina settlement. The terms included a supervised cease-fire that would halt all American bombing and mining and bring about withdrawal of all U.S. forces within two months; separate future cease-fires were expected in Laos and Cambodia. Prisoners of war would be exchanged. A series of mixed political commissions, composed of elements from the Viet Cong, the Saigon government, and neutralists, would then be established to work out a new South Vietnamese political order leading to a new constitution and the election of a new government. Provisions and personnel were to be supplied on a one-to-one basis for both sides.

The Nixon administration felt it had achieved an "honorable peace." The North Vietnamese, after having declared for years that the Thieu government would have to go as a precondition for a cease-fire, now accepted Thieu as the leader of the government faction. Thieu remained in control of a sizable army and large police forces with which he administered most of the country and all the urban centers, leaving only minor areas and a small percentage of the population under the control of the Viet Cong and the approximately 145,000 North Vietnamese troops. The Thieu faction therefore seemed to have a good chance to compete politically and militarily with the communists after the fighting ended. But Thieu stalled in agreeing to this tentative October 1972 settlement because the United States had accepted the presence of North Vietnam's troops in areas of the South during the period of cease-fire. Although Thieu could object, he held no veto.

When Thieu stalled, so did the North Vietnamese; both sides appeared eager to strengthen their positions as the final stage of peace talks resumed in Paris. In response, Nixon ordered some of the heaviest bombing of the North, including civilian centers in Hanoi and Haiphong. The incessant "Christmas bombings" of late 1972 continued for several days. Nixon defended the bombardment against an outcry from the public and by the newly elected Democratic majority in Congress. He argued that they were necessary to demonstrate American resolve against North Vietnam in the crucial final days of conflict. Simultaneously, Nixon made it clear that Thieu did not have a veto over U.S. policy.

The end of the Vietnam War came in January 1973 when the North Vietnamese returned to the negotiating table and both sides signed a cease-fire agreement in the Hotel Majestic in Paris. Twelve nations, including the United States, the Soviet Union, and China, formally approved the treaty in March. The administration could now focus its primary attention on improving relations with China and the Soviet Union, and the United States would no longer pour its resources into a war that deeply divided the country.

Two years after the Paris conferences, however, North Vietnamese troops launched a final offensive against the remnants of the South Vietnamese army. Although Thieu insisted that Nixon had pledged continued U.S. support in the event of such an offensive, Nixon had resigned under the cloud of the Watergate scandal and President Gerald Ford, under great pressure from Congress and public opinion, refused to recommit American resources to Vietnam. Thieu resigned on April 21, 1975, and nine days later Saigon fell to the Viet Cong as the last American officials in the city were hurriedly shuttled away by helicopter. South Vietnam then surrendered unconditionally. Twenty years after the failed Geneva accords of 1954, Vietnam was again reunited.

For the United States the "Vietnam syndrome" lingered until the Cold War's sudden collapse in 1989. In terms of foreign policy, it meant that the country was far less willing to commit itself to military intervention abroad. Equally worrisome, the syndrome entailed a growing skepticism and distrust toward the government and its military leadership. It did not help that Richard Nixon's administration was shamed during this period by the Watergate scandal. But even without Watergate, for the first time the United States was confronted with the prospect that its power in the world had peaked. For many Americans, disillusionment with Vietnam led them to believe that their country's reputation as the world's "beacon of democracy" had been tainted, and that during the war their leaders had been guilty of misjudgment, deception, and wanton destruction of human life.

CHAPTER SEVEN

U.S-Soviet Détente and the 'China Card'

The United States emerged from the Vietnam War with new doubts about its role in foreign affairs. Having assumed the status of a global superpower for only one generation, America found its traditional antipathy toward world politics quickly reasserting itself as the debacle in Vietnam raised serious doubts among many Americans about using anticommunism as the basis for the country's foreign policy. Before Vietnam, the United States could be mobilized to stop communist aggression; after Vietnam, the nation sought to avoid engagement in such overseas adventures.

Even more basically, the anticommunist effort had been weakened by the increasing pluralism of the formerly cohesive Sino-Soviet bloc. It was one thing to fight communism as long as it appeared monolithic, but when communism became fragmented globally, and in some cases internally divided, the appropriate Western response became more difficult to define. Did the United States now have to distinguish among the communist states, determining which posed a true threat? More specifically, what changes in the distribution of power could America safely allow, and where, if anywhere, and against whom did it still have to draw frontiers? These questions were more difficult to answer in the years that followed the Vietnam War than during the earlier days of more easily defined bipolarity because each case would now confront policy makers with several policy options, thereby arousing great debate and intense controversy. In addition, anticommunism would no longer be as useful a means of eliciting popular support because the United States might well be supporting one communist state against another.

FROM *IDEALPOLITIK* TO *REALPOLITIK*

One crucial question the decline of anticommunism posed for the future conduct of American foreign policy was whether, in the absence of anticommunism, the United States would dirty its hands by conducting diplomacy on the basis of traditional "power politics." When during the early Cold War *realpolitik*, based on power, was synonymous with *idealpolitik*, based on ideology, it had been easy for the United States to be a leader and to organize various coalitions against the ideological foe. The state system's requirement to maintain the balance of power could be performed by the government of the United States so long as it could disguise from its own people what it was doing and pretend it was engaged in a noble task. But could a nation that historically had condemned power politics adapt its outlook and style to a world in which justifying foreign policy in terms of ideological crusades was outmoded? Or would America, no longer believing it had an ideological mission, lapse into its traditional withdrawal from great-power politics?

In 1968 the incoming Nixon administration confronted a novel postwar situation: how to conduct foreign policy without a domestic consensus. The administration thought it could turn to a foreign policy based on the traditional logic of the state system. This dramatic shift away from a style that stemmed from the nation's domestic values and experiences to a balance-of-power rationale was somewhat surprising because Nixon, as U.S. representative, senator, and vice president, had been virulently anticommunist and possessed by an inflexible moralism that rejected having anything to do with communists. But as president, he and his national security adviser Henry Kissinger, a German-born Jewish immigrant and Harvard professor who also became secretary of state in Nixon's second administration, rejected the traditional American justification for participating in foreign affairs.

Indeed, the administrations of Nixon and his post-Watergate successor, Gerald Ford, might well be called the Kissinger era. Kissinger articulated and justified the Republican approach to foreign policy; he personally carried out much of its private as well as public diplomacy; and he provided an element of continuity amid the transfer of power. Kissinger so dominated these eight years that one wag noted that he was the only national security adviser and secretary of state ever served by two presidents.

THE KISSINGER PHILOSOPHY

The philosophy underlying American foreign policy during the Kissinger years from 1969 to 1977 began with the assumption that international politics was not a fight between the good side and the bad side. All states, communist or noncommunist, had the right to exist and possessed legitimate interests. A nation, therefore, did not launch crusades against an adversary on the assumption that differences of interests represented a conflict of virtue and evil. The better part of wisdom was to learn to live with other states, to defend one's interests if encroached upon, but also to attempt to resolve differences and build on shared interests. International politics was not just conflict, but cooperation as well. Differences, admittedly, would not be easily or quickly reconciled; statesmen's views of their interests were usually deeply held and not easily relinquished. Summit meetings were important as part of a negotiating process, but one summit could not solve all problems, and to raise false hopes that it would was to produce the cynicism and disillusionment that would endanger diplomacy itself. Good personal relations among leaders might smooth this process, but they were not a substitute for hard bargaining, and accords basically reflected the ratio of power between the nations that the leaders represented.

How then should the United States deal with a communist dictatorship whose values and practices it abhorred? The most the United States could expect was to influence its international behavior in a responsible direction. American power was too limited to transform another superpower's domestic behavior. American demands would be resisted, which, in turn, would jeopardize accords on international issues that might otherwise have been resolvable. The United States was not omnipotent and had to abandon its habit of crusading to democratize adversaries. Coexistence with a communist regime such as that of the Soviet Union was necessary if peace and security were to be preserved. The key, of course, was the balance of power, and the United States had to try to accommodate the legitimate needs of the principal disturber of that peace. Power neutralizes opposing power, and by satisfying the interests of other great powers the United States would be more likely to produce acceptance of the present international system than continued frustration with and hostility to an international system in which they had little vested interest. No state could be completely satisfied, but it could be relatively satisfied.

Kissinger's view, then, concentrated on the powerful actors in the state system. Although he brought the rhetoric and style of American foreign policy more in line with the operational norms of the international system, there also was a fundamental continuity in policy. The Soviet-American balance remained the preoccupation; it was still the Soviet Union, as a great power, whose influence needed to be contained and behavior moderated. This unity of rhetoric and action—the explanation of U.S. policy in terms of power, balances, spheres of influence, national interests, and the limits of American power, as well as the specific rejection of ideological justifications and crusades—represented the "socialization" of American foreign policy by the state system.

THE DECLINE OF AMERICAN POWER AND PRESTIGE

The Nixon and Ford administrations pursued détente because changes in the United States and the state system called for a relaxation of tensions. The United States had changed to become, during and after Vietnam, a nation weary of its foreign policy burdens. This mood was illustrated by the attacks on the "imperial presidency"; by the 1973 War Powers Resolution, which restricted the president's ability to deploy U.S. forces abroad; by cuts in the defense budgets; and by restrictions on covert operations by the Central Intelligence Agency (CIA). The president was to be restrained by a more assertive and watchful Congress; the freedom to use the instruments of overt and covert intervention abroad were to be limited.

In the pre-Vietnam era of containment Congress had rarely questioned the president's authority to use the armed forces or the CIA to carry out U.S. policy. But after Vietnam, America's "global policeman" role was criticized widely and emphasis was placed on the nation's limited power, suggesting a more restricted role in what was popularly regarded as the post-Cold War era. For Nixon and Ford, then, détente was a course to be pursued until the nation could once again play the leading role they felt was required to protect U.S. interests against Soviet expansion.

Another change, around 1970, was in the balance of power—a longer-term reason for détente. Simply put, the Soviet Union had caught up with the United States. The balance between the two superpowers had long been between the U.S. Strategic Air Command (SAC), later supplemented by the navy's nuclear submarines, and the Red Army. American bombers and missiles deterred the Soviet Union by threatening to destroy its cities. The Soviet Union gained its intercontinental capability and capacity to destroy the United States from its massive buildup that began after 1964.

From the 1950s to the late 1960s, however, America's strategic power had been balanced not by Moscow's bomber and missile force, which had been relatively small, but by the Red Army. The powerful Soviet army, it had been believed, could overrun Western Europe and quickly defeat North Atlantic Treaty Organization (NATO) forces. Thus the American-Soviet balance had been asymmetric: the United States had held strategic superiority and an intercontinental reach; the Soviet Union had maintained conventional superiority and a regional reach. But by 1969 the balance had become symmetric; the Soviet Union's strategic power had achieved parity with that of the United States, and the Soviets could now hold America's population, as well as Western Europe's, hostage. Moreover, this Soviet buildup showed no sign of slowing down, not even after the number of Soviet intercontinental ballistic missiles (ICBMs) had matched the number of American missiles.

Even during the period of U.S. strategic superiority, Moscow had been willing to risk limited challenges, such as in Berlin and Cuba, but it had remained cautious during confrontations. If there was resistance, it retreated and called the challenge off. U.S. power had set limits to how far the Soviets felt they could push. But because the strategic balance was now shifting, a continuation of the containment policy by means of threats of force would become riskier. Soviet leaders had gained a new sense of confidence in their power. Indeed, the Soviet Union now belonged to the most exclusive club in the world, but the potential danger of its membership was clarified when the Soviet foreign minister informed the world that no important issue anywhere could be resolved without the Soviet Union.

In addition to its growing strategic power, the Soviet Union also had engaged in a parallel massive *conventional* buildup, particularly of a modern surface navy and airlift capability. Thus as the Soviet Union's ability to neutralize America's nuclear force grew, its capacity to project its conventional power beyond Eurasia also grew. The Soviet naval buildup, which by the late 1970s had produced a navy that exceeded that of the United States in numbers of combat ships, was not needed for defense. Would the Soviet Union, in these new circumstances, be content to expand its influence only on land and in nearby areas? Or would it, as a result of its new might, feel a confidence that had been absent before and act more boldly? Now that it had lost its strategic superiority, would the United States, by contrast, be more reluctant to react?

Kissinger compared the Soviet Union's emergence as a world power to Germany's appearance on the world scene in the early twentieth century. In both cases the challengers were land powers. The symbols of their aspiration and determination to expand were the navies they built; nothing could have carried greater symbolic weight for Great Britain and the United States, the two greatest naval powers in their respective times. Germany's emergence and desire to be a world power with its overseas colonies resulted in World War I. How could the Soviet Union's newly gained power and its determination to pursue a *weltpolitik* (global policy) be managed peacefully so as not to threaten American security interests? Clearly, as a badge of its newly achieved equal status, Moscow also sought overseas clients, basically Marxist-Leninist states that would become members of the Soviet "empire." As they had been for Germany, these territories, usually of limited strategic and economic value, were geopolitically important as symbols. Thus the Soviet Union's massive military buildup raised questions not just about the military balance and its stability but, more fundamental, about its ultimate intentions.

MANAGING THE NEW RELATIONSHIP

Nations whose power has declined normally adjust by reducing their commitments or by seeking new allies or greater contributions from current allies. They generally also seek to reduce threats to their interests by diplomacy. When it lost its strategic superiority, the United States did not curtail its obligations but sought to preserve them through détente. As a political means of managing the superpowers' adversarial relationship, this strategy sought to secure American interests at a lower level of tension and cost than those required by the policy of Cold War confrontation and frequent crises. The American-Soviet balance would still be bipolar, but it would be somewhat more complex and fluid than in the earlier Cold War era. Indeed, U.S. foreign policy was now explained differently: Nixon's predecessors, while also pursuing a balance-of-power policy, had felt compelled to justify their policy as a moral crusade. From Truman on, U.S. presidents frequently had been trapped by their anticommunist rhetoric and had felt compelled to be more inflexible and interventionist than perhaps they otherwise would have been. For twenty years they had been unable to abandon the fiction that Taiwan was China and to establish a formal diplomatic relationship with the real China on the mainland, the People's Republic. The Nixon-Kissinger balance was to include the PRC. Beijing could be used to get the Soviets to act with restraint and to show greater willingness to compromise if they wished to avoid closer Sino-American relations and collusion against the Soviet Union.

Furthermore, the bipolar balance was to be supplemented by a network of agreements and a set of rules of mutual restraint beneficial to both powers. The key Kissinger word was *linkage*. If a series of agreements and understandings on such matters as arms control and trade could be arrived at, the more expansionist-minded Soviet Union, because of the benefits of these agreements and understandings, would gain a vested interest in good relations with the United States. While the Soviet Union was to be faced, as before, with continued parity and a strong American military, this "stick" was to be supplemented with enough "carrots" to make a restrained foreign policy more appealing. Indeed, military sanctions against the Soviet Union at a time of strategic parity were becoming riskier for the United States. Fortunately, then, the offer of economic rewards for restraint or self-containment was particularly appealing to the Soviets.

Linkage also had another meaning: the various U.S.-Soviet issues would be linked together diplomatically. Progress on one front would be tied to progress on another; the Kremlin could not expect to make gains on one issue that interested it but refuse to meet American interests on others. If it did so, there would presumably be a penalty exacted by a lack of progress on issues of interest to the Soviet Union or by withholding benefits Moscow was seeking. Cooperation and mutual concessions were obviously preferable. The adversarial part of the relationship was to be balanced by the partnership element in a new adversary partnership. The overall purposes were to lower tensions between the superpowers, to confront fewer crises, and to encourage diplomatic negotiations.

For Kissinger, then, détente was not only a strategy selected to secure American interests at a lower level of tensions and costs but also a continuation of containment at a time when the United States had lost its strategic superiority and its extensive role in world affairs was widely questioned by its citizens. Détente was to achieve its purpose by exploiting the Sino-Soviet split and by using American technology and food as nonmilitary "weapons." But this political-diplomatic strategy was not utopian; it did not assume that the Soviet Union had become a benign power or that the Cold War was over. Détente was intended to be a realistic strategy for a time when, because of neo-isolationism at home and the shift in power internationally, the United States was no longer in a position to compete as vigorously with the Soviet Union as in the days before the Vietnam War. Détente was the continuation of containment by other means.

THE OPENING TO CHINA

When the Nixon administration came into office in January 1969, the United States had no official relationship with the PRC. Its government was opposed to resuming relations with the United States as long as Washington recognized the Nationalist regime on Taiwan, which it regarded as PRC territory. But Nixon recognized the changing circumstances and considered it vital to bring mainland China into the diplomatic constellation. By calling the regime by its chosen name, the People's Republic of China, ending regular patrols of the Taiwan Straits by the Seventh Fleet, and lifting trade and visitation restrictions against China, Nixon opened the way for a personal visit to China in February 1972. This visit served in part to symbolize to the American public and Congress, long hostile to dealing with Beijing, the dramatic shift of American policy. By playing the "China card," Nixon and Kissinger began clearing away mutual hostilities and defining some of the more outstanding issues and problems impeding improved Sino-American relations.

Thus détente applied not just to the relationship between the United States and the Soviet Union but also to the relationship with China. Indeed, it may be argued that détente with China was the greater U.S. achievement because of the tremendous hostility that had existed between the two countries since 1950. At least with the Soviet Union the earlier period of high tension, confrontation, and recurring crises, particularly since the Cuban missile crisis, had been balanced by increasing cooperation in arms control. In any event, there can be little doubt that détente with China was a prerequisite to détente with the Soviet Union: by bringing China into the superpower balance, Nixon and Kissinger would increase the Soviet Union's incentive to improve relations with the United States.

The Nixon administration was able to exploit the rivalry between the Soviet Union and the PRC because relations between these two allies had become deeply embittered. For too long the Soviets had dominated the communist world. As the capital of the first communist-controlled nation, Moscow had since the early 1920s controlled the international communist movement and formulated its policies. Moreover, after World War II it had established control over the states of Eastern Europe. Of these states, only Yugoslavia was controlled not by Moscow but by its indigenous communist party. When Yugoslavia resisted Joseph Stalin's efforts to impose control, it was ejected from Stalin's empire. The birth of communist China—another state controlled by the indigenous party—thus represented a real problem for the Soviets. The Chinese leadership, while communist, was like that of Yugoslavia, highly nationalistic and therefore not likely to subordinate itself to the Kremlin. The potential for a schism, then, was built into the relationship. That the leaders of these two huge communist states shared an ideological framework did not dampen their growing policy differences toward the United States and the Third World—with Moscow generally taking a more accommodating attitude and Beijing a more hard-line one. To the contrary, it accented their rift. A schism was therefore inevitable, despite the treaty of friendship signed by the two countries in 1950.

By the late 1960s the Sino-Soviet split was dramatically visible. The epithets hurled between Beijing and Moscow reached a ferocity unknown since the early days of the Cold War. The Soviets called Mao "Hitler" and compared the Chinese to the Mongol hordes who overran Russia a millennium earlier; the Chinese talked about the "Soviet revisionist clique" as a "dictatorship of the German fascist type" and quoted Karl Marx as saying that Russia's aim had been, and always would be, world hegemony. As the struggle against the Soviet Union intensified, Mao and his followers were more careful to avoid conflict with the United States. During the war in Vietnam, for example, China continually counseled Hanoi that revolutions had to be self-suffi-cient; it repeatedly stated that only an American attack on China would pre-cipitate Beijing's intervention. In brief, North Vietnam should not and could not count on active Chinese help to help defeat American forces in South Vietnam. Rhetorically, Mao's policy was militantly anti-American, but in ac-tion it was restrained. Thus the incoming Nixon administration had a grand opportunity to exploit the Sino-Soviet conflict, to bring about closer U.S.-Sino relations, and to end a hostile twenty-year relationship that had been strategically very harmful, if not disastrous, for the United States.

U.S. EFFORTS TO OUTFLANK THE SOVIETS

The Sino-Soviet split gave the United States more opportunities to bring pressure to bear on the Soviet Union. The clearly implied message to the So-viet leadership was that their obstinacy would compel Washington to align it-self more closely with Beijing. To the Soviets, already fearful of China, such an alignment had to be a nightmare. It might encourage China to be more hos-tile, as well as renew tension on the Soviet Union's other front in Europe. Similarly, Beijing had for years complained loudly about alleged American-Soviet collusion to isolate and contain China. But as the Soviet Union began to move huge numbers of troops eastward to defend its frontier with China, and on occasion let a rumor slip about the possibility of an attack on China, Beijing, apparently convinced that Nixon was pulling out of Vietnam, began to look toward detaching Washington from any possible cooperation with Moscow against China. Even more important, better relations with the United States would presumably restrain the Soviet Union from attacking China, for the Kremlin could not be sure that Washington would not support Beijing in such an event.

In the Shanghai communiqué released at the end of Nixon's historic visit to China in 1972, the United States and China declared their opposition to the hegemony of *any* power in Asia—but they were clearly referring to the Soviet Union. Thus Sino-American relations began on a firm foundation of mutual self-interest. Moreover, the communist position had long been that Beijing would not establish any relationship with Washington before official U.S. ties with Taiwan were cut—such ties with the rival claimant to power being, Bei-jing claimed, interference in a domestic matter. That, in these circumstances, the People's Republic would reverse itself and sign the Shanghai communi-qué constituted evidence of its fear of the Soviet Union. As for the United States, the eagerness to attract China into an anti-Soviet coalition was reflect-ed in America's declaration that it would gradually remove all its forces and installations from Taiwan and would not interfere in a "peaceful settlement" between the communists and Nationalists.

President Nixon's trip to Beijing in 1972 symbolized a dramatic change in Sino-American relations, ending once and for all the irrationality of a situation in which the United States for almost a quarter-century had ignored the existence of the world's most populous country, a nation with great potential power and an ideological rival of the Soviet Union. And just as Washington, during the 1950s, had feared the Sino-Soviet coalition, and Beijing, during the 1960s, had frequently pointed to alleged Soviet-American collusion to isolate China, so Moscow now became apprehensive of closer Sino-American relations because such relations gave the United States a persuasive lever—if used skillfully—in its negotiations with the Kremlin. The American shift of policy from Taiwan to Beijing was long overdue. U.S. domestic politics had too long blocked a rational adjustment and exploitation of the Sino-Soviet conflict, a conflict in which tensions constantly shifted in intensity, but one that was likely to continue despite leadership changes in both communist countries. Sino-Soviet quarrels reflected historic and entrenched differences of interest more profound than mere differences of personalities.

Indeed, the succession struggle in China and the change in the presidency in the United States did not stop progress toward full normalization. On January 1, 1979, the People's Republic of China and the United States exchanged diplomatic recognition and ambassadors. This was followed in March by an official visit to Washington by China's strongman, Deputy Premier Deng Xiaoping. The timing of this last step toward normalization had come from Beijing, which, with increasingly obsolete weapons, confronted large modern Soviet forces along its 4,500-mile northern frontier. At the same time it looked to the West to help it modernize everything from its hotel and steel industries to exploitation of its enormous oil reserves. For the United States the final shift from Taiwan to Beijing meant ending diplomatic recognition of Nationalist China and abrogating the Taiwan defense treaty, requiring the withdrawal of the last American military personnel stationed in Taiwan. In return, Beijing accepted the American position that the Taiwan problem be resolved peacefully. (The United States could easily resort to force and defend Taiwan should Beijing some day violate the understanding about the peaceful resolution of this problem.)

With recognition of the mainland came new directions in trade. Although at first the United States did not sell arms to Beijing in order not to provoke Moscow, it was willing to let its European allies sell China arms, such as jet fighters and antiaircraft and antitank missiles. The United States limited its own sales to dual-purpose equipment such as radar, trucks, and transport planes, which could be put to either civilian or military use. Later, Ronald Reagan's administration, in an effort to forge stronger links with China against the Soviet Union, offered to sell Beijing arms. But as China had limited funds to buy arms on a large scale, the significance of this move was more political than military; it signaled to the Soviets the growing Sino-American links. The United States and China also cooperated in jointly operating an electronic intelligence-gathering station in China to monitor Soviet missile tests.

ARMS CONTROL AS THE CENTERPIECE OF DÉTENTE

Arms control over the years gained increasing importance in relations between the United States and the Soviet Union, and for very good reason. The two powers had been rivals since the closing days of World War II; indeed, their rivalry reached into almost every region of the world. As a result, profound distrust and mutual fear, if not hatred, characterized their relationship. The arms race was an expression of their deep political differences. But the danger was, of course, that the arms race, fueled by continuing conflict, would at some point spill over into a nuclear war. To avoid such a cataclysmic end, each side built up its nuclear forces as a defense, and negotiated agreements that reduced the chances of war breaking out. But as the basic conflict continued and as nuclear weapons were unlikely to be abolished, the next best tactic was to "manage" the nuclear balance by instituting arms control agreements and promoting *deterrence*.

During the 1960s arms control had dealt largely with such issues as the establishment of a "hot line" between the Kremlin and the White House for quick communication in a crisis, a limited ban on testing nuclear devices, and, through the United Nations, an agreement on the nonproliferation of nuclear weapons. In the 1970s these negotiations shifted to each side's strategic forces. The Strategic Arms Limitation Talks (SALT) stood at the center of détente.

SALT had four objectives. Its first was to make the arms race more predictable by establishing and documenting the numbers of strategic weapons for each side. It was hoped that such knowledge would reduce the anxiety of the arms race; uncertainty and the fear that the opponent might be gaining superiority in military strength fueled competition.

SALT's second aim was to ensure parity. The assumption was that if the two sides had approximately the same number of warheads and bombs, neither side could launch a crippling strike against the other. More specifically, parity was a condition in which no matter who struck first, the attacked side would still have the capability to retaliate and destroy the aggressor. When each power possessed missiles with single warheads, even with reasonably accurate warheads, a two-to-one superiority was needed to launch a devastating first strike. Short of such a superiority, the United States and the Soviet Union

would each retain a sufficient "second-strike" capability to ensure the continuation of deterrence.

The third purpose of arms control was to reduce threats to each side's deterrent forces. By the early 1970s the deterrent balance was threatened not
only by the continuing Soviet strategic growth but also by technological innovations that were widely believed in the United States to be undermining the
stability of American-Soviet deterrence. One matter of concern was the development of a new defensive weapon. The Soviets had deployed antiballistic
missiles (ABMs) around Moscow and were thought to be working on a sec-
ond-generation ABM for possible nationwide deployment. If ABMs could
shoot down enough incoming American ICBMs and reduce the destruction
inflicted on the Soviet Union to an "acceptable" level of a few million casualties, the ABMs would undermine U.S. deterrence, which depended on its capacity to impose "assured destruction."

This defensive weapon stimulated the United States, in turn, to improve
its offensive technology by developing the multiple independently targeted
reentry vehicle (MIRV)—an ICBM with multiple warheads that could separate in flight, change trajectory, and fly independently to assigned and dispersed targets. The advantage of MIRVs was that the large numbers of warheads would be able to overcome any ABM defense, enabling the United
States to destroy Soviet society in a retaliatory blow. But MIRVs also threatened to destabilize the deterrent balance: multiplying the warheads and providing them with greater accuracy placed a premium on attack. Whichever
side got in the first blow was likely to win because it might be able to prevent
any major retaliation. "Use them or lose them" could become a tempting
strategy for either side.

The fourth reason for SALT was that it was necessary for détente. On the
one hand, the failure to arrive at an agreement or at least to continue the
SALT dialogue was bound to have a deteriorating effect on the overall U.S.-
Soviet political relationship. On the other hand, only a relaxation of tensions
could provide the diplomatic atmosphere that would enable the two nuclear
giants to arrive at an arms agreement that would leave them feeling more secure, sanctify the strategic parity between them, and avoid new costly offensive and defensive arms races. SALT, in brief, became a symbol of détente.

The first set of agreements, known as SALT I, was signed by President Nixon and Soviet Communist Party leader Leonid Brezhnev in May 1972. SALT I
had taken two and a half years to negotiate and incorporated two agreements.
The first, a treaty, limited each nation's ABMs to 200 launchers, later to be reduced to 100 each. For all practical purposes, by eliminating the ABM, the
two powers ensured that their deterrent forces would be able to retaliate in response to a nuclear attack. The second agreement, a five-year interim agree-

ment, essentially froze offensive missiles at the number each side possessed at the time. Each side retained the right to improve its weapons within the overall quantitative agreement, thus preserving parity. Although no on-site inspection to check for violations was established, both sides pledged not to interfere with each other's reconnaissance or spy satellites, which would be the principal means to check compliance with both accords.

SALT II was regarded as critical to a long-term effort to stabilize mutual deterrence. President Gerald Ford, after Nixon's resignation, arrived at the guidelines for SALT II at a 1974 meeting with Brezhnev in Vladivostok. This time each side would have an equal number of strategic weapons: 2,400 missiles and bombers; 1,320 of these delivery systems could have MIRVs. Despite this broad agreement, it was seven years after SALT I that Brezhnev and President Jimmy Carter signed SALT II. It was a complex series of agreements, carefully balancing the varying interests and different force structures of the two powers. But SALT II became controversial in the United States.

Proponents said it provided for some reduction of strategic launchers from the Vladivostok ceiling of 2,400 to 2,250. This change meant that the Soviets would have to reduce their force levels by about 150 older missiles, thereby setting a precedent for SALT III, whose main purpose was to bring about a major reduction of strategic forces. Critics noted, however, that the SALT II ceilings were so high that it was the very opposite of any reasonable interpretation of the words *arms control;* other critics asserted that, despite the equal numbers provided for both sides, the treaty would give the Soviet Union strategic superiority because Soviet missiles were considerably larger, could carry more and bigger warheads, and were becoming more accurate (though less accurate than U.S. missiles). The Soviets, therefore, would by the mid-1980s be capable of destroying up to 90 percent of America's ICBMs.

The debate over SALT II became moot in the late 1970s after the Soviet Union sent troops into neighboring Afghanistan to shore up a pro-Soviet military regime. The U.S. Congress refused to ratify the treaty and, reversing his earlier plans to reduce U.S. defenses, Carter promised to counter the Soviet invasion with a U.S. military buildup. But despite heated rhetoric coming from both Washington and Moscow, the terms of SALT II were generally observed into the 1980s while new efforts to reduce nuclear stockpiles accelerated under President Reagan during his second term in office.

LINKING TECHNOLOGY AND TRADE TO SOVIET RESTRAINT

In the early days of détente American policy makers were willing to fortify the incentives for Soviet political and military restraint with economic help. The Soviet economy as it entered the 1970s was in serious trouble. After its

rapid advancement in the 1950s and early 1960s, the economy saw its 5 percent growth rate headed down to 2 percent by the early 1970s. The economic
decline was particularly notable in those branches of industry associated with
the "second" industrial revolution: computers, microelectronics, and petro-
chemicals. In short, the Soviet Union was behind and falling further behind
the West in those industries that were most important for economic growth.
The implications of this decline could not be ignored; it damaged the Soviet
Union's appeal as a socialist state, hampered its ability to compete with the
United States, and threatened its future superpower status.

Even in agriculture the growth in production had fallen sharply below expectations and official plans. Workers on the land, like workers in the factory,
were far behind their American counterparts in per capita production. The
Soviet Union's continued inability to provide a balanced diet—indeed, in
some years just to avoid widespread hunger—was not just the result of poor
weather, but of the ideologically determined organization of a command
economy administered by a rigid bureaucracy. By contrast, the small private
plots that peasants were allowed to own produced much of the Soviet
Union's poultry, pork, vegetables, and other staples. Thus just as the regime
was failing to live up to its promise of more consumer goods, it also was falling short of its goal of a more nutritious and varied diet, including more
meat. As for the Soviet workplace, during the 1970s it was characterized by
high absenteeism, drunkenness, corruption, and shoddy production. Moreover, the Soviet Union was the only industrial society in which the peacetime
life expectancy of males was declining and infant mortality was rising!

Brezhnev could not forget that Nikita Khrushchev's promises of a higher
standard of living had played a large part in his fall from power. He had raised
popular expectations and then failed to meet them. The same thing could
happen to Brezhnev. In a system where the leadership was determined to
maintain a monopoly on political power and control, it sought popular approval by providing multiple social benefits at low costs: jobs, housing, health
care, retirement benefits, and similar social services. The Soviet standard of
living might not have been high by Western standards, but as long as it improved gradually the regime could claim to be fulfilling its aim of enhancing
the lives of its citizens. Conversely, a decline had serious implications. The
Kremlin had to look no further than Poland. In 1970 the poor state of the Polish economy and worker dissatisfaction with food shortages and a lack of
consumer goods had led to riots in several cities and the collapse of the government, which, even in a communist-controlled state, had to be replaced.
(Similar unrest occurred in 1980-1981 and again in the late 1980s.)

Soviet concerns about an ailing economy and lack of progress in the scien-
tific-technological revolution presented the Kremlin with two choices: to
look toward the West for a "technological fix" to help stimulate the economy

or to attempt a basic structural reform of its highly centralized and rigidly bureaucratized system. Not surprisingly, the Soviet leadership chose Western technology, machinery, food, and the Western credit proffered to buy them. Structural reform was rejected because it was not only antithetical to the regime's basic ideological beliefs about private property, the profit motive, and free market, but also contrary to the deeply vested interests of the governmental bureaucracies committed to central planning, a command economy, and self-preservation. Decentralization of authority—devolving authority to factory and farm managers and their work forces—was judged to be too risky because it might threaten the party's control of political power. Importation of Western goods and food was considered less risky than such a fundamental reform.

Trade with the United States, with its enormous mass-production capabilities, technological advances that the Soviets envied, and its agricultural abundance, was especially desirable to Moscow since it also saw the benefits in broader collaboration. Because it had little to sell the United States, it offered to let Americans develop and exploit the huge Soviet deposits of raw materials, especially in Siberia; the American capital to help finance this extraction would presumably be repaid in oil, natural gas, and other mineral resources in the future. The Soviets also looked to the United States for food in years of shortages, which occurred more and more frequently.

The Nixon-Ford administration believed these economic problems would give the United States leverage. Trade obviously was profitable for American industry and agriculture, but the main reason for permitting it was political. American productivity, it was hoped, would provide a powerful material reinforcement for a Soviet foreign policy of restraint and accommodation made necessary by the desire to prevent closer Sino-American "collusion," to achieve strategic arms agreements to stabilize mutual deterrence, and to gain American recognition of Soviet parity and equal status with the United States. According to Kissinger, economic relations could not be separated from the political context. The United States should not be asked to reward hostile conduct with economic benefits. In return for the expansion of trade, it was not unreasonable to require the Soviets to restrain themselves on key foreign policy issues. In other words, the linkage strategy would give Moscow the incentives to practice self-containment.

But Kissinger's idea of using economic means to achieve political purposes was undermined by the Senate, which approved offering the Soviets trade and credits on the condition (specified in an amendment offered by Sen. Henry Jackson and Rep. Charles Vanik) that Moscow would allow more Soviet Jews to emigrate. Considering the amendment to be an intervention in its domestic affairs, the Soviet Union rejected the trade agreement. No great power—let alone the Soviet Union, which claimed to be a nation in which class dis-

tinctions and religious and other forms of prejudice no longer existed—
would admit publicly that it mistreated part of its population and allow itself
to be placed on probation by a foreign nation in return for trade. As a result,
the Soviet Union conducted its business with Western Europe instead of the
United States, and a potentially powerful American weapon remained largely
useless. And to the extent that the Soviets' primary motive for détente was
economic, as many observers thought, the lack of payoff reduced their incentives for maintaining détente.

THE LIMITATIONS OF DÉTENTE

While the superpowers negotiated over the size of their nuclear arsenals in
the "spirit of détente," much of the outside world remained torn by internal
unrest and regional conflict. The ideological rivalry of the Cold War had infected their already unstable societies, dividing their populations into hostile
ideological camps, prompting their leaders to undertake ever greater forms of
repression, and undermining their prospects for democracy and economic
growth. The resulting calamity in Vietnam already has been reviewed at
length. Among the other Third World flashpoints, the failed experiment with
democracy in Chile and the civil wars in Angola and Ethiopia clearly demonstrated the limitations of détente.

CHILE'S MILITARY TAKEOVER

After the declaration of the Monroe Doctrine in 1823, the United States regarded South America to be within its sphere of influence. Although Washington gradually became more accommodating to the nationalism of its Latin
neighbors, it remained sensitive to what it perceived to be radical left-wing
revolutions and regimes that might bring Soviet influence close to America's
shores. When in 1970 Chile elected the Marxist Salvador Allende to the presidency, the Nixon administration sought first to prevent Allende from becoming president and, when that failed, to make life difficult for him and encourage a military coup d'état. Ironically, the reasons for the Chilean coup, when
it came, stemmed essentially from Allende's own actions and the domestic reactions they precipitated. Although the CIA helped to hasten the coup, the
causes of the crisis were primarily internal, and by 1973 Allende's end was
merely a matter of time. Indeed, Chile provided a most persuasive example of
why the United States should *not* have intervened given that the outcome was
largely predetermined and that, in the coup's aftermath, the U.S. role became
the subject of widespread criticism.

Allende came to power in 1970 with 36 percent of the vote, only two points
ahead of his next competitor in a three-way race. In the runoff vote in the
Chilean Congress, he received the support of the centrist Christian Demo-

cratic Party. At the outset of his rule the opposition supported much of his program, including land reform and the nationalization of the American-owned copper mines, banks, and major industries. Thus it should have been possible for him to work within Chile's constitutional norms with a democratic consensus. But Allende believed in class struggle, and he deliberately pursued a policy of polarizing Chileans, which did more to consolidate the professional middle and lower-middle classes in opposition to him than to broaden his worker-peasant base of support. As a result, his vow to maintain constitutional rule fell by the wayside; he survived only by increasingly by-passing the Congress and the courts. When the Christian Democrats then joined the rightist opposition, the class polarization was at long last paralleled by the divisions between the executive and legislative branches.

The military during this period became increasingly politicized. Asked by Allende at several points to participate in his cabinet to reassure those worried about law and order, the military at first served Allende, as it had his predecessors. What precipitated the military's intervention was the rapid growth of paramilitary forces among Allende's followers, who had always believed in armed confrontation against "reactionaries," and the call for an insurrection in the navy by a close Allende friend and party leader. Both events apparently occurred with Allende's complicity. The country was on the verge of civil war when the military struck. It did not need American urging.

After the expropriation of American property without compensation, Washington had cut off American credit for Chile and pressured international financial institutions to follow suit. But Allende had more than made up for his American losses with credits from communist states, other Latin American countries, and West European countries. Chile also had rich copper mines. Had Allende imitated Egypt's Nasser, he would likely have survived U.S. pressure and hostility by arousing his people's nationalist ardor. But that was why Allende did not survive; he declared himself to be president of only some Chileans—against other Chileans. Had the CIA (and some powerful U.S.-based multinational corporations) abstained from meddling, responsibility for the Chilean coup would properly have fallen on Allende. Instead, the United States reaped widespread condemnation for its intervention, and Chile became for many critics a symbol of American imperialism.

REGIONAL CONFLICT IN AFRICA

A second example of détente's limitations came in 1975 in Angola, a country rich in oil and mineral resources and one that geographically divided "white supremacist" Africa—Rhodesia and South Africa, which controlled South-West Africa, or Namibia—from black Africa. As a Portuguese colony, Angola had helped to protect the two racist states from black liberation movements. But as Portuguese colonialism came to an end, Angola's interim government, which was composed of three factions based on tribal allegiances, underwent a power struggle. This rivalry continued after Angola became independent, and the leftist Popular Movement for the Liberation of Angola (MPLA) attracted Soviet support and thousands of Cuban troops. Some claimed that the Cuban military intervention occurred after repeated South African military strikes into Angola, as well as intervention by Zaire. To the Ford administration, however, it was the Soviets who financed the deployment of Cuban military advisers and who later provided massive volumes of jet fighters, mortars, rockets, armored cars, and ground-to-air missiles. The administration—including Secretary of State Kissinger—viewed the Cubans as Soviet proxies and their intervention in Angola as an outgrowth of Soviet expansionism.

The result was the reintroduction of great-power rivalry and confrontation into southern Africa. Rejecting U.S. military intervention, Washington provided covert arms to the faction opposing the Soviet-supported ones. But not only did this effort not match that of the Soviet Union, it also was cut off by the Senate, fearful of another Vietnam in an area that did not constitute a vital American interest. Rejecting the contention that Angola might become another Vietnam, Ford and Kissinger conceded that Angola was not a significant American interest. They emphasized, however, that Soviet behavior could not for that reason be ignored. Angola might be far away, but, in their view, it was a test case of the new superpower relationship. Soviet actions were simply incompatible with détente; it was another case of their selective détente, of the Kremlin seeking unilateral advantage from the general relaxation of tensions. Kissinger went on to point out that Angola was far beyond any Soviet sphere of influence and that the Soviet action constituted a military intervention to impose a regime of Soviet choice. The Soviet Union's response was to defend its behavior by asserting that support of national liberation movements, including armed intervention, was not incompatible with détente—a view rejected by the United States.

Moscow's next move in Africa came in 1977 in Somalia, the Soviet Union's closest African ally and home to its naval base at Berbera. Using Soviet-supplied arms, Somalia was supporting the Western Somali Liberation Front in the Ogaden region of Ethiopia (Somali troops had invaded Ethiopia to fight alongside the Front) because it had long claimed that this area, populated by ethnic Somalis, was part of Somalia. Ethiopia, already facing disintegration as it confronted other rebellions and secessionist attempts, especially the attempt by Eritrea to establish itself as an independent state, rejected the claim. Like other African and Third World nations, it recognized the borders existing at the time of independence—that is, borders drawn by the colonial powers—as its legal national boundaries. Because Ethiopia was about ten times as large as Somalia with its population of just over 3 million, the Soviet Union supplied Ethiopia with Soviet military advisers, 20,000 Cuban advisers and troops, and an estimated $1 billion in military supplies to squash the Ogaden rebellion. Thus it was willing to risk alienating Somalia and losing its naval base and some air facilities facing the Indian Ocean because the stakes were even greater in Ethiopia than in Angola.

There was irony in a Soviet-supported Marxist regime attacking another Soviet-supported Marxist regime, which the Ethiopian government had become after the overthrow of Emperor Haile Selassie in September 1974. But as Soviet relations with Washington worsened, Moscow saw its opportunity to enhance its influence in the strategic Horn of Africa—which was just across the Gulf of Aden from Saudi Arabia. Washington feared, therefore, that the Soviet Union might gain control of the southern entrance to the Red Sea, which led to the Suez Canal and Israel, and that it would pose a threat to the important oil routes from the Persian Gulf to the West.

The Carter administration's reaction to both crises was divided, reflecting its ambivalence toward the Cold War and its projection to the Third World (see Chapter 8). National Security Adviser Zbigniew Brzezinski, like Kissinger, tended to see the Soviet-Cuban activities in Africa in the context of the American-Soviet rivalry. Secretary of State Cyrus Vance and the State Department's African desk, however, saw the problems as indigenous and warned that American intervention would likely lead to deeper involvement. The U.S. response, therefore, was limited to covert assistance to its perceived allies in the region, and continued rhetorical attacks against Soviet interference.

THE EROSION OF U.S. ALLIANCES

The whole concept of détente was bound to pose several problems for the United States. Alliances are normally drawn together by common perceptions of an overriding external threat. But what cements the bonds of such relationships when that threat is no longer seen as great—indeed, is vastly reduced—by the principal members of the coalition? Is it not inevitable that the strands of such "entangling alliances" become untangled? In Europe, among America's most important allies, that appeared to be the situation.

In the days when all members of NATO had seen the Soviet threat as serious, the alliance had been a reasonably cohesive organization. To be sure, NATO had become strained because its European members, although still dependent on the United States for their security, had recovered from the war and wanted a greater voice in the alliance. But the common perception of external danger had been enough to keep the bonds of the alliance close.

In the era of détente, however, various member nations were no longer so willing to give priority to alliance interests. Washington, for example, now negotiated directly with the Kremlin on key issues, as relations with Moscow became in some respects more important than those with NATO members. Not surprisingly, the European states also went their own way, and economic issues proved especially divisive within the Atlantic community. During the immediate postwar era economic policies such as the Marshall Plan had been consistent with and supported American political-military policy. But now economic relations were at odds with the other strands of NATO policy.

As the 1970s began, Europe was no longer the weak, divided, and demoralized continent it had been after 1945. Indeed, the emerging Common Market had become an increasingly powerful economic competitor. During the Cold War the United States had been a leading proponent of European union; a strong United States of Europe would be a significant contribution to the U.S. balance with the Soviet Union. The competitiveness of an economically unified Europe was thought to be worth the risk. In a period of détente, however, as the European unification movement stalled and differences between the United States and Europe grew, past policy often appeared flawed because of the economic losses it entailed.

The European-American relationship also was strained by the continued sense of vulnerability of the Europeans, fostered by their ongoing dependence on the United States for defense. Their concern revolved, on the one hand, around their fear of abandonment. As U.S. territory became more vulnerable to Soviet attack, the Europeans wondered if they could continue to rely on American protection. Without sufficiently large and credible nuclear forces of their own, their security was entirely in American hands. But, as Soviet intercontinental missile forces grew, what would happen if the Soviets made demands considered vital by the Europeans but not by Washington? Could the small British or French strategic force deter the Soviet Union? The U.S. management of the Berlin crises from 1958 to 1962 had not reassured them—especially France and West Germany—of Washington's steadfastness as its risks and costs of defending the alliance rose. On the other hand, Europeans also feared entrapment. They had been deeply concerned about the diversion of U.S. resources and attention away from them during the Korean and Vietnamese Wars. While Europeans worried about U.S. recklessness, the United States resented their lack of political support for U.S. ventures outside of Europe. This feeling deepened U.S. disappointment over the failure of the Europeans to play a far greater role in their own defense.

The alliance was further divided by the psychological fact that while the United States had become a global power, the European states, having shed most of their empires, had largely relinquished their former extra-European role and had concentrated on their economic growth and their European role. As former great powers, the European states naturally resented their rapid postwar decline in prestige and status and their dependence on a vigorous, self-confident, and, in their eyes, youthful and often impetuous new-comer who might disregard their counsel—advice that, the Europeans felt, was based on their greater experience and wisdom. They seemed mainly to be preoccupied with restraining the United States from doing anything that they perceived as rash and endangering détente, regardless of Soviet behavior.

While the NATO alliance was straining, the Southeast Asia Treaty Organization (SEATO) and the Central Treaty Organization (CENTO) collapsed completely. Indeed, the era of "pactomania" initiated under the Eisenhower administration came to an abrupt halt in the 1970s. SEATO formally dissolved in 1975 after the fall of South Vietnam and its takeover by the North. All expectations had been that Hanoi would make its big push for victory in 1976 during the American presidential campaign. But a rather routine fight in 1975 turned into a rout as President Nguyen Van Thieu of South Vietnam was forced to resign and his army surrendered unconditionally. Given that SEATO's primary *raison d'être* was the conflict in Southeast Asia, its conclusion, even on terms contrary to its members' desires, made the demise of SEATO inevitable.

The Central Treaty Organization died more slowly. First, with the splitting off in 1972 of Bangladesh from Pakistan, which also had been a SEATO member, India emerged as the dominant power on the subcontinent. Pakistan, which had joined both alliances primarily to receive U.S. arms for its adversarial relationship with India, no longer had much interest in either. In the meantime, it had moved close to China, a regional rival of India. Turkey, at the other end of the alliance's geographical area, was grappling with domestic conflicts along with a U.S. arms embargo, which was imposed after the escalation of fighting between Turkey and Greece over control of Cyprus. In between, Iran had become the only reliable friend of the West in Southwest Asia. The fragility of this friendship, illustrated by the overthrow of the American-backed shah and the seizure of American hostages in 1979, was ample evidence of the weakness of CENTO in its final days.

DISILLUSIONMENT WITH DÉTENTE

Any evaluation made of détente in the 1970s reflected one's expectations. In the context of America's national style, it was not surprising that views of détente swung from euphoria as the decade began to increasing disillusionment as early as 1973 or 1974. The nation always had wavered between such opposite and mutually exclusive categories: isolation or intervention, peace or war, diplomacy or force, idealism or realism, harmony or strife, optimism about America's destiny or cynicism about an evil world that resists reform.

The Nixon administration's overselling of détente and such slogans as "negotiation, not confrontation" reinforced the expectation that the Cold

War was over and that the two superpowers had put their conflicts and crises and the danger of war behind them. But raising people's hopes too high was bound to lead to disillusionment when later events did not live up to expectations. The problem was that each administration tended to package its foreign policy in slogans that emphasized how its policy differed from that of its predecessors. And, anticipating the next election, it wanted to make that policy look appealing and successful. Despite the high degree of continuity of American foreign policy, the United States had indulged itself by turns in the rhetoric of containment, liberation, frontiersmanship, and détente. In addition, détente as a state of existence that combined both conflict and cooperation was more difficult to understand than the Cold War. It was easier to explain a relationship that was essentially one of confrontation or cooperation. The Cold War aroused people; détente relaxed them, as if it were the same thing as *entente,* meaning friendship. In fact, détente means a reduction of tensions, not an absence of tensions or superpower rivalry. To regard it as if it were a harbinger of harmony was bound to inflate expectations.

Indeed, it is critical to remember that in its conception détente was intended to serve as another form of containment for a period of domestic neoisolationism, superpower parity, and Sino-Soviet schism. The Cold War stick was to be supplemented by the carrot of détente, and issues were to be linked, explicitly or otherwise. The Soviet Union was to be constrained from foreign adventures with force, or the threat of force, plus the withholding of agreements it desired. The United States hoped that Moscow, enticed by Western goods, technology, and credits, would restrain itself to avoid the loss of such benefits and of agreements such as SALT. In other words, Moscow would be given the incentives to practice self-containment.

But if the United States adopted détente as a diplomatic strategy because of the country's pervasive mood of withdrawal and its relative decline after the Vietnam War, these factors made containment of the Soviet Union at the moment it had become a global power very difficult. Détente was not a set of self-denying rules. If the Soviet Union faced favorable situations to exploit, should it shun those opportunities just because the United States was in no mood to resist? Self-restraint as a policy was asking a great deal of any major power, especially one that had just achieved strategic parity.

Within the United States the Watergate scandal and Nixon's resignation in 1974 combined to weaken the presidency as an institution. The passage of the War Powers Act in 1973, restricting the president's ability to use force, was symbolic of the shift of power from the executive to the legislative branch, whose purpose was clearly to restrain the U.S. role in international affairs. As the "Vietnam syndrome" took hold, Americans were increasingly reluctant to project the nation's power. It was the exercise of *American* power, not the expansionist efforts of the Soviet Union, that was seen as the main problem.

Restraint of the United States, not the containment of communism, emerged as the chief task if the world were to become a more peaceful place. The "limits of American power," the constant refrain after Vietnam, were widely proclaimed among critics of American foreign policy in the public and in the U.S. Congress.

The built-in executive-legislative conflict resulting from separate institutions sharing power always has made the formulation of U.S. foreign policy difficult. World War I, America's first major experience in great-power politics after a century of isolationism, ended in a peace treaty that the Senate defeated. It was Congress's strong isolation during the interwar period that led President Franklin Roosevelt to resort increasingly to executive agreements in his conduct of foreign policy from 1939 to 1941. During the early stages of the Cold War, shared perceptions of great external threats and U.S. aims generally restrained the conflict between the two branches and increased the president's influence with Congress. But in the absence of a clear and present danger during the détente years, and amid intense disagreements about the use of American power in the wake of Vietnam, the White House and Congress pulled in different directions. Almost every policy became caught in a bitter dispute, often raising the most basic constitutional questions.

The Soviet Union's aggressive behavior during this period was understandable; probably any great-power rival would have behaved as it did under the circumstances. After all, during the heyday of détente the United States had bombed Moscow's ally, North Vietnam. And after renewed hostilities in the Middle East in 1973 (see Chapter 8), the United States had promoted a Middle East peace settlement by making itself the arbiter between Israel and the Arabs and excluding the Soviet Union from playing a key role in the area. In this context, Moscow was especially likely to exploit America's paralysis of will and any opportunities to enhance its own influence. The Soviet Union believed itself to be engaged in an irreconcilable struggle with international capitalism led by the United States. For the Soviet Union détente did not mean an end of the competition; it only meant competing at a lower level of tension so that the rivalry would not erupt in nuclear war. It was not its fault if Americans did not want to hear the message that the "class struggle" would go on and that Moscow would give its blessings and assistance to national liberation movements in the Third World. The Soviet leaders had no intention of betraying their historical obligation to assist the inevitable struggle of peoples for freedom from Western neocolonial controls.

Indeed, détente was a particularly favorable situation in which to promote this struggle. Détente, to the Soviets, was the product of a shift in the balance of power as a result of the new strategic parity in nuclear weapons. Before parity, U.S. strategic superiority had allowed Washington to intervene all over the world and to intimidate Moscow and compel it to be cautious. But now that U.S. nuclear forces had been neutralized and deterrence had become truly mutual, the United States had to act more cautiously. In fact, that was why Washington pursued détente. Note the cause and effect carefully: it was the growth of Soviet nuclear forces that induced the United States to behave with greater self-restraint. And consider the obvious corollary: the greater the military power the Soviet Union acquired, the more American compromises and concessions in negotiations would be offered. This perception of American behavior—and the breakdown of consensus in Washington—was nothing less than a rationale for a continuing struggle for preeminence. The world had become a safer place for Soviet expansion. Strategic parity and the newly acquired Soviet outposts in the Third World, like the Soviet navy, were the geopolitical status symbols of the Soviet Union's new standing in international politics. Thus, the United States, despite its successful playing of the "China card" and its widening economic advantage over the Soviet Union, remained mired in the Cold War struggle that would far outlast the Kissinger era in American foreign policy.

Jimmy Carter grasps hands with Egyptian president Anwar Sadat and Israeli prime minister Menachem Begin at the signing of the Camp David accords in 1978. It would be one of Carter's final foreign policy achievements.

CHAPTER EIGHT

Jimmy Carter and World-Order Politics

In times of national self-doubt citizens often turn to an outsider who appears untarnished by past government actions and who promises a fresh approach to domestic and foreign policy making. In the 1976 U.S. presidential campaign this role was filled by Jimmy Carter, a peanut farmer and former governor of Georgia. Carter seemed to epitomize the moral virtues Americans found lacking in previous presidents. Drawing on his experience as a Sunday school teacher in his Baptist church, Carter eloquently described the country's need for moral rejuvenation and spiritual rebirth after the traumas of Vietnam and Watergate. His words struck a chord with the American people, who elected him as president over the seemingly lackluster incumbent, Gerald Ford.

Carter's world views differed profoundly from those of his predecessors. Rather than emphasizing the Cold War and East-West conflict, Carter paid more attention to global "interdependence" and the need for closer cooperation between North and South. His views reflected widely perceived trends in world politics, such as greater concern about the environment and recognition of the growing importance of economic versus military power. Carter denounced foreign adventures that caused death and destruction abroad; he also reflected the view of America's first generation of leaders that such adventures threatened democracy at home and invited tyranny. Drawing on the idealism of President Woodrow Wilson, he proclaimed the needs of the "world society" to be superior to selfish national interests, and he espoused universal standards of morality as the appropriate basis of foreign policy.

In this manner Carter offered a way out of what he called the national "malaise" in the United States. The best course for the country, he proposed, was to reject power politics, seek renewal and purification by concentrating on domestic affairs, and build a fully free and socially just society whose example would radiate throughout the world. Power politics would be replaced by social politics; America's foreign policy would be an extension of its domestic policy. In the words of a former chairman of the Senate Foreign Relations Committee, America should "serve as an example of democracy to the world" and play its role in the world "not in its capacity as a *power,* but in its capacity as a *society.*" [1] Virtue, not power, would be the hallmark of foreign policy; American influence in the world was to be derived from the nation's moral standing as a good and just society. Other nations would be attracted to the United States by its principles, not its strength.

THE SEARCH FOR CONSENSUS AND HUMAN RIGHTS

History has proven that democratic states cannot effectively conduct foreign policy in the absence of a domestic consensus. For most of their history Americans have enjoyed such a consensus, which has centered around the need for detachment from foreign affairs and the primacy of domestic economic and political development. In the absence of an external threat, the United States historically has wanted only to be left to its own devices. When provoked, however, its citizens have been easily mobilized and united for its foreign policy crusades. But in the wake of Vietnam and in the midst of détente, no such provocation appeared on the horizon, and the American penchant for withdrawal prevailed.

The task of re-creating consensus on foreign policy was embraced by Carter, who thought he could find it in America's self-proclaimed historical role as the defender of democracy and individual liberty. Human rights became the platform on which he expected to mobilize popular support; the liberal

1. J. William Fulbright, *The Arrogance of Power* (New York: Vintage Books, 1967), 256.

tradition, which former secretary of state Henry Kissinger was accused of having abandoned in favor of his amoral geopolitics, was to be reunited with American foreign policy. Carter pledged to condition American relations with other countries, rich and poor alike, on their respect for human rights, but he largely directed his human rights campaign toward the Third World. That was where the majority of humanity lived, where living conditions were the worst, and where population growth was the most rapid. To pursue his vision of "world-order politics," Carter would focus on the relationship between the Western industrial democracies and the poorer Third World.[2] In its preoccupation with the ideological struggle of the Cold War—in Carter's words, the "inordinate fear of communism"—the United States had neglected these impoverished areas. Indeed, the superpowers, Carter felt, by extending their Cold War to many "frontiers" in the Third World, had encouraged military dictators on both sides of the ideological spectrum, undermined the prospects of the developing countries for democracy, and further retarded their economic development. In short, the Cold War had only made the already miserable conditions in the developing countries worse.

The United States thus once more stood for something, having reclaimed its democratic heritage and a moral basis for its foreign policy. American flirtations with the Machiavellian world of great-power diplomacy during the "high" Cold War had only confirmed the Founders' dire warnings. Indeed, the United States had learned its lesson; it would no longer search for "monsters to destroy." A new foreign policy more consistent with its traditional style would be adopted. Jimmy Carter, the born-again Christian, had become the redeemer of the American way.

THE RECOGNITION OF INTERDEPENDENCE

By 1976 the nations of the world had become more interdependent, meaning that their fates were more closely connected than ever before. Shifts in economic production, the growth and movement of populations, and environmental decay did not respect national frontiers. Even in the area of national security, the continuing appeal of nuclear weapons meant that any large-scale war would affect all corners of the world—no nation was any longer "an island, entire of itself." The attraction of interdependence was its prospect of a more peaceful and harmonious world consistent with American values and an escape from the more troublesome world of power politics. Moreover, it was claimed, transnational economic and technological forces made this more cooperative world inevitable. The expansion of the global economy into a single marketplace, the perils of nuclear proliferation, and the

2. See Stanley Hoffmann, *Primacy or World Order* (New York: McGraw-Hill, 1978).

effects of pollution and the population explosion collectively made interdependence not just an aspiration but a reality in world politics.

Four central assumptions underlay interdependence as a model for the future—and they continue to influence American foreign policy as it enters the twenty-first century.[3] First, it was asserted that, in an ironic paradox, nuclear weapons had ensured the peace. The superpowers' strategic nuclear arms were weapons of denial and deterrence, and their existence made the use of conventional arms less likely because of the danger of escalation of hostilities. Thus the likelihood of major war between the superpowers, even among their allies and friends, was minimal. When wars occurred, however, as in the case of Vietnam, the conflicts were likely to last a long time and to be expensive in terms of lives lost, money, and increased social divisions—in short, the costs might be excessive in relation to the combatants' goals. Thus future Vietnams were unlikely, especially after the disastrous American experience.

The second and related assumption underlying interdependence was that economic or welfare issues (collectively referred to as low politics) had become at least as important to national security as military protection (high politics). This occurred not only because security seemed more assured but also because the democratic societies of the West had become more and more preoccupied with economic growth rates, consumerism, and ever-higher standards of living. The developing countries, too, were bent on modernizing and on satisfying their own people's expectations for a better life, an effort that Carter promised to support generously. The key issues were economic and social, in his view, and by their nature they promoted such values as social justice and human dignity rather than violence and destruction.

Third, under conditions of interdependence nations could not fulfill their socioeconomic goals by themselves. Western societies, for example, ran largely on oil imported from non-Western countries, which, in their turn, sought Western capital, technology, and food. All countries, rich and poor alike, suffered from cyclical downturns in the world economy and prospered when these cycles reversed themselves. Thus nations no longer completely governed their own destinies, and no government by itself could meet the aspirations and needs of its people for a better life; only cooperation would enhance each nation's prosperity. More specifically, whereas in zero-sum military matters one nation's increase in power was seen by its adversary as a loss of power, on positive-sum economic issues each country's welfare was dependent on the existence of prosperity in other countries. Precisely because nations were vulnerable to one another, they needed to work out problems together. Such cooperation required a greater willingness to resolve disputes

---

3. For a detailed examination of this topic, see Robert O. Keohane and Joseph Nye, Jr., *Power and Interdependence*, 2d ed. (New York: HarperCollins, 1989).

peacefully and a higher degree of mutual understanding and international harmony.

Fourth, and very important, great-power coercion was said to play a minimal role in resolving welfare issues, again in strong contrast to the primary role it might play in security issues. Even if coercive threats were effective once or twice, their frequent use would only alienate countries whose support was needed on other issues. Although many of the nations with which the United States had to deal were comparatively weak militarily, they were not helpless or without leverage of their own. Their economic troubles would require commitments of American aid; their social problems would send thousands of refugees to American shores and cities. Furthermore, they possessed commodities that, if production were shut off, would hurt the consuming nations. And together they had considerable political influence. The traditional way of calculating power—by adding manpower, industrial capacity, military strength, and other factors—did not reveal this.

It was not surprising that this vision of transnational interdependence strongly influenced the Carter administration's policy. Carter came to power just after South Vietnam's final collapse, when the United States was sick and tired of the war and the power politics that had presumably been responsible for the country's involvement. Many of the administration's top officials, who as leaders or members of the bureaucracy under Lyndon Johnson or Richard Nixon had participated in the decision making about the war, shared the widely felt sense of shame about that conflict. They felt guilty about this apparent abuse of American power, as well as about other misuses (such as covert political interventions). Henry Kissinger's balance-of-power approach, therefore, was dismissed as obsolete; the world had moved beyond the days when this "European" approach seemed relevant. The incoming administration claimed that it would be more sensitive to the "new" realities of a more complex world and no longer a prisoner of the old Cold War myth of superpower competition and confrontation, which in the past had received strategic priority and had led the United States to support right-wing dictatorships in the name of freedom.

East-West matters, then, were no longer regarded as a central concern except in the sense of working together for arms control to reduce the superpowers' nuclear arsenals, to prevent the outbreak of a catastrophic war, as well as to reduce the spread of nuclear weapons to nations that did not yet possess them. Détente remained a prerequisite for doing "good works" in the developing areas of the world.

This image of the post-Vietnam War world, with its distaste for national egotism and the use of power, represented more than the reassertion of an older and more "moral" American approach to foreign policy. To many it signified the ultimate transformation of world politics.

When social and economic strength supplemented military power as the foundation of national security in the 1970s, the *instruments* of foreign policy changed as many countries increasingly turned to the tools of "economic statecraft" in advancing their foreign policy goals.[4] For example, the United States often dangled the "carrots" of trade and technology (see Chapter 7) before Soviet leaders to induce their compliance in arms control negotiations. Other instruments included international organizations, particularly the United Nations, where Third World countries had become numerically dominant and where their proposals for closer North-South collaboration would attract worldwide attention. Regional organizations such as the European Community, Organization of American States (OAS), and Organization for African Unity (OAU) brought their leaders together to devise common strategies for political stability and economic growth. Flows of foreign aid, in both military and economic forms, increased dramatically during this period. These growing volumes of aid served the foreign policy interests not only of the recipients but also of the donors themselves, who often competed for aid supremacy among Third World states. Finally, and perhaps most dramatically, the "weapon" of petroleum was used by Middle Eastern states, which exploited the vulnerability of industrialized countries on oil for their economic stability.

THE NEW INTERNATIONAL ECONOMIC ORDER AND NONALIGNMENT

Before Carter's rise to power, Western leaders often argued that the causes of the persistent poverty in so many of the developing countries were of their own making: the fragility of nationhood; inefficient farming techniques, resulting in widespread hunger; high birth rates, which defeated the most valiant efforts aimed at economic growth; large defense budgets, often used to prop up dictators and repress citizens; and, all too often, widespread inefficiency and corruption. The developing countries rejected the argument, however, that they were responsible for their failure to modernize. They pointed to the external system—the international economy—in which they were the sources of raw material for Western industry, as the culprit. When supplies or demand declined, or when Western industries found substitutes or synthetics, the prices of developing country products went down. As prices declined, so did the capacity of the developing countries to earn foreign exchange with which to buy Western industrial products. This prevented them from devel-

---

4. For an elaboration, see David Baldwin, *Economic Statecraft* (Princeton, N.J.: Princeton University Press, 1985).

oping their own industries and urban centers, which were widely viewed as the catalysts of heightened prosperity, higher levels of education and literacy, and improved living conditions.

In short, the earnings of the world's poorest countries declined while the cost of goods from industrialized societies steadily rose. In addition, when these countries were able to develop some industry and export to the West, they often ran into protective tariff barriers. Thus even when they worked harder, it was of little use; the structure of the international economy was biased against them and kept them in a subordinate position as suppliers of cheap raw materials for the rich Western states and as consumers of their finished products. Third World countries seemed condemned to poverty and to continuing political weakness.

As their leaders saw it, they were dependencies. They may have gained political independence, but they remained chained economically to the Western industrialized economies. Their status remained *neocolonial* because their economies were geared not to the needs of their own markets but to those of the developed countries' markets. That is why, they claimed, that after decades of working hard and despite large infusions of foreign aid they remained impoverished. Their dependent status in an international system dominated by the North, as the Third World nations perceived it, hindered their ability to grow economically. Their integration into the global economy only benefited the dominant Western nations and left the developing countries behind.

The developing countries were arguing not just that the Western-controlled international economic order gave an advantage to the strong over the weak; their main point was that they were poor because they had been exploited by the West. They had been plundered during the colonial days, and this plunder continued as they sold their resources cheaply on the international market. In this context their demand for a "new international economic order" was a claim for a redress of past wrongs. Having used their power unfairly to take from the poor countries what rightfully belonged to those countries, the argument went, the rich nations were obligated to make restitution in the name of past abuses. The transfer of wealth from the West to the Third World was therefore seen as repayment of a moral debt, and as an overdue investment in their ravaged economies.

Among Third World countries the demands for a new international economic order included calls to stabilize commodity prices, index those prices to Western inflation rates, increase foreign aid, and establish preferential tariffs so that they could sell their products in Western markets. They felt they had the resources Western industry needed, and they vowed to press their demands through collective action. Toward that end and recognizing their numerical superiority in the United Nations, the developing countries organized themselves into a cohesive bloc, the Group of 77 (G-77), as a vehicle to make their voices heard. As for their relations with the two superpowers, they reaffirmed their earlier adherence to "nonalignment" in the Cold War and to freedom from superpower interference.

While nonalignment was the geopolitical buzzword for much of the Third World, in reality the bias of these countries toward the Soviet Union was clearly visible. The Soviets had charged all along that the poverty and misery of the non-Western world were the results of Western capitalism and imperialism. Still, it seemed odd to find Vietnam, Afghanistan, North Korea, and Cuba accepted as nonaligned nations and odder still that the 1979 conference of these nations was held in Havana. Furthermore, the support given by G-77 countries to most Soviet positions in the UN General Assembly raised doubts about their independent status. It seems oddest of all that when Vietnam, after its victory in the war, was cruelly driving its Chinese population out of the country, usually in boats that would not survive long ocean journeys, its behavior was not condemned. Meanwhile, the G-77 states routinely voted against the United States in the General Assembly and openly criticized American actions in the United Nations Conference on Trade and Development, which had been established in 1964 to promote greater cooperation between rich and poor countries.

All this being said, this unofficial coalition between the Soviet Union and the nonaligned nations was largely tactical. The nonaligned countries were, above all, nationalistic; they had not fought for national independence only to lose it to Soviet imperialism. Yet it was a sign of the times that this coalition existed and that only a small number of Third World governments criticized the direction of the nonaligned movement and defended American policies.

FOREIGN AID AND NORTH-SOUTH RELATIONS

The developing countries benefited from the Cold War in many ways, although they often criticized the superpowers for their Cold War preoccupations and their consequent neglect of the poorer nations of the world. Far from neglecting them, however, the United States, the Soviet Union, and other industrialized countries gave them attention and resources in the form of foreign aid that were wholly disproportionate to the Third World's power. The reason was the bipolar distribution of power, which conferred on these new nations, most of whom were not only poor but also weak, greater leverage than their own strength and influence warranted. Confronted by two nations competing for their allegiance and loyalty, the Third World countries could lean first toward the East, thereby attracting Western economic and military aid and political support, and then toward the West, thereby attracting similar assistance from the East.

The developing countries' exploitation of this "foreign aid rivalry" continued throughout the Cold War. But even beyond the superpower competition, many wealthy states, particularly those in Scandinavia and later along the Pacific Rim, offered billions in aid to further their own designs for North-South relations. As the era of "low politics" took hold, foreign aid became tantamount to an obligation of affluent states. It was not a question of *whether* they would contribute foreign aid, but how much, to whom, for what purposes, and under what terms. By the mid-1990s these donor states had contributed more than $60 billion annually in Official Development Assistance (ODA) to poor countries. Japan "caught up" with the United States in 1989, and other industrialized countries increased their aid flows to carefully selected recipients in pursuit of widely varying national interests.[5]

The flow of foreign aid was expected by many to diminish with the end of the Cold War. Indeed, during the 1970s many industrialized states already had become disappointed by the results of previous assistance efforts. It had become clear after two decades that the optimistic expectations of "instant development" had underestimated the difficulties of modernization. Moreover, foreign aid had not even been particularly successful in winning friends and gaining influence. As a result, not only did American aid fall to its lowest point by 1980—less than half of 1 percent of the gross national product (GNP)—but the emphasis shifted from capital development to technical assistance and an increasing role for private enterprise, meaning basically the multinational corporations. (In 1979 U.S. aid was only 0.2 percent of GNP, behind the aid given by Sweden, Norway, the Netherlands, France, Britain, West Germany, and other donors.) In surveys, Americans consistently identified foreign aid as their least favorite government program.

In any event, as the 1990s began, prospects for the developing countries appeared grim. With few exceptions they were still far from modernized. The optimism had faded that foreign aid would stoke their modernization or, later, that "trade, not aid" would permit them largely to earn their own way and to finance their own development. Food shortages in Africa and Asia were stark reminders of what could happen. Thus the expectation of the former colonial states that they could realize their dream of better and more rewarding lives for their peoples was unfulfilled. Illiteracy, starvation, and disease continued to coexist with dreams of national dignity and material welfare. For a variety of complex reasons, the billions of dollars in annual support from the North had little or no impact in the Southern Hemisphere. And the latter's best hope for stoking their development through exploiting their own natural resources failed.

---

5. See Steven W. Hook, *National Interest and Foreign Aid* (Boulder, Colo.: Lynne Rienner, 1995).

It was in the context of yet another Arab-Israeli war in 1973 (described in the next section) that the Organization of Petroleum Exporting Countries (OPEC) raised oil prices fourfold, from $3 to $12 a barrel, and that its Arab members embargoed shipments of oil to the United States and the Netherlands, both supporters of Israel. The oil companies, which were supposed to be such powerful multinational corporations that they dominated the countries in which they operated, were shown to be without much power. Indeed, they were at the mercy of the governments of the countries in which they operated. The so-called imperialist states, whose governments were presumably controlled and directed by the capitalists, did not mobilize to squash the governments that were said to be their puppet regimes. Confronting a vital threat to their well-being and security from countries that had no military power to speak of, the industrial democracies did not even debate the issue of military intervention. This was the era of "low politics" in which economic and social issues took precedence over "high" or security issues. The Western countries instead talked of accommodation and acquiesced. Had this event occurred a few decades earlier, they would not have hesitated to resort to force rather than face the possibility of being destroyed economically.

OPEC's action at the time was widely viewed in the Third World as symbolic of a general protest against the industrialized countries. The organization became a kind of vanguard of the world's poorest nations. They shared a mood of anger, resentment, and revolt that was clearly directed against the North, particularly the United States. Ironically, however, the effects of the quadrupling of oil prices were felt most keenly by developing countries by threatening their plans to industrialize and handicapping their efforts to grow more food with technologically intensive, petroleum-based agricultural techniques. But whatever fears they had about the future, these countries stood united with OPEC.

Despite the increased suffering brought on by the steep rise in oil prices, the Third World countries did not form a coalition with the United States, Western Europe, and Japan to force lower oil prices. This can be explained in part by their fear of irritating OPEC, in part by their hope for promised but largely undelivered OPEC economic help (most went to fellow Muslim nations, where it was spent on arms), and in part by their desire to imitate OPEC. But the basic reason was that the Third World identified emotionally with OPEC. The organization's action was widely perceived by these countries as "getting even" for past exploitation. It gave them a good feeling that for once the weak had turned the tables and made the strong suffer. (The German word *schadenfreude* says it best: pleasure received from seeing someone who deserves it really suffer.)

The sharp rise in oil prices left no country untouched. In the United States and among its principal industrial allies, high oil prices slowed economic growth, brought on unemployment, created "stagflation" (simultaneous inflation and recession), lowered standards of living, created large Western imbalances of trade, and sharply lowered the value of the dollar. The energy crisis of the 1970s did not merely cause occasional inconveniences such as long lines to buy gas or higher prices at the gasoline pump; it profoundly upset entire economies and changed ways of life, as evidenced by smaller cars and lower speed limits in the United States. Moreover, the energy crisis raised the question of how the Western states, which had paid for welfare programs by means of rapidly growing economies, could still afford such programs, and whether they would have to reduce defense expenditures in order to continue such programs. Or would they be able to maintain strong defenses only by cutting social expenditures? Plenty of "guns" and "butter" no longer appeared affordable.

When Mao Zedong once said that "power grows out of the barrel of a gun," he would have been equally correct had he referred to a barrel of oil, an irreplaceable commodity that cannot be recycled. Large-scale capital investments and many years are required to explore, find, and drill for new oil. Similarly, new technologies to exploit solar energy or shale oil also require enormous investments of time and money. Other energy sources such as nuclear power are controversial or are, like coal, deemed environmentally undesirable. No short-run substitute is readily available for economies that have long depended on relatively cheap oil and have neglected the development of alternative energy sources.

Is it any wonder, then, that the developing countries were delighted and held high hopes in the wake of the oil shocks of the 1970s? Indeed, OPEC's actions gave rise to three expectations: first, that OPEC would use its leverage to raise the prices of natural resources from the other Third World countries; second, that the other commodity producers would follow OPEC's example by organizing their own cartels; and, third, that the OPEC "petrodollars" would flow to the Third World in the form of foreign aid. But to the chagrin of these countries, none of the three expectations materialized. OPEC fragmented as its members reverted within a decade to their previous patterns of undercutting the cartel oil prices. And its example was not adopted by producers of other commodities, who remained consumed by their own competition for Western markets. Finally, OPEC profits were not shared with developing countries in the form of aid. After being deposited in New York banks, they were lent instead to many developing countries (particularly Mexico and Brazil) at market rates, which the borrowers could not repay, thus contributing to the debt crisis that afflicted much of the Third World in the 1980s.

Four years before Carter took office, in the waning days of the Nixon administration, tensions in the Middle East had erupted in warfare that threatened to draw in both superpowers. In 1973 Egypt and Syria attacked Israel on the highest of all Jewish holy days, Yom Kippur or the Day of Atonement. Egypt, which was ruled by Anwar Sadat, the Egyptian nationalist who had succeeded Gamal Abdel Nasser, attacked because it had become increasingly frustrated by Israel's continued occupation of Egyptian territory up to the East Bank of the Suez Canal, which Israel had captured in the Six-day War in 1967. The Egyptians achieved initial success in crossing the Suez Canal and driving into the Sinai Desert. Fearing that it would lose influence in the Arab world by remaining neutral, the Soviet Union delivered offensive arms to the Arab states. When indeed the Egyptian and Syrian armies proved successful in the opening round of fighting, the Soviets began a huge airlift of war materiel and opposed any cease-fire calls that were not linked to a pullback by Israel to the 1967 frontiers. Moscow also called on other Arab governments to join the war and approved the OPEC oil embargo.

U.S. INTERVENTION AND NUCLEAR CRISIS

The United States, under President Nixon, responded with its own massive airlift of military supplies in the face of enormous Israeli fighter plane and tank losses. Once Israel had recovered from its shock and had driven the Syrians back from the Golan Heights, its forces concentrated on Egypt, crossed the Suez Canal to the West Bank, and moved to cut off supplies to the Egyptian forces on the East Bank and to encircle them. At this point the United States and the Soviet Union agreed on a cease-fire resolution in the UN Security Council. But the shooting continued, and the Israelis drove to encircle and destroy the Egyptian army on the eastern side of the Suez Canal.

Sadat then asked the United States and the Soviet Union to use their own forces to impose their cease-fire resolution. The United States declined to intervene with its forces, but the Soviet Union threatened to do so unilaterally. Thus the two superpowers now confronted one another, and American military forces were placed on a worldwide nuclear alert. Moscow backed off, however, and the United States, also eager to avoid an escalation, pressured Israel to end its military advance. These moves assured the cease-fire.

For Henry Kissinger, the urgency of reaching a Middle East settlement was obvious, and the time seemed favorable. He campaigned actively for a settlement, engaging in "shuttle diplomacy" as he crisscrossed the Middle East mediating the dispute. Indeed, Sadat was the first Egyptian leader to declare his willingness to accept the existence of Israel and make peace with it on the basis of the 1967 frontiers. Moreover, an Arab-Israeli peace would prevent an

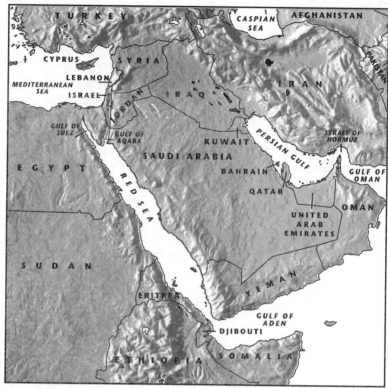

THE MIDDLE EAST

American-Soviet confrontation that could escalate into a superpower war. Each Arab-Israeli war had held the possibility of such a confrontation; in 1973 that possibility had come the closest yet. Kissinger also was determined to avoid the past pattern of an Israeli military victory, which could not be translated into an acceptable political settlement, and an Arab defeat, which left the Arabs humiliated, resentful, and more determined than ever not to accept Israel's right to exist and use oil as a weapon against the West.

CARTER'S MIDDLE EAST BREAKTHROUGH

In 1976 the incoming Carter administration viewed the Mideast situation with alarm. Time was of the essence because Egypt was now isolated in the Arab world. Carter therefore proposed that all parties resume the negotiations that had begun at Geneva after the 1973 war.

In the final days of the Ford administration, Secretary of State Kissinger had fashioned his strategy to bring the Arabs and Israelis together step by step and exclude the Soviets; only at the final conference would the Soviet Union be invited for symbolic reasons. But Carter decided to approach the Soviets and enlist their cooperation in achieving a peace settlement. Moscow had influence with the more militant Syrians and within the Palestine Liberation Organization (PLO), which had formed to press the cause of renewed statehood for Palestine. The Soviets, therefore, could cause a lot of trouble and block negotiations. If Moscow participated in the peace negotiations, however, it would retain a degree of influence in the Arab world if and when a peace treaty were signed, the possibility of a superpower clash would be reduced, and détente with the United States would be strengthened, a prerequisite for a U.S. focus on the developing countries.

The two superpowers reached agreement on Middle East conflict resolution late in 1977, but neither Jerusalem nor Cairo was happy with the Soviet-American accord. Israel did not want to face all its enemies again simultaneously, and Egypt already had broken with Moscow, which now favored Syria, Egypt's rival. Thus Israel and Egypt decided to bypass Moscow and Washington and negotiate directly. In a dramatic and internationally televised visit to Jerusalem in November 1977, during which he addressed the Israeli Knesset (parliament), Sadat extended recognition to the Arabs' archenemy. The mood afterward was euphoric; a comprehensive peace, a peace with all of Israel's Arab enemies, seemed near.

The mood did not last long, however. Sadat apparently believed peace was achievable easily and quickly because he had taken the significant psychological step of reassuring the Israelis that his peace offer was genuine, not a trick. Israel would withdraw to its 1967 frontiers from the Sinai, the West Bank, Syria's Golan Heights, and Jordan's East Jerusalem and would recognize the Palestinians' legitimate rights. In return for their land, the Arabs would sign a peace treaty and Israel would gain the legitimacy and peace with security it had sought since birth. The Israelis always had asserted that if only the Arabs would negotiate with them directly, implying recognition, they would be willing to return the territories taken in 1967. In fact, Israel had specifically disclaimed annexationist ambitions. After the 1967 war its Labor government had accepted UN Resolution 242 committing Israel to the withdrawal from the captured land (or, given some adjustments for security reasons, from almost all of these areas).

But Israel's new coalition government was led by Prime Minister Menachem Begin, leader of the principal opposition party, Likud. He proposed an Israeli withdrawal from the Sinai Desert, but offered the Palestinians on the West Bank and in the Gaza Strip only autonomy, or self-rule, not self-determination. Moreover, Begin referred to the West Bank by its ancient Hebrew names, Judea and Samaria, and he claimed that it was not occupied territory to be returned but liberated territory to be kept as a part of the Greater Israel of which he had long dreamed. He left no doubt that he expected to establish Israeli sovereignty over both the West Bank and Gaza, each of which contained large Arab populations. In the meantime, the Israeli government announced that Jewish settlements in the Sinai and West Bank would remain, and it encouraged more settlements.

When, to no one's great surprise, bilateral negotiations broke down, the United States reentered the negotiating process. Carter felt that Sadat was offering Israel the security and peace it had so long sought, and that if this opportunity were not seized the result would be politically disastrous for Israel and economically disastrous for the West. The president thought three conditions were necessary for a solution in the Middle East. First, Israel had to abide by UN Resolution 242, and return most of the Arab territory it had captured in 1967. Only minor adjustments for security reasons could be allowed. Second, because the key to peace was the Palestinian issue, the Palestinians had to participate in the peace-making process. Carter himself declared that the Palestinians had a right to a "homeland," a deliberately vague term but one that nevertheless carried great symbolic weight. Third, in return for such Israeli concessions, the Arab states had to commit themselves not only to ending their state of hostilities with Israel but also to signing a peace treaty.

Begin was at odds with the first two conditions. He reinterpreted UN Resolution 242 to mean that Israel was not required to withdraw from the West Bank and Gaza. He also was opposed to a Palestinian state, which he—and indeed most Israelis—felt would endanger the existence of Israel. Moreover, he promoted his own plan for Israeli settlements in the occupied lands. Since 1967, however, the United States had consistently opposed these settlements as illegal. The Carter administration repeated this while it watched in disbelief as the Israeli government, in the middle of the peace process, actively encouraged new settlements on the land the Arabs claimed to be theirs. Washington was convinced that the Israelis were acting in bad faith in the midst of peace negotiations.

Repeated American efforts to halt this policy were in vain. By contrast, Sadat appeared reasonable and conciliatory. He had with great courage provided the psychological breakthrough with his trip to Jerusalem. He had shown sensitivity to Israel's security needs and had been willing to accept Israel's demands for a peace treaty and the subsequent normalization of relations—not after twenty-five years, or even five years, but immediately. The stalemate continued.

As the three-year, interim Sinai agreement was about to run out in October 1978, Carter gambled and invited Begin and Sadat to meet with him at Camp David, the Maryland presidential retreat. The invitation was a gamble because had this summit meeting produced no results, the president's prestige, already low, would have been even more seriously impaired, American mediating attempts would have run their course, and Israeli-American relations would have been set back even further. But the president, for one of the only times in his administration, showed persistence and skill and after twelve days of patient negotiations emerged with a series of agreements, including a commitment by the two leaders to sign a peace treaty within three months.

Sadat made most of the concessions. He did not gain a commitment to an eventual Israeli withdrawal from the West Bank and Gaza Strip, or full Palestinian self-determination. The Israelis, however, promised to recognize "the legitimate rights of the Palestinians," to permit West Bank and Gaza Palestinians to participate in future negotiations on these areas and ratify or reject a final agreement, and to halt temporarily new Israeli settlements on the West Bank. In return, Israel gained a separate peace treaty with the strongest of its Arab neighbors; without Egypt the others could not by themselves take on Israel. Thus for a seemingly small investment Israel had gained the enormous dividend of a real sense of security.

Sadat hoped that a peace agreement would start momentum for further agreements with Israel. The first Arab reaction to the Camp David accords, however, was negative. Jordan, and even Saudi Arabia, joined Syria, Iraq, Libya, Algeria, and South Yemen in condemning Sadat, who became more isolated than ever. Under these circumstances, Carter's courageous personal intervention—his trip to Egypt and Israel—produced the necessary diplomatic breakthroughs and brought peace between these two long-term enemies. Yet the subsequent treaty did not bring a stable peace to the area. Israel quickly resumed and accelerated its settlements policy in the West Bank; the Arab states, except Egypt, became more hostile to American "meddling" in the region; the key Palestinian issue remained unresolved; and all sides continued to import large volumes of military hardware in preparation for the next conflagration.

THE COLLAPSE OF CARTER'S FOREIGN POLICY

The emergence of interdependence as the newly accepted world view coincided with the Soviet Union's achievement of nuclear parity with the United States and Americans' "crisis of confidence" in their government, brought on by a series of domestic problems. Thus, while the new Carter administration was deemphasizing the East-West conflict and focusing on North-South cooperation, the Soviet Union, perceiving the global balance of power to be shifting in its favor, saw opportunities to exploit and expand its influence militarily in the Third World.

The East-West struggle was not just an old, bad memory. It was still very much alive, even if the United States preferred not to compete actively and told itself that containment no longer seemed relevant in the face of the diffusion of power in the world, growing nationalism in the developing countries, and the shift in emphasis from power politics to "world-order" politics. The Soviets showed that they shared neither the belief that international politics had changed nor the view that military force had become an increasingly irrelevant instrument of policy. In the late 1970s the Soviet Union was estimated to be outspending the United States on its military forces by at least 25 percent, perhaps by as much as 50 percent. Given an economic base believed to be about half that of the United States, this heavy emphasis on "guns" at the cost of "butter" for the Soviet people suggested that these forces were intended for more than just defense. In the Third World the Soviet Union used its growing political-military involvement to exploit hostility among developing countries toward the North and to offer its model of communism and centrally directed industrialization for the developing countries to emulate.

During the "high" Cold War, the United States had often erred by overemphasizing East-West relations. Indeed, some of its mistakes, particularly with regard to China, were costly. But experience also had shown that grave danger lay in ignoring or downplaying these relations. It was one thing to learn from the past and correct errors; it was quite another to dismiss the very nature of international politics, whose chief characteristic, arguably, was its strong sense of continuity. In the last half of Carter's presidency this lesson was painfully learned. His restraint in foreign affairs and appeals to universal moral standards were followed by the Soviet invasion of Afghanistan, a Marxist revolution in Nicaragua, and the seizure of American diplomats as hostages in Iran. These three concurrent events, along with a second energy crisis, seemed to offer strong testimony to the limitations of world-order politics and raised the question of whether the Nixon and preceding administrations had been so wrong in giving priority to American-Soviet competition, in emphasizing military power, or in thinking that the East-West struggle by necessity intersected with North-South relations.

THE SOVIET INVASION OF AFGHANISTAN

Divisions within the Carter administration between adherents of détente and hard-liners continued to fester. This division was symbolized by Secretary of State Cyrus Vance, on the one hand, and National Security Adviser Zbigniew Brzezinski, on the other. After Soviet troops and tanks poured into Afghanistan in late 1979, Vance's influence waned and Brzezinski's rose. The Soviet-inspired coup that had occurred a year earlier in Afghanistan had been overlooked, but the 85,000 Soviet troops that had arrived there during the last week of 1979 were hard to ignore. Fierce resistance by Muslim tribesmen to radical and antireligious reforms appeared to threaten the Soviet-supported regime.

Among their other concerns, the Soviets feared that the Islamic fundamentalism then sweeping Iran and Pakistan might engulf Afghanistan, which lay between these two countries, creating an insecure situation on the Soviet Union's southern border where approximately 50 million Soviet Muslims lived. In response to the situation, Moscow invoked the Brezhnev Doctrine, which asserted that once a nation had become socialist, it was not to be surrendered to counterrevolution (as the Soviets defined these terms). The march of history toward socialism was inevitable and irreversible. Earlier, this doctrine had been invoked only in Eastern Europe—in Hungary in 1956 and Czechoslovakia in 1968. Now the Red Army was to ensure history's progress outside of the Soviet sphere in a Third World country.

The Soviets probably expected no more of an American response than a condemnation of the Soviet action as deplorable, but no action. Clearly the Soviets believed that vital security interests were at stake and did not give much thought to American reactions. In truth, there was little to lose. Carter, to rescue the SALT II treaty in the Senate, had promised to increase defense spending and modernize American strategic forces. And the Soviet Union had received little of the trade, technology, and credits it had expected from détente; indeed, it had been denied most-favored nation commercial status, which China had received. Nevertheless, such a disregard for American reaction, implying contempt for American power, was rather new.

For Carter and Vance, who had pinned so much of their hopes for world-order politics on superpower cooperation, the Soviet invasion was a shock. Chagrined, Carter called the Soviet action the greatest threat to world peace since World War II and said the Afghanistan invasion "made a more dramatic change in my opinion of what the Soviets' ultimate goals are than anything they've done in the previous time I've been in office." No president in the postwar era has testified more dramatically to his own naiveté.

The president, swinging with events, now became a hard-liner. He stepped up military spending, halted high-technology sales, embargoed grain shipments, and imposed a U.S. boycott on the Olympic Games scheduled for Moscow in the summer of 1980. The Senate, meanwhile, refused to ratify the SALT II treaty. Most important of all, Carter announced his own doctrine: the United States would henceforth consider any threat to the Persian Gulf to be a direct threat to its own vital interests. It would be one of many steps in Carter's anguished transition to a more aggressive, militaristic, and Cold War-oriented foreign policy.

Détente thus came to an end in 1980 as superpower relations disintegrated. Carter undoubtedly had been correct that not all regional conflicts were tests of superpower strength and credibility. In truth, however, few purely regional quarrels existed in the context of global Cold War. Détente ultimately collapsed because of a series of regional conflicts that the administration had attempted to isolate from the American-Soviet rivalry—only to find that it could not do so. As Soviet activities in the Third World showed, the Soviet Union did not consider this rivalry over. Quite the opposite: it took advantage of America's post-Vietnam reluctance to act and its illusion that Third

World problems could be separated from the superpower competition.

COMMUNIST REVOLUTION IN NICARAGUA

History also was unkind to President Carter in Central America, where decades of economic distress, military dictatorship, and ideological polarization spawned a variety of revolutionary movements. These were often directed not only against the reigning rulers but also against the United States, whose support for dictators in the name of containing communism engendered widespread resentment throughout Latin America and the Caribbean. The United States, the self-proclaimed protector of the region under the Monroe Doctrine, was widely viewed by many as more of a menace than a supportive patron. Carter hoped to change this perception by reforming U.S. policy and establishing a new reputation as a truly "good neighbor."

In Nicaragua, Carter opposed the long-standing military dictatorship of Anastasio Somoza, whose family had ruthlessly controlled the country for nearly five decades (after the departure of U.S. Marines from the country). Carter's reversal of American policy was consistent with his overall effort to shift attention from Cold War concerns to internal social and economic problems in the Third World. Continuing U.S. support for right-wing dictatorships, he felt, would certainly doom U.S. interests in the region and throughout the developing world. Popular resentment and anger would eventually lead to the overthrow of such dictatorships, and American identification with the status quo would only alienate the new rulers. Unlike in Vietnam, the argument went, the United States had to place itself on the "right side of history." Thus the Carter administration favored social and political change and tried to identify U.S. policy with such change rather than oppose it.

The rebellion against Somoza accelerated in the late 1970s despite the leader's increasingly brutal use of the Nicaraguan National Guard. His overthrow also was encouraged by the Organization of American States, which called for a democratic government and the holding of free elections as soon as possible. As a result of all these forces, Somoza's regime finally collapsed in 1979. At first, Carter favored the coalition of anti-Somoza forces led by the Sandino Liberation Front, which during Somoza's days were domestically supported by such elements as the Catholic church, the educated middle class, and the business community. In its first years under the coalition, Nicaragua received allotments of $90 million in foreign aid from the United States and promises for long-term support. "If you do not hold me responsible for everything that happened under my predecessors," Carter told Nicaragua's new leader Daniel Ortega, "I will not hold you responsible for everything that happened under your predecessors."

The new regime in Nicaragua, however, did not live up to Carter's expec-

tations. The broad-based anti-Somoza coalition rapidly dissolved as the Sandinistas centralized authority within a nine-member directorate. Free elections were delayed, the press was (again) censored, and other political
restrictions were imposed by the junta, which turned increasingly to Marxist-
Leninist rationales for building a self-sufficient communist state. In addition,
the Sandinistas offered to assist their allies in El Salvador, where a similar civil
war was erupting between its military dictatorship and left-wing guerrillas.
The El Salvadoran government responded by sending "death squads" into
the impoverished countryside and murdering suspected insurgents. When
their victims included three American nuns, the Carter administration re-
scinded U.S. aid to El Salvador and watched as the civil war became bloodier.
Nicaragua and El Salvador remained battle zones into the 1980s and became a
central preoccupation of Ronald Reagan's presidency.

The unrest in Central America further demonstrated the limitations of
Carter's efforts to redirect American foreign policy. To some degree, he was
captive to the unstable conditions that had developed in the region before
and during the Cold War. No immediate reversal of American policy, however well intentioned, was likely to counteract the bitterness and resentment
that had developed for so long toward "*yanqui* imperialism." Far from en-
gendering newfound trust between the United States and Central America,
Carter's efforts instead provided an opening for anti-American forces to assume power and translate their resentment into revenge. As Carter attempted
to purify American foreign policy, he discovered that the outside world was
continuing to pursue the same *realpolitik* he had eschewed. Ideological tensions only increased during his tenure, despite his best efforts to focus on areas of cooperation between the United States and its Latin American
neighbors.

AMERICA 'HELD HOSTAGE' IN IRAN

The low level to which American credibility and power had fallen was further symbolized by the storming of the American embassy in Teheran in November 1979 by a mob of militant students, who seized fifty-two American
personnel. This outrage occurred after the longtime, pro-American shah,
who had been overthrown and who was suffering from cancer, was admitted
to the United States for medical treatment. (He died a few months later in
Egypt.) The newly installed revolutionary authorities, hoping to create an Islamic theocracy in Iran, gave the unprecedented action their blessing and
support.

The seizure of American hostages paralyzed Carter, and his subsequent efforts to gain their safe release became high public drama. Nightly, U.S. television networks exposed the American public to pictures of crowds, like well-
rehearsed choruses, chanting their hatred of America, the "Great Satan," as it

was called by the Ayatollah Ruhollah Khomeini, Iran's chief religious leader and *imam*, or leader, of all Shiite Muslims. "Death to America" was the battle cry as Carter was burned in effigy on the streets of Teheran.

Carter, who had stressed human rights in his election campaign and who had pointed to the shah, among others, as an example of his predecessors' amoral, if not immoral, policy, was as usual caught between conflicting views. The disagreements in Washington were such that the fall of the shah and Khomeini's triumph were greeted with relief. But as had happened so often before, the Carter administration's understanding of Khomeini was superficial, consistent with its own hopes of what would happen. Yet perhaps Carter's confusion was understandable, for, after all, who in Washington or any other Western capital in that secular age would have given serious consideration to the strength of a religious movement and the possibility that it would transform Iran into a medieval theocracy? The possible emergence of an Iran dominated by the clergy was so alien to all Western thinking that it was not taken seriously; there was no precedent for such a reaction to efforts at modernization.

In the 444 days following the taking of the hostages, the world watched as the Carter administration tried one means after another to gain their release. Among other things, appeals were made to the United Nations and the International Court of Justice and a series of economic sanctions was applied. But all was in vain. The holding of the hostages was a symbolic act of defiance and revenge for the shah, who was portrayed by the new regime as an American puppet who had cruelly exploited Iranians in behalf of U.S. interests. As the administration's patience wore thin, it attempted a rescue mission in the spring of 1980. The mission was called off, however, when three of the eight helicopters malfunctioned in a desert sandstorm. Even worse, one helicopter collided on the ground with the refueling aircraft for the flight out of Iran, killing eight servicemen and injuring five others. To a nation on edge, the mission's failure dramatically symbolized the apparent helplessness of the United States, as well as the low level of readiness, competence, and reliability of its armed forces. Cyrus Vance resigned in protest of the mission, revealing deepening divisions within the Carter administration over foreign policy.

Fortunately, two events helped to gain the hostages' release on January 20, 1981, the day Carter left office. The first was the Iraqi attack on Iran in the fall of 1980. The war suddenly made the U.S. economic sanctions, especially the freeze on Iranian money in U.S. banks, painful for Iran because its military forces were largely American equipped. The need for spare parts and the cash to buy them and other goods grew as oil production in Iran fell to almost nothing. The second event was the November victory of Ronald Reagan, the former governor of California, in the U.S. presidential elections. Because he had run on a tough foreign policy platform and had denounced the Iranians as "barbarians" and "kidnappers," the Iranians expected harsher measures from Reagan, including military action.

In these circumstances diplomacy finally proved successful. The fifty-two diplomats and marines were released just after Reagan's inauguration in a gesture fraught with symbolism. A humiliating chapter in American history, coming so shortly after the Vietnam trauma, had ended. In the exuberance of the welcome that the ex-hostages received on their return to America, one could almost hear the refrain "never again," for, in a real sense, America itself and the U.S. government had been taken captive and held hostage. Combined with national frustrations over Afghanistan, Nicaragua, and the second oil crisis of the decade, which was precipitated by the turmoil in Iran, the Iranian debacle deepened the perception of an American "decline," which Reagan vowed to eradicate upon his assumption of the presidency in January 1981.

THE TRIUMPH OF REALISM OVER IDEALISM

As we have seen in this chapter, the Soviet invasion of Afghanistan, the Sandinista revolution in Nicaragua and its spin-off rebellion in El Salvador, and the hostage crisis in Iran collectively undermined Carter's attempt to promote world-order politics on the basis of global interdependence, universal standards of morality, and peaceful cooperation. Along the way, these events dispelled much of the post-Vietnam malaise and led to a demand for a more vigorous American foreign policy. In this respect, Leonid Brezhnev, Daniel Ortega, and the Ayatollah Khomeini may have done the United States a favor, just as it had taken German submarine attacks on U.S. ships (World War I), a Japanese attack on Pearl Harbor (World War II), and a Soviet seizure of power in Czechoslovakia (Cold War) to mobilize the nation when the public mood was one of disengagement and relaxation. After America's years of withdrawal, these challenges in 1979 and 1980 may have been necessary to demonstrate that isolation from the unsavory realities of world politics, far from rendering such realities inconsequential, perhaps encouraged their spread and resulted in sustained assaults on U.S. interests and prestige.

Carter sensed this shift in mood as he took a harder line toward the Soviets during his final year in office. For example, he elevated the stature of Brzezinski. And on Capitol Hill the U.S. Congress enthusiastically approved Carter's requests for a large increase in American defense spending. Thus began the process of national rearmament that Ronald Reagan would continue and accelerate well into the 1980s. In all of these efforts Carter was strongly supported by the American public, which drew a connection between his previous condemnation of power politics and the calamities that befell his administration in its final two years.

Paradoxically, it was not the *recognition* of Carter's moralistic values but their *repudiation* that pulled the country out of its post-Vietnam "malaise." The widely perceived consequences of American introspection and self-doubt, which included humiliations and challenges to its interests on virtually every continent, mobilized public opinion and political consensus where appeals to universal moralism had fallen short in previous years. The American style of foreign policy, it appeared, seemed to require more than good intentions; support for democratic values and global progress would not be sustained at the cost of American national interests.

Carter was clearly anguished by the spreading challenges to his foreign policy. For weeks he refused to leave the White House while he considered ways to get the hostages home from Iran; in December 1979 he refused to light the White House Christmas tree while the hostages remained in captivity. Moreover, the downward spiral of events took a visible physical toll on the president, who was forced to reconcile his most basic spiritual beliefs with the unavoidable challenges of overseas competition. In response to these challenges and to the shift in American public opinion away from world-order politics, Carter abandoned many of his foreign policy beliefs and programs.

Conversely, Reagan received the full benefit of this shift in mood. He had long taken a hard line toward the Soviet Union, and, although inflation and the weak state of the U.S. economy may have been important factors in Reagan's election, the fact remains that because of OPEC and the collapse of the shah, the domestic economic issue was inseparable from American foreign policy and the U.S. position in the world. Whereas Carter was forced to acknowledge that the events of 1979 and 1980 undermined his idealistic world view, Reagan was able to argue that they confirmed his realism. "Historical forces" were not moving in the direction of transnational cooperation, as Carter had claimed previously; they had never diverted from their consistent path, which was littered with conflicting interests and tests of strength.

Ronald Reagan, often called the "great communicator," promoted hard-line policies toward communist countries during the early 1980s.

CHAPTER NINE

The Revival of Superpower Confrontation

Just as Jimmy Carter's rise to power reflected the introspective American mood of the Vietnam-Watergate era, Ronald Reagan captured the more assertive national spirit of 1980. A former movie star and pitchman for General Electric, President Reagan was known neither for his intellect nor for long hours spent in the Oval Office. The contrast with his predecessor was widely apparent. Whereas Carter's world view emphasized the complexities of interdependence, Reagan's was unabashedly one-dimensional. Whereas Carter pored over background reports and anguished over policy choices, Reagan literally dozed through high-level meetings. But he brought to the office two skills that were to help transform American-Soviet relations: strong anticommunist instincts and a powerful ability to mobilize public opinion. Both skills served him well.

Reagan attempted to restore the country's battered stature and the national pride of Americans by reviving the notion that an active U.S. role in world affairs was essential to world peace. Soviet leaders, he felt, had exploited détente, the Vietnam syndrome, and Carter's conciliatory gestures to advance America's global strategic interests. As Reagan's supporters saw it, a clear line could be drawn from Carter's idealism to the Soviet invasion of Afghanistan, the Sandinista revolution in Nicaragua, and the seizure of American hostages in Iran. Believing the United States must match the Soviet nuclear and conventional military buildup of the 1970s, Reagan proposed a massive buildup of U.S. armed forces. A concerned Congress approved his proposals to double American defense spending in his first term. This included matching recent Soviet deployments of intermediate-range nuclear missiles in Europe with a new round of North Atlantic Treaty Organization (NATO) deployments.

Reagan often boasted that he was blessed with the luck of the Irish. Indeed, he certainly had the good fortune to take office as the torch was being passed in Moscow from the old guard to a new generation of reformers ultimately led by Mikhail Gorbachev. The reduced tensions between the superpowers, so unexpected at the beginning of the decade, have often been attributed to Gorbachev, who took over the Kremlin in 1985. The new Soviet leader was said to be the first enlightened ruler since the 1917 Revolution. His generation of Soviet elites hailed from urban rather than rural backgrounds and had some exposure to foreign countries; it was thus more aware of the failings of the Soviet system and critical of its internal defects. Had Brezhnev or his two immediate successors survived, Gorbachev's domestic and foreign policy changes might not have occurred. Nor would the Cold War likely have ended on terms that were as peaceful or as beneficial to the West.

To some, the collapse of the Warsaw Pact and the Soviet Union in 1991 was a fait accompli, a historical inevitability that would have occurred no matter who was the president of the United States in the 1980s. The ossified Soviet system already was in an advanced stage of decline; its internal problems were growing severer daily and its hold on its clients in Eastern Europe and beyond was becoming more tenuous. Thus Gorbachev—or any leader of the country—had to implement drastic reforms in the Soviet Union's political and economic system; permit the restive populations in Warsaw, Prague, and East Berlin to express themselves; and adopt a more cooperative posture toward the United States. These measures would, in this view, only magnify the deficiencies of the Soviet system and hasten its self-destruction.

But this interpretation of events, which minimizes the roles of both Reagan and Gorbachev, does not quite tell the full story. It fails to recognize the crucial part that Reagan played in raising the costs of the superpower competition and in forcing the Soviet Union to reform its system. The Reagan military buildup, which had actually begun in Carter's last year, required greater Soviet investments in arms at a time when the dwindling resources of the Soviet Union were needed for domestic priorities. Moreover, new NATO missile deployments in Europe negated the strategic advantages of recent Soviet installations. The president's proposals for a Strategic Defense Initiative further worried the Soviets because, whether or not it succeeded in creating a missile-proof shield over the United States, the research might lead America to a quantum leap in technology at a time when the Soviet Union was struggling with growing economic problems at home. Finally, the Reagan Doctrine of supporting guerrillas against Soviet-backed Marxist regimes further increased the costs of Soviet expansion.

In short, the Brezhnev foreign policy, which at first had appeared so successful, had become counterproductive: it had provoked a strong American reaction, held NATO together, and left the Soviet Union surrounded by enemies (including Japan and China). Reagan had increased the strains on the Soviet Union so much that it could no longer muddle through. Moreover, he had eliminated any flexibility that Gorbachev might have had and forced him to retrench abroad, cut military spending, and subordinate foreign policy to domestic affairs. Initially thought to be reckless and widely condemned as a cowboy (especially in Europe) because he appeared trigger-happy, the president left office with the superpower relationship on the best terms it had been since 1945. Thus, despite some setbacks and a huge federal budget deficit that helped to make the United States, once the world's largest creditor nation, its greatest debtor, Reagan left office in January 1989 with the highest public approval of any postwar president.

REAGAN'S RHETORICAL OFFENSIVE

When Reagan came into office, the national disillusionment with détente was widespread and the term *Cold War II* was heard often. The president's longtime hostility toward communism in general and the Soviet Union specifically fit the new post-détente mood. He denounced Soviet communism as "the focus of evil in the modern world" and announced to Americans, "There is sin and evil in the world, and we're enjoined by Scripture and the Lord Jesus to oppose it with all our might." [1] Soviet leaders would "lie, steal, cheat, and do anything else to advance their goals," warned Reagan.[2] Opposition to the Soviet Union was, therefore, a religious as well as a political imperative. Reagan spoke of the march of freedom and democracy leaving "Marxism-Leninism on the ashheap of history." Of Eastern Europe he said, "Regimes planted by bayonets do not take root"—that is, the communist regimes had no legitimacy. The United States could not accept the "permanent

1. Remarks to the National Association of Evangelicals, March 8, 1983, in *The Russians and Reagan*, ed. Strobe Talbott (New York: Vintage Books, 1984), 113.
2. *New York Times*, January 30, 1981.

subjugation of the people of Eastern Europe," he asserted.[3] In making the point that democracy and freedom were the waves of the future, the president was not just giving the Soviets a dose of their own medicine, for the Soviets regularly denounced the United States and forecast the "inevitable end" of Western capitalism. More important, he was questioning the legitimacy and longevity of communism as a social and political system in Eastern Europe and the Soviet Union.

Many American critics rejected Reagan's predictions about communism being swept aside by the tide of democracy as empty rhetoric. By the end of his second term, however, as noncommunist tyrannies were being swept away and communist regimes were being exposed to greater demands for liberties from within, Reagan's prediction looked less like right-wing rantings than accurate insights into historical development. While far from being a political theorist, Reagan was a spirited polemicist whose expectation of communism's demise in Europe was fulfilled under his watch.

The harsh denunciations of the Soviet Union were not mere statements of the president's personal ideology; they served two tactical purposes. First, they were intended to remobilize American public opinion after the years of détente. Reagan, to whom détente had all along been an illusion based on the unwarranted belief that the Soviets had changed their character, sought to arouse American opinion for the longer term. Second, the president's war of words was intended to send the Soviet leaders a message, one that probably was heeded all the more because the Soviet leadership was in the throes of a geriatric crisis. First, Soviet leader Leonid Brezhnev died in late 1982; his successor, Yuri Andropov, died just over a year later in early 1984; and his successor, Konstantin Chernenko, in ill health when he took over, died just over a year later in 1985. Gorbachev, who had risen rapidly to the top of the Communist Party hierarchy, now became the Soviet Union's fourth leader since Reagan had assumed office. Reagan's blunt declarations were intended to send the new Soviet leadership the signal that the Vietnam syndrome was a thing of the past, that America's will to resist Soviet expansion was back. But the president hoped to avoid confrontations and possible military clashes by sending signals that were intentionally sharp so that the Soviet Union would not act, as it had during the 1970s, in the belief that America would not react. Minor U.S. military actions against small Soviet proxies such as Libya and Grenada—actions that the United States could not lose and were not costly—were intended to drive this message home. In that sense, the tough words were essentially a substitute for riskier deeds.

3. Address to members of the British Parliament, June 8, 1982, in Talbott, *Russians and Reagan*, 89-104.

In fact, the early Reagan years were characterized by rhetorical confrontations but no direct encounters or crises. In policy terms they were quiet years. Despite his reputation for machismo, the president was operationally cautious. Indeed, to the extent the Soviets saw him as a leader spoiling for a fight, they were no doubt strengthened in their conviction that they needed to act with restraint. Reagan's foreign policy was basically a return to the containment policy of the immediate postwar years. The primary emphasis was on East-West relations, on the Soviet Union as a communist expansionist state, and on the need to contain that expansion, including in the Third World, by force if necessary.

THE U.S. MILITARY BUILDUP AND OPPOSITION TO ARMS CONTROL

The 1970s in the United States were rife with antimilitary sentiment, neoisolationist hopes, and cries for domestic priorities and for reductions of the defense budget. Indeed, those years witnessed "the most substantial reduction in American military capabilities relative to those of the Soviet Union in the entire postwar period." [4] American defense expenditures had fallen to the 1950 (pre-Korean War) low of 5 percent of the nation's gross national product (GNP) at a time when the Soviet Union, despite having an economy only half the size that of the United States, was spending substantially more than the United States on defense.

By 1981 any president would have been concerned about Soviet intentions and capabilities. Carter's defense secretary, Harold Brown, already had noted that "as our defense budgets have risen, the Soviets have increased their defense budgets. As our defense budgets have gone down, their defense budgets have increased again." And Reagan had once asked, "What arms race? We stopped, they raced."

After a decade and a half of Soviet efforts to exploit America's Vietnam-induced isolation and a weakened American presidency, the Soviet Union possessed the strategic and conventional forces needed to project its power beyond Eurasia. It was in the context of Soviet perceptions of a changing "correlation of forces" that the Soviets had exploited Third World situations to increase their influence by means of military advisers and arms, proxies such as the Vietnamese in Cambodia and the Cubans in Africa, and, of course, their own troops in Afghanistan.

The Reagan administration was especially worried about the state of America's deterrent forces. The vulnerable land-based Minuteman intercon-

---

4. John Lewis Gaddis, *Strategy of Containment* (New York: Oxford University Press, 1982), 320-322.

tinental ballistic missiles (ICBMs) and the aging B-52 bombers and Polaris submarines had been built in the 1950s and mid-1960s. American strategic forces needed to be modernized to ensure their continued deterrent capability. At the center of the administration's rearmament program was the MX (missile experimental) ICBM with ten warheads. Highly controversial because it appeared to have the same first-strike capability attributed to Soviet ICBMs, the MX would create a mutual hair-trigger situation that, in turn, could lead to a nuclear war that neither side wanted. Each would feel it had to take that risk because if it failed to strike first, its ICBMs might be destroyed.

Even more disturbing was the administration's talk of nuclear warning shots, "protracted" nuclear war, nuclear "war fighting," and "prevailing" in a nuclear war. The Reagan administration, more than its predecessors, speculated about such scenarios publicly, including Secretary of State Alexander Haig. Thus the administration's five-year, $1 trillion defense program (which actually totaled almost $2 trillion over Reagan's two terms) stimulated enormous controversy. It conveyed the impression that by relying too much on military strength the administration was flirting with disaster, and it reinforced the impression that the United States was largely responsible for the arms race. The momentum of the Soviet Union's arms program since the mid-1960s and its impact on the balance of nuclear and conventional balances often appeared forgotten in the uproar over the administration's rearmament program.

This uproar was intensified by Reagan's strong opposition to arms control, the centerpiece of both Nixon's and Carter's policies toward the Soviet Union. Rejection of the SALT process reflected the Reagan administration's strong distrust of the Soviets and its conviction that past arms control efforts had led to America's alleged decline. It announced that it would postpone any arms negotiations until the United States could "negotiate from strength." But postponing new arms control talks proved difficult since public opinion equated arms control with disarmament and even more so with a sincere search for peace. The pressure on the administration therefore grew. When negotiations finally started in 1982, the administration claimed it was shifting the emphasis from arms limitation—setting ceilings on launchers—to drastic reductions. Thus it changed the name of the process from SALT (Strategic Arms Limitation Talks) to START (Strategic Arms Reduction Talks). The administration's real motive for this change was to make its approach politically appealing at home, to deflect domestic criticism, and to weaken the newborn nuclear freeze movement while the buildup continued. The initial proposals, then, were clearly propagandistic and meant to be rejected by Moscow, thereby winning time for the administration.

That is how many Americans saw it too, and Reagan therefore inspired a widespread "peace movement" in the early 1980s. Its adherents ranged from academics to religious leaders, especially the Catholic and Methodist bishops, who questioned the morality of nuclear deterrence, a policy based on the threat to use nuclear weapons in order to prevent their use. Both sets of bishops condemned not only the use of nuclear weapons, but also their very presence in the arsenals and military doctrines of both superpowers. Yet if such weapons could not be used even in retaliation, how could deterrence be made credible? Was the goal of peace moral but the means of preserving it immoral? In the meantime, antinuclear books and films became popular, climaxing in an ABC-TV movie entitled *The Day After* which depicted the nuclear devastation of an average American city.

Besides the immorality of nuclear deterrence, the second major theme of the peace movement was that nuclear war would mean the end of civilization, the "last epidemic" as a doctors' organization phrased it. This theme was supported strongly by new scientific arguments that the smoke produced by the many fires resulting from nuclear attacks would shut out sunlight, plunging the world into darkness for several months and causing a prolonged freeze, or "nuclear winter," leading to the extinction of most plant and animal life. Regardless of who "won" a nuclear war, climatic catastrophe would follow and spread over the globe.[5]

Despite their widespread appeal, these books and films contained little that was new. By 1980 the horror of nuclear war had been common knowledge for thirty-five years. That was, after all, why the United States had adopted a deterrent strategy. And it was the suicidal nature of these nuclear arms that had encouraged the belief that nuclear deterrence would prevent an all-out Soviet attack on the United States and preserve peace among the superpowers. Moreover, although deterrence could fail, it had a historical record. The superpowers had not exchanged as much as a rifle shot in Europe where they confronted one another; their nuclear power and their mutual fear of suicide had given Europe thirty-five years without hostilities, its longest period of peace in the twentieth century. Indeed, nuclear weapons had eliminated war among *all* the great powers, not just the superpowers.[6]

Although the antinuclear movement appeared to confuse the issue of threatening nuclear force to bolster deterrence with its use, that did not stop the movement from gaining enormous momentum by 1982. The danger of nuclear war appeared to be the nation's first concern. In New York City three-quarters of a million people turned out for the largest political gathering in American history. For those demonstrators and the others marching, meeting, and debating the nuclear issue across the country, the ultimate goal

5. See Carl Sagan, "Nuclear Winter and Climatic Catastrophe: Some Policy Implications," *Foreign Affairs* (Winter 1983-1984): 257-292.

6. See John Lewis Gaddis, "The Long Peace: Elements of Stability in the Postwar International System," *International Security* (Spring 1986): 99-142.

was to eliminate nuclear weapons, but the immediate goal was to achieve a nuclear freeze. Proposals for a freeze on the testing, production, and deployment of nuclear weapons to stop the arms race were passed (or almost passed) by many town-hall meetings and by voters in ten of the eleven states on whose ballots it appeared in the midterm 1982 election. Congress, especially the Democratic House, reflected this antinuclear mood, and, after coming within two votes of endorsing a nuclear freeze in 1982, it endorsed a modified version of the freeze in 1983. In 1984 all Democratic presidential candidates but one came out in favor of a freeze.

THE STRATEGIC DEFENSE INITIATIVE

Reagan first introduced his Strategic Defense Initiative (SDI) in the midst of the controversy about arms control. The proposal was quickly dubbed "Star Wars" by its critics because of its reliance on sophisticated space-based technologies glimpsed only in movies, such as lasers and particle beams. SDI was intended to render nuclear missiles "impotent and obsolete," presumably protecting America's population. According to official descriptions, SDI would be a layered defense using different technologies to destroy attacking missiles during each phase of the ballistic trajectory. Mutual assured survival would replace mutual assured destruction. Was it not better to save lives on both sides, the president asked, than to kill the population of the aggressor in revenge for a first strike?

For the president the SDI plan served several purposes, the first of which was domestic and political. Criticized for increasing the defense budget while cutting social services and assailed for being a warmonger, Reagan was able to seize the initiative with SDI. Instead of always defending himself, he could pose as a man of vision who would end the threat of missile attacks and ensure that the population of the United States, of the Soviet Union, and, indeed, of the world would survive. He had gone arms control advocates one better, not by stabilizing the balance of offensive missiles, but by banishing their life-threatening potential.

If the churches condemned nuclear deterrence as immoral, was his scheme for a strategic defense not the reincarnation of morality? And if the movement condemning nuclear deterrence spread to other Western societies, would strategic defense not be the most politically acceptable option? With SDI, in fact, Reagan undermined the antinuclear movement by stealing its thunder. He may have been the nation's most conservative postwar president and he did promote a large-scale rearmament program, but on nuclear issues he was an abolitionist, who often spoke of a world devoid of nuclear weapons as his ultimate goal. Reagan dismissed the distinction between stabilizing and destabilizing nuclear weapons, as he did the role they had played in deterring war. He clearly was uncomfortable with the deterrent strategy to which all of his predecessors had been committed, and he condoned the addition of new nuclear stockpiles only as a means to hasten arms control efforts. At the Reykjavík (Iceland) summit in 1986 Reagan had come close to agreeing with Gorbachev to the total elimination of all nuclear weapons within a ten-year period. (Ironically, it was his refusal to postpone research on SDI that undermined that agreement.)

Second, SDI's utopian side was matched by a more pragmatic consideration: if it worked, it would outflank the Soviets. For years the Soviets had invested heavily in first-strike missiles, which also were the basis for the Soviet claim to superpower status. SDI now threatened the value of this Soviet investment in ICBMs and claims to equality with the United States. What would be the point of a Soviet attack if its missiles could not penetrate the defensive shield above the United States?

Third, although defense of the population and elimination of all ICBMs were the fundamental and long-term goals of SDI, it could potentially defend U.S. ICBMs in the future. A defense against missiles would relieve the American fear that its ICBMs were vulnerable and increase Soviet uncertainty that they could launch a successful first strike. Thus there would be no point in a Soviet strike at all. SDI could make mutual deterrence—the reciprocal hostage relationship—safer.

SDI was denounced by critics for many reasons: it would be enormously expensive; it would accelerate the arms race; it would have to work perfectly the first time it was needed; it would tempt a Soviet first strike if the Soviets felt they were on the verge of becoming "nuclear hostages" to an unassailable United States. In short, SDI would only lead to new arms races, offensive and defensive, in which the defensive technologies, even if they gained the upper hand, would do so only temporarily. Moreover, the system would be so expensive that it would threaten U.S. budgets for other strategic and conventional forces. Therefore, it was doubtful that the United States or the Soviet Union would be any more secure. Arms reductions through bilateral negotiations were the better course.

But if the critics were correct, why did the Soviets denounce Reagan's "arms race in space"? Why, after previously walking out of all arms control negotiations, were the Soviets so eager to resume talks? Clearly SDI worried them; they really were as fearful of an American first strike as the Americans had been of a Soviet first strike since the early 1970s. The Soviets perceived SDI to be part of an offensive, not defensive, strategy, a prelude to an American strike. They also were aware that SDI research and development would result in American technology taking a huge step forward at a time when Soviet technology already was behind. With its domestic economy in shambles, the Soviets could not afford to accelerate the arms race on so great a scale.

The Soviets thus were eager to delay, if not stop, the deployment of SDI. The United States, meanwhile, continued to worry about the Soviet first-strike capability. A compromise seemed the obvious solution: a drastic cut in Soviet ICBMs in exchange for SDI, or at least a delay of SDI. Reagan, however, refused to turn SDI into a bargaining chip and trade it for Soviet ICBMs. After he walked out of the Reykjavík negotiations, no strategic arms control agreement was possible. Such a deal became possible only after Reagan left office. Nevertheless, he approved the more modest START I agreements signed by his successor.

THE REAGAN DOCTRINE IN THE THIRD WORLD

Although Reagan refocused the attention of American foreign policy on the East-West struggle, this did not eliminate the Third World as a matter of concern. Among Reagan's top priorities on taking office was a reversal of what he saw as Soviet gains during the 1970s in such areas as Angola, Ethiopia, Yemen, Afghanistan, and Cambodia after the Vietnam War. The Soviets and their allies had been using force to make inroads in these areas—direct force in Afghanistan, indirect force through proxies elsewhere. And in Central America the Marxist Sandinista government in Nicaragua consolidated its power and sought to extend its influence to neighboring countries, especially El Salvador.

Past administrations had been committed to containment and had not hesitated to intervene to save a friendly regime from being attacked from outside or from within by the Soviet Union or its friends. But, except for episodic efforts such as Harry Truman's effort to "liberate" North Korea, or John Kennedy's Bay of Pigs operation in Cuba, it had never been the official policy of the U.S. government to unseat Soviet-supported regimes. Dwight Eisenhower's administration had spoken of the "liberation" of Eastern Europe and the global "rollback" of communism but had never acted on those words; containment remained a fundamentally defensive doctrine. The new Reagan policy, however, was offensive.

Dubbed the "Reagan Doctrine," it aimed to undo the results of recent Soviet expansion. States such as Nicaragua, Angola, and Afghanistan had established Marxist governments that had not yet consolidated their power, and all faced resistance movements. The Soviets had justified their Third World expansion with the doctrine of "national liberation" and then asserted that communism was irreversible once a society had become Marxist. Reagan now adopted his own national liberation strategy against governments that had not come to power by means of democratic processes. In his eyes such regimes lacked legitimacy. Moscow had placed them in power and, unlike his predecessors (with the partial exception of Jimmy Carter in Afghanistan, where a U.S. program of largely covert assistance for resistance fighters already was in progress), he refused to accept Moscow's claim that the civil wars were over once governments were in place. The domestic conflicts were not over until popular governments, acceptable to the people (and presumably to Washington), were in power. In short, the Reagan Doctrine set out to disprove the Brezhnev Doctrine's claim that once a nation had become part of the Soviet bloc, it could never leave.

The president's version of national liberation was not applied to all Third World states—only to some of the Soviet Union's recent acquisitions. The doctrine was based on certain assumptions: that the Soviet Union had become overextended in the 1970s; that the global balance of military power, after favoring Moscow in the 1970s, was shifting back to the United States; that the Soviet Union's most critical problems were domestic; that, except for Afghanistan, only peripheral Soviet interests were involved; that the Soviet Union would not want to risk a confrontation with the United States; and that a democratic tide was sweeping through the Third World. In practice, the Reagan Doctrine amounted to little more than bleeding the targeted governments and especially Moscow; if they wanted to stop the hemorrhaging, they would have to negotiate a political solution with the insurgents. The insurgencies were not strong enough to overthrow the Marxist regimes, but with American help they could keep the wars going.

ROLLBACK IN THE DEVELOPING COUNTRIES AND THE SALVADORAN PRECEDENT

As noted, the Reagan administration turned Marxist ideology on its head by arguing that "historical forces" were on the side of Western democracy and capitalism, not socialism. For evidence, the administration pointed to Latin America, where during the Reagan years (1981-1989) Argentina, Bolivia, Brazil, Guatemala, Honduras, Peru, and Uruguay had become, at least nominally, democratic, in addition to El Salvador, Grenada, and Haiti. Whatever the reason for this phenomenon—administration policy, global social and political trends, economic development, or sheer coincidence—the administration expressed its optimism that this was part of an irreversible process. The Soviet bloc, by denying human freedom and dignity to its citizens, was running against the tide of history.

Drawing on the traditional hemispheric preoccupation of the Monroe Doctrine, Reagan identified Central America, South America, and the Caribbean as vital U.S. interests and vowed to turn back any outside (that is, Soviet) incursions into America's backyard. To demonstrate his resolve, Reagan intervened directly on the tiny Caribbean island of Grenada, where a military coup had led to the installation of a Marxist regime in 1983. The U.S. military operation, which ostensibly was designed to liberate American medical stu-

dents from the island, took longer than expected because of logistical problems and a considerable amount of bungling by U.S. Army, Navy, and Marine forces. But it achieved its main objective of eliminating the Marxist
regime.

The U.S. invasion of Grenada was intended to raise the risks and the costs
for the Soviets and Cubans should they continue to try and extend their political and military control in the Western Hemisphere, as well as elsewhere. Asserting that it had intervened to prevent Grenada from becoming a "Soviet-
Cuban colony," the administration called Grenada a "warning shot" that was
actually targeting the Sandinista regime in Nicaragua. The administration
was convinced that the Sandinistas harbored ideologically motivated ambitions beyond their own frontiers. Because they also accepted support from
Havana and Moscow, Washington saw them as a continuing source of instability and tension for the vulnerable states in the region. The Sandinistas'
pledge to confine themselves to Nicaragua was regarded with skepticism by
those who recalled their earlier pledges to promote political pluralism, a
mixed economy, and a nonaligned foreign policy.

What the Reagan administration sought in Nicaragua was to undo the
Sandinistas' increasing monopolization of power and to return the country to
its immediate post-1979 state when the popular anti-Somoza revolution had
produced a new coalition government composed of the major groups that
had helped to overthrow the dictator, including religious groups, entrepreneurs, and large segments of the middle and working classes. Once in power,
however, the Sandinistas began to consolidate their hold on government,
gradually suppressing the voices of criticism. They postponed general elections, censored the news media while building an army larger than Somoza's,
restrained activities by other political parties, extended control over worker
and peasant organizations, and strengthened their police and security apparatus. They also turned toward Cuba and the Soviet Union for diplomatic support and economic assistance. But the question was not how *Marxist* the regime would become as it turned against the Catholic church, the business
community, professional organizations, trade unions, and student groups
that had helped it to depose Somoza. The question was how *dictatorial* it
would become and how closely it would align with Havana and Moscow.

The United States, which initially supported the new regime in Nicaragua
with foreign aid, was increasingly distressed by its consolidation of power and
militaristic behavior. Thus after Reagan took office, he authorized the formation of an anti-Sandinista army known as the "contras." Trained by U.S. military advisers in neighboring Honduras, these soldiers staged a series of military offenses against the Sandinista regime from Honduras, which received
increased U.S. military assistance for these purposes, even though Reagan encouraged the public to view the contras as an indigenous, independent army

of "freedom fighters." Later, however, this policy backfired against the Reagan administration and dealt a serious blow to its credibility at home and abroad.

The Reagan administration also placed the Central American country of El Salvador, a country the size of New Jersey with a population of 6 million, within the context of the superpower conflict. Adapting the Eisenhower administration's domino theory of communist expansion to Latin America, Reagan expressed concerns that the Sandinista revolution in Nicaragua would spread to El Salvador, and ultimately the rest of Central America would follow. Furthermore, the threat was defined as applying to the wider U.S. position throughout the world. "If Central America were to fall," the president asked, "what would the consequences be for our position in Asia, Europe, and for alliances such as NATO? If the United States cannot respond to a threat near our own border, why should Europeans or Asians believe that we are seriously concerned about threats to them?"[7] Specifically, Reagan alleged that the Nicaraguan government was shipping weapons to rebels in El Salvador, and he proposed increased U.S. arms transfers to El Salvador to match the reported Sandinista arms transfers.

Whether El Salvador was the right place to take a stand against Soviet communism and its proxies, or whether the revolution should have been allowed to follow its natural course, was energetically debated in the United States. Critics of the administration's plans, especially the Democrats in opposition, argued that the Nicaraguan arms were not the principal cause for the civil war but, rather, the appalling domestic social and economic conditions and political repression. As was the case throughout the Third World (see Chapter 5), the seeds of revolution were often sown in poverty and despair, which were byproducts of despotic rule. In the view of these critics, the United States should not support the privileged few who had long exploited the poor. Social justice demanded nonintervention; so perhaps did self-interest if the United States wished to avoid being identified with the losers, as it had been so many times before. The Vietnam War frequently was cited as a reminder of the dangers of supporting the wrong side—an unpopular political elite whose vested interest lay in the preservation of the status quo. In any event, no purely military solution was possible.

Locating a moderate center in El Salvador was the key to the Reagan administration's effort to mobilize support domestically and achieve success. In the Third World the United States had often appeared trapped between reactionary forces, on the one hand, whose rigid commitment to the status quo only intensified revolutionary sentiment and endangered American interests,

7. Ronald Reagan, "Central America: Defending Our Vital Interests," *Current Policy* (U.S. Department of State), April 27, 1983.

and radical forces, on the other, which tended to be Marxist and to look to Havana and Moscow. The administration was saved from this trap in El Salvador by Napoléon Duarte, who was in power for most of the Reagan years and sought to pursue democratic reforms while preventing the radical left from capturing power. Duarte strengthened the Reagan case for assistance to El Salvador because Reagan could rightfully claim that the United States was not supporting the right wing as an alternative to the radical left. Washington hoped, by sending Duarte economic and military aid and by encouraging domestic reforms, it could avoid both another Cuba in Central America, as well as another Vietnam. The fighting, however, continued.

The Salvadoran precedent of support for a democratic center was widely recognized after the events of 1986 in the Philippines, where the United States had long supported the dictator Ferdinand Marcos. But his despotism, economic mismanagement, transparent corruption, and the military's abuses had fueled public discontent and a rebirth of the communist guerrilla force called the Nationalist People's Army. In the absence of basic reforms, it appeared that the guerrillas might defeat the poorly trained and badly led Philippine army. Nevertheless, Marcos refused to heed suggestions for reform and, to prove his legitimacy, called for snap elections. He was confident that he could manipulate and control such elections as he had done before, but in this case the opposition proved overwhelming. The opposition candidate, Corazon Cojuangco Aquino, was the widow of the popular opposition leader Benigno Aquino, who in 1983 had been assassinated at the Manila airport upon returning from exile in the United States. After the assassination, Corazon Aquino, whose tempered manner and conciliatory approach attracted worldwide support, became both a symbol of democracy and a rallying point for the opposition. When it became obvious that he would not win the election, Marcos tried to alter the results with widespread fraud, but, because the election was closely monitored by international observers and the news media, the fraud was clearly visible. Thus Marcos lost his legitimacy even while "winning" another term. The United States encouraged him to step down. When top army commanders defected, Marcos fled to Hawaii and Corazon Aquino became president.

Also in 1986 the Reagan administration helped the Haitian people to oust Jean-Claude "Baby Doc" Duvalier, who had succeeded his father as dictator of the Western Hemisphere's poorest state. The United States first advised Duvalier not to use force against protesting crowds and then furnished him with an airplane to flee to France. Previously, the U.S. government had backed the military juntas in Haiti in the name of communist containment, and it had often looked the other way as vicious dictators tortured, killed, and otherwise silenced their enemies, real or imagined. The Reagan administration now declared its new policy: "The American people believe in human rights and oppose tyranny in whatever form, whether of the left or the right." [8] Under this variation of Carter's human rights policy, the United States would support those struggling for democracy and oppose not just radical Marxist regimes but also pro-American military dictatorships.

And it did so. In 1987, after considerable turmoil in South Korea which had flared on and off for years, the military government was persuaded to promise free elections for the presidency. Administration pressure on South Korea, a key U.S. ally and beneficiary of U.S. aid, had encouraged the long-awaited transition. Similar pressure on Chile resulted in an election that displaced its military leader, Gen. Augusto Pinochet, and opened the way for the establishment of democracy.

WAS THE REAGAN DOCTRINE A SUCCESS?

Although the Reagan administration invoked its claim of a global pro-democratic tide to support the resistance movements in Afghanistan, Angola, and Nicaragua, the insurgencies it supported in the name of spreading freedom often fell considerably short of that virtue. Indeed, the administration's emphasis on human rights in many cases was compromised by the absence of moderate factions that had any chance of taking power. For Reagan it became a matter of identifying and supporting the lesser of evils. In Afghanistan the opponents to Soviet rule were Islamic fundamentalists, who, if they won, were more likely to establish an Iranian-style theocracy than a democracy and to fragment the Muslim world further. Still, that they were a genuine resistance movement could not be doubted. In Angola, Jonas Savimbi, the rebel leader representing Angola's largest tribal group, was trained in the People's Republic of China and was quite willing to rely on racist South Africa for help. And in Nicaragua some of the principal contra commanders were former members of Somoza's detested National Guard. Reagan was ultimately pragmatic in these cases; he supported all opponents of the Soviet Union in order to weaken it.

The contrasts between Afghanistan and Nicaragua were, in this respect, instructive. In Afghanistan the resistance to the Soviet-imposed government had genuine popular support. These so-called freedom fighters fought courageously and successfully against the Soviet army despite their general lack of modern weapons. As a result, many nations were sympathetic to the rebels; in fact, the Muslim states were largely united in their condemnation of Moscow. As for the United States, unlike its support for the contra war in Nicaragua, which most states in Latin America and elsewhere opposed, America's covert assistance to the Afghan resistance was not condemned by neighboring states. Moreover, at home it had congressional and popular support.

8. President Reagan's March 14 Message to Congress, *New York Times*, March 15, 1986.

Lack of congressional and public support for the Nicaraguan contras left Reagan with only one option when the presidents of Costa Rica, Nicaragua, El Salvador, Honduras, and Guatemala agreed to a regional peace plan in 1987. He had to support the Contadora initiative because if the plan failed and if its failure could be clearly attributed to the Sandinistas' unwillingness to open up Nicaragua to genuine democratization, as stipulated by the peace plan, he might regain support for further financial assistance of the contras. But the Democratic-controlled Congress remained disenchanted with the contras, whose ties to the U.S. government were obvious despite administration denials, and used the peace plan as a reason not to fund any more military aid. Such assistance, it was claimed, would only thwart efforts to bring peace to Nicaragua and the region. Thus the administration's plan to overthrow the Sandinistas seemed doomed to failure. This appeared even more certain after the five Central American presidents, over the protests of the United States, called for the disbandment of the contras, most of them in Honduras, by December. But there was no enforcement provision, so the contras remained alive.

But, more important, Sandinista leader Daniel Ortega and his military aides had consolidated power during their ten years in office, and they expected to be able to use their control of the government, including the police and army, to ensure an electoral victory that would give them international legitimacy and eliminate any possible rationale for further U.S. assistance to the contras. Like Marcos in the Philippines, they certainly did not expect to lose and to relinquish their power; as good Marxists, they believed they represented the masses. But lose they did. Despite Sandinista control of the government and efforts to intimidate opposition candidates and rallies, as well as the holdup of congressionally approved funds for the opposition, Ortega lost to Violeta Chamorro, widow of the anti-Somoza newspaper editor whose assassination had rallied the Sandinista-led revolution that brought the dictator Somoza down.

Whoever should have received the credit for the defeat of the Sandinistas—the contras and Ronald Reagan, or the five Central American presidents led by Costa Rica's Oscar Arias, or the Nicaraguan people who had the courage to vote against an oppressive regime, or the Sandinistas themselves for believing they could survive an unpopular draft and a mismanaged economy in a relatively free election—there was no doubt of the consequences. For the Salvadoran guerrillas, the loss of Nicaraguan political support and military assistance constituted a serious setback to their campaign to overthrow the government or negotiate a favorable settlement that would give them a share of the power. For Castro, who had served as an idol for the Sandinistas and a source of help and support, it meant further isolation as he was the only remaining revolutionary in Latin America. As for Nicaragua, the solid defeat of the Sandinistas gave that country a second opportunity to build a democracy, to reintegrate the contras into the fabric of Nicaraguan society, to reconcile political opponents, and to reestablish cordial relations with the United States.

Whether the results of the Nicaraguan elections were attributed to the Reagan Doctrine or not, the doctrine had to be judged at least a partial success. It was a cost-effective means of putting pressure on Moscow, which had to spend an estimated $10-20 billion a year (compared with less than $1 billion annually for the United States) to preserve the gains it had achieved in the 1970s. In 1988, therefore, a number of the regional conflicts in which the United States and the Soviet Union had been engaged came to an end. In Afghanistan, Gorbachev, realizing that the war was an unending drain and a political embarrassment, decided to withdraw Soviet forces. In Angola, after years of fruitless negotiations, the Cubans agreed to pull out their forces, and the South Africans agreed to pull back their forces and grant independence to neighboring Namibia, which they had governed since World War I. These arrangements were followed by a settlement of the Angolan civil war and a largely effective effort by the United Nations to hasten the region's democratic transition. In Cambodia the Vietnamese agreed to withdraw their army, which had invaded that country earlier and overthrown the pro-Chinese Pol Pot regime, responsible for the genocide of over 1 million of its own 8 million people. Gorbachev had to resolve these regional quarrels because by 1987 it had become clear that he needed to conserve his resources for investment in the stagnating Soviet economy. The prerequisite was an armistice in the Cold War so that the Soviet leader could greatly reduce spending on the huge Soviet military establishment and unpromising foreign policy involvements. But the Soviet Union did not suffer a set of total defeats or the United States a series of unqualified triumphs. In Afghanistan, Angola, Ethiopia (where America's Arab friends, notably Saudi Arabia, had supported the opposition), and Cambodia, Marxist regimes retained power. The United States had compelled the Soviet and Vietnamese withdrawals, but it had not achieved its declared goal of replacing Marxist regimes with democratic governments.

ABUSES OF THE REAGAN DOCTRINE: THE IRAN-CONTRA SCANDAL

In one area of its execution the Reagan Doctrine tarnished the president's reputation among the public. In 1987 Reagan's competence, integrity, and sense of judgment were laid open to question when it was revealed that profits from secret arms sales to Iran, now an anti-American Islamic theocracy, had been used to fund the Nicaraguan contras from late 1984 to 1986, a period when the U.S. Congress had expressly forbidden the use of U.S. funds for this purpose. In fact, in an end run around Congress the administration had shifted the conduct of the contra war from the Central Intelligence Agency (CIA) to the National Security Council (NSC) staff. Both operations were reputedly run by the CIA director, William Casey, and his point man in the NSC, Oliver North, a marine lieutenant colonel.

Referred to in the later congressional investigation as the only "five-star" lieutenant colonel in the U.S. military, North supervised the arms sales made to Iran in the hope that U.S. hostages, seized in Lebanon by pro-Iranian terrorists, would be released. He also directed the raising of private funds for the contras from tax-exempt organizations and from wealthy U.S. citizens and foreign governments. Moreover, North commanded a vast network of arms dealers, ships, and airplanes to supply the contras, for whom he also provided tactical intelligence and advice on how to conduct the war. The NSC thus became a "shadow government," which, in turn, organized the secret campaign to direct and fund the contra war effort. When the operation was discovered, the NSC attempted a coverup to minimize the president's role in these events—relevant documents were shredded or smuggled out of NSC offices. Moreover, throughout the operation the administration kept any knowledge of what it was doing from Congress; indeed, it lied to Congress. Furthermore, as the story broke, the president first denied knowledge of many of the details of these events, making it appear as if his deputies had taken the foreign policy of the United States into their own hands.

Public opinion polls showed that most Americans thought Reagan was lying, and the congressional hearings held made it plain that he was actively involved and informed, especially on the contras. Thus he suddenly reversed gears and claimed that he knew about everything except the diversion of funds, but he further argued that the congressional restrictions did not apply to him or his staff. The secrecy with which the Iran and contra operations were carried out, however, suggested that the administration knew very well that it was breaking the law even though when Congress had first forbidden military assistance, the administration had claimed repeatedly that it was obeying the law. All the participants, once they were caught, claimed to be acting only out of patriotic motives; in several cases, however, their patriotism seemed well greased by private gain.

Reagan damaged himself badly by this affair. He was, after all, the presidential candidate who had accused his predecessor of weakness in dealing with the Iranian hostage situation. Under his own leadership, Reagan vowed, the United States would "never negotiate with terrorists," let alone sell them weapons. He had consistently projected an image of toughness and confidence, and he had claimed that the nation could "stand tall" again. Many Americans shared this new sense of patriotism and regarded the president as the man who made them proud again and who could—and did—stand up to the Soviets. But Reagan had almost done the impossible by making Carter's hostage policy look good; Carter had not sent arms to Khomeini in the hope that U.S. hostages would be returned in exchange. Even President Reagan's admirers and supporters were puzzled. They knew that if congressional investigators had been able to find a "smoking gun" linking the scandal to the Oval Office, Reagan might, like Nixon before him, have faced impeachment for his violation of federal laws. As it was, he emerged from the crisis and left office with a clouded reputation, and the Iran-contra scandal haunted the administration of Reagan's successor, George Bush.

ALLIANCE POLITICS IN THE LATE COLD WAR

The Reagan administration's early attacks on détente, its preoccupation with rearmament, its reluctance to engage in arms control negotiations, and its vigorous pursuit of the Reagan Doctrine exerted great pressure on the Soviet Union throughout the 1980s. This pressure exacerbated the already strong tensions within the Warsaw Pact, where long years of political repression and economic stagnation had left its people increasingly frustrated and restive.

Along the way, the renewed Cold War also strained the Western alliance and provoked public demonstrations from Washington to Bonn. Old questions resurfaced about the status of Western Europe as a potential superpower battleground, about the dominant role of the United States in NATO, and about the freedom of each member of NATO to pursue its own foreign policy. But the most important confrontation came over the issue of new Soviet missile deployments, which compelled the United States to propose its own series of new installations of intermediate-range missiles in Europe. With both alliances wavering, the outcome was very much in doubt: Would NATO disintegrate first because of its members' internal differences? Or would the Warsaw Pact succumb to its own deficiencies and to the mounting pressure from the West?

Thus the 1980s was a decade of great volatility on both sides of the iron curtain. What few people anticipated, however, was that this latest round of alliance posturing was a prelude to resolution of the post-World War II division of Europe. The curtain was rapidly falling on the Cold War.

POLAND AND THE RISE OF SOLIDARITY

The first crack in the Soviet empire came in Poland, where in 1980 a labor union, asserting first its economic rights and then its political demands, led the Soviet-backed communist government to impose martial law. This crackdown, reminiscent of past actions in Eastern Europe, further inflamed East-West hostilities.

It was ironic that it was in Poland, a so-called people's democracy and a communist state that purported to represent and protect the interests of the working class, where a truly spontaneous workers' revolution against their exploiters occurred and threatened the Communist Party's monopoly of power and control. Stimulated by a failing economy stemming from poor political leadership, inefficient bureaucratic planning, and mismanagement, Polish workers demanded the right to form their own independent trade union, which would have the right to strike. Such a demand was unheard of in a communist country where the party claimed to embody the workers' aspirations. In wanting their own union, the Polish workers rejected this claim and challenged the basis of the party's legitimacy.

After strikes brought the government down, the new political leadership recognized the right of the workers to form their own union, called Solidarity. In effect, this eliminated the party's monopoly of power. Solidarity then began to issue its demands—demands that were not only economic but also political. As the party-controlled government retreated before each demand, the demands increased and the party withdrew further in the face of threatened strikes. With each success, Solidarity grew more militant, publicly asserting that it was "the authentic voice of the working class" and announcing support for other East European workers who might wish to form independent unions. Domestically, it favored free parliamentary elections, free speech, and a voice in government policy, including the running of the economy. Although the Soviets accused Solidarity of provocative behavior—seeking "political power"—they refrained from invading Poland.

This restraint contrasted sharply with Soviet behavior in Hungary (1956) and Czechoslovakia (1968), where the Soviet army had intervened when the Communist Party's monopoly of power was threatened. And Poland, the nation through which every Western invader of Russia had marched and through which the Soviet Union had projected its power into the center of Europe since 1945, was geographically far more critical than those two countries had been. As the situation grew more intolerable in Moscow's eyes, the danger of the Polish "disease" spreading to other East European states, perhaps even to the Soviet Union, led the Soviets to hold very visible Warsaw Pact military maneuvers in hopes of frightening the Poles. The Soviet Union could afford neither a weakening nor a collapse of its hold on central and Eastern Europe, nor a dilution of controls at home.

But the risks and costs of intervention also were great. The Soviets recognized that Solidarity was not just a trade union seeking better working conditions; it also represented a well-organized mass movement. In suppressing Solidarity, the Soviets faced the real possibility of a clash with units of the Polish army, the costs of occupation, and the difficulties of pacifying the population and getting it to work. In addition, the cost of paying off Poland's $27 billion debt to the West would be a drain at a time when the Soviet economy was in trouble; maintaining the separate détente with America's European allies would become more difficult; and the possible establishment of a better relationship with the new U.S. administration would be jeopardized. Reagan could exploit a Soviet invasion of Poland to rally the NATO allies. Thus for more than a year Moscow demonstrated remarkable restraint. When the move against Solidarity finally came, probably as a result of Soviet pressure, it was the Polish military and police who arrested the union leaders and imposed martial law in Poland.

Whether Moscow ordered the intervention or the Polish government acted on its own to forestall Soviet action, there can be little doubt of increasing Soviet pressure on the Polish authorities to crack down on what the Soviets called "counterrevolutionary" elements. Solidarity, by winning the sympathies of almost 10 million members, about one-third of the population, was a living refutation of the party's claim of representation; it symbolized the bankruptcy of communism. Unable either to produce a decent standard of living or to tolerate a minimal degree of freedom, communism in Poland had forfeited its legitimacy. The lesson was not lost on other parts of Eastern Europe, where the struggle by Solidarity served as an inspiration and a precursor of greater challenges to come.

THE MISSILE DEBATE IN EUROPE

In Western Europe one almost heard a collective sigh of relief that the Red Army had not invaded Poland. The Polish army's crackdown was considered a domestic affair, not a matter over which détente was to be sacrificed. This reaction reflected anxieties in the region about the growing hostilities between East and West, with the Western Europeans finding themselves trapped in the middle. Indeed, it had become apparent in the early 1980s that the Western Europeans wanted to pursue an independent political policy while still counting on the United States for their defense; they wanted, it was said, to "uncouple" themselves politically from Washington but to remain "coupled" to it militarily. But even the military relationship was called into question when West European opinion appeared to go back on a decision, collectively agreed to by the United States and Western Europe, to meet the threat of new intermediate-range Soviet missiles (SS-20s) with a new generation of NATO missiles (Pershing IIs).

Since the beginning of NATO the Europeans had wanted the alliance strategy to emphasize deterrence. Europe had had more than enough wars in the twentieth century. The NATO army, therefore, was to serve as a "plate glass" that, once the Soviet invasion occurred, would sound the alarm and call in the U.S. strategic forces. The army's purpose was not to fight a long war like World War II, even when it was reinforced by 300,000 American soldiers. The presence of the troops emphasized America's stake in Europe and clarified to Moscow that any attack would result in war with the United States. The fear of nuclear retaliation by the United States, it was reasoned, would deter the Soviet Union from invading Western Europe.

After the first Soviet missile test in 1957, the key question had been: Would the United States risk its own survival for the defense of Europe? Some observers had said no, but most had been uncertain, although U.S. strategic forces at the time had been superior to those of the Soviet Union. After the 1970s and the emergence of strategic parity, the answer to this question had grown even more doubtful. It had been one thing for the United States to attack the Soviet Union when the Soviets could not attack the United States, or when America had a vast strategic superiority; it was quite another to do so when the Soviet Union could retaliate fully. Was America's strategic deterrence still credible? Washington's standard reply was yes, but in Western Europe there was more doubt than ever that this was really so.

The intermediate-range nuclear force (INF) deployments were supposed to reassure the allies, who were troubled by the Soviet SS-20s. Instead of being strengthened by new American resolve, however, the NATO "marriage," in the words of the French foreign minister, came close to a divorce. Huge crowds throughout Western Europe (except in France) demonstrated for months against the proposed deployment of the American missiles, with the greatest opposition in West Germany. There the Protestant churches, the universities, the Social Democratic opposition party, and a new political movement, the pacifist and environmentalist Green Party, were all opposed to the deployment. The street demonstrators' accusations were many: America was stoking the arms race; America intended to fight a war limited to Europe; America was the aggressive party in the Cold War. Moscow was not considered the chief threat. It was Washington, which had defended Western Europe since 1949 and had not yet deployed a single Pershing II, that was charged with being the bigger menace to peace.

Certainly the demonstrators did not represent the majority opinion in their respective countries. In all NATO countries support for the alliance remained generally strong; so did faith in deterrence. Nevertheless, the peace movement reflected widespread concern about Reagan's antidétente foreign policy and an increased fear of war. The Soviets shrewdly exploited the protests. By repeatedly saying they were eager to negotiate the issue, the Soviets appeared reasonable and put the United States on the defensive.

Reagan felt compelled to respond to the demonstrations in Europe and to the Soviet initiative. He proposed a "zero option" whereby the United States would not deploy any of its Pershings and cruise missiles if the Soviets dismantled all of their intermediate-range missiles, which had a maximum range of 1,500 miles, including the SS-20s. It sounded good; all such missiles were to be eliminated. What could be more beneficial for peace and more moral than doing away with a whole class of dangerous weapons? The United States, however, did not expect Moscow to accept this offer. The zero-zero option was a public relations move; by turning it down, the Soviets would enable the U.S. deployment to go ahead as a clearly necessary and defensive move, the street demonstrations would decline, and the blame for the American missile buildup in Europe would be placed at the Kremlin's door.

The intra-NATO "missile crisis," however, had by then done considerable damage to the alliance. For many Europeans the protests against deployment expressed their concern about Reagan's foreign policy and, more generally, their desire to reduce the risk of war. For many Americans the protests were a reminder that the Europeans did not appear ready to take the measures necessary for their own defense. Although their combined population and industrial output exceeded that of the Soviet Union, America's European allies were still unwilling to raise the size of their conventional forces. They wanted to continue relying on the American strategic deterrent at a time when the superpowers strategically neutralized one another.

In the United States demands began for the withdrawal of some or all American forces from Europe over a period of several years. Most of the American defense budget allocated for hardware and maintenance was not spent on strategic forces; half went for the upkeep of the more expensive conventional forces whose primary mission was the defense of Europe. When the alliance had been formed, the European nations had vividly remembered the failure of appeasing a totalitarian regime, the defeats and suffering of World War II, their postwar collapse, and the need for American protection against the new threat from the East. By the 1970s and 1980s the memory of having appeased Nazi Germany was fading; the story of this appeasement was not even a part of the history or consciousness of the new generation that had grown up in a peaceful Europe. Protected by the United States, that generation, like many older Europeans, had seemingly forgotten the realities of international politics and took peace for granted.

Only in France, which had deployed a growing independent deterrent force, was the popular historical association of national independence and pride in the nation's armed forces still alive. There were no massive antinuclear and anti-American demonstrations. Indeed, Socialist president François Mitterrand told the West German parliament in 1983, "I'm against the Euromissiles. But I notice two terrible simple things about the current debate: Pacifism is in the West and the Euromissiles are in the East. I consider this an unequal relationship." [9] Such an imbalance, he predicted, would ensure war, not avoid it.

But elsewhere in Western Europe, defense had apparently become an

9. Quoted in Flora Lewis, "Missiles and Pacifists," *New York Times,* November 18, 1983.

American responsibility. Parties that were formerly stalwart defenders of
NATO, such as the British Labour Party and the West German Social Democrats, now deserted the alliance. Given the changes in the four decades since
World War II, one had to wonder whether, if NATO had been proposed in
the 1980s, there would be an alliance at all, and if so, which countries would
have joined it?

NATO THREATENED FROM WITHIN

By the mid-1980s one thing had become very clear: the intermediate-range
nuclear weapons issue was not primarily a military issue but a critical political
one. The decision to deploy the new generation of ground-based nuclear missiles in Europe had been an alliance decision. But Moscow refused to accept
any American deployment and rejected the principle of superpower equality.
The Soviet purpose was clearly to manipulate Europe's fear of war to drive a
wedge between the NATO allies, especially between Europe and the United
States. Would the alliance survive? The Soviets had no reason to compromise
in separate arms control negotiations on this issue; they had every reason to
test the strength of the European peace movement in the hope of aborting the
American deployment. The Soviets could deploy their missiles and target every European capital, but the United States could not deploy missiles in Europe that could hit the Soviet Union. What Moscow had was not negotiable;
what NATO had, was.

In Moscow's attempt to undermine the alliance through the missile debate, NATO had not confronted such a serious issue since German rearmament in the early 1950s and the Berlin crisis after 1957. These two issues had
involved the future of the alliance, its ability to face down intimidation and
remain united. Above all, they had involved a struggle for West Germany,
NATO's strongest European member, without whose territory the alliance
could not defend itself. Moscow obviously wanted to detach West Germany
from NATO, and Washington wanted to keep that country within the alliance. Given the political stakes for each superpower, should it have been surprising that American-Soviet relations reached a low point in the early 1980s,
regardless of who the leaders were? Neither side was willing to compromise in
what it regarded as a fundamental test of wills. Despite considerable pressure
on Reagan to be more accommodating, he insisted on going ahead with the
deployment. When that began during the winter months of 1983-1984, was it
really a surprise that Moscow walked out of all arms control negotiations in
order to raise the fear of war in Western Europe and to push it into a greater
neutralism and pacifism?

For a time, however, the missile crisis faded as the deployment occurred.
Then in a complete turnabout, Gorbachev accepted the earlier Reagan proposal for the complete elimination of intermediate-range missiles for both

powers. The Soviet leader needed a relaxation of international tensions in order to give priority to domestic affairs and rebuilding the Soviet economy. The administration's determination had paid off. It had not abandoned the deployment, nor, when the Soviets responded by walking out of all arms control negotiations, had it delayed deployment, despite widespread calls to do so. Unable to achieve Soviet goals with threats, Moscow capitulated.

The "zero-zero" solution was a significant achievement, trading about 1,400 Soviet warheads for just over 300 U.S. warheads. This move eliminated an entire class of weapons rather than—as in SALTs I and II—placing limits on their deployment. Moscow also accepted intrusive verification procedures to monitor the agreement. More fundamentally, in retrospect *the Soviet turnabout was the first sign that the Soviet Union needed a cease-fire in the Cold War.* U.S. resolution had paid off, undermining not the NATO position but that of the Warsaw Pact.

But it also was clear that Europeans' confidence in the United States had severely eroded since Vietnam. During the Nixon-Ford détente years they had complained about possible U.S.-Soviet deals at Europe's expense; during the Carter years, of vacillation and weakness; and during the Reagan years, of too much machismo or "Ramboism." Europe's fear of war also had risen. Not Soviet behavior but the arms race itself was seen as the critical danger, as was "provocative" American behavior in remote regions that could ignite a head-on clash in Europe. These attitudes translated into growing public doubts about the value of NATO.

The European members of the alliance remained unwilling to reexamine the assumption they had accepted for more than forty years—namely, that the Soviet Union was the naturally dominant Eurasian power against which Western Europe could not mobilize sufficient counterbalancing power without outside help. Such an assumption was demeaning for states that had for centuries been the leading international actors and that, by the 1980s, had become the dependents of an overseas protector. Ironically, their growing skepticism toward NATO coincided with its victory over the Warsaw Pact.

At home, many Americans by the late 1980s had recaptured much of their confidence in America's mission of defending and, where possible, advancing democratic values. Although Reagan's talk of a turning of the communist tide and the inevitable global sweep of democracy was at first widely dismissed as self-serving propaganda, such were the emerging trends in his final year as president.

FROM CONFRONTATION TO CONCILIATION

Although the tensions of the 1980s ruptured the cohesion of both alliances, in the end, as Reagan left office in January 1989, U.S.-Soviet relations were better than they had been since the two had been allies against Nazi Germany during World War II. How could that be? How, in a few years, could such a profound transformation of superpower relations have occurred?

The rapidity of the change in the two superpowers' relationship was astounding. The Cold War had spanned more than four decades, exceeding the time that elapsed from the beginning of World War I (1914) to the end of World War II (1945). The transformation of superpower relations was even more surprising because the 1970s had been a period of great confusion and self-doubt for the United States. Having withdrawn from Vietnam without victory—some would say defeated—the United States was domestically divided. The Watergate scandal had undermined public trust in the presidency. The U.S. economy and that of the other Western nations had suffered oil shocks and stagflation in 1973 and 1979—the year the Somoza government fell to the Sandinistas in Nicaragua; the Iranians seized the U.S. embassy and fifty-two American hostages; the Soviets invaded Afghanistan; the Vietnamese, after invading Cambodia in December 1978, established a pro-Soviet government there; and a pro-Soviet communist faction seized power in Grenada. It was a decade to deflate any country's self-confidence. By contrast, the Soviet Union had appeared confident and optimistic about the future course of international politics.

Soviet policy was at a high point in the 1970s. The Soviet Union had attained strategic parity and a conventional capability to project Soviet power beyond Eurasia; and it sought to gain a geopolitical advantage to exploit America's mood of withdrawal. The Soviet leadership saw the Soviet Union's growth of military power as part of a shift in the "correlation of forces" from West to East. That strength would allow Moscow to exploit opportunities it saw in the Third World to weaken the West while simultaneously deterring American military countermoves. Leonid Brezhnev and his colleagues believed that the more military power they acquired, the greater would be the American need to be accommodating. In addition, by encouraging Third World governments to adopt Marxist-Leninist one-party governments, Moscow believed that Soviet gains would be irreversible and cumulative. Convinced that the United States was a declining power, Moscow calculated that Washington had no choice but to adjust to these new circumstances and accept the consequences.

The apparent successes of the Soviet Union were, however, deceptive for two reasons. The first was the failure of the Soviet economy. Its economic growth rate, 5 percent in the 1960s and only 2 percent by the early 1970s, had stagnated by 1980. Capable only of producing a plentiful supply of weapons, the Soviet economy could no longer supply basic goods and public services. By the late 1980s the Soviets were importing many necessities and basic foodstuffs were rationed. After harvests failed repeatedly in the 1970s, grains and produce had to be imported from the United States and other countries. The centralized Soviet economy was nearing a breakdown. Gorbachev, who when first appointed general secretary in 1985 had believed that economic growth could be stimulated by more discipline in the workplace, less worker absenteeism and drunkenness, and higher productivity, by 1987 realized the severity of the crisis he faced. The second reason for the Soviet turnabout was the cost of Brezhnev's foreign policy. With a gross domestic product (GDP) half that of the United States and a military budget that the CIA then estimated at 16 percent of GDP (compared with 6 percent for the United States and 3 percent for Western Europe), the civilian economy was starved. In fact, later Soviet figures showed that military spending was between 25 percent and 30 percent of Soviet GDP.

Outside the Soviet Union, Moscow's unrelenting arms buildup and expansionist activities in the Third World had produced fear and suspicion of Soviet intentions. The result was the very encirclement the Soviet Union had long feared. In Asia the growing Soviet threat allowed the United States to play divide-and-rule, attracting China to the West in a major shift of power. Thus the Soviet Union, like Germany at the turn of the century, created its own worst nightmare and increased its sense of vulnerability.

The United States played no small role in this scenario. American-supplied weapons raised the price of the Afghanistan intervention, placing victory out of reach, and prolonged the civil war in Angola. Although the administration did not succeed in overthrowing the Sandinistas in Nicaragua, the Soviet effort to sustain the latter was the only bargain in an otherwise unending financial drain, as was the continuing civil war in Ethiopia. The imperial outposts that had looked so promising only ten years earlier had now lost their luster, and support for such proxies as Cuba and Vietnam had become prohibitively expensive. Gorbachev had no choice but to see what Marxists always had prided themselves on recognizing: objective reality. The Soviet Union, with a structurally unsound economy, surrounded by a Western coalition of NATO, Japan, and China, and led by the United States with a resurgent economy (despite its rapidly increasing federal and trade deficits), was forced to recognize the need for rapprochement with the United States.

The Soviet weakness and consequent desire to end the Cold War first became apparent in 1987 when the Soviet delegates walked back into the INF talks they had earlier walked out of and accepted virtually the entire package of U.S. demands. Even more significant, in a series of pronouncements Gorbachev and his supporters contradicted long-held Soviet doctrine and positions by stating that: (1) the "all-human value of peace" took precedence over the class struggle, meaning that the unilateral pursuit of advantage to extend socialism could jeopardize the peace; (2) Soviet (and American) security could not be achieved unless there was "common security," suggesting that if one side armed and then the other responded in kind, as in the past, the initiating side would be left less, not more, secure; (3) force and the threat of force should no longer be instruments of foreign policy; (4) security should be achieved by political means—that is, resolving disputes by compromise; (5) in the future "reasonable sufficiency" would be the new standard by which the Soviet Union would judge the military strength it needed; (6) Soviet forces along the iron curtain would be reorganized in a "nonoffensive defense" so that NATO, whose war plans called for no advance eastward, could feel reassured; and (7) negotiations between NATO and the Warsaw Treaty Organization should reduce the levels of troops and arms and, wherever asymmetries favored one side, the stronger power—such as the Soviet Union in tanks and personnel carriers—should reduce to the level of the weaker side rather than the opposite.

In the Third World Moscow deemphasized the revolutionary struggle for national liberation and raised questions about the future of socialism in the developing countries. In addition, by withdrawing from Afghanistan and helping to resolve several other regional conflicts, Gorbachev reduced Soviet foreign policy costs and diminished the likelihood of new conflicts with the United States and the chances that the current ones would undermine the emerging improvement in U.S.-Soviet relations. More broadly, Gorbachev sought to deprive the American-led coalition encircling the Soviet bloc of an enemy. His "charm offensive," including visits abroad, was very effective in Europe, especially in West Germany, where "Gorby" rated far higher as a statesman and peacemaker than either Reagan or his vice president and successor, George Bush. The Soviet leader also normalized relations with China in 1989. Among two of the many dramatic moves made to improve the Soviet image, Moscow confessed that its intervention in Afghanistan had violated Soviet law and international norms of behavior, and, after years of denying accusations that it had violated the 1972 ABM treaty, admitted the violation.

Gorbachev therefore changed priorities and launched his program of *glasnost* (openness) and *perestroika* (restructuring) to revitalize Soviet society and the economy. He realized that the two were intimately related: without more openness in Soviet society, without harnessing the energies of the Soviet people, long used to suppression and obedience, the Soviet economy would not recover from its stagnation. Thus Gorbachev advocated strengthening civil liberties—more freedom in the press, arts, literature, scholarship, and even in the reexamination of the darker side of Soviet history, long kept secret. He also called for decentralizing the economy, cutting back on the pervasive role of the Moscow-based central planning bureaucracy, and permitting the profit motive and market forces a greater role in stimulating production, including a degree of private ownership and entrepreneurship. And he urged the removal of the Communist Party from the daily management of the economy and other sectors of Soviet life, permitted real but limited competition in party and legislative elections, and allowed the Soviet parliament to assert itself, plus a host of other reforms.

But despite Gorbachev's exhortations and reform efforts, there was strong resistance from the 19 million party and government bureaucrats who had a vested interest in the status quo. Change threatened their jobs, status, and privileges. Opposition to Gorbachev was further fueled by the fear that the loosening of central controls would be harmful, if not fatal, politically. It was the Russians who in the Soviet Union, as in czarist Russia, had controlled most of the levers of power and were particularly concerned that such a devolution of power away from Moscow might result in more political self-determination by the more than 100 non-Russian nationalities. Economic decentralization would then spill over into political decentralization. In other words, the fundamental structural reforms required by the Soviet Union might threaten not only the party's sole control of power but also Moscow's imperial control over its own vast country. The ongoing unrest in the Baltic republics (Estonia, Latvia, and Lithuania), especially the demands for independence, and similar agitation in Georgia and the central Asian republics, were in this respect very worrisome. This uneasiness was compounded by the successful efforts of the countries of Eastern Europe to throw off their communist yokes. Quite contrary to Marxist analysis, the political system determined the fate of the economy rather than the other way around. The Soviet political system had become the greatest obstacle to economic modernization. That was why, preoccupied at home, Gorbachev needed to end the Cold War.

To many, the dismantling of the Berlin Wall in 1989 symbolized the end of the Cold War.

CHAPTER TEN

Ending the Cold War: Negotiating the Terms of Peace

The collapse of the Soviet bloc already had begun by the time George Bush became president in January 1989. Mikhail Gorbachev's reforms were rapidly undermining the Communist Party's hold in Moscow, while the Baltic states were demanding independence and the first streams of East Europeans were making their way across the iron curtain with the reluctant assent of their crippled political leaders. Indeed, many analysts (including George Kennan, the founding father of the containment policy) proclaimed that the Cold

War was effectively over. Others suggested more cautiously that it was coming to a close.

President Bush, a lifelong politician who lacked Ronald Reagan's flamboyance or his convictions, was otherwise a capable and pragmatic leader. His experience as director of the Central Intelligence Agency (CIA), ambassador to China, and U.S. representative to the United Nations left little doubt that he was competent in foreign affairs. When he became president, Bush said he would not use the term *Cold War* to characterize America's relationship with the Soviet Union. He referred instead to a period of U.S.-Soviet relations "beyond containment" in which the principal task would be to integrate the Soviet Union into the "community of nations." In 1990, however, after referring to the "Revolution of '89" in his State of the Union address, Bush said the changes in Eastern Europe had been so striking and momentous that they marked "the beginning of a new era in the world's affairs." This proclamation, though grandiloquent, proved to be an understatement.

In truth, very few observers, including the most experienced and perceptive analysts of international relations, anticipated the sudden collapse of the Soviet system. Most predicted either a prolonged stalemate, a gradual convergence of the capitalist and communist systems, or, more gloomily, an apocalyptic military showdown. The suggestion that one of the two superpowers would simply default and disappear from the world map without a shot being fired and virtually without preconditions would have been rejected as sheer fantasy. For Bush, the principal task of American foreign policy would be to manage this historic transition as smoothly as possible to ensure that the Warsaw Pact's demise would not be overwhelmed by an even greater cataclysm. If that were accomplished, Bush looked forward to a "new world order" in which the attributes of the Western political and economic system could be extended into the former communist bloc and provide the basis for global harmony.

BUSH'S MANAGEMENT OF THE SOVIET IMPLOSION

With the benefit of hindsight, what were some of the signs that the Cold War was, in fact, drawing to a close? At first, the Bush administration was not sure what to believe. In the context of forty years of Cold War and of previously dashed hopes that the Cold War was ending, the administration—and especially the president—tended to be cautious. If Gorbachev were to fall and be replaced by a hard-line conservative, the United States did not want to be caught off guard. Nevertheless, Secretary of State James Baker, a holdover from the Reagan team, acknowledged that Soviet "new thinking" in foreign and defense policies promised possibilities that ten years earlier would have been unimaginable. Uncertainty about Soviet reforms was all the more reason to seize the opportunities represented by Gorbachev. Thus after a period of hesitation the Bush administration followed Reagan's lead and embraced Gorbachev; his continuation in power was good for the United States.

Events, already moving rapidly, only accelerated both within the Soviet Union and beyond as the 1980s ended. In these circumstances, predicting what lay ahead for the Soviet Union was risky business because the changes had come so quickly and had been so unexpected. The year 1990 witnessed growing upheaval in Moscow as the communist system, seventy-three years after its inception, began to crack. It became apparent that the Soviet Union was operating from a position of grave weakness, that Gorbachev's foreign policy amounted to a diplomacy of retreat and damage control. The result was that regardless of who held power in Moscow, the United States had a golden opportunity to exploit its advantages. Any ruler of the Soviet Union, if it survived essentially intact, would face debilitating domestic constraints on the conduct of foreign policy.

As the "victorious" power in the Cold War, the United States had to give thought to its terms of peace: What kind of post-Cold War world did the United States wish to see? It had, therefore, to define its own goals. Even if Gorbachev did not survive, the United States needed to take advantage of the time he was in office to codify Soviet concessions to ensure that future Soviet foreign policy would be as irreversible as possible. Granted, American influence on Soviet internal affairs was limited, and the ultimate success of *perestroika* (restructuring) depended on events in the Soviet Union, but if the United States were responsive to Gorbachev's policies and proposals, it could support and assist the process of domestic reform and bolster his position in the Kremlin. Washington's principal recourse, therefore, was to lend its support for the peaceful reform of the Soviet state given that both superpowers were moving beyond the Cold War toward an unknown future.

Although the Soviet Union's negotiating position was weak—a problem that was to worsen as Eastern Europe defected, ethnic nationalism grew, and communism as a political and economic system vanished—the country had not surrendered unconditionally. Nor had the United States won a total victory, as it had in World War II against Germany; it could not impose its terms on Moscow. Moreover, a victory that humiliated the loser would result in a peace built on sand. World War I had ended with a victor's peace imposed on Germany, but it had lasted only as long as Germany remained weak. After World War II both Germany and Japan were treated in a more conciliatory fashion. Neither, therefore, had been bent on revenge. For a durable peace, the Soviet Union, too, had to find the emerging international order hospitable. Thus the two powers engaged in complex negotiations about the terms on which the Cold War was to be ended, as well as about the construction and shape of the new balance of power.

The ending of the Cold War depended basically on the fulfillment of three conditions: (1) the dismantlement of Joseph Stalin's empire in central and Eastern Europe, (2) the decolonization of Leonid Brezhnev's Third World outposts, and (3) a reduction in arms and a stable nuclear balance. When these conditions were fulfilled, Bush was thrust into the tenuous position of managing the disintegration of the Soviet Union and directing the transition of U.S. bilateral relations toward the largest successor state, Boris Yeltsin's Russia.

DISMANTLING STALIN'S EMPIRE

Events in China during the summer of 1989 served as a prelude to the popular uprisings in Eastern Europe and suggested that the erosion of communism's appeal and legitimacy had extended to the world's most populous communist state. As in Moscow, dissidents in Beijing were granted greater freedom to express their grievances in public and to exercise some degree of political freedom. After they erected a miniature Statue of Liberty in Tiananmen Square, however, the communist government moved in with tanks and brutally squashed the growing rebellion. The worldwide television audience that witnessed these events was understandably horrified by what it saw. But China's decrepit regime dismissed the condemnation of foreign governments and intensified its crackdown on pro-democracy activists. Thus when their time came, the East Europeans were inspired by the Chinese example to accelerate their revolution and guarantee that it could not be turned back.

One key sign of Soviet willingness to end the Cold War was its acceptance of Eastern Europe's rapid moves away from Communist Party control. The conquest and subsequent Stalinization of Eastern Europe, together with the division of Germany, had split the continent after World War II. This division was at the heart of the Cold War confrontation, and only self-determination for Poland, Hungary, Czechoslovakia, and other Eastern European states could end it. Events in the region were critical because each of the major wars of the twentieth century had broken out there. The disintegration of the Austro-Hungarian empire had led to the eruption of successive Balkan wars and World War I; Germany's absorption of Czechoslovakia and attack on Poland had sparked World War II; and the de facto Soviet annexation of Eastern Europe had led to the Cold War.

American foreign policy during World War II had been sensitive to Soviet security concerns in Eastern Europe, but the United States also had been committed to national self-determination, and President Franklin Roosevelt had presumed that after the war Soviet security could be compatible with democratic freedoms. Where communist parties did well, they could be included in coalition governments, reflecting the popular will. Critical in the president's thinking was the knowledge that smaller countries living in the shadow of the Soviet Union would take its security concerns into account in formulating their foreign policies. Roosevelt's thinking reflected that of a traditional great power: small nations living within a superior power's sphere of influence do not have to have governments that reflect the latter's ideological and political values. They *must*, however, be willing to make a virtue out of necessity: to make the best of their geographic situation, to be aware of their constrained freedom and maneuverability, and to acquiesce to the wishes of the regionally dominant power. Finland provided the most concrete example of this relationship.

But Soviet ideology defined security in Marxist terms. Security could be ensured only if potential class enemies were kept out of power altogether. The governments bordering the Soviet Union therefore had to be communist. Even coalition governments in which the Communist Party controlled the major levers of power—military and police—were unacceptable. Eastern Europe, then, was to become a sphere of dominance, with each country having not only communist governments controlled by Moscow but also ideological conformity. As for the Soviet troops stationed throughout Eastern Europe, they were intended not merely to protect these states from perceived Western threats, but also to assure Soviet dominance and adherence to Soviet-style socialism. Without this military presence and occasional Soviet interventions, these governments, unpopular with their people, would not have survived as long as they did.

Could Moscow now separate its ideology from its definition of security? That was the main question in 1989. The initial answer to that question came when the Communist Party in Poland was unable to form a government after its disastrous showing in the relatively free June elections in which the Solidarity movement claimed overwhelming popular support. Because the communists had been repudiated, Solidarity, which had in effect received a mandate to govern, was asked to organize the government. Poland thus formed its first noncommunist—indeed anticommunist—government in the post-World War II era. The military forces, including the security police, were left in communist hands, however, to reassure Moscow about the future course of Poland, a country the Germans had twice marched through in the twentieth century to invade the Soviet Union. In addition, Lech Walesa, Solidarity's leader and spokesman, stated that Poland would remain a member of the Warsaw Pact—just the kind of political sensitivity that Roosevelt had had in mind.

Gorbachev appeared willing to accept such a noncommunist Poland and a more traditional sphere of influence in Eastern Europe for several reasons. One was his preoccupation with worsening domestic matters. Another was that Eastern Europe had not proved to be a "security belt"; instead, it had added to Soviet *insecurity*. Its people were sullen and resentful of the Soviet-imposed regimes, and they had not forgotten that earlier efforts to rid themselves of these regimes had been suppressed militarily. Gorbachev did not want to be confronted with an explosive situation, which, among other things, would be a major, if not fatal, setback to the reemerging détente with the West. The installation of more acceptable and legitimate governments would avoid this confrontation and thus enhance Soviet security. Furthermore, given the strains on the Soviet economy, he could not afford continued subsidies to Poland and the rest of Eastern Europe, all of whose economies were in trouble. It made eminent sense, therefore, to unburden his straining economy and "dump" Eastern Europe on the West, especially West German bankers. Finally, by accepting a more modest sphere of influence, he could resolve a principal issue that had precipitated and prolonged the Cold War.

The dominoes continued to tumble throughout 1989. In Hungary the parliament dropped the word "People" from the country's formal name, and the Communist Party renamed itself the Democratic Socialist Party in order to survive a Polish-style disaster in the upcoming multiparty elections. (Even so, the party was able to keep only 30,000 of its original 720,000 members.) Similarly, Czechoslovakia dropped "Socialist" from its name, and the East German Communist Party also sought to shed its Stalinist skin to better compete in the 1990 elections. In a decision of critical importance, the Hungarian foreign minister opened his country's borders with Austria on September 10, 1989. A free fall ensued when 200,000 East Germans, mostly young skilled workers vital to its industry, fled their country—via Czechoslovakia, Hungary, and Austria—for West Germany. These events demonstrated vividly that communism had lost its grip on the Eastern Europeans. Indeed, the events of 1989 suggested that the legitimacy of all communist regimes throughout the area was in doubt. Even those who had grown up under communism rejected its philosophy and were now able to say so openly. The direction of these events became obvious during what Zbigniew Brzezinski called the "terminal crisis of Communism." [1]

To make the best of the situation, Gorbachev announced that socialist countries had no right to intervene in each other's affairs; each country was responsible for its own destiny. The clear implication was that the Brezhnev Doctrine was dead. To make the point clearly, in late 1989 Gorbachev paid a symbolic visit to Finland, a country that always had been sensitive to Soviet security interests, yet had maintained a relatively autonomous democracy. He presented Finland as a model of a relationship between a big and little coun-

1. Zbigniew Brzezinski, *The Grand Failure* (New York: Scribner's, 1989).

try that were neighbors but had different social systems. Gorbachev also visited East Germany to observe its fortieth anniversary as a communist state.
There he restated the new doctrine of nonintervention that further propelled
the Warsaw Pact's demise. The process gained even more momentum after
Moscow and its four Warsaw Pact allies that had jointly invaded Czechoslovakia in 1968 condemned that invasion as "illegal" and pledged a strict policy
of noninterference in each other's affairs. Moscow issued its own declaration
of repentance.

Gorbachev's actions were most keenly felt in East Germany, where the
hemorrhage of its youth threatened to depopulate the country of 16 million
and mass demonstrations finally led to the removal in December 1989 of its
despotic communist leader, Erich Honecker. In what was a genuine people's
revolution, Soviet troops stood by instead of propping up the regime, and the
new party leader promised radical changes, including free elections in May
1990. Among the first reforms, all restrictions on travel and emigration were
lifted, inciting hundreds of thousands of East Germans to swarm across the
Berlin Wall in the hours after that announcement. Altogether, 1.5 million East
Germans poured across the wall that first weekend to celebrate. As for the
wall itself, entire sections were leveled with sledgehammers, and fragments
were taken home as souvenirs. From its construction in 1961, the wall had
been the symbol of what the Cold War was all about—tyranny versus freedom. Its collapse on November 9, 1989, exactly fifty-one years after Hitler had
unleashed his storm troopers against German Jews in Berlin and throughout
Germany, thus symbolized more than any other event the ending of the Cold
War.

After the fall of the Berlin Wall, the winds of change swept over Czechoslovakia. What was happening there also had great symbolic importance, although it was not widely noted at the time because of the tumult elsewhere.
The great powers had inflicted tremendous injustices on Czechoslovakia, the
only central European democracy before World War II. It was betrayed by
France and England in their efforts to appease Hitler in 1938 and, a decade later, was violently transformed into a communist nation by the Soviets. Its efforts to humanize Czech communism during the Prague Spring of 1968 were
crushed by Soviet tanks. The collapse of the communist regime in Prague,
therefore, also was a sign of the times.

Everywhere in Eastern Europe—in what Ronald Reagan had once called
the "evil empire"—people were saying openly just how evil that empire had
been. They demanded not just the reform of communist parties but their removal from office, ending what many of them viewed as a forty-year-long
foreign occupation. They also called for free elections and interim governments composed mainly of noncommunists. Only in Bulgaria and Romania
did the local communist parties manage to run under new names, with

claims that they had reformed, and easily win the first free elections after the collapse of the Soviet-supported governments.

The United States responded by expressing support for the governments seeking to liberalize, and President Bush provided a visible show of support by visiting Poland and Hungary in 1989. Beyond this effort, however, the Bush administration did not want to arouse Soviet security concerns. Gorbachev, therefore, sought a tacit understanding with Bush: the Soviet leader would continue to support, if not encourage, the transformations in Eastern Europe, and he would not resist the changes even if they went further down the road to "decommunization" than he would have preferred. In short, the United States agreed not to exploit the geopolitical transformation then under way in the Soviet empire in return for Soviet nonintervention. Nor would it jeopardize Soviet security or humiliate Moscow more than already was being done by the popular rejection of communism among its Warsaw Pact allies. Bush also agreed to make concessions—on trade, for example—to help Gorbachev to rebuild the Soviet economy and to show some tolerance for his internal problems. Because it was in the U.S. interest to manage the changes in the Soviet Union and Eastern Europe peacefully, the Gorbachev-Bush bargain held. This deal even applied for a time to the Baltic republics. Gorbachev considered them part of the Soviet Union, while the United States had never recognized their annexation.

Nonviolence was chosen not only by the East European rulers but also by the masses. For forty years the Soviet-imposed regimes had exploited and oppressed their peoples. Violence from below would have been natural as these regimes relented. Instead, the transitions to democracy were almost unnaturally peaceful. Revolutions—for that was what was going on in Eastern Europe—are rarely so orderly. After all, 1989 was the bicentennial celebration of the French Revolution, an act of popular liberation that degenerated into a reign of terror. But, as everyone seemed to understand, such violence in the liberation of Eastern Europe would jeopardize the whole process of change.

Only in Romania was there violence because the regime used force in its attempt to stay in power. Hundreds of people were killed as its dictator, Nicolae Ceausescu, sought in vain to buck the trend in the rest of Eastern Europe. But he failed, as army units defected to the opposition and fought his security forces. Captured as they attempted to flee, Ceausescu and his wife, Elena, were executed after a hasty trial on Christmas Day. With that single exception, it was nonviolence that prevailed. Czechoslovakia's new president, the playwright Vaclav Havel, set the tone by calling on his fellow citizens to act with dignity, honesty, and honor. The slogan of the demonstrators massed in the streets of Prague was "we are not like them."

Equally important, Washington thought it best to allow Eastern Europe's evolution to occur within the broader European context. Even before the

1989 revolutions, the European Community (EC) had decided to revive its movement toward a single market. It was a wise move given the likelihood that U.S. economic problems as well as a diminished Soviet threat would lead to a significant reduction of American forces in Western Europe. The EC also was mindful of stiff Japanese—and to a comparable extent, U.S.—economic competition in the last decade of the century. A single market and currency, the coordination of foreign policies under the Maastricht accords of 1993, and other cooperative efforts represented steps toward a possible European political confederation.

If the task of helping Eastern Europe was now an additional motive for an enlarged EC role, another—and perhaps more important one in the long run—was the rebirth of the German problem. For more than forty years East and West had lived with a divided Germany. They preferred a partitioned Germany, each controlling its part, because it would ensure that Germany would not initiate another war. The terminal crisis of communism in Eastern Europe, however, undermined this division. Two thousand East Germans continued to pour into West Germany, further crippling the East German state, its economy, and its delivery of basic social services. Moreover, as the East German government's authority waned, the calls in East Germany for unification grew stronger every day. To everyone's surprise, the East German election held in March 1990 (earlier than planned given the mounting crisis) was won by the followers of West German chancellor Helmut Kohl, thereby ensuring reunification. The large votes for the Christian Democrats and the Social Democrats, both tied to their West German counterparts, amounted to a death sentence for the German Democratic Republic and an endorsement of a "buyout" by the richer and more powerful West Germans.

But a reunited Germany, even a democratic one, posed all sorts of problems and potential instabilities. In fact, the collapse of the Warsaw Pact and the inevitable, increasingly imminent, reunification of Germany meant constructing a new European balance of power. To make a united Germany acceptable to Moscow, the West proposed that it be a member of NATO. This proposal also offered Moscow two reassurances. First, no Western armies, including German troops assigned to NATO, would be stationed on former East German territory in view of Moscow's certain opposition to the presence of NATO troops on the Polish border. Second, during a three- to four-year transition period, the 380,000 Soviet troops already in East Germany would remain there. Germany also would guarantee its neighbors' borders, restate West Germany's pledge that it would not seek to acquire nuclear weapons, and agree to limit its armed forces to 370,000, below West Germany's 474,000 in 1990 and well below the 667,000 level of the two Germanies.

Gorbachev's initial proposal to the West was based on memories of the German defeat of czarist Russia in World War I and of the 20 million Soviet lives lost repelling the German invasion in World War II. He therefore insisted that a reunited Germany be a neutral, disarmed state. But this was unacceptable to virtually everyone else, and it probably was not even thought to be the best solution by Moscow. The real question was whether a united but neutralized Germany would become once more a nationalistic, dangerously destabilizing force on the Continent. Pushed by his former allies to accept a NATO Germany, Gorbachev then proposed a reunited Germany that would be a member of both the Warsaw Pact and NATO. This too was rejected as merely another formula for neutrality. The United States felt confident that Moscow would eventually accept the NATO Germany favored by all members of the Western alliance, the West German government, the new East German one, as well as most Warsaw Pact members. The Soviets, having obviously lost the Cold War, were thought to be in too weak a bargaining position to insist on anything else.

But Gorbachev, weak or not, continued to resist the Western solution. He realized that when it came, the collapse of East Germany would spell the end of a major Soviet Cold War goal, hegemony over Europe by neutralizing West Germany. Indeed, all the Soviet Union's gains in World War II had been lost. Even more humiliating, a reunited Germany would likely emerge as the financial and economic center of Europe, the dominant power in Eastern Europe, and the principal source for capital and machinery for the Soviet Union. Thus the post–Cold War period, when economic considerations and power would be more significant and the Soviet Union would need German help, was likely to see the Soviet-German relationship reversed, resembling that found before the First World War.

In July 1990, only four months after declaring that German membership in NATO was "absolutely out of the question," Gorbachev bowed to the inevitable, accepting a reunited Germany in NATO. His acceptance was made easier by the promise of $8 billion in German credits to help the failing Soviet economy. Nevertheless, like his acceptance of a larger number of U.S. troops than Soviet troops in the new Europe, Gorbachev's acquiescence to German membership in NATO was tantamount to Soviet surrender. Although it had none of the drama of VE Day and VJ Day, which marked the end of the war in Europe and in the Pacific in 1945, *history will note July 16, 1990, as the day the Soviet Union gave up, effectively ending the Cold War.* Indeed, the American insistence on Soviet acceptance of Germany's admission to NATO appeared in large part driven by the need to clarify this issue.

The reemergence of modern Europe's central problem—that of Germany—was imminent. The only issue had been what kind of security arrangements could be established to contain German power in the new post-Cold War Europe. The two superpowers agreed on a framework for ending the division of Germany. First, merger of the two governing Christian Democratic parties was scheduled for October 1, and formal German reunification was set for October 3. Second, in November the reunification issue would be submitted for formal approval to the thirty-five-nation Conference on Security and Cooperation in Europe.[2] Finally, an all-German election of an all-German parliament was set for December 2.

The new year would start therefore with the convocation of the new parliament and the formation of the new government. As for the future, the reunited Germany would assume the role of Europe's most powerful economic actor and, like Japan, the other country vanquished in World War II, would quickly become a principal actor in the newly emerging multipolar international system. The world hoped, however, that Germany's preponderant size, population, and economic power would be directed not just toward fulfilling selfish interests but also toward serving as a catalyst for political stability and economic growth throughout Eastern Europe and, indeed, within the Soviet Union itself.

DECOLONIZING BREZHNEV'S THIRD WORLD OUTPOSTS

The second condition requisite to ending the Cold War was Soviet cooperation in resolving regional conflicts in the Third World. As noted earlier, Soviet expansionism in the Third World had hindered U.S.-Soviet relations for decades, but now the Soviet Union's desire to avoid trouble with the United States was likely to prevent further expansionism.

Gorbachev's reversal of Soviet expansionism was dramatic. The Soviets withdrew from Afghanistan and later admitted that the invasion had been a mistake, a result of their foreign policy's overreliance on force. In Angola, after prolonged negotiations failed to achieve the exit of 50,000 Cuban troops from that country in return for South Africa's withdrawal from Namibia (South Africans had frequently attacked Angola in pursuit of guerrilla forces operating in Namibia), a deal was struck under which the Cubans would withdraw in return for the independence of Namibia. In Southeast Asia, with Soviet encouragement, Vietnam withdrew from Cambodia. Vietnam had invaded Cambodia to overthrow its murderous Khmer Rouge government, which had slaughtered more than 1 million of its own population of 8 million people. In both Angola and Cambodia the backing of the Cuban and Vietnamese operations in support of Marxist governments had been costly to the Soviet Union both economically and in terms of credibility. Moscow wanted

2. The Conference on Security and Cooperation in Europe (now known as the Organization on Security and Cooperation in Europe) comprised sixteen NATO countries, seven Warsaw Pact nations, and twelve neutral states. It was founded in Helsinki in 1975, when its signatories promised to respect existing frontiers (including the East German-Polish border) and to observe human rights.

to cut its losses from these seemingly unending struggles; its overseas empire was proving unmanageable.

Even in the Middle East, Moscow moved, initially, toward rapprochement with Israel—it had broken diplomatic relations in 1967—and later to the reestablishment of relations. It also supported the U.S. objective of an Israeli-Palestinian dialogue and raised the possibility of increased Jewish emigration from the Soviet Union to Israel. Instead of supporting the more radical parties and obstructing American peace efforts, the Soviet Union indicated that it preferred partnership with the United States.

But in one important area, Central America, the Soviets continued to supply arms to anti-American forces despite soothing words about seeking peaceful settlements. Soviet arms shipments to the Nicaraguan government, although reduced, continued; shipments from Cuba and Eastern Europe made up the difference. Soviet-made weapons also reached the Salvadoran guerrillas, who launched a number of attacks in the capital city of San Salvador in 1989.

The Bush administration strongly protested these policies of support as "Cold War relics," calling these countries "Brezhnevite clients" during the informal summit meeting that Gorbachev and Bush held in December 1989 off the Mediterranean island of Malta. Gorbachev denied sending weapons to Central America, but Bush would have none of it. Cuba and Nicaragua were Soviet clients. Washington clearly expected Moscow, which elsewhere had pressured its proxies to reach regional settlements, to do the same in America's backyard. Undoubtedly, Cuba's Fidel Castro, who had denounced the Soviet Union's retreat from socialism and considered himself one of the few true remaining socialists, would resist counsels of restraint. Even without Soviet arms shipments, Cuba and Nicaragua had enough weapons to ship to the Salvadoran guerrillas.

The more critical issue was the February 1990 election in Nicaragua, which, if fairly and freely conducted, held out the promise of easing regional tensions in Central America. Gorbachev reportedly prevailed on the Sandinistas to permit free elections such as those held in Eastern Europe. The Sandinistas, like Ferdinand Marcos earlier in the Philippines, were confident of a victory in an election while they held the reins of power. Such a victory promised them greater legitimacy and would discredit any further U.S. support for the contras.

But the Sandinistas completely underestimated the chances that the opposition in a country wracked by civil war, drained of young men, and disabled by huge inflation and a ruined economy might win such an election. In a stunning upset for the Sandinista leadership, the Nicaraguans, tired of civil war and economic stagnation, voted the Sandinistas out of office in an election supervised by the United Nations. The contra issue was now moot.

Moreover, the election results isolated the leftist guerrillas in El Salvador and Cuba's Castro, weakening them both. As for Nicaragua, national reconciliation, disbanding the contras, rebuilding the economy, ensuring a democratic and more just society, and reestablishing good relations with the United States were to be the new tasks.

What happened to the Sandinistas and, more broadly, the collapse of the Soviet empire in Eastern Europe and in the Soviet Union itself, were not lost on the rebels in El Salvador. Suddenly, long-standing but previously unsuccessful negotiations to end that country's civil war became more productive, and in 1991, with the help of the United Nations, the government and guerrillas agreed to end the conflict. Many details remained to be worked out on the guerrillas' role in Salvadoran politics after peace was reestablished, but, given the unusually harmonious spirit of the times, such negotiations proceeded without significant acrimony.

The only remaining source of real friction between Washington and Moscow was Cuba. Castro swore that socialism would continue to be practiced on his island even if it had been betrayed by Gorbachev and even if it were abandoned virtually everywhere else. Moscow discontinued its multibillion dollar subsidy to Cuba in 1991, announcing that future economic relations between the two countries would be on a trade-only basis. The Soviet military training mission also would be withdrawn. The Soviet Union, itself seeking economic help from the West, was responding to the Bush administration's insistence that it would not consider such assistance while Moscow continued to provide Castro with the equivalent of $5 billion annually. Thus the Soviet retraction of power from the Third World continued.

REDUCING ARMS AND STABILIZING THE NUCLEAR BALANCE

The third condition for ending the Cold War was a reduction in superpower arms and a stable nuclear balance. A consistent U.S. goal in the evolving new superpower relationship was to provide for a stable security environment through appropriate arms control agreements. More specifically, U.S. policy had three objectives. The first, especially in view of Gorbachev's uncertain tenure, was to reach agreements to reduce strategic and conventional arms; once achieved, such arms reductions would be politically and economically difficult to reverse. The second objective was to reduce the likelihood of surprise attack, a goal that was pursued by both sides through a variety of confidence-building measures. And the third objective was to reduce the burden of defense spending and to realize a "peace dividend" to be spent on domestic needs. (For Gorbachev, this financial benefit was probably the driving force behind all his arms proposals. As the U.S. budget deficit grew, Bush also wanted to see a reduction in defense spending.)

From the beginning of the SALT process, SALT III was intended to cut drastically the strategic arsenals of both powers. Renamed START (Strategic Arms Reduction Talks) by the Reagan administration to emphasize radical reductions—a 50 percent cut—the treaty was aimed at cutting Soviet land-based missiles, which, with their multiple and accurate warheads, were the principal threat to the survival of American intercontinental ballistic missiles (ICBMs). In short, reductions per se were not the objective; the aim was *stabilizing* reductions. By the time Reagan left office, the START negotiations were substantially completed. Each side had agreed to a ceiling of 1,600 delivery vehicles, an aggregate of 6,000 strategic weapons, and a ballistic missile warhead limit of 4,900. Although the overall cut in strategic forces was closer to a 30 percent reduction, the most destabilizing forces, the ballistic missiles with multiple warheads, had been cut by 50 percent.

The chief obstacle from the very beginning was SDI, the Strategic Defense Initiative (see Chapter 9). The Soviets insisted that they would not reduce their ICBM force until they knew whether they would have to cope with American strategic defenses. But Reagan clung to his vision of SDI, and therefore the Soviets refused to sign the START treaty. To break the deadlock, Moscow announced in 1989 its willingness to sign the treaty on the condition that the United States abide by the 1972 antiballistic missile (ABM) treaty. While the two issues were finally severed, at least formally, START's fate again depended on Washington's decisions about SDI development. The program had lost its main advocate, however, and faced great technical difficulties and increasing congressional disenchantment at a time of a huge federal deficit. Thus support for SDI steadily eroded, and it no longer posed an obstacle to arms control negotiations.

As for conventional forces, after 1987 Gorbachev had talked repeatedly about a shift from an offensive to a defensive military doctrine, as well as sizable military budget cuts as the Soviet Union scaled its forces back to "reasonable sufficiency." He promised and carried out unilateral reductions of Soviet forces, including the withdrawal of troops and tanks facing NATO. For Warsaw Pact forces to shift to a strategy that could repel an attack but not launch a massive surprise attack on NATO was obviously very much in the West's interest. Such a shift would greatly relieve Western fears stemming from the Soviet Union's sizable forces and Soviet military doctrine, and it would be a tangible sign that Soviet intentions had fundamentally changed.

The conventional arms reduction negotiations, or CFE (Central Front Europe) negotiations, sought to reduce Soviet forces in Eastern Europe and American forces in Western Europe to 275,000. CFE also sought equal numbers of tanks, armored personnel carriers, artillery pieces, and combat aircraft for the two military alliances. But events in Eastern Europe were moving so fast that in January 1990 President Bush called for a further U.S.-Soviet troop reduction in central Europe to 195,000, with 30,000 more American troops outside of that area. Surprisingly, Gorbachev accepted the U.S. proposal, even though this cutback would, for the first time since the war, leave the United States with more troops in Europe than the Soviet Union. Militarily this was unimportant, but politically and psychologically it was further evidence of Soviet weakness. In any case, the 195,000 troop ceiling was unlikely to be the last word on reductions because of the strong domestic pressure in the United States to cut U.S. forces further to about 75,000.

Such reductions appeared possible because by 1990 the Soviet-led alliance, organized to protect the Soviet-imposed socialist systems, had fewer systems to defend as Eastern Europe defected from the Warsaw Pact. In these circumstances Moscow could no longer count, if it ever could, on the armies of Czechoslovakia, Hungary, Poland, East Germany, Bulgaria, and Romania for any joint military action against the West. In 1990 Moscow agreed to withdraw its forces from Czechoslovakia, Hungary, and Poland by the end of 1992, but this pledge became irrelevant as the Warsaw Pact died shortly afterward, to be formally buried in 1991.

Would NATO also disappear? That was unlikely, at least in the short run, because the alliance continued to have several functions. One was to continue to guard the West against the possibility of a renewed Soviet or Russian threat. There was at the time widespread concern that Gorbachev might be overthrown by the old communist guard, which then would reimpose Soviet hegemony in Eastern Europe. (Even after the attempted coup in August 1991 against Gorbachev, which led to the Soviet Union's own demise, Russia, the successor state, retained significant military power—see next section.) Another function of NATO, not spoken of openly for diplomatic reasons, was to restrain the new Germany. After twice calling on American power to defeat Germany, Europeans were unsure that they alone could manage a unified Germany. Retaining NATO would keep American power in Europe. Finally, the United States wanted the alliance to serve as an institutional link through which it could influence the shape of the emerging new order in Europe as the European Community moved toward greater economic and political integration.

Bush's arms control initiatives continued even after the Soviet Union itself dissolved in late 1991. Under the rubric of the START II negotiations, Bush carried on with Russian president Boris Yeltsin. At their June 1992 summit meeting, the two sides agreed to even deeper cuts in nuclear arms, among them, the most destabilizing nuclear weapons, including multiple warhead missiles which had become a headache to strategic planners in Moscow and Washington. Both sides would be allowed to retain about 3,000 missiles by the year 2003, or sooner if the United States could assist the financially strapped Russians in dismantling their weapons.

In 1990 there was no question that the Soviet Union itself was undergoing a rapid and profound transformation. With the disintegration of the economy, the political regime lost its legitimacy and was further weakened by internal conflicts between Moscow and a number of Soviet republics. Demands for autonomy, if not independence, erupted in many republics, and ancient ethnic feuds reemerged. These events threatened the integrity of the Soviet state and compelled the regime to move Soviet tactical nuclear warheads out of the Baltics and the volatile southern republics to parts of the Russian republic it considered more politically stable.

Even more worrisome, the Communist Party was showing growing signs of disintegration and was losing its authority to impose decisions on the nation. In the Baltics it was faced with the Lithuanian Communist Party's defection from the Soviet party and its identification with Lithuania's demand for independence. In Azerbaijan the Soviet army had to be sent in not only to restore order between the Azerbaijanis and Armenians, but also to prevent the communist government from falling into the hands of the Azerbaijani popular front—much as communist regimes in Eastern Europe had fallen to the opposition groups. In several cities and regions, party officials had to resign because of popular outrage over their corruption and privileges. Indeed, in Moscow, Leningrad, and other cities the emerging democratic political opposition inflicted embarrassing defeats on the communists by winning majorities in local elections.

Gorbachev, alert to popular disenchantment with the party, gradually shifted his base of power from the Communist Party (whose conservative apparatus continued to resist his reforms) to the elected Supreme Soviet and the presidency, a post he held in addition to that of general secretary of the party. He went even further by calling on the party to give up its seventy-year constitutional monopoly of power, although he clearly considered the party to be the most capable of guiding the nation through its turmoil. For the party to remain the political vanguard, however, it would have to earn the Soviet people's trust, and this would require it to restructure itself. Gorbachev even suggested that at some future point rival political parties might be established.

Equally revolutionary was Gorbachev's embrace of the free market as an alternative to the failed communist economy. Having already repudiated Lenin, Gorbachev now dumped Marx as well. Thus seventy-three years after the Bolshevik revolution, the Soviets reversed themselves; markets would replace bureaucracy, and capitalism would succeed socialism. But Gorbachev, however revolutionary his rhetoric and declarations, hesitated to implement his reforms because they would surely propel the flow of power away from Moscow and the central government he headed. A social explosion might occur as well if the withdrawal of subsidies for industry and to Soviet citizens for rent, food, health care, and education resulted in sharp rises in inflation and unemployment. Moreover, Gorbachev could not discount the old guard's opposition.

In principle, then, the party had renounced both its political-economic dictatorship and its intellectual heritage, but the real question was whether it all had happened too late. Could a political leadership that no longer enjoyed sufficient political authority or popularity because of five years of growing economic shortages, which now included even bread and cigarettes, take the tough measures required to implement wholesale economic changes? Had Gorbachev become the captain of the Soviet *Titanic* as the party increasingly lost control to the Supreme Soviet, the legislatures of the republics, municipal governments, popular fronts, and increasingly assertive workers' unions, all of which sought a greater devolution of power and policy?

The strongest challenge to Gorbachev's power came from Boris Yeltsin, who in May 1990 was elected president of the Russian republic. Russia occupied two-thirds of the territory of the former Soviet Union and had almost half of its population and most of its oil, natural gas reserves, and coal. Yeltsin was quick to sense the popular disaffection with the power and privileges of the Communist Party. Once Gorbachev's protégé, Yeltsin became his fiercest critic and arch rival because the Soviet leader had not, in Yeltsin's judgment, moved quickly enough to change the system.

On the day after his election by the Russian parliament, Yeltsin challenged the system by proposing Russia's economic autonomy and a radical decentralization in which republic law took precedence over Soviet law and the president of the Soviet Union would have no greater authority than the presidents of the fifteen republics. Indeed, not only would Russia claim sovereignty and determine the prices of its natural resources, but also it would make its own agreements with the other members of the Soviet Union. And just to make his challenge clear, Yeltsin announced that he would seek to make the Russian presidency a popularly elected office, which he won overwhelmingly. His victory provided another contrast to Gorbachev, who had been elected only by the Supreme Soviet. By being elected president of the Soviet Union's largest republic by the people for the first time in its thousand-year history, Yeltsin acquired a legitimacy Gorbachev never had.

A few weeks later, Yeltsin, together with the reformist mayors of Moscow and Leningrad, resigned from the Communist Party. Their resignations were symptomatic of growing national disenchantment with the party and Gorbachev's declining popularity. Next, the Ukraine, the Soviet Union's second largest republic and its "breadbasket," with a population of more than 50 million, declared its sovereignty and its laws above those of the Soviet Union. It also claimed an independent foreign policy role by stating it would be a neutral state; it would not participate in military blocs; and it would ban the production and deployment of nuclear weapons on its territory. The Ukraine's action was followed by a similar declaration from Byelorussia (now renamed Belarus). And eventually all of the Soviet Union's fifteen republics issued sovereignty declarations, asserting either outright independence or more cautious assertions of their rights. Gorbachev's Soviet Union crumbled around him, republic by republic.

By late 1990 Gorbachev had become more and more irrelevant in domestic affairs. Yeltsin was setting the pace and scope of change by supporting the drive for independence by the Baltic republics and by proposing a 500-day plan for the transformation of the Soviet economy into a market economy. Gorbachev found himself maneuvering between the increasingly radical forces on the left and the forces of reaction on the right, represented by the traditional instruments of Soviet power—the military, secret police, and Communist Party bureaucracy—which had survived all his attempts at reform. They were the elite and therefore had a strong vested interest in the status quo. In the meanwhile, Gorbachev had his hands full just trying to hold the union together, to stem the republics' nationalism. Thus he shifted his original direction and aligned himself with the forces of "law and order." He dismissed many of his former liberal allies in the struggle for *glasnost* and *perestroika*, began cracking down on the Baltic republics, and reimposed censorship.

Gorbachev's new allies, however, tried to limit his power and enhance their own because they felt that he was leading the country to chaos and anarchy. Moreover, they despised him because he had retreated from Eastern Europe and had given up the Soviet Union's World War II gains. In reaction, Gorbachev swung back to ally himself once more with the reformers. He made his peace with the republics and promised the presidents of the nine republics who agreed to stay within the union, including Yeltsin, to turn the Soviet Union into a new voluntary federation that all republics would have the right to join or not join. They also would be free to choose their own forms of government and exercise most of the power over their natural resources, industry, foreign trade, and taxes. He promised a new constitution and a newly elected central government.

But just as the new All-Union Treaty was about to be signed, the hardliners struck. Fearing that their power was waning and that it soon would be too late to do anything about it, they launched a coup in August 1991, arresting Gorbachev while he was on holiday. But the coup plotters failed to understand the effects of the six years of Gorbachev's policies. Led by the popularly elected Yeltsin, who showed enormous courage, the people of Moscow rallied behind Gorbachev, resisting those who would reimpose the old dictatorship. Even units of the military and secret police opposed the coup, which quickly collapsed. This event proved to be the death blow of the Soviet Union.

All the republics now wanted their independence from Moscow and central authority. The three Baltic republics were let go and their independence was recognized by Moscow. At this point, seven of the twelve remaining republics, including Russia, planned to stay together in a loose confederation because they were still economically interdependent, although the agriculturally and industrially important Ukraine would not commit itself to creating a "common economic space" and a single currency, the foundation of a free-market economy.

What was absolutely clear in these times of uncertainty was that the old regime had disgraced itself by the coup attempt. Statues of Stalin and Lenin were removed from public squares; the old imperial flag designed by Peter the Great once again flew over the Russian parliament, the center of the resistance to the coup. Leningrad was renamed St. Petersburg, its prerevolutionary name, in accordance with the wishes of its citizens. Many said that it also was time to remove Lenin's body from the mausoleum in Red Square. But the major victim of the failed coup was the Communist Party. Yeltsin took sweeping measures against the Russian Communist Party, closing all of its offices and newspapers. Gorbachev, acknowledging the mood of the country and trying to salvage some of his authority, ended the party's role as watchdog of the military, secret police, and government bureaucracy, and disbanded its leadership. For all practical purposes the Communist Party as a governing body was dead. It could no longer block the path to democracy and radical economic reform. The revolution of 1917 had been undone in a stunning sequence of events.

The republics, however, were still grappling with their fates. At the moment of decision the seven republics that had endorsed the new union would not commit themselves, leaving its fate in the hands of their national parliaments. When the Ukraine voted on December 1, 1991, for independence and became Europe's fourth largest nation, it became clear that nothing could stop the process of Soviet disintegration. With even a weak confederation now dead, Russia was left as the successor state to the Soviet Union. Indeed, this status had become overwhelmingly clear when the central government declared bankruptcy in November 1991 and Russia assumed its debts and promised to fund what remained of the central government's ministries. In capitalist language, this act constituted a buyout of the former Soviet Union. Russia also claimed the Soviet Union's permanent seat as one of the five permanent members of the UN Security Council.

The Soviet Union was formally buried on December 8, 1991, when, in an act of desperation to stop the complete disintegration of the nation, the presi-

COMMONWEALTH OF INDEPENDENT STATES, 1992

dents of the three Slavic republics—Russia, Ukraine, and Byelorussia—representing 73 percent of the population and 80 percent of the territory of the Soviet Union, decided to establish a commonwealth and invited other republics to join. The new Commonwealth of Independent States (CIS) assumed all the international obligations of the Soviet Union, including control over its nuclear arsenal. Coordinating bodies would be established to decide on cooperative policies in foreign affairs, defense, and economics. Subsequently, the commonwealth agreement was signed by eleven of the remaining twelve Soviet republics after the defections of the three Baltic states; the twelfth republic, Georgia, was consumed by civil war. On December 25, 1991, the red hammer and sickle flag that had flown over the Kremlin was lowered, seventy-four years after the Bolshevik revolution. The Soviet Union had disappeared from the world's map.

DID THE UNITED STATES 'WIN' OR
THE SOVIET UNION 'LOSE' THE COLD WAR?

Throughout his presidency George Bush was dogged by the notion that he lacked a coherent vision of the future of world politics. Further, he was criticized for what seemed to be an overcautious approach to U.S.-Soviet relations, his continuing embrace of Gorbachev after the Soviet leader lost legitimacy, and his resistance to immediate deep cuts in American defense spending. Bush, the lifelong government bureaucrat, the manager, the caretaker, presumably lacked the panache to seize such a profound historic opportunity.

Twenty-first century historians probably will be kinder to Bush because a careful review of his performance reveals how skillfully he manipulated one of the crucial turning points in history not only to the advantage of the United States, but also in the interests of global stability. The three-year free fall of the Soviet system was by no means a certainty when Bush arrived in office, and its peaceful course was without precedent. In assisting Gorbachev when he urgently needed outside support, in insisting on German unification on Western terms, and in exploiting the opportunity for drastic nuclear disarmament, Bush successfully navigated the United States and its allies through a complicated phase of international relations, toward their ultimate victory in a half-century conflict of global proportions. Bush was chastised for adhering to the most "prudent" approach to world politics, but history may suggest that prudence was precisely the quality the world required.[3]

Ironically, once the Cold War was over, the question was raised of whether the United States had "won" the war and whether its containment policy had been successful. Or was it more accurate to say that the Soviet Union had "lost" the Cold War and that its defeat had been basically self-inflicted? These questions—which were not conducive to definitive answers—produced a contentious debate among scholars, journalists, and policy makers.[4] But it was not merely an academic exercise, for the answers to these questions would reveal the central lessons of the Cold War, which in turn would help in the establishment of guidelines for future American foreign policy.

THE CONTENDING ARGUMENTS IN PERSPECTIVE

Advocates of the view that the United States had "won" the Cold War claimed that the Western system of political, economic, and military organi-

---

3. A more thorough review of Bush's performance is provided by Michael Beschloss and Strobe Talbott in *At the Highest Levels* (Boston: Little, Brown, 1993).

4. For a consideration of this debate, see Charles W. Kegley, Jr., "How Did the Cold War Die? Principles for an Autopsy," *Mershon International Studies Review* (Summer 1994): 11-41. See also, John L. Gaddis, *The United States and the End of the Cold War* (New York: Oxford University Press, 1992).

zation was superior to that of the Soviet Union and its allies. Furthermore, the U.S.-led containment policy and the half century of competition had overwhelmed Soviet capabilities. Those believing that the Soviet Union had indeed "lost" the war argued that the containment policy did not play an essential role in bringing about Soviet defeat; if the United States had "won," it was merely because the Soviet Union's flawed system made its demise inevitable. Its excessive centralization of power, bureaucratic planning, and supervision of every detail of Soviet life, economic and otherwise, and its command economy and ideological oppression contributed to its undoing.

Such observations call for a closer look at the Soviet experience in converting the aspirations of the 1917 Russian Revolution into practice. Seventy years after the revolution and at a staggering cost in lives (estimated at more than 50 million), the Soviet standard of living was so low that even Eastern Europe, with its own economic problems, appeared affluent by contrast. According to the former Soviet Union's statistics, about 40 percent of its population and almost 80 percent of its elderly citizens lived in poverty. One-third of its households had no running water. Indeed, the Soviet Union was the only industrialized society in which infant mortality had risen and male life expectancy had declined in the late twentieth century. In Zbigniew Brzezinski's words, "Perhaps never before in history has such a gifted people, in control of such abundant resources, labored so hard for so long to produce so little." [5]

The Soviet economy, which was supposed to have demonstrated the superiority of socialism, sputtered for decades and then collapsed. Deliberately isolating itself from what it saw as the global capitalist economy, the Soviet Union had intended to build an economy that was self-sufficient and productive, assuring a bountiful life for the workers and peasants who so long had been deprived. Instead, the centralized command economy meant no domestic competition among firms, and its self-exclusion from the international economy ensured that it remained unchallenged by foreign competition. The Soviet economy thus became a textbook case of what free traders have long argued are the results of protectionism: inefficiency, lack of productivity, unresponsiveness to consumer needs, and technological stagnation.

Soviet communism was efficient only in producing military hardware. But this, ironically, also contributed to its defeat. As a state with few natural protective barriers, frequently invaded throughout its history, first Russia and then the Soviet Union kept sizable standing forces for its defense. Its twentieth-century experiences with Germany did nothing to relieve the longtime Russian sense of insecurity, fueled by the Marxist conception of politics as a constant struggle and its perception that enemies were everywhere. But

5. Zbigniew Brzezinski, *Game Plan* (Boston: Atlantic Monthly Press, 1986), 123. See also Brzezinski, *Grand Failure.*

whether Soviet expansionism stemmed from a defensive preoccupation with security or from an offensive ideological goal of aggrandizement, Moscow's drive for absolute security left other states feeling absolutely insecure. It is no wonder, then, that such insecurity drove all of the Soviet Union's great-power neighbors (Western Europe, on one side; China, Japan, and South Korea, on the other) into an encircling alignment with the United States. Indeed, under these circumstances, it would have been a surprise if the Soviet Union had not driven itself into bankruptcy. It has even been argued that Soviet accomplishments, such as its inroads in the Third World during the 1970s, considered at the time as setbacks for the United States, were actually setbacks for Moscow. Angola in 1976, Ethiopia in 1977, and Afghanistan, Grenada, and Nicaragua in 1979 were supposed to have given the Soviet system a bad case of digestion. The logic of this thesis that the more the Soviet Union expanded, the greater the cost, was that the containment policy was not an essential ingredient in stopping Soviet expansion; indeed, it was precisely when containment *failed* that the Soviet Union's burden became too great to bear. Soviet expansion, this suggests, would have reached its limits even in the absence of American countervailing power.[6]

Strobe Talbott, *Time*'s former Soviet expert and an undersecretary of state in the Clinton administration, even asserted that the Soviet threat was a "grotesque exaggeration" and claimed in retrospect, "The doves in the great debate of the past 40 years were right all along." [7] The Soviet "meltdown" in the Cold War was self-inflicted, "not because of anything the outside world has done or not done or threatened to do." Thus American and Western policies had little to do with the Soviet defeat in the Cold War since its cause was purely internal. Talbott's analysis was characteristic of the revisionist view that follows every major American war: that there really had been no major danger to this country; that the nation's long, intense, and dangerous involvement in the post-World War II world had not been necessary; and that instead of playing a key role in the defeat of America's adversary, the containment policy had merely prolonged the Cold War. Soviet power "was actually Soviet weakness," and the conflict itself "distorted priorities, distracted attention and preoccupied many of the best and the brightest minds in government, academe, and think tanks for nearly two generations." Thus it would have been better to have avoided the "grand obsession" with the "Red Menace," to have remained isolated from the power politics that diverted resources from domestic reforms to military preparations and war. Gorbachev, Talbott claimed, not only helped show that the Soviet threat was not what it used to be, but "what's more, that it never was."

6. John Mueller, "Enough Rope," *New Republic,* July 3, 1989, 15.
7. Strobe Talbott, "Rethinking the Red Menace," *Time,* January 1, 1990, 66-71.

Soviet communism surely deserves some of the credit it has been given for contributing to its own collapse. But to conclude from this that the containment policy was not necessary, or, if necessary, was not a key ingredient in the Soviet Union's demise, is to differ from the conclusions drawn by its potential victims. As the United States attempted to withdraw from Europe after World War II, countries such as Iran and Turkey, followed by those in Western Europe, pleaded with the United States to help them. All saw their independence and national integrity at stake; America's continued presence was their only protection. The collapse of the former great powers of Western Europe left the Soviet Union as the potential hegemon throughout Eurasia. Had the United States retreated into isolationism, as it did after World War I, the countries on the periphery of the Soviet Union would have been exposed to Soviet control.

Western Europe remained the pivotal strategic stake throughout the Cold War. The Soviets repeatedly tried to intimidate these nations, to divide them (especially West Germany from the United States), and to drive the United States back to its shores. But the containment policy made Moscow cautious about expanding its power. From this perspective the ancient rule of states is a prudent one: power must be met by countervailing power. A balance among states is the only guarantee that they will retain their independence and preserve their way of life. Without containment, the inefficiencies of the Soviet system might not have mattered as much; the Soviet Union would not have had to engage in a costly, ongoing arms competition.

Containment, however, was not aimed just at blocking Soviet domination of Western Europe and the rest of Eurasia; it also was intended to win time for the Soviet leadership to reexamine its goals and moderate its ambitions. Thus the American strategy in the Cold War rested largely and correctly on a tactical assumption of Soviet behavior. In George Kennan's original explanation, the United States had

it in its power to increase enormously the strains under which Soviet policy must operate, to force upon the Kremlin a far greater degree of moderation and circumspection than it has had to observe in recent years, and in this way *to promote tendencies which must eventually find their outlet in either the breakup or the gradual mellowing of Soviet power. For no mystical, messianic movement—and particularly that of the Kremlin—can face frustration indefinitely without eventually adjusting itself in one way or another to the logic of that state of affairs.*[8]

In retrospect, these words were prophetic. The Cold War experience demonstrated the virtue of patience in foreign policy. While interpreting the Soviet threat as the country's paramount concern, Kennan foresaw no quick fixes

8. George Kennan, *American Diplomacy, 1900-1950* (Chicago: University of Chicago Press, 1951), 127-128 (emphasis added).

and recommended no immediate solutions to the problem. To the contrary, he anticipated a prolonged, low-intensity struggle along several distant frontiers. The conflict would be settled most effectively—and most peacefully— through the gradual exposure of contradictions within Soviet society. Soviet communism, in his view, would ultimately self-destruct under the weight of these contradictions. In the meantime, however, the United States would need to pursue a "long-term, patient, but firm and vigilant containment of Russian expansive tendencies." From Truman to Bush, that is what U.S. presidents did.

The importance of the containment policy becomes even more evident when the period of its implementation is contrasted to the period before it was put into effect. If the principal causes of the Cold War were the structure of the postwar state system and the Soviet style in foreign policy, then America's national style made its own contribution. By failing to take a firm stand against Soviet policy during World War II, after it had become evident from repeated episodes that it was impossible to accommodate Soviet interests in Eastern Europe and Asia, the United States has to accept some of the blame for the Cold War that followed. This is not to say that the United States passively accepted Soviet expansionism, but only that it did not oppose Stalin early enough, that it continued to cling to its hope for postwar amity with the Soviet Union despite Soviet behavior in the late stages of the war, and that after hostilities had ceased, it dissipated its strength immediately in a helter-skelter demobilization. Stalin respected American power and was a cautious statesman, but when President Roosevelt informed him that American troops were to be withdrawn from Europe after two years, Stalin knew that he did not need to concern himself about American protests against Soviet actions in Eastern Europe. Protests were one thing, action another. Not until after the war did the United States act and draw the lines beyond which Soviet expansion would not be tolerated.

The American containment policy, then, played a critical role in the defeat of the Soviet Union. If the United States had not resisted Soviet expansion, Moscow, believing that communism represented the wave of the future, would have become more assertive and aggressive; perceived weakness always invited efforts to expand. For example, when Khrushchev initially claimed that the balance of power had turned in favor of the Soviet Union, he precipitated a series of crises over the West's presence in West Berlin that stretched from 1957 to 1962. And later, when Brezhnev's Soviet Union did attain strategic nuclear parity while also fielding a sizable army and building a growing navy, it exploited America's "Vietnam syndrome," using its own forces in Afghanistan, Soviet and East German advisers plus Cuban troops in Africa, and supporting Vietnamese forces in Cambodia. It was U.S. policy that, in the final analysis, compelled Soviet caution and moderation. If this country and its allies, especially NATO, had not opposed Soviet expansionist efforts and imposed penalties to counter such efforts, there would have been no need for Gorbachev to reassess his predecessors' policy and call off the Cold War.

EXCESSES OF THE CONTAINMENT POLICY

Containment was not, of course, a flawless policy. Once the Cold War started, U.S. misperceptions, like those of Soviet leaders, fed the superpower conflict. For example, Washington frequently exaggerated Soviet military capabilities. Fears of Soviet superiority—the bomber gap in the 1950s, the missile gaps a few years later, the ABM gap in the mid-1960s, and "the window of vulnerability" in the 1970s and 1980s—propelled the arms competition already well under way because of Soviet insecurity. In addition, the U.S. emphasis on anticommunism meant American policy often was insensitive to the nationalism of the new nations. As a result, the Middle East Treaty Organization (METO) and Southeast Asia Treaty Organization (SEATO) alliances proved weak reeds for containing communism, alienating important states such as Egypt and India, which shifted toward the Soviet Union, aggravating regional rivalries, and aligning the United States with discredited regimes such as Nationalist China. Indeed, in the name of anticommunism Washington often supported authoritarian, right-wing regimes in the Third World; it saw no democratic alternatives to the regimes it backed other than left-wing pro-Soviet or Chinese ones, which were unacceptable.

The U.S. government also consistently exaggerated the monolithic nature of international communism. The fall of Nationalist China, the Korean War, and the communist Chinese intervention in that war transformed the containment policy, which originally was limited to responding to Soviet moves in the eastern Mediterranean and Western Europe, into global anticommunism. The events of 1949 and 1950 led to virulent anticommunism in the United States, with the Republicans (notably Sen. Joe McCarthy) accusing the Democrats of being "soft on communism" and engaging in paranoid witch hunts. Future Democratic administrations therefore would not be able to exploit the growing differences between the Soviet Union and China; instead, seeking to avoid being charged with the "loss of Indochina," as they had been with the "loss of China," Democratic administrations intervened militarily in Vietnam.

The American penchant for crusading, already vividly demonstrated in two "hot" wars, was not to be denied in the Cold War. Its failure to distinguish between vital and secondary interests—or to discriminate between different communist regimes—resulted in a war that the United States could not win, dividing the country deeply and undermining the domestic consensus that had been the basis of the Cold War. Ironically, Vietnam destroyed American anticommunism, and U.S. policy shifted back toward the containment of Soviet power—but this time in "alliance" with China. Finally, as noted in Chapter 9, the overzealous pursuit of the Reagan Doctrine resulted in the Iran-contra scandal, which raised new doubts about the lengths to which the U.S. government would go to fulfill its mission of defeating communism.

A FINAL APPRAISAL

Its shortcomings aside, on the whole, American foreign policy must be pronounced a success. The expansion of American power and influence in the world has by and large been associated with the promotion of democracy. America's World War II enemies, once dictatorial, are today stable, free societies. If one looks at the societies liberated by the Soviet Union during World War II, the contrast is striking. No East European country, until Gorbachev, could have been described as a "free society"; past attempts to move toward greater freedom had been squashed by the Soviet army in East Germany, Hungary, and Czechoslovakia, and by the Polish army in Poland. East Germany had to build a wall across Berlin and a barbed-wire fence along its entire border with West Germany to prevent its citizens from escaping. It was symbolic, too, that in the summer of 1989, when the pro-democracy movement in China was culminating in Beijing, student leaders erected a "goddess of democracy" modeled after the Statue of Liberty. After the movement was violently crushed by the authorities, this goddess became the symbol for its sympathizers all over the world.

Over the four decades of the Cold War the United States acquired many authoritarian allies, mostly in the Third World, which weakened Washington's democratic rationale and laid open its foreign policy to the charge of hypocrisy. It would have been preferable, of course, to have democratic allies, but that was not always possible in a world in which most developing countries were not democratic in the Western sense of the term. Security and democracy occasionally were bound to appear as conflicting values (as today the values of economic growth and jobs conflict with concerns about human rights). Which value was to be given priority presented a difficult, often agonizing choice.

The basic fact remains, however, that the principal thrust of American foreign policy after World War II, as before the war, was to preserve a balance of power that would safeguard democratic values in the United States and other like-minded states. Indeed, this has been a consistent policy since World War I, whether the threat has come from the expansionism of the right or of the left. American policy makers in the twentieth century have opposed both types of regimes, for they have threatened not just U.S. security but, more broadly, the international environment in which democratic values can prosper. And this was the crux of American opposition to the Soviet Union: that its great power constituted a threat to Western values and Western-style open societies, for communism, especially as reflected in the organization of pre-Gorbachev societies, was antithetical to societies that believed in individual freedoms, whether of speech or religion, in free party competition and genuine political choice, and in a distinction between state and society. It was America's power, not simply its democratic ideals, that protected these values.

Indeed, the end of the Cold War was witness not only to the end of the Soviet challenge but also to the defeat of the second totalitarian challenge to Western-style democracy in this century. The Nazis will be forever identified with the concentration camps of Auschwitz, Bergen-Belsen, and Treblinka, where they systematically murdered millions of people, including 6 million Jews, and with the unleashing of World War II, which, before it was over, cost the lives of 17 million soldiers and 34 million civilians. Just as the Nazi system was epitomized by Hitler, the Soviet system remains identified with Stalin and his cruel collectivization of the Soviet peasantry, the deliberate starvation of the Ukrainian peasants in the early 1930s, and the purges and other crimes that claimed the lives, conservatively estimated, of 20 million people and imprisoned and deported 20 million more. Stalin, not Hitler, was the great mass murderer in history; he also was in power twice as long.[9] Thus, while the "de-communization" of Eastern Europe and the collapse of Soviet power were to be celebrated, the defeat of the two regimes that had been the greatest suppressors of human rights had global significance.

The U.S. victory in the Cold War coincided with its own economic woes, and the country needed its own *perestroika*, but the nation still had reason to be proud of its overall record. During the forty-five-year Cold War in which it was the leader of the Western coalition, there was no nuclear war, Soviet expansionist ambitions were checked, and democracy flourished while the United States preserved and revitalized its own democratic traditions and guarded those of its allies in Western Europe. Surely this record testifies to the power of democratic ideas in the conduct of American foreign policy. The United States also had avoided treating its former enemies, Germany and Japan, in a vengeful manner; indeed, it helped them back on their feet economically and welcomed them into the Western alliance of democratic nations. Similarly, after winning the Cold War, it refused to gloat, seeking instead to attract the Soviet Union, or its successor state, as a partner in the creation of a more secure Europe and a post-Cold War international order. All in all, not a bad record.

9. Robert Conquest, *The Great Terror* (New York: Oxford University Press, 1990).

The UN peacekeeping mission in Bosnia proved less than effective. Internal dissension prevented the UN from taking significant action against the Bosnian Serbs, who continued their "ethnic cleansing" of the area's Muslims into 1995.

CHAPTER ELEVEN

Old Tensions in a New Order

Great expectations flourished as the Cold War unwound between 1989 and 1992. Democratic values and institutions were likely to thrive now that the Soviet bear had been slain, and, given the historically pacific relations among democracies, the frequency of wars would probably decline.[1] Perhaps even international organizations, particularly the United Nations, would finally overcome the ideological divisions that previously had blocked collective action. In the United States the "peace dividend" was expected to translate into lower taxes or better-funded social programs, or both. Most important, the United States would play a more modest role in world politics, a development that was welcomed by many Americans.

1. Bruce Russett, *Controlling the Sword* (Cambridge: Harvard University Press, 1990).

But contrary to these expectations, international tensions increased in the early 1990s as countries large and small adapted uneasily to the post-Cold War environment. Given the central role played by the U.S.-Soviet rivalry in world politics for nearly half a century, its sudden demise was bound to be destabilizing. *Interstate* wars did indeed become less frequent, but *civil* wars broke out in many parts of the world, inflicting widespread destruction and threatening to draw in neighboring states, great powers, and transnational peace-keeping forces. Challenges to the emerging global power structure, which arose even before the Soviet Union dissolved, foreshadowed a sustained pattern of regional crises that tested the fragile, makeshift security arrangements devised for the new era.

As noted in Chapter 10, President George Bush focused his energies on supporting the transition of the Soviet Union and its Eastern European satellites to democratic rule and market economics. But even as he heralded the coming of a "new world order," Bush was confronted with far-flung regional conflicts, particularly in developing areas of the world where disruptions of political order were accompanied by social upheaval and economic disarray. Although Bush initially hoped to avoid U.S. involvement in these flashpoints, they nevertheless demanded his attention, and in some cases drew direct U.S. military action. Some crises persisted beyond Bush's electoral defeat in November 1992 and served as legacies to his successor, Bill Clinton, whose goal of focusing on domestic economic concerns "like a laser" was upended by the string of conflicts overseas.

One of these trouble spots was the Persian Gulf, where the absence of superpower rivalry left a power vacuum that one regional leader, Iraq's Saddam Hussein, attempted to fill. Hussein's bid for hegemony in August 1990, between the collapse of the Warsaw Pact and that of the Soviet Union, effectively produced the first post-Cold War world crisis. The strong international response—involving sharp condemnations in the UN Security Council, economic sanctions, and, ultimately, an overwhelming show of multilateral military force—would not have been possible amid continuing rivalry between the United States and the Soviet Union. In the end, Hussein's attempted seizure of neighboring Kuwait was turned back quickly, but he remained in power, determined to threaten regional stability whenever the opportunity arose.

IRAQ'S CHALLENGE IN THE PERSIAN GULF

At least $80 billion in debt from the Iran-Iraq war, Saddam Hussein ordered his battle-tested army to invade the oil-rich emirate of Kuwait on August 2, 1990. The Iraqi army quickly overran the largely undefended Kuwaiti capital. With his troops poised on the border of Saudi Arabia and many Arab neighbors afraid of him, Hussein sought to intimidate the Persian Gulf oil

kingdoms and assert his dominance over the Gulf, goals that he had tried to
achieve in his costly war against Iran.

Unfortunately, there really was no one in the Middle East to oppose Hussein's bid for power. Egypt, traditionally the leader of the Arab states, had lost
that status when it made peace with Israel. Moreover, in an era in which
"petrodollars" produced political and military power, Egypt, not an oil producer, was weaker than other Arab states in the region. Syria, another frequent rival for Arab leadership, was left isolated as its patron in Moscow disappeared. Thus Hussein reasoned that by establishing Iraq as the dominant
power in the region, he could then launch his long-sought "holy war" against
Israel, the moderate Persian Gulf oil kingdoms (Saudi Arabia, Bahrain, Qatar,
the United Arab Emirates, and Kuwait), and rival Arab states such as Egypt.

As Iraqi forces massed near Saudi Arabia's border, the possibility that
Hussein might soon control 40 percent of the world's oil reserves and dictate
the terms of production by the Organization of Petroleum Exporting Countries (OPEC) forced the industrial democracies to act. Aware that their economic growth depended on stable oil prices and uninterrupted supplies, Japan and the member countries of the North Atlantic Treaty Organization
(NATO) froze Iraqi assets and those of the deposed government of Kuwait.
This was accompanied by a UN-sanctioned embargo on Iraqi oil and Iraqi-
controlled Kuwaiti oil, to be enforced by a naval blockade of the Gulf. The
two key questions, however, were whether Iraq's customers would honor the
embargo long enough to bankrupt the Iraqi economy, and whether Hussein
would ultimately succumb to the economic sanctions or allow his people to
suffer indefinitely, as Fidel Castro had done in Cuba.

Meanwhile, the Bush administration proceeded with the largest U.S. troop
buildup, called Operation Desert Shield, since the Vietnam War: 250,000
troops to deter an attack on Saudi Arabia. The administration hoped the
prospect of war with U.S. and other coalition forces might persuade Hussein
to withdraw from Kuwait and restore its government. If it did not, the coalition forces would be large enough to force the Iraqi army to leave Kuwait.

The stakes were clear in this confrontation: Hussein's control over oil production and prices and the survival of moderate Arab regimes opposed to his
attempt to become a regional hegemon. Having accepted the challenge, the
United States could not afford to back off without endangering its security, its
economic future as well as those of its major trading partners and allies, and
its status as the world's lone superpower after the Cold War. If it neglected its
Arab allies and Israel in their moment of peril, they might never trust the
United States again. Thus the stage was set for a showdown. The United Nations gave Hussein a mid-January 1991 deadline to withdraw from Kuwait. If
he refused, force would be used to eject him. This remarkable UN unanimity
was not matched by the U.S. Congress, however, which insisted that Presi-

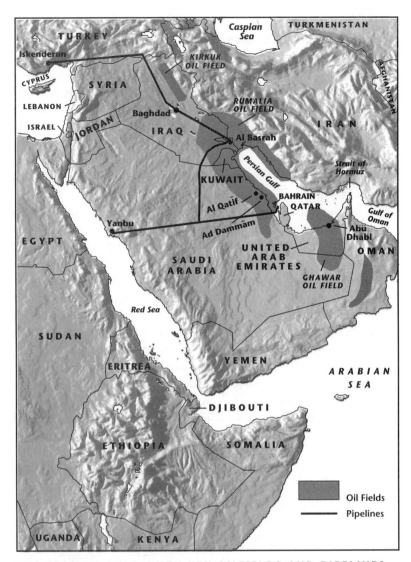

THE PERSIAN GULF, WITH KEY OILFIELDS AND PIPELINES

dent Bush gain its assent before he used force. At first, Bush tried to avoid the Democratic-controlled Congress, fearing that it would reject the mission, embarrass and humiliate the United States, and undermine its goals. Many members of Congress, still haunted by memories of Vietnam, argued that economic sanctions would be sufficient to dislodge Iraq. But in early January 1991, with the UN deadline nearing, Bush decided he needed congressional approval before taking the nation into war. After intense debate, Congress narrowly approved the military operation.

When the January 15 deadline passed and Iraq had not withdrawn, the United States and its allies transformed Operation Desert Shield into Operation Desert Storm. Their massive air and land assault sent Hussein's forces fleeing for cover. In an air war that lasted five weeks, allied air forces flew more than 100,000 sorties, devastating Iraqi targets from the front lines to Baghdad. In phase one they took out Iraqi command and control posts, air fields, and other military installations. In phase two they destroyed bridges and roads to stop all supplies from reaching the Iraqi forces in Kuwait. In phase three these forces, now cut off, were subject to constant pounding. Only in the final phase did the ground forces launch their attack, and within 100 hours they surrounded the Iraqi forces and defeated them. Prisoners flocked in from the beginning of the ground assault; most were only too glad to surrender and receive some food and water. The war had lasted forty-three days, and U.S. casualties were limited to fewer than 300. Hussein was forced to revoke his annexation of Kuwait.

The war, however, did not result in Hussein's removal from power; that had not been the United Nations's goal. Indeed, had the United States marched on Baghdad, the coalition might have come apart. The Arabs wanted to end Hussein's threat to his neighbors, but they were against his overthrow. And Washington wanted no part of governing a nation in civil war. Such a conflict broke out in the wake of Hussein's defeat when Iraq's Kurds and Shiite Muslims, who constituted the majority of the country's population, rebelled against their ruler, a Sunni Muslim, but were not strong enough to defeat the remnants of Hussein's Republican Guard. Yet despite Hussein's undisguised brutality toward his own people, Bush and the coalition partners did not want to see Iraq disintegrate; they expected it to continue to play a role in the regional balance of power. They did not want the surrounding countries, especially Iran and Syria, to carve up the country in their own bids for regional dominance.

After the war Hussein defied a series of international demands, making it clear that despite the coalition's victory he would remain a threat. Hussein affirmed this late in 1994 when he again massed troops on the Kuwaiti border, this time to protest continuing UN sanctions against Iraq. The United States responded by mobilizing its own forces in the Persian Gulf and deploying

thousands of new troops to the region. This time Hussein backed down and
ordered his Republican Guards to return to their bases. He then acknowledged the sovereignty of Kuwait and recognized the existing border between
the two countries, concessions that were calculated to induce a relaxation of
UN sanctions. But his earlier provocations, and the frenetic response they
produced, proved that Iraq was still a viable and volatile force in the region.

AMERICAN INTROSPECTION AFTER
THE COLD WAR

The U.S.-led victory in the Gulf War distracted the world's attention in
1991 from the more important but less dramatic process of adapting to a
transformed international system. The former Warsaw Pact states of Eastern
Europe continued their difficult transition to democracy and market economies, while Mikhail Gorbachev's Soviet Union stumbled toward its collapse
at year's end. In the People's Republic of China, where the communist regime
remained in power, a sustained economic boom—fueled by capitalist "enterprise zones" along the Pacific coast—was under way and helped to finance a
major military buildup. Meanwhile, Western Europe and Japan remained
linked to the United States through mutual security treaties, but these arrangements were overshadowed by the growing economic competition
among these states and many newly industrialized countries (NICs). The nature of the emerging balance of power was far from clear; indeed, it was not
even clear what constituted power in the new era.

In the United States many people sensed that the costs of the Cold War,
reflected in record U.S. budget and trade deficits and a skyrocketing national
debt, had yet to be fully paid. American industries floundered as foreign competitors—particularly Western Europe, Japan, and other East Asian "ti-
gers"—assumed a growing share of the global market. Across the country, social problems such as crime, failing schools, and urban decay were attributed
to national neglect during a period when fighting communism was the national passion. Finally, the wounds inflicted on the country in its hot wars in
Korea and Vietnam, in its crisis-prone relations with the Soviets, and in its es-
trangement from many developing countries and the United Nations, remained deeply felt. The country was in many ways exhausted by the Cold
War, and, despite its success against the Soviet Union (and more recently
Iraq), basic questions about the country's future role in the world remained
open.

Soon after Iraq's defeat these questions began to revive old debates in the
United States about the country's appropriate "mission" in foreign affairs.
Thus the American people faced yet another period of self-appraisal in the
early 1990s. Always ambivalent about the country's world role, they wondered

whether the American experience in world leadership had come at a prohibitively high price. Some waxed nostalgic about the country's earlier status of "splendid isolation" when the vagaries of great-power politics were left for others to resolve. Others countered that the United States was destined to remain a strong force because of its predominant power and proven success during the Cold War.

Into this void came the closely contested presidential campaign of 1992. Of the three candidates, who had widely varying views on the country's future role, Arkansas governor Bill Clinton captured the nation's introspective mood and promised to pursue domestic priorities rather than foreign policy. As a result of this and other positions, he defeated incumbent George Bush and independent Ross Perot, becoming the first president born after World War II and the first to take office after the Cold War.

In some respects Clinton resembled Jimmy Carter. He too was a relatively obscure southern Democrat and a devout Christian, who was not averse to infusing his political rhetoric with biblical pronouncements. A self-described "policy wonk" who immersed himself in scholarly analysis and debate, Clinton exploited the public's soul-searching to turn the country's attention inward, to resolve important domestic problems as a prerequisite to restoring America's vitality and credibility abroad.

In other respects Carter and Clinton were very different. Carter was more driven by foreign policy goals than Clinton, and his world view—based on universal moral principles, protection of human rights, transnational interdependence, and North-South cooperation—shaped his approach to all facets of government. The opposite could be said of Clinton, who admitted that foreign affairs were less compelling to him than domestic concerns such as deficit reduction and health care reform. In fact, beyond his vague comments about global economic integration and his equally ambiguous declaration that the "enlargement" of democratic rule would replace the containment of communism as the primary U.S. objective, it was difficult to discern what, if anything, amounted to a world view for Bill Clinton.

After a fumbling start, during which a debate over gays in the U.S. military became the national preoccupation, Clinton slowly settled into the presidency. His popularity ratings crept upward as the economy showed signs of sustained recovery for much of 1993 and 1994. Housing construction increased, as did spending by Americans on other expensive items such as furniture, televisions, and automobiles (more of which were American-made). While many factory and white-collar jobs were lost, the U.S. unemployment rate remained low, as did the inflation rate. Clinton even made progress in lowering the federal deficit, a prerequisite for sustained economic growth.

The good economic news was offset, however, by a steady stream of international crises. Ethnic tensions and economic problems within the former

Soviet bloc demanded Clinton's attention, together with humanitarian disasters in Africa and Latin America and a confrontation with North Korea over its apparent efforts to build nuclear weapons. These problems diverted Clinton from his stated objective of focusing on domestic reforms. Rather, he was forced to give foreign policy major attention and to defend American interests against challenges that, in many ways, were as complex as those posed by the Soviet Union.

As Clinton grappled with these developments, the new president faced a continuing challenge from his political opponents at home, who questioned his ethical behavior as Arkansas's governor and raised public doubts about his character. At the same time, they argued that many of Clinton's domestic reforms, particularly in the area of health care, were destined to expand rather than curb the role of "big government." The Republican Party's takeover of the U.S. Congress in the 1994 midterm elections served to seriously weaken Clinton's presidency. Yet among the many consequences of this political watershed, Clinton found foreign policy a reliable source of national, bipartisan support—more beneficial to his image than wrangling over health care or education reform on Capitol Hill. Clinton thus looked beyond his domestic agenda and became comfortable playing the role of statesman on the world stage. Predictably, he achieved his greatest success in the area of foreign *economic* policy, involving such issues as U.S. trade flows, economic assistance, and the encouragement of overseas private investment. In earlier years such policies had been managed by cabinet secretaries or congressional committees. But in the 1990s, when a global economic market was rapidly forming and wealth, not military might, was becoming the basis of national security, foreign economic policy had become "high policy." Moreover, it was in this area that Clinton was able to fuse his goal of national economic revival with the opportunity to exploit the political benefits of engagement in foreign affairs.

ECONOMIC LIMITATIONS AND
GLOBAL COMMITMENTS

On the campaign trail Clinton had made the U.S. economy the centerpiece of his bid for the presidency. He had reasoned that in a country still reeling from a recession and high unemployment, the economy would be the issue that would defeat George Bush, whose foreign policy skills seemed less relevant in the new era. In his campaign Clinton laid out a program of domestic reforms and emphasized that without a strong and growing economy, accompanied by declining budget and trade deficits, the United States could not afford to play an influential role in world politics, regardless of what that role would be in specific instances.

But, as Clinton acknowledged, the "decline" of the U.S. economy during the Cold War had been inevitable. America's economic preeminence immediately after World War II, when it accounted for nearly half of global production, had stemmed largely from the decimation of the Western European and Pacific economies. And it had lasted only until they recovered. On a broader scale, the U.S. share of the world gross national product (GNP) was about 22 percent before World War I; after its dramatic rise in the 1940s it returned to that level and stabilized in the 1980s. Thus the country's predominance after World War II was a historical aberration; the *relative* decline of the U.S. economy—on an absolute basis it continued to grow—was not a harbinger of economic collapse.

From this perspective the apocalyptic fears of many observers about the U.S. economy were unfounded. The country, however, was facing many daunting economic problems, a number of which were self-inflicted. Many long-complacent American industries were unprepared for the sudden burst of overseas competition. Meanwhile, American consumers had gone on a protracted spending spree which had stimulated manufacturing and retail sales but had drained the country of a savings base from which industry could draw for expansion. The U.S. government, having built and equipped a military superior to any other, had funded growing social and entitlement programs while the economy surged during the 1950s and 1960s. In response to political pressure, however, it had restrained tax increases to pay for the new programs, producing large budget deficits. Finally, state and local governments, with more responsibility for education than Washington, had allowed schools to deteriorate and students to become uncompetitive in the global economy. (Japanese and West German school children attended school longer each day and up to two months longer a year. These children also learned more science and mathematics, the basis of all contemporary innovations.)

Because almost every sector of American society bore some responsibility for the problems confronting the U.S. economy in the 1990s, Clinton argued that their resolution would require an equally widespread effort. In focusing on problems at home that went beyond economics—to include social divisions and widespread public cynicism toward government—Clinton was ready to accept a more modest American presence in world politics. Thus only those issues that affected U.S. economic recovery and growth, such as the reform efforts in Eastern Europe and regional trade, held his attention early in his presidency.

THE COURSE OF AMERICA'S ECONOMIC FAILURES

In the wake of World War II American policy makers rarely raised the issue of affordability when responding to a foreign country or regional crisis that was of "vital interest" to the United States. A few occasionally asked whether the United States could afford a Marshall Plan or expanded military programs. And the Eisenhower administration was particularly concerned about costs, federal deficits, and balanced budgets. But in the words of President John Kennedy, the country could "bear any burden" that was thought necessary. Although funds were limited, the assumption was that the nation was wealthy enough to support a high standard of living at home and an activist policy abroad.

The 1950s and 1960s were decades of unprecedented economic growth in the United States. Wages rose rapidly as trade unions grew powerful and negotiated sizable annual raises paid by an American industry that apparently could afford such raises while still earning handsome profits. Meanwhile, in the 1960s the Kennedy and Johnson administrations vastly expanded the welfare state in their effort to build a "Great Society," leading to the establishment of new entitlement programs, as well as higher costs for such older programs as Social Security. Some new programs, such as Medicare, started small but grew rapidly as their responsibilities multiplied.

The bubble burst for the U.S. economy in the early 1970s. The enormous expense of the Vietnam War, plus the dramatic rise in oil prices, produced high inflation and large-scale unemployment and put a brake on the generation-long economic expansion. Instead of growing rapidly, the economy stagnated. Meanwhile, the war-ravaged industrial economies of Western Europe had largely recovered and new competitors in East Asia had entered the global marketplace. After Vietnam, it was obvious that the United States could no longer afford an unlimited supply of both guns and butter. It had to make choices; an economy that was growing slowly could not afford rapidly rising annual welfare costs and expensive foreign policy commitments. In the late 1970s Jimmy Carter attempted to revive the economy by reducing military spending and keeping taxes in line with the growing entitlement programs (see Chapter 8). But a second oil shock in 1978 and 1979 produced a new burst of inflation, punctuated by double-digit interest rates and unemployment. The resurgence of Soviet adventurism and anti-American revolutions in Nicaragua and Iran then forced Carter to reverse his military cutbacks. Ronald Reagan accelerated this military expansion in the early 1980s while cutting taxes for many Americans, both of which were campaign promises. Despite his efforts to reduce domestic spending on social programs and to crack down on "waste, fraud, and mismanagement," government expenditures continued to mount.

But free spending is usually followed by a free fall. The long-term expectation of the Reagan administration's "supply-side economics" was that a U.S. economy stimulated by lower taxes would grow as rapidly as it had during the 1950s and 1960s. But the American economy had changed greatly since the 1960s. Although American agriculture was the most bountiful in the world, by the mid-1980s its overseas markets were declining. Other industrialized countries and many developing states such as India, China, Thailand, and Indonesia became food exporters. More important, traditional American smokestack industries such as steel and automobile manufacturing were caught off guard as newly industrialized countries (NICs) produced superior goods at less cost and increased their shares of important markets.

Thus, in addition to the growing budget deficits recorded in Washington, a string of trade deficits in the 1980s and early 1990s plagued the U.S. economy. Its annual trade deficits with Japan alone exceeded $50 billion, and in 1994 China exported $30 billion more in goods to the United States than it imported. Reasons for the trade deficits were similar to those for the overall decline in American industry: low capital investments in nonmilitary research and development; the preoccupation among corporate leaders with quarterly profits and dividends to the detriment of long-term growth; and the decline of the American labor force, a byproduct of lower educational standards. In addition, there was a lack of corporate enterprise. During the 1980s capital investment and modernization took second place to a merger mania and hostile takeovers of companies. Even though this shuffling of paper was profitable financially for a small group of investment bankers and lawyers, it did not add one whit to economic growth. As for American consumers, despite the stagnation of disposable income, they continued to spend freely, often with credit cards.

Finally, much of American industry was going overseas where it could gain access to new markets and where wages were lower, especially in Third World countries. American manufacturers also could avoid the European Community's tariff wall by building factories in Western Europe. Industry considered these policies rational, but they contributed to growing unemployment in the United States and other problems that could not be attributed simply to economic cycles. It appeared that "structural problems"—a euphemism for intensified global competition—confronted the U.S. economy, and they would not recede on their own.

But not all of the blame for America's economic lethargy could be directed inward. The economies of Western Europe and East Asia had recovered in large measure by violating the terms of the liberal international economic order promoted by the United States under the Bretton Woods regime. Members of the European Community (now called the European Union—EU) may have opened their internal markets, but they discouraged exports from overseas through high trade barriers such as those enacted through its Common Agriculture Policy. The Japanese government also actively promoted the expansion of its key industries, particularly automobiles and consumer electronics, by providing them with generous tax breaks and research subsidies and protecting them from foreign competition through punitive tariffs.[2] These practices incited charges of "neomercantilism" from the United States, Japan's primary export market, which was unable to sell its products in Tokyo at competitive prices. Relations between the two countries suffered as a result, especially after the Cold War when Japan's strategic role as a bulwark of containment ended. More troubling to American leaders and workers, the NICs along the Pacific Rim emulated Japan's "industrial policy" and served as additional role models for developing countries in Africa and Latin America. Even the People's Republic of China got into the act, flooding international markets while erecting high tariff walls against imports. In so doing, the Chinese communist regime gave new meaning to the term "central planning" in economic development.

RESPONSES BY THE CLINTON ADMINISTRATION

Clinton was widely praised for recognizing that the country's eroding economic base represented a clear and present danger to U.S. national security. America's superior productive capability may have underwritten its victory in World War II and its successful postwar campaign against the Soviet Union, but economic stagnation in the 1980s and 1990s raised the critical question of whether the economy could still support a foreign policy that maintained 300,000 U.S. soldiers in Western Europe, defended Japan and South Korea, policed the Persian Gulf and the Middle East, and retained its traditional sphere of influence in Latin America. Could the United States do all this while supporting ever-growing domestic programs and keeping up with interest payments on the national debt, the fastest growing area of federal spending?

Clinton argued that the United States must "reinvest" in its domestic base in order to compete more effectively with the outside world. By reinvestment, he meant that the federal government should take a more active role in reforming the national health care system, improving the quality of American schools, combatting crime, and restoring the country's basic infrastructure such as roads and bridges. Furthermore, he vowed to improve the antagonistic relationship that had prevailed between the federal government and many large industries. Toward this end Clinton met with leaders from the U.S. automobile industry in 1993 and proclaimed a "new partnership" between the federal government and auto makers. These two groups would act as allies rather than adversaries in promoting economic growth, much as they did in Japan. In promoting his own version of industrial policy, Clinton was ready to play by the same rules as his economic competitors.

Among Clinton's early priorities in foreign economic policy was the pro-

2. Chalmers Johnson, *MITI and the Japanese Miracle* (Palo Alto: Stanford University Press, 1982).

motion of U.S. participation in regional trading blocs. The early 1990s witnessed a wave of regional economic integration, much of it based on the success of the European Union, which had linked its member states together in a single economic market.[3] By removing barriers to trade and investment within the blocs, by encouraging the movement of workers across national borders, and by standardizing health and safety regulations, these states hoped to increase economic efficiency and raise overall levels of production and commerce.

The first such achievement for the United States was the passage in 1993 of the North American Free Trade Agreement (NAFTA), which integrated the economies of the United States, Canada, and Mexico. Proposed and negotiated under the Bush administration, NAFTA was aimed at reducing or eliminating the tariffs that had limited trade among the three countries. American critics of NAFTA charged that it would encourage U.S. manufacturers to relocate their factories in Mexico, where labor was far cheaper, thus crippling American firms and their surrounding communities. Others claimed NAFTA would reward the Mexican government, its one-party rule, and neglect the country's largely impoverished population (including Indian groups in southern Mexico, which staged an armed rebellion in 1993). NAFTA supporters countered that the treaty would stimulate economic growth in Mexico, relieve the plight of most Mexicans, create new markets for American goods, and move Mexico toward democracy. They further argued that the Canadian market had been neglected because of the cross-border restrictions and that both economies would benefit by their integration. Finally, they proclaimed NAFTA to be consistent with the laissez-faire principles of free markets that the United States had long espoused. In the end, pro-NAFTA forces prevailed; the treaty passed narrowly in Congress and went into effect on the first day of 1994. By year's end, NAFTA had increased U.S. exports by $9 billion and had created 100,000 new jobs. The Mexican deal, however, suffered a major setback when a sudden and deep devaluation of the peso provoked a fiscal crisis early in 1995, requiring a $40 billion international loan guarantee ($20 billion from the United States) to prevent a financial collapse and adversely affected U.S. exports and jobs. NAFTA remained intact with strong support within the U.S. government.

Before this occurrence, Clinton had broadened his campaign for economic integration when in December 1994 he embraced a hemispheric free trade

3. The European Union, formerly the European Community, expanded to fifteen member states in 1994 when Austria, Finland, and Sweden voted to accept membership. The twelve other members of the EU are Belgium, Denmark, France, Germany, Greece, Ireland, Italy, Luxembourg, the Netherlands, Portugal, Spain, and the United Kingdom. In December 1994 the EU members pledged to increase their number still further, offering future membership to Bulgaria, the Czech Republic, Hungary, Poland, Romania, and Slovakia. The three Balkan states and Slovenia also were added to the "pre-accession" list.

zone extending from Alaska to Argentina. At the Summit of the Americas held in Miami, the leaders of all thirty-four countries in the Western Hemisphere except Cuba pledged to reach an accord on regional trade by 2005. They also promised to adhere to worldwide trade reforms and to undertake economic development sensitive to environmental and social concerns. Encouraging this momentum, the United States announced during the summit that it would begin talks with Chile in 1995 about its entry into NAFTA. This opens the doors for other South American states, most notably Brazil and Argentina, unless reaction to Mexico delays the development of the single economic market in the Western Hemisphere.

In yet another step toward regional economic integration, the United States supported a fifteen-nation program of Asia-Pacific Economic Cooperation (APEC), designed to coordinate trade and investment within the region. The Pacific market had emerged as the most dynamic area of economic activity for the United States, growing faster and producing more jobs than Europe. In fact, according to President Clinton, exports across the Pacific had become the "lifeblood" of U.S. economic growth. When Clinton attended an APEC summit meeting in Indonesia in late 1994, he restated his interest in expanding commerce throughout the region. Distrust lingered among many APEC members over each other's political and economic practices, and serious questions remained about future security arrangements in the Pacific region. But as economic relations climbed to the top of the foreign policy agenda, these concerns were swept aside.

All these efforts were designed to fuse the U.S. economy to that of the rapidly expanding world economy. Indirectly, they also contributed to the market-driven world economy sought by the United States since World War II. A giant step in this direction was taken late in 1994 when the U.S. Congress ratified the most recent round of the General Agreement on Tariffs and Trade (GATT), approved by nearly every other country earlier in the year. The agreement, which resulted from GATT's Uruguay Round and was designed to reduce tariffs on most products sold overseas, was hailed by Clinton as the "largest tax cut in world history." Passage of GATT, which had seemed assured, was briefly placed in doubt after several members of Congress criticized its provisions for a World Trade Organization (WTO) to monitor trade practices and enforce compliance. These criticisms were silenced, however, after Clinton assured Congress that the United States would not surrender its sovereign authority to the WTO. In fact, with its record of relatively open trade practices, the United States would be in a strong position to use the WTO in the pursuit of its ultimate goal of globalized free trade. After Clinton's Republican rivals finally endorsed GATT, it was ratified easily by both houses of Congress.

Economic integration was not the only response by the Clinton administration in the key area of trade. Clinton was faced with a second important issue in the spring of 1994 when questions again arose over trade with the People's Republic of China, one of the world's fastest-growing economies in the 1990s. In response to U.S. concerns about China's dubious human rights practices, Clinton's predecessors had linked China's "most-favored nation" (MFN) trade status to its progress in respecting human rights. But in 1994 China's leaders openly declared that their domestic behavior would not be tailored to satisfy American concerns and demands. Their defiance trapped Clinton, who was aware of the economic value of U.S. trade with China and of the important stakes and jobs at issue in the trade relationship. When push came to shove, Clinton backed down on the political demands, and, taking matters a great leap forward, he announced that human rights would no longer be directly linked to U.S. trade with the Chinese. Instead, he predicted that the "carrot" of continuing trade would better elicit reforms in China than the "stick" of trade sanctions. His decision, while angering human rights groups, sent a message that in the future the United States would consider its economic self-interest along with humanitarian concerns in making foreign policy decisions.

Indeed, Sino-American relations worsened in early 1995 over strictly economic matters, especially China's infringements of international copyright and patent laws. A trade war was narrowly avoided. Clinton made a similar pragmatic shift in U.S. policy when he lifted Washington's twenty-year trade embargo against Vietnam. Clinton was persuaded by economic projections indicating that trade between the United States and Vietnam would triple to more than $8 billion by 1999 if the embargo were lifted. Again, he used the argument that closer economic ties between the two countries, which still had deep ideological differences and lingering disputes over the issue of missing American servicemen, would contribute more to their resolution than political and economic estrangement. (Ironically, when such a policy of "constructive engagement" was employed by the Reagan administration in its approach to South Africa, it was widely criticized by Democrats.)

Clinton's emphasis on "geoeconomics" and his support for American material interests over idealistic crusades struck a chord with the American public and among many conservatives who otherwise opposed him. But just as global influence was dependent on a sound domestic base, the reverse also was true: the United States required a relatively stable world order for it to remain attentive to domestic needs. Yet Clinton's economic focus did not signify the end of international crises nor the end of America's traditional interests as a great power. In his first years as president a growing number of problems overseas—many of them social, political, and military in nature—demanded a coherent U.S. response. And in these areas Clinton was far less adept, with serious implications for the country's credibility as a great power.

During the post-World War II period, the number of nation-states in the international system grew dramatically, from 55 in 1946 to nearly 200 in 1995. Most of these new countries were created from former European colonies in Africa and southern Asia. Others, such as the detached Czech Republic and Slovakia, emerged during the 1990s in Eastern Europe, while still others—including the three Baltic states, Ukraine, and Kazakhstan—were carved out of the former Soviet Union.

This proliferation of nation-states, part of a longer-term process of "self-determination" which received its impetus from President Woodrow Wilson after World War I, dramatically changed the face of world politics during the late twentieth century. The new countries, often located in the world's poorest areas, received large volumes of economic assistance from wealthier nations and accepted their help in the complicated task of "state building." In the newly established United Nations the new states united with other developing countries to form a majority within the General Assembly, which served as a vehicle for their collective campaign in the 1970s for a "new international economic order." Most dramatically, the fragile new states often became regional flashpoints for confrontation between the United States and the Soviet Union (see Chapter 5), from whom they received a steady infusion of military weapons, ammunition, and training, which fueled civil wars and strengthened repressive rulers.

As already explained, the early 1990s witnessed the addition of many new countries to the state system, mostly in Eastern Europe and the former Soviet Union, and continuing struggles within some of the younger states in the developing world. Both processes, often accompanied by political disorder and widespread violence, were byproducts of the Cold War's abrupt conclusion and the power vacuums it left, which were filled by often bloody struggles among rival ethnic groups. Among the earliest examples was that of the former Yugoslavia, a polyglot society which had been held together under the repressive control of its communist leader, Marshal Tito, but which fragmented violently after Tito's death and the subsequent demise of communism across Eastern Europe. The dissolution of the Soviet Union itself produced more than a dozen new countries, including a dominant Russian republic that struggled to sustain its transition to an open-market economy and democratic political system. While this was going on, many poor countries such as Somalia and Haiti, which had relied on support from the Cold War superpowers, found themselves suddenly adrift. As living conditions worsened and political leaders were powerless to meet growing demands for relief, they lapsed into anarchy and carnage.

All of these developments confronted the U.S. government at a time when its attention had turned to domestic reform and economic recovery. But the widening bloodshed and potential for further chaos demanded a response by the United States, the world's most powerful state and the recent champion of the Cold War. Uncertain of its role in the post-Cold War world, however, and skeptical that these crises threatened its national interests, the United States responded tentatively. Rather than taking a lead role, it turned to other great powers and the United Nations for concerted action. Their inability to resolve the growing number of crises, as described below, signaled a turbulent new era in world politics and a widening array of challenges to U.S. foreign policy.

'ETHNIC CLEANSING' IN THE BALKANS

Yugoslavia's violent disintegration served as the most frightening example of what could occur in other countries in which Cold War divisions had given way to nationalist rivalries. Yugoslavia, as elsewhere in Eastern Europe after World War I, was a diverse state composed of several national and religious groups: mainly Serbs (Eastern Orthodox), Slovenes and Croats (Catholic), and Bosnians (Muslim). The dominant Serbs, who controlled the capital in Belgrade, the government, and the formidable armed forces, resisted the country's disintegration. When Slovenia and Croatia declared independence in 1991, the Yugoslav army intervened in both territories and a bloody war ensued.

Serbian troops inflicted great damage on Slovenia and Croatia. But they were unable to prevent the secession of the two nations, both of which were promptly admitted into the United Nations. The Serbs then directed their military campaign to the heart of Bosnia-Herzegovina, the most multinational of the former Yugoslav territories, which declared its independence in February 1992—a move unacceptable to the Serbs in Belgrade and in the territory itself, who had no intention of living in a nation dominated by Muslims. In the brutal campaign that followed, the Bosnian Serbs pursued a self-described policy of "ethnic cleansing," which consisted of driving the non-Serbs from their communities in order to expand the Serbs' territory. In doing so, the Serbs burned and looted villages, tortured non-Serbs in concentration camps, systematically raped women of all ages, and besieged the Bosnian capital, Sarajevo, for three years, depriving its citizens of food, water, and electricity.

These actions appalled outside observers and drew widespread condemnation. Many Americans, including 1992 presidential candidate Bill Clinton, called for military intervention in Bosnia. They asserted that by looking on passively while the Serbs committed such flagrant aggression, the United States and the European powers were undermining the very principle that had underlaid their war against Iraq: the inviolability of frontiers. According to the prevailing expectations of the immediate post-Cold War world, no borders were to be changed by force. Indeed, aggression would simply not be allowed to stand, President Bush stated at the height of the Persian Gulf crisis. In Bosnia, many observers charged that the systematic expulsion of Muslims constituted genocide, which was explicitly prohibited by the UN Charter, and called on all countries to act immediately to prevent mass slaughter on the basis of racial or cultural differences.

Opponents of outside intervention countered that the Balkan conflict was a civil conflict, not an international war, despite the recent establishment of new states that were recognized by the United Nations. Furthermore, military intervention would require a massive commitment of between 200,000 and 400,000 troops, heavy fighting, and extensive casualties to separate the combatants and preserve order. Such a military presence in the treacherous mountain territory would likely be required for many years, and no coherent "exit strategy" was in view. But, most important, the conflict appeared to be contained within the Balkan peninsula, imposing little or no threat to the national interests of the great powers, including the United States. The Bush administration generally adopted this view while promoting a diplomatic solution to the crisis. Once elected, Bill Clinton suspended his verbal campaign for U.S. intervention and reluctantly stood by while the onslaught continued.

An international arms embargo was imposed on Yugoslavia when the fighting first erupted. This, however, favored the Serbs because the Yugoslav army—well equipped from its years of association with a communist dictatorship—supplied the Serbs in Croatia and Bosnia-Herzegovina with weapons from its arsenal, while the Muslims were unable to acquire sufficient arms to protect themselves. European leaders opposed lifting the embargo, arguing that it would only broaden the violence and endanger their own peace-keeping forces, which were gradually introduced to provide humanitarian aid to so-called "safe havens" in the remaining Muslim-held areas. The arms embargo continued into 1995, along with a broader economic boycott against the Serbian regime in Belgrade, which claimed to be independent of the Bosnian Serbs.

Clinton occasionally advanced proposals for multilateral military action in the Balkans—and for lifting the arms embargo against Bosnia—but they were strongly opposed by most Western European governments and many influential members of the United Nations, including Yeltsin's Russia, a natural ally of the Slavic Serbs. Even within the U.S. Defense Department, most experts opposed a military response because, in their view, air strikes alone would not be decisive and large U.S. ground forces would soon be required once the air attacks had failed. Within Congress, domestic problems were of greater concern than the seemingly intractable problems in the Balkans. In short, many Americans asked the same question: If the Europeans did not feel sufficiently threatened by events in Bosnia to intervene, why should the more distant United States? For all of these reasons, Clinton was unwilling to assert himself and demand action within NATO, as his predecessor had done in Kuwait. Rather, he waffled, sometimes threatening to intervene with air power and to lift the arms embargo, at other times retracting these positions, citing allied unwillingness to go along as his reason for inaction. He knew that if the United States intervened unilaterally, the war would soon become "America's war." Like President Johnson in Vietnam, he might become stuck in military quicksand, jeopardizing his domestic priorities, stimulating a peace movement, and endangering his reelection chances in 1996.

Meanwhile, the United Nations pressed forward with a plan to partition Bosnia-Herzegovina along ethnic lines. The scheme was constructed to give the Serbs nearly 50 percent of Bosnia while granting the Muslims and Croats control over the remaining lands. Negotiations over this plan foundered, however, as the Serbs continued shelling Muslim enclaves, which the United Nations had declared to be safe havens. The United Nations assured their residents of protection and brought them medicine and food in an effort to mitigate the impact of the Serb sieges; this, in turn, interfered with the Serbian campaign to win the war. The Serbs, therefore, continued to test the limits of UN patience by persevering with their shelling of population centers. Only the threat of UN-authorized air strikes against Serb positions in the mountains surrounding Sarajevo, to be carried out by NATO warplanes, temporarily brought relief to that city and other safe havens. But Serb defiance resumed when the relatively few and ineffective air strikes convinced the Serbs that the United Nations and NATO did not have the will to stop them. Indeed, the air strikes only provoked the Serbs and increased their determination to push on as they watched divisions grow within the anti-Serb coalition, which registered only verbal protests unsupported by firm collective acdion.

For a brief period late in 1994 it appeared the tide was turning against the Serbs. After the Muslims and Croats joined forces and established a combined federation in Bosnia-Herzegovina, Serbian leaders in Belgrade broke with their kinsmen and imposed their own arms embargo against the Bosnian Serbs—a move clearly designed to persuade the United Nations to lift its debilitating economic sanctions against Belgrade. The United States then announced that it no longer would enforce the arms embargo against the Muslims and Croats. This move, dictated by Congress, essentially told the Europeans that if they insisted on depriving the besieged population of Bosnia-Herzegovina of weapons, they would have to enforce the embargo themselves. The United States could, of course, take this position because none of its soldiers were exposed to the consequences of its action.

But the embargo remained largely intact as the Serbs regrouped and retaliated near the safe haven of Bihac in northwestern Bosnia, one of the last Muslim-Croatian strongholds in the region. To deter future air strikes, the

Serbs seized hundreds of UN peace-keepers and held them—and UN/NATO strategy—hostage for several weeks. By 1995 it appeared that the Serbs not only had accomplished their goal of displacing the Muslims from most of Bosnia, but also had succeeded in humiliating the United Nations by demonstrating that its peace-keeping forces never had a peace to keep and that the Serbs could with impunity overrun UN-protected safe havens. Then, in a final turn of the screw, the Serbs announced a ban on UN military escorts of humanitarian convoys, making it almost impossible for aid to reach Sarajevo and other towns and depriving the United Nations of its principal reason for being in Bosnia at all.

The discrediting of the United Nations mirrored the impotence of NATO, whose leaders had earlier stated their intention to play a critical military role in the Balkan conflict. The alliance that had for forty-five years deterred a Soviet attack on Western Europe stood paralyzed before the Serbs in the post-Cold War world, when the alliance no longer was held together by a common enemy and the organization was searching for a new role. The United States, while condemning the Serbs as aggressors and viewing the Muslims as victims, was willing to provide only aerial support—not ground forces—to the anti-Serb effort. Other NATO members, including Britain and France, blamed all parties for the war and atrocities. Moreover, because they had troops on the ground in Bosnia (in noncombat roles), they greatly feared that their soldiers would be imperiled if NATO undertook strong actions against the Serbs. Thus a political deadlock emerged within NATO that reinforced the diplomatic deadlock between the Serbs and Muslims in Bosnia, ensuring that the besieged Muslims would spend a third winter without heat, water, or adequate food supplies. With only a few pinprick air attacks by NATO forces on Serb positions, themselves evidence of the inability of NATO to act collectively and forcefully, a Serbian victory was practically assured.

Thus the Yugoslav debacle revealed critical shortcomings in the system of collective security that was supposed to guarantee peace in the post-Cold War era. The United Nations was shown incapable of harnessing a united response to aggression, much less ending such transparent "ethnic cleansing." NATO was deeply divided by a crisis in which none of the great powers, although horrified by the human tragedy and outraged by the Serbs' conduct of the war, felt their vital interests to be at stake. Despite months of visible discord within NATO about its role in the Balkan conflict, the objective of containing Serbian aggression was ultimately subordinated to the objective of preserving the alliance, although it was unclear what role, if any, the alliance should play at a time when its raison d'être had disappeared. The price of this solidarity, in any case, was essentially inaction in Bosnia.

In late 1994, with victory in sight, the Bosnian Serbs asked former president Jimmy Carter to help restart diplomatic negotiations for a settlement of the war while both sides observed a four-month-long cease-fire. From the beginning, however, the fact that sporadic fighting continued while talks were under way raised the question of whether such a cease-fire would last any longer than the many earlier ones. One reason was the Muslims. Their continued resistance and hopes for a settlement in which they would keep half of Bosnia's territory had long been fueled by the hope—raised by President Clinton—of active U.S. intervention. Would they finally recognize that NATO, which could not be counted on to rescue them, had little choice but to recognize the Bosnian Serbs' conquest? The other reason was the Serbs. Had they offered to talk only as a public relations ploy and to win time to consolidate their territorial control because the winter weather made fighting difficult anyway, or perhaps because they too were weary of the war? Would they be willing to surrender enough of their 70 percent territorial control to entice the Muslims to accept peace? Or were the talks intended merely to legitimate these gains, or, worse, to buy time while the campaign of ethnic cleansing widened further?

NATO, reluctantly acknowledging the result of its unwillingness to act, was by now eager to see the war end and to extricate itself from this unhappy situation by recognizing the Serbs' gains. By contrast, the Serbs' principal weapon in their successful campaign had been their singleness of purpose and their indifference to world opinion as long as their critics kept their powder dry. The longer they did, the more arrogant the Serbs became. Thus unless the cease-fire was intended only to allow both sides time to recuperate until spring when they could resume fighting, or to give the American government, pressured by the Republican majorities in Congress, time to lift the arms embargo and use U.S. air power to its fullest, the Serbs were likely to get what they had wanted all along: the opportunity to govern themselves or, more likely in the longer run, to create the Greater Serbia they had sought since before World War I.

RUSSIA'S ECONOMIC AND POLITICAL TURMOIL

The collapse of Soviet rule, which was widely hailed by foreign observers and many Russians in 1992, exposed deep fault lines within the former Soviet Union and across its vast periphery. Just as the breakup of decrepit empires had ignited World War I, and just as the dismantling of the European colonial empires after 1945 had set off violence between and within many new states, the same potential for violence attended the end of the Soviet empire.

First, the fall of the iron curtain and the Berlin Wall released forces of nationalism in the former Warsaw Pact countries and in Western Europe. Czechoslovakia broke up, peacefully, into the Czech Republic and Slovakia as each ethnic group sought its own state. To the south, a Hungarian political leader claimed that he was "in spirit" responsible for all Hungarians, including sizable numbers living in Romania, Slovakia, and Serbia. To the west, in Germany, where East and West had just been reunited, many Germans became openly critical of the country's open immigration policy and hostile toward the waves of refugees that flowed in from war-torn regions to the south and east. Neo-Nazi "skinheads" assaulted immigrants and firebombed their apartments in many cities. Nationalist groups also gained prominence, and political power, in other Western European countries, including France, Great Britain, and Italy where economic problems persisted.

Second, the Soviet Union fractured into fifteen republics, all claiming sovereignty, with the Baltic states of Estonia, Latvia, and Lithuania reclaiming their pre-World War II independence. Since the Russians had long controlled both the czarist and communist states, ethnic Russians were left scattered throughout the Commonwealth of Independent States (CIS), the loose amalgamation of the eleven non-Baltic republics. In addition to the Russians, more than 100 other nationalities that had composed the Soviet Union inhabited its vast frontiers. This intermingling of nationalities inflamed the hatreds between the Russians and the peoples they had long dominated, particularly Muslims living in the southern tier of CIS states. In Russia it gave xenophobic nationalists and former communists, bent on destroying the liberal state and market economy the reformers were creating, a strong emotional issue with which to bring down the centrist regime of Boris Yeltsin. In Moldova and Georgia, there were secessionist movements; Ukraine was internally divided between its own ethnic group and a sizable Russian population; Tajikistan was engulfed in civil war; and Armenia and Azerbaijan fought a costly war over an enclave seen as the rightful possession of both groups.

After the Soviet Union disappeared from the map, Russia remained a potentially formidable military power with the ability to destroy the fragile political arrangements that were emerging in the early 1990s. The Russian government continued to command an army of more than 1 million soldiers, of which 200,000 remained outside its borders within the CIS. Boris Yeltsin, the Russian leader, attempted to institute political and economic reforms, but these proved to be difficult to impose on a society that had never been exposed to democracy or the free market. From the U.S. perspective, then, Bush had succeeded in managing the Soviet Union's fall; the Clinton administration faced the equally foreboding task of assisting its peaceful transition to democracy.

Yeltsin, the first freely elected leader in Russia's thousand-year history, proclaimed his commitment to a free market and democratic political reforms. But the Russian communists, who were elected under the old Soviet constitution when the Communist Party still governed, still dominated the legislature and state bureaucracy, and they blocked all attempts at reform. Also opposed to Yeltsin's efforts were Russian nationalists who shared the communists' resentment at the loss of empire and status. Yeltsin was clearly caught in the middle. In October 1993 an attempted parliamentary coup failed when Yeltsin, supported by security forces and the army, succeeded in dissolving the parliament (and destroying its headquarters). But the parliamentary elections that followed only made matters worse: a majority of the new parliament was dominated even more by extremists from both the left and right. The most outspoken nationalist, Vladimir Zhirinovsky, pledged to restore the old Russian empire, even suggesting that he would press for the return of Alaska! As conditions worsened across the country, many Russian citizens welcomed this message and openly longed for the more "orderly" system under Stalin and Brezhnev.

In the United States and Western Europe questions were raised about the continuing flow of Western aid to Russia and its neighbors. Should the new Russia be treated as a defeated power, left mired in its own economic misery and political stalemate, perhaps to emerge some day as a resentful state, as Germany did after World War I? Or should its former adversaries be conciliatory and support Russia so it could grow economically and stabilize itself politically, as Germany did with American help after World War II? Multinational corporations also questioned whether the Russian market could profitably absorb their capital. The consensus among the Western powers was that Russia must be provided economic assistance, but only as long as the money was being used effectively. They demanded that Yeltsin's political reforms move forward, that Russian leaders stop subsidizing inefficient industries, and that the country's rate of inflation be held in check. Although faced with their own economic problems, the Western powers (led by Germany) promised more than $30 billion in aid to Russia but limited their actual disbursements as they waited to see what would become of Yeltsin's reforms.

Russia's economic problems, however, were increasingly overshadowed by the problems stemming from the approximately 25 million Russians who lived in the fourteen non-Russian republics, 11 million of them in Ukraine. When Yeltsin's Russia actively supported these populations, which were frequently persecuted in their new countries, fears were raised that Russia might be trying to subdue its neighbors and build a new empire. "Regrettably, the imperial impulse remains strong and even appears to be strengthening," observed former national security adviser Zbigniew Brzezinski.[4] The impulse reverberated far beyond Moscow. Most leaders of the CIS republics were former communists, and in 1994 several, including the newly elected leaders of Belarus and Ukraine (the Slavic nucleus, with Russia, of the CIS), openly considered relinking their countries with Russia. Thus the Clinton ad-

4. Zbigniew Brzezinski, "The Premature Partnership," *Foreign Affairs*, March/April 1994, 72. For an opposing view, see Stephen Sestanovich, "Giving Russia Its Due," *National Interest* (Summer 1994): 3-13.

ministration confronted two potential dangers: the loss of Russia to anti-democratic forces, and, even more ominous, the possible restoration of the former Soviet Union.[5]

An additional and equally volatile issue was Russia's role in a proposed expansion of NATO to include members of the former Warsaw Pact. Many observers worried that the pact's demise had created a power vacuum in central Europe that must be filled by including the region in NATO.[6] Others disagreed, arguing that such an expansion would only weaken the NATO alliance's already fragile cohesion, undermine a sense of common purpose, and drag NATO members into a host of "out-of-area" conflicts in which they had little vested interest. For President Clinton, who was reminded of the alliance's fragility by the morass in the Balkans, no clear solution that would satisfy all NATO members was in sight. The decision was further complicated by the issue of Russian involvement. One suggestion was that NATO be expanded gradually, beginning with Poland and perhaps Hungary and then adding new members as their cases warranted. But such a piecemeal expansion would likely antagonize the Russians, historically alarmed at the prospect of "encirclement" by hostile neighbors. Moreover, if the Eastern European states but not Russia were incorporated into NATO, the process would only further inflame Russian nationalism and destroy hopes for stability in a region still fearful of Russian expansionism.

Thus Clinton and other NATO leaders arrived at a compromise solution. Under the rubric of a "Partnership for Peace," the former Warsaw Pact members and the CIS republics were invited to become auxiliary members of NATO. By May 1994 eighteen of these countries had agreed to join the partnership. As auxiliary members, they were allowed to participate in some NATO deliberations and training exercises, but key strategic decisions were left to the original members. If the larger collaborations proved successful, NATO officials suggested, these auxiliary states might at some future date become full-fledged members of the NATO alliance. Yeltsin first rejected the partnership concept, but later insisted that if Russia were to join, it should receive preferential treatment given its greater military strength, its former role as a superpower, and its continuing status as a permanent member of the UN Security Council. NATO officials resisted this demand, however, arguing that Russia should assume the same role as other partnership members while long-range negotiations over the alliance's role continued. Finally, Yeltsin reluctantly agreed to these conditions and accepted a muted Russian role in the Partnership for Peace.

5. Adrian Karantnycky, "Back to the U.S.S.R.," *Wall Street Journal,* June 30, 1994.
6. See Thomas L. Friedman, "Not Red, But Still a Bear," *New York Times,* February 27, 1994.

But this fragile arrangement began to unravel in late 1994 after NATO members agreed to consider an accelerated schedule for Polish and Hungarian entry into the alliance. Yeltsin loudly protested this plan at a December meeting of the fifty-two-member Organization on Security and Cooperation in Europe (OSCE). Exploiting the tensions within NATO, Yeltsin warned all Europeans, from both east and west, about subjecting themselves to the American military control that had been a central element of the NATO alliance. He then declared that the "Cold Peace" that was emerging between Moscow and Washington would thaw only after the proposed eastward expansion of NATO was suspended. The United States and its NATO allies rejected Yeltsin's thinly veiled threats, which they attributed largely to the Russian leader's need to appease nationalists at a time when his hold on power was threatened.

Yeltsin's internal problems mounted in December when he felt compelled to deploy thousands of troops to the oil-rich republic of Chechnya in southern Russia. The Islamic territory, which had long struggled against Moscow's hegemony, had unsuccessfully sought independence after the Soviet Union collapsed in 1991. When Chechnya's leader, Dzhokhar Dudayev, declared in December 1994 that "our independence is forever," Yeltsin sent Russian troops to the Chechen capital, Grozny, and the Russian air force bombed residential neighborhoods. After the poorly organized and under-equipped Russian troops faltered against the more determined Chechens in early January, Yeltsin escalated the Russian offense in defiance of protests from the United States and other major powers. In defending their actions, Russian leaders diminished the significance of Chechnya as an oil producer, although its annual production of more than 10 million tons was a vital resource. More important to Russia was the dangerous precedent that Chechnya, a republic the size of Connecticut located near Georgia in the Caucasus Mountains, would set for other dissatisfied republics if its demands for independence were met. After bringing in reinforcements and escalating the bombardment of Grozny, Russian troops seized control of the presidential palace, which was largely reduced to rubble. The Chechen rebels refused to surrender, however, and vowed to continue fighting in the surrounding hillsides. As a result, a protracted guerrilla war appeared likely, which would further drain Russian resources and weaken Yeltsin's standing among the U.S. and Western European leaders he badly needed for political and economic support.

Thus for the moment the issue of Russian relations with the United States and NATO was overshadowed as Yeltsin struggled to keep his own house in order. The fact that Yeltsin had found it essential to bomb his own cities spoke volumes about his tenuous hold on the country's transition to democracy. In the aftermath of Grozny's collapse, however, Western leaders were restrained in condemning Yeltsin, fearing that his overthrow would only lead to a more repressive regime.

THE CRISES OF 'FAILED STATES'

"When two elephants fight, the grass suffers," says a familiar African aphorism. Such was the case during the Cold War in many poor countries, which served as regional theaters of superpower conflict. But the propensity of the superpowers to intervene in these countries' civil and regional conflicts abruptly ended along with the Cold War.[7] In this respect the Cold War's end brought relief to many Third World leaders, who looked forward to more constructive relations with the industrialized North. By the mid-1990s, however, the leaders of many poor states were expressing concern that their social and economic problems actually had *worsened* now that the Soviet Union had dissolved and the United States was more concerned with its own economic needs. Many of these countries witnessed the same revival of ethnic clashes and political unrest that occurred in the former Soviet bloc. In addition, they suffered from the same high levels of malnutrition, infant mortality, and inadequate education that had persisted throughout the Cold War. Some observers suggested dismantling what was left of these governments and putting them under UN trusteeship. Such a response was highly unlikely, but it revealed the depths to which many of these countries had fallen. Overall prospects for the world's poor were more uncertain than ever.

This pattern—partly a byproduct of the Cold War's collapse but also an extension of longer-term trends—had devastating effects on many political and economic institutions in the developing world. Indeed, in many areas the post-Cold War era witnessed the emergence of the "failed state":

From Haiti in the Western Hemisphere to the remnants of Yugoslavia in Europe, from Somalia, Sudan, and Liberia in Africa to Cambodia in Southeast Asia, a disturbing new phenomenon is emerging: the failed nation-state, utterly incapable of sustaining itself as a member of the international community. . . . [T]hose states descend into violence and anarchy—imperiling their own citizens and threatening their neighbors through refugee flows, political instability, and random warfare.[8]

One of the first such states to arouse international attention was the impoverished country of Somalia, located along the Horn of Africa at the entrance to the Red Sea. During the Cold War the Soviets had supported its ruler because its large neighbor to the north, Ethiopia, was aligned with the United States. When a pro-Soviet military regime came into power in Ethio-

---

7. The U.S. Agency for International Development reflected this view in 1993 and 1994 by curtailing aid packages to many failed states and outright cancelling assistance to others.

8. Gerald B. Helman and Steven R. Ratner, "Saving Failed States," *Foreign Policy* (Winter 1992-1993): 3.

pia, Gen. Muhammad Siad Barre, Somalia's ruler, switched sides as well. When the Cold War ended and Barre was overthrown, Somalia, despite sharing a common ethnicity, language, history, and religion, descended into a civil war between rival warlords and clans fighting for succession. The government then disappeared and chaos prevailed. When the rival militias prevented farmers from planting new crops and killed most of the nation's livestock, starvation spread, affecting about one-third of the population.

After months during which the world looked the other way—toward the plight of the Kurds in Iraq, the civil wars in the Sudan and Liberia, the life-threatening droughts in other parts of Africa, the brutal war in Bosnia—media attention compelled a U.S. and Western response through the United Nations: a humanitarian action with a limited objective. More than 28,000 troops, at first mainly American, were dispatched in late 1992 to provide order and food. After they had achieved the mission of Operation Restore Hope, the American forces were to be withdrawn and replaced by UN forces drawn from various nations.

The problem, however, was that once these forces were withdrawn, the warlords would reignite the struggle for power and the killing and the hunger would soon resume. Thus the UN mission was changed in 1993 from one of humanitarian relief to one of rebuilding Somalia's political and economic structures. But the country's principal warlord, Gen. Mohammed Farah Aidid, who controlled Somalia's capital, resisted the enlarged UN mission because it called for the warlords' removal and disarmament. In the fighting that followed, twenty-four Pakistani peace-keepers were ambushed and killed. Later more UN troops were killed, including U.S. soldiers from forces sent in to capture the elusive General Aidid as well as Somali civilians. As the number of deaths of U.S. soldiers mounted—and after one dead soldier was dragged through city streets before cheering crowds and television cameras—calls for the withdrawal of U.S. troops began. Clinton responded by accelerating their departure, and the United Nations announced in late 1994 that the failed peace-keeping effort would be suspended by the spring of 1995.

The critical downfall of the Somali operation was that the international peace-keepers, initially dispatched for the humanitarian purpose of feeding the people, ignored the political situation that had created the hunger in the first place. The hunger had not stemmed from a natural disaster; it was man-made. Indeed, it should have been clear from the beginning that resolving the anarchic political situation was a prerequisite to resolving the humanitarian crisis. But because that was not clear, what was believed at the outset to be a short mission ended up taking two and a half years, underlining the point that there was no such thing as an apolitical, purely humanitarian mission. A lasting solution to the Somalian conflict could be achieved only by "state building," which proved to be a far more difficult, if not impossible, under-taking. Thus a worthy, moral effort to help the Somali people—which it did in the near term—turned into an open-ended commitment with minimal prospects for success.

His experience in Somalia still fresh in his mind, Clinton was faced with another humanitarian nightmare in the African state of Rwanda, where vio-lence between the rival Hutu, who dominated the government, and Tutsi tribes had resulted in more than 500,000 casualties, mainly Tutsi, over a peri-od of less than three months in 1994 (this death toll far exceeded that in Bos-nia, where the killing of about 200,000 Muslims by the Serbs was often re-ferred to as "genocide"). Given that the multilateral response was proving unworkable in Somalia, a concerted peace-keeping effort in Rwanda was out of the question. Thus the United Nations was largely silent in the face of the Rwandan tragedy. Responsibility for outside intervention fell on the French government, which had considered francophone Africa part of its sphere of influence even after its colonial control had ended. (Although Rwanda was a Belgian colony, it had been incorporated into France's sphere of influence af-ter its independence.) But by the time French troops intervened in Rwanda— perhaps to save the Hutu government France had long supported—it was too late. Rwanda's rivers were choked by slain bodies, many horribly hacked to death with machetes. Moreover, the victory of the Tutsi army and the estab-lishment of a Tutsi-led government provoked one of the world's greatest hu-man migrations. Fearing vengeance, the Hutus virtually emptied Rwanda, half a million fleeing to Burundi, another half million to Tanzania, and a mil-lion to Zaire. This relentless flow of humanity overwhelmed local and inter-national efforts to help and led to widespread deaths from starvation, cholera, dehydration, and exhaustion.

The Clinton administration was confronted with yet another crisis in the failed state of Haiti, the poorest country in the Western Hemisphere. Ruled by the U.S.-backed Duvalier dictatorship until 1986, the Haitian people had their first experience with democratic elections in 1990 when they elected Jean-Bertrand Aristide to be the country's president. But Aristide's proposed reforms, including his plans to demilitarize the country and redistribute wealth, resulted in his overthrow six months later by the military. With Aris-tide in exile in the United States, the military leaders, ruled by Gen. Raoul Cé-dras, launched a campaign of terror across the island, killing, torturing, and imprisoning those who had fought for reforms and who continued to resist the new rulers. As a result, thousands of Haitians constructed makeshift boats and fled to the United States. In his final months in office, President Bush an-nounced that the United States was unprepared to accommodate these "boat people" and ordered the U.S. Coast Guard to turn them back. His decision angered many human rights groups, as well as candidate Bill Clinton, who declared on the campaign trail that as president he would allow the Haitians to seek asylum in the United States.

But just as in other areas of foreign policy, Clinton's position on Haiti changed once he took office. Suddenly he shared Bush's reservations about absorbing the mass emigration of Haitians. Thus while continuing to demand Aristide's return to Haiti and denouncing the military rulers, Clinton also announced that he would not allow Haitian refugees to enter the United States. Instead, a UN-sponsored economic embargo was imposed on Haiti, and it was hoped that the embargo would force Aristide's restoration.

In July 1993 the Clinton administration reached an agreement that would have brought about Aristide's return to power in exchange for the amnesty of Cédras and other military leaders. But when the 270 U.S. and Canadian peace-keepers arrived on the U.S.S. *Harlan County* in October to oversee the transition back to civilian rule, they were greeted at the waterfront by a handful of armed thugs who denounced their arrival. The ship then beat an ignominious retreat. An angry and disappointed Aristide publicly condemned the Clinton administration's reversal and was joined by many liberals on Capitol Hill, including the Congressional Black Caucus, which saw a racial bias in Clinton's acceptance of Cuban refugees, while Haitians, of African origin, were turned back in open waters.

The tentative American response to disorder in Haiti became a symbol of the Clinton administration's lack of resolve in foreign policy. Even the *New York Times,* which supported most of Clinton's domestic initiatives, expressed dismay at his reversals in handling the deepening crisis in Haiti. "After months of vacillating from one policy to another, America faces the troubling prospect that Mr. Clinton is drifting into using troops in Haiti because he wants to compensate for other policy embarrassments and does not have a better idea."[9] Clinton also was condemned by conservatives, aghast at a retreat at the first sign of opposition by a weak and corrupt military regime and at the squandering of U.S. prestige which had been elevated by America's Cold War victory and its more recent spectacular military victory over Iraq.

The turmoil in Haiti continued into the fall of 1994 even while Haitian refugees were being diverted to an overcrowded settlement camp on the Guantánamo naval base in Cuba, then to temporary facilities as far away as Panama City. As for President Clinton, he finally concluded that the Haitian problem could only be resolved by U.S. military intervention, and he issued the Cédras junta a public ultimatum. His threat of war was widely denounced in the United States, where congressional opponents demanded time to debate and vote on the impending invasion, but Clinton had gone beyond the point of no return. Yet even as American jets were taking off toward Port-au-

9. "Which Haiti Policy?" (editorial), *New York Times,* July 7, 1994.

Prince, he dispatched to Haiti a high-level mission, headed by former president Jimmy Carter, to confront Cédras, offer him a final opportunity to leave peacefully, and prevent a military clash. Cédras accepted the offer, but reportedly only after being notified that the invasion was in progress. Thus the mission was transformed into a "semi-permissive occupation" of Haiti that extended well into 1995. As in Somalia, the United States was thrust into the role of state builder. Aristide was returned to power, but stability on the island was largely dependent on the presence of U.S.—and subsequently UN—troops and a long-term commitment of foreign aid to Haiti.

The American public's response to Clinton's efforts in these cases was overwhelmingly negative. The failed states of Somalia and Haiti became synonymous with failed American foreign policy; many members of Congress and the public openly doubted that the United States had vital interests in these areas. The terms of the Haitian settlement—recognition of the military junta, amnesty for Cédras, and a comfortable retirement for him and his henchmen, whom Clinton had consistently denounced as criminals—were viewed as excessively generous, granted only because Clinton needed a face-saving alternative to invasion. While Haiti was a success in that no American soldiers were killed in combat (in contrast to Somalia), the nation breathed a sigh of relief at having avoided another disaster. But, most important, widespread rejection of American actions in Somalia and Haiti—coupled with Clinton's rebuke in the 1994 congressional elections—spelled further doom for the notion that humanitarian interventionism would serve as the orienting principle of American foreign policy after the Cold War.

BREAKTHROUGHS IN THE MIDDLE EAST

As described in earlier chapters, Cold War tensions often spilled over into civil and regional conflicts in the developing world, undermining the tenuous steps that had been taken toward political and economic development in that region. Indeed, many regimes in the Third World exploited the U.S.-Soviet rivalry by accepting economic or military aid from the highest bidder. Thus the end of the Cold War was widely expected to erase this pernicious pattern and reduce the likelihood of crises and violence.

But quite the opposite occurred in the Persian Gulf. For while the United States and the Soviet Union frequently escalated local quarrels, domestic and external, they also restrained the proxies they had aided politically and militarily to prevent a confrontation that might escalate and risk nuclear war. The disappearance of this superpower restraint, however, meant that ambitious regional leaders like Iraq's Saddam Hussein now had the freedom to try and realize their aims. The Gulf War was thus the direct result of the Cold War's end.

Indeed, the end of the Cold War and the collapse of the Soviet Union radically changed the political situation and strategic choices for the former client states. The first sign of this change in behavior was exhibited by Syria during the Gulf War. It was a surprise when even moderate Arab states, although threatened by Saddam Hussein's action, aligned themselves with the United States, Israel's strongest and staunchest supporter. But when a radical Arab state like Syria, long a Soviet client and militantly anti-Israel, did so it was plainly shocking. Unlike Iraq, Syria had calculated that without Soviet support and weapons it had better ingratiate itself with the only remaining superpower. Thus Syria, an enemy of Iraq, joined the anti-Saddam Hussein coalition, where its participation lent credibility to the Arab coalition with the United States and symbolized the changing nature of Middle Eastern politics.

After Iraq's defeat, in fact, the Bush administration judged the time right for a major effort to gain a comprehensive peace between Israel and its neighbors (only Egypt had made its peace with Israel and recognized the Jewish state). But despite the favorable conditions, Secretary of State James Baker had to make many trips to the region to cajole all the parties, including the Palestinians, to come to Madrid, Spain, for their first face-to-face conference. Since Israel always had refused to deal directly with the Palestinian Liberation Organization (PLO), which it regarded as a terrorist organization, the Palestinians participated as part of the Jordanian delegation.

The breakthrough in the talks—which was totally unexpected—came in September 1993 when the PLO and Israel agreed to recognize each other. In this historic agreement, negotiated with the help of Norway, the PLO abandoned its call for the destruction of Israel and renounced terrorism. In return for Palestinian recognition of the right of Israel "to exist in peace and security," Israel would withdraw from the Gaza Strip and the West Bank town of Jericho and allow the Palestinians to begin governing themselves. It was assumed that, over time, the Palestinians' authority in education, health, social services, taxation, and tourism would be extended over the West Bank except in the areas settled by the Israelis. A further assumption was that the Palestinians would keep order, police themselves, and, in particular, end the *intifada* (holy war) against Israel and its supporters. If these expectations were realized, then the two sides would eventually negotiate the future of the occupied territories—whether the Palestinians would be allowed to establish a state of their own—and the status of East Jerusalem, which the Palestinians claimed as their capital and the Israelis claimed as part of the united capital of their state.

Why did these two deadly enemies finally decide to negotiate their differences? The end of the Cold War had deprived the PLO of a strong political supporter, and the Gulf War, in which PLO leader Yasir Arafat made the di-

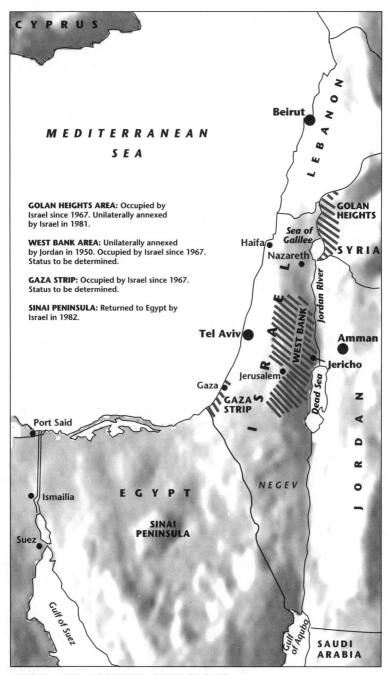

GOLAN HEIGHTS AREA: Occupied by Israel since 1967. Unilaterally annexed by Israel in 1981.

WEST BANK AREA: Unilaterally annexed by Jordan in 1950. Occupied by Israel since 1967. Status to be determined.

GAZA STRIP: Occupied by Israel since 1967. Status to be determined.

SINAI PENINSULA: Returned to Egypt by Israel in 1982.

ISRAEL AND OCCUPIED TERRITORIES

sastrous decision to support Saddam Hussein against the oil kingdoms that had provided the PLO with most of its finances, had left the organization almost broke, unable to pay its supporters and fund its extensive social-welfare activities. Iranian-supported Islamic radicals moved into the vacuum as the PLO's support on the West Bank and Gaza Strip declined. But even before these events, the spontaneous outburst of the *intifada* among West Bank Palestinians frustrated by the continued Israeli occupation and Arafat's inability to solve their problems already had demonstrated his declining hold on his followers. That is why in 1988 Arafat had declared the establishment of a Palestinian state in the occupied areas, thereby suggesting a two-state solution instead of Israel's elimination. On their part, the Israelis were tiring of the constant conflict, and the costs—physical, economic, as well as moral—of the six-year-old *intifada*. But more than that, they too were worried by the increasing support among Palestinians for extremists. Thus talks with the PLO had become more and more inevitable. Finally, if Israel could achieve a stabler peace, the country's economy, aided by the large influx of skilled Russian immigrants who were fleeing the antisemitism that was flourishing once more in their homeland, would prosper.

But as many had anticipated, one obstacle after another blocked implementation of the Israeli-PLO accord. Tensions between Palestinians and Israelis continued, and massacres committed by militants on both sides threatened to cripple it entirely. Would the ongoing attacks on and killing of Israelis by Islamic fundamentalists undermine the efforts by Prime Minister Yitzhak Rabin to seek a solution to the impasse and embolden opponents of the accord within the Israeli government? At the same time, would the radical Islamic groups succeed in destroying Arafat's authority and legitimacy as the PLO's leader?

But despite the opposition of extremists in Israel, the Middle East peace process achieved further success by late 1994 when Israel resolved its differences with Jordan. Under the terms of the agreement, both countries acknowledged the right of the other to exist, bringing their de facto state of war to an end. In addition, Jordan's King Hussein and Israeli prime minister Rabin agreed on the boundaries between the two neighbors, divided control over underground water reservoirs and other natural resources, and established the basis for bilateral trade and tourism.

Although the Middle East peace process had its own momentum, the United States played its traditional mediating role. Secretary of State Warren Christopher, though criticized for his lack of dynamism in such trouble spots as Bosnia and Haiti, was credited by both sides with hastening the agreements through repeated, often unpublicized trips to the region. The United States also agreed to forgive Jordan's foreign debt, which played a key role in procuring the country's cooperation given its continuing economic distress. King

Hussein and Prime Minister Rabin therefore invited Christopher and President Clinton to be present at the signing of the accord.

Clinton, suffering from a series of domestic setbacks, was only too happy to assume this highly visible role. His act of statesmanship was overshadowed, however, by his decision to visit Damascus and meet personally with Syrian leader Hafez al-Assad, long considered by the U.S. government to be a primary sponsor of international terrorism. Clinton, emulating Jimmy Carter's quixotic approach to diplomacy, hoped he could gain Assad's cooperation through personal appeals to good faith. But Assad did not take the bait. He conceded little to Clinton while enjoying the enhanced prestige and legitimacy that came with being recognized, for the first time, by an American president. Thus rather than achieving a more comprehensive Middle East peace through his high-stakes gamble, Clinton only provided more ammunition to his critics, who assailed his befriending of international outlaws.

THE PRICE OF PEACE WITH NORTH KOREA

Clinton's willingness to bargain with anti-American dictators was evident again in 1994 as he was forced to resolve yet another crisis, this time in North Korea, where its Stalinesque dictator, Kim Il Sung, threatened to build nuclear weapons in open defiance of North Korea's earlier pledge to respect the terms of the Nuclear Non-Proliferation Treaty (NPT) Sung had signed. The prospect of nuclear weapons in North Korea was disturbing to the United States, and to much of the world, for several reasons: the possibility that such weapons might stimulate an arms race in East Asia—South Korea and Japan could not ignore such a threat to their security; the encouragement such weapons might give other radical anti-American regimes, such as Iran, to build their own nuclear bombs or obtain help from regimes like North Korea; and, above all, the role such weapons would likely play in undermining the NPT, due to be renewed in 1995, and in setting loose the forces of mass destruction.

The Clinton administration, vowing that North Korea would not be allowed to become a nuclear power and insisting that it would not negotiate with its government until after it permitted inspection of its nuclear facilities, threatened to impose economic sanctions against North Korea. Kim responded by declaring that such sanctions would be regarded as an act of war and by deploying troops to the border with South Korea. For several weeks a reprise of the Korean War of the 1950s became a possibility. Moreover, the North Korean standoff raised a number of questions about the roles that Russia and China, North Korea's allies during the Cold War, might play in the situation, and it heightened concerns in Japan about its own security, which had been protected by the United States during the Cold War.

All of this presented an additional challenge to Clinton, who dispatched Jimmy Carter to North Korea for personal meetings with its dictator. After several discussions in June 1994, Carter announced that Kim had agreed to limited inspections of his nuclear program. It became clear, however, that Sung already had diverted enough plutonium to build at least one nuclear bomb. In October the United States announced that North Korea had agreed to "freeze" its nuclear program. But the price for maintaining North Korea, not as a nonnuclear state but as an infant nuclear power, was incredible: U.S. payment of $4 billion for the construction of two nuclear power generators that would not yield plutonium; a free supply of oil for eight to ten years (since China was no longer willing to supply oil at "friendship" prices); and diplomatic relations with the United States and Japan.

When the details of this astounding arrangement were disclosed, many questions were raised about its credibility. What had the United States received in return for reviving North Korea's failing economy with free oil, ending its diplomatic isolation, and building its nuclear reactors gratis? Only a promise: to allow inspections within eight years and shut down the plutonium reprocessing plant, a promise North Korea had made years earlier and then violated. In short, North Korea's nuclear program remained intact, only "frozen," keeping any weapons it might already have made while buying time to build more if the North Koreans decided later to up the ante. Moreover, the United States had to hope that in the intervening years North Korea would not produce more nuclear weapons from the fuel rods it controlled. And not least, it had to assume that Sung's successor, his son, Kim Jong Il, who assumed power upon his father's death in July 1994, would respect the agreement. (Doubts about this were raised in early 1995 when North Korea threatened to scuttle the agreement if the United States and South Korea proceeded, as in the past, with joint military maneuvers, or the latter were to construct the reactors. But one point about this outcome was not in doubt: North Korea, economically and politically vulnerable, had effectively demonstrated for other potential proliferators how diplomatic intransigence and threats of war will be rewarded by an irresolute superpower fearful of confrontation.

OVERSEAS REFUGE FOR THE 'DOMESTIC PRESIDENT'

At the midway point in Bill Clinton's term as president, the United States remained at peace and most of its people were benefiting from an extended economic recovery. Yet many Americans remained anxious about the country's direction and were openly skeptical about Clinton. They questioned his political judgment, with the aborted health care initiative serving as Exhibit

A, and they harbored ongoing suspicions about his character. Further, they were dismayed by reports of internal disarray within the Clinton administration and by the president's inability to assume more forceful leadership.[10] Finally, beyond their personal distaste for Clinton, they rejected the continuation of "politics as usual" in Washington and sought relief from the gridlock and corruption that seemed to epitomize the federal government.

Clinton's political enemies in the Republican Party seized on this public dissension, calling for such dramatic reforms as term limits and a balanced budget amendment. These critics ridiculed First Lady Hillary Rodham Clinton, who had led the unsuccessful health care reform effort, and demanded full-scale investigations of the first family's financial dealings. In a stunning reversal of congressional power, the GOP routed the Democrats from Capitol Hill in the November 1994 midterm elections. For the first time in four decades, the Republicans held majorities in *both* the Senate and the House of Representatives. Thus in the mid-1990s, at the tail end of a historic political realignment in American party politics, the GOP's dominance was well entrenched. Led by the outspoken Newt Gingrich, who became Speaker of the House in January 1995, Republicans took over the leadership of congressional committees and, confident of their ability to override presidential vetoes, pursued their own legislative agenda with little regard for Clinton's wishes.

In foreign policy Republican leaders vowed to reduce foreign aid and curb support for the UN and its peace-keeping missions, particularly those of marginal strategic interest. Although vague about the specific threats confronting the United States, Republicans pledged to boost defense spending after several years of budget cuts and base closings. Some talked of taking a harder line with Serbia. Others argued that the unpredictable behavior of Boris Yeltsin in Russia—his insecure hold on power, his declaration of a "Cold Peace" in U.S.-Russian relations, and his brutal assault on Chechnya—warranted a restoration of many military programs. But specific contingencies were rarely raised in this debate; the larger Pentagon budgets were more often advocated in the general interest of enhanced combat readiness of American troops. To that end, and to appear to be taking the lead on this issue, Clinton announced in November 1994 that he would authorize the spending of an additional $25 billion on U.S. defenses to be spread over several years. The Republicans, predictably, complained that this was too little, if not too late.

Reeling from the electoral sea change, which extended to many state assemblies, Clinton discovered what a welcome refuge foreign policy could be from the storms of domestic politics. Heads of state historically have gained

10. For a representative critique, see Bob Woodward, *The Agenda* (New York: Simon and Schuster, 1994). Also see Elizabeth Drew, *On the Edge* (New York: Simon and Schuster, 1994); and David Maraniss, *First in His Class* (New York: Simon and Schuster, 1995).

credibility—and public approval ratings—by meeting with foreign leaders. In this role they serve as the personal embodiments of their country and are generally supported at home, and they usually play to a receptive international press corps. No doubt with this in mind, Clinton traveled to Indonesia only a week after the elections for meetings of the Asia-Pacific Economic Cooperation countries, and he announced plans to visit U.S. allies in Europe in December. Thus the "domestic president" had taken a 180-degree turn, finding foreign affairs more hospitable to his political image than tinkering with health care or welfare reform in Washington. Especially where he could focus on economic issues, which were indirectly related to his plan to revive America's domestic base, Clinton became an avid foreign policy president.

The critical and still unresolved issue remained what orienting principle would guide U.S. foreign policy in the transformed world of the 1990s. Since the anticommunist, mainly anti-Soviet guidelines were obviously no longer applicable, what, if anything, would take their place, unless the administration intended to continue to react to each international crisis on an ad hoc basis? The ambiguous new order demanded a restatement of American purpose, which would reconcile the competing requirements of global leadership and self-restraint. As Henry Kissinger observed in 1994,

Indiscriminate involvement in all the ethnic turmoil and civil wars of the post-Cold War world would drain a crusading America. Yet an America that confines itself to the refinement of its domestic virtues would, in the end, abdicate America's security and prosperity to decisions made by other societies in faraway places over which America would progressively lose control.[11]

This was the central dilemma of American foreign policy in the mid-1990s. In the absence of a coherent statement of U.S. interests, the steady stream of challenges and crises that besieged Clinton was destined to continue. And the country's response to these developments would continue to be tentative, inviting criticism from within the government and further provocations from overseas. The consequences of this for U.S. interests as well as international stability would be enormous.

11. Henry Kissinger, *Diplomacy* (New York: Simon and Schuster, 1994), 833.

To comply with the original terms of START, the U.S. Air Force has begun dismembering B-52 bombers, which are then left for ninety days so that Russia can confirm the destruction with satellite photos.

CHAPTER TWELVE

The Renewed Search for America's Mission

The United States entered the twentieth century as a rising industrial power that remained, deliberately, outside the circles of great-power diplomacy. It stood by while the Concert of Europe was established in 1815, while that agreement's participants overcame internal social revolutions, and while the European states scrambled for African colonies. In the meantime, with its considerable freedom to maneuver, the United States established itself as a major political and economic power, extending its territory into the Pacific Ocean and its sphere of influence across the Western Hemisphere.

Although many observers saw this territorial expansion as proof of America's "manifest destiny," the rapid growth of the United States would not have been possible without a widely recognized balance of power in Western Europe. This balance contributed to the century of relative calm that followed the Napoleonic Wars (1803-1815), which in turn permitted the United States to focus on its internal state-building efforts and continental expansion. The American dream of permanent isolation from great-power politics proved impossible, however, after Germany's challenge to the balance of power provoked total war in Europe in 1914. The specter of German control over Europe was viewed as a clear and present danger to the United States, which was forced to intervene in behalf of Great Britain and France. The United States, along with its Western European allies and the Soviet Union, was thrust into an even greater role in the Second World War, fending off simultaneous challenges from the fascist states of Germany, Italy, and Japan. And during the Cold War the United States assumed the responsibilities of a political, economic, and military superpower—the linchpin of Western security in a protracted bipolar struggle with the Soviet Union.

With each of these conflicts settled in its favor, the United States approached its third century with the same ambivalence about foreign affairs maintained by early leaders. The international system of the 1990s was fraught with direct challenges to American leadership, along with old, unsettled rivalries that resurfaced after the Soviet Union's collapse. "Ours is a period of 'international deregulation,' " foreign policy analyst Richard Haass observed, "one in which there are new players, new capabilities, and new alignments—but as yet, no new rules." [1] As in the past, many Americans sought to turn their energies inward, to resolve domestic maladies, and to allow the convulsions of the Old World to work themselves out. Others felt the United States should exploit its political, economic, and military preeminence and impose its will on the outside world. In short, the new era revived old controversies about America's role in the system of states, controversies that had been largely dormant while the country bowed to the imperatives of containing communism.

REALISM VERSUS MORALISM:
THE REVIVED DEBATE

It was emphasized in Chapter 11 that the turbulent international system of the early 1990s did not wait patiently while the United States resolved its latest

1. Richard Haass, "Paradigm Lost," *Foreign Affairs*, January-February 1995, 43.

identity crisis. Upheavals in several regions shattered the widely anticipated "new world order" and forced American leaders to respond in the absence of an overriding redefinition of national purpose. Crises in Kuwait, Somalia, the Balkans, Rwanda, Haiti, North Korea, Russia, and Mexico drew varying U.S. responses, but the overriding question loomed: What was the role of the United States in the post-Cold War world? Anticommunism could no longer serve as a basis for intervention, nor could the bipolar division of power that had compelled the United States to react to Soviet moves.

Americans' widespread desire to concentrate once more on domestic affairs was reinforced by deepening social and economic problems. Moreover, they also recognized that, given the end of the Soviet threat, the old superpower role was too expensive to maintain, not to mention unnecessary. To balance its ends and means, the United States had to lower its international profile and to be more selective in its commitments. The issue, then, was not so much *whether* the United States would be involved internationally, but what new orienting principle would guide U.S. foreign policy. Of the two general approaches that had vied for supremacy in the past, would it be realism or moralism?

At one pole were the realists, whose outlook had by and large guided U.S. Cold War policy. They envisioned a United States that was motivated by consistent and well-defined national interests, rooted in the country's need for self-preservation in a hostile system of nation-states. During the Cold War the ideological fissure between the superpowers had allowed the United States to disguise what essentially had been a balance-of-power policy—based on bipolarity and global networks of alliances, satellite states, and regional proxies—as a moral crusade. But realism had guided George Bush to repel Saddam Hussein's threat to the West's vital oil supplies and the moderate Arab governments, which, despite America's friendship with Israel, were pro-Western. Realism also had led the same George Bush, despite his sense of personal horror at the bloodshed in the Balkans, to avoid U.S. involvement because no strategic or material interests were at stake.

At the other pole was the traditional moralism that had so often in the past fueled America's sense of mission. To many observers, moral imperatives rendered U.S. foreign policy distinct from the power politics of Old World diplomacy. American idealists equated the country's national values—democracy, religious tolerance, human rights—with universal values, and, given its considerable assets, the United States was in a favorable position to project these values on the outside world. But by its nature, moralism was unable to distinguish between the country's vital interests, which might require action and the use of force, and secondary or lesser interests, which would not. Moralistic sentiments provoked President Woodrow Wilson to pursue a world "safe for democracy"; in the late twentieth century it animated President Jimmy Carter in his efforts to reconcile long-standing disputes between the United States and many developing countries.

THE IMPACT OF GLOBAL TELECOMMUNICATIONS

In the "high-tech" era, this moralistic impulse was increasingly driven by the satellite images conveyed by news networks, many of which featured grisly pictures of famine, military carnage, and violations of human rights. In effect, these images promoted activism in cases of otherwise marginal relevance to American national interests. During his tenure in the Oval Office, George Bush admitted that he was influenced by television's ability to bring into American homes pictures of human suffering and misery. Such pictures appeared after the victory over Iraq, when Saddam Hussein persecuted his Kurdish minority, who had rebelled during the war and sought to secede from Iraq. The televised footage of 1.5 million Kurdish refugees, from the very young to the old, fleeing their homes with whatever they could carry and living in the mountains in the bitter winter cold, were wrenching to a global television audience. Its moral outrage, already strong against Saddam Hussein, created public pressure to act, leading to an American-led UN relief effort and a declaration that the Kurd-held regions of northern Iraq were off-limits to Iraqi forces.

Televised images of the Somali famine also were instrumental in rallying an international response. But when the American troops sent to Somalia on a humanitarian mission began to be killed or injured—all before the TV cameras—public and congressional pressure to withdraw became intense. In response, President Clinton, in an about-face from his earlier enthusiasm for the UN peace-keeping mission, ordered a hasty retreat. In this respect, it was television that brought the United States to Somalia, and it was television that brought it out.

Thus in the post-Cold War period, as Americans preferred to concentrate on domestic problems, the CNN type of globalization of news strengthened traditional American humanitarian concerns and tended to define, in piecemeal fashion, what constituted the U.S. "national interest." Television pictures often focused on what might be called "lost causes"—those of the Kurds and the Shiite Muslims in Iraq, the Muslims in Bosnia, the waring tribes in Rwanda, and the Somalis—and illustrated the human misery that resulted from the brutality of governments, from ethnic hatreds and ambitions, and from intramural fights for power among leaders who cared little for the pain and suffering of their victims.

CONSEQUENCES FOR U.S. INTERVENTION

The debate over whether or not to intervene in Bosnia-Herzegovina was at the center of the problem of what principles should guide the nation's foreign policy, especially the use of force, in the post-Cold War era. For Bush, the criterion was whether U.S. vital interests—that is, strategic or material interests—were involved. They were in the Persian Gulf; they were not in Bosnia. The stakes in the latter were largely humanitarian, as in Somalia. But in Somalia the initial assumption had been that the United States could satisfy its moral urges at a relatively minor cost since UN forces from other countries would take over from the United States after a couple of months. In Bosnia moral principles could not be so easily satisfied. The intervention might not be successful, but even if it were, it would probably be very costly in lives, dollars, and presidential popularity. For Bush, Bosnia was not another Desert Storm; it was potentially another Vietnam.

There was a tremendous paradox and irony in this, for the very people who had opposed going to war against Saddam Hussein were by and large the same people who advocated intervention in Bosnia. If only Bosnia had oil, some of them said. That was a very revealing comment since it suggested that Bush would have intervened had there been material interests at stake. For those advocating intervention in behalf of the Muslims, however, such intervention was necessary precisely because *no* material interests were involved. Neither oil nor strategic position should sully America's cause. Refusing to accept humanitarianism as a reason for not intervening, they claimed that it was just for that reason that intervention was urgently required. What did America stand for if not democracy and human rights? Had these not been America's reasons for fighting Nazi totalitarianism and then opposing the Soviet Union? How, therefore, could the United States stand by, expressing its shock and outrage about Serbian behavior but doing no more than making empty threats of intervention? Would not such inaction encourage other leaders to follow the Serbs' example since they would know they could do so with impunity and that aggression would be rewarded?

The post-Cold War world appeared to be turned upside-down. After Vietnam, many liberals had rejected President John Kennedy's avowal that the United States would "pay any price, bear any burden, meet any hardship, support any friend, oppose any foe to assure the survival and the success of liberty." The Vietnam War had turned many of them into foes of military intervention and had pushed many others toward pacifism and isolationism. America's moral standing, in their view, had been irreparably damaged by that conflict. Until then, the Cold War, like World Wars I and II, had been fought for a moral cause. But Vietnam demonstrated that in containing Soviet power the nation's anticommunism had led it to overreact and had corrupted its cause. Therefore, the post-Vietnam problem was not how to contain Soviet expansion but how to restrain U.S. power. Most liberals therefore opposed every post-Vietnam use of force until President Bush asked the U.S.

Congress for authorization to go to war against Iraq—a resolution that passed the Senate by only three votes.

If fighting against Saddam Hussein was not a pure cause, fighting for the Muslims in Bosnia was—one of conscience, unadulterated by geopolitics or material interests. And in such desperate areas as Somalia and Haiti, where political disintegration had produced brutal violence and highly visible human suffering, American military preeminence could, for once, be put to appropriate use. Thus the post-Vietnam doves, overwhelmingly liberal and Democratic, plus a few moderate Republicans, transformed themselves into hawks. Humanitarian intervention, at least where it could be achieved successfully at limited cost, was to be the guide in these civil conflicts.

Were reasons of conscience good enough for using force? According to this viewpoint, they were, precisely because they called for "disinterested" intervention. The use of force to secure U.S. interests was not a sufficient justification. Indeed, as one critic claimed, self-interest was tainted and, rather than acting as an indispensable reason for using force, it disqualified the use of military power.[2] Thus many liberals became interventionists, enthusiastically urging action in Bosnia and initially supporting the Somali and Haitian interventions, not only to relieve the human suffering in those areas but also to redeem the United States by making it an instrument of justice. Moral crusading, then, had not died with the end of the Cold War; rather, it had gained a new lease on life and renewed strength.

As in the past, however, a foreign policy based on moralism proved difficult to sustain. The lesson of Somalia, fears of involvement in Bosnia and Rwanda, and ongoing confrontations with the dictators of Iraq, North Korea, and Cuba led to an American effort under Bill Clinton to find a middle course, combining moralism with realism. As part of the "enlargement" strategy announced by National Security Adviser Anthony Lake in 1993, promoting the global diffusion of democratic rule would be the cornerstone of American foreign policy. But in practice this priority was pursued selectively. In many cases (such as trade with China and Vietnam) a pragmatic concern for self-interest superseded America's normative agenda. If concern for human rights and democracy was to be a major concern of American foreign policy, the fact remained that not all nations were of equal importance, nor were all nations equally able to support democracy. U.S. policy thus gave priority to maintaining and strengthening relations among the key Western industrial powers. In addition, it sought to extend the fold of democratic and market economies to Eastern Europe, where U.S. security interests were most directly involved.[3]

2. Charles Krauthammer, "Essay," *Time*, May 17, 1993.
3. Thomas L. Friedman, "Clinton's Security Aide Gives a Vision for Foreign Policy," *New York Times*, September 22, 1993.

Ultimately, moral outrage over Serbian atrocities proved to be an inadequate basis for U.S. intervention in the Balkans, which were not, as Secretary of State Warren Christopher initially admitted, a vital interest. Western European leaders, who would be the most adversely affected by events there, did not seem worried, asserting that bloodletting among the Balkan peoples was not a new phenomenon and that outsiders could not do much to end it. Moreover, even if they tried, the rugged terrain and harsh climate in the region mitigated against an Iraqi-style quick victory. Finally, if a government's inhumane treatment of its own people became the sole or principal moral cause for another country intervening militarily in its affairs, where would the latter draw the line? Why not also intervene in other areas where ethnic conflicts and attendant cruelties were going on at the same time—Armenia/Azerbaijan, Georgia, the Sudan, Rwanda, Liberia, Tibet, Sri Lanka, or a dozen other places? "Our planet will be filled with barbarism for a long time to come," said one distinguished historian, but "in many cases we must accept the sad necessity of living with tragedies that are beyond our power to control and our wisdom to cure. . . . We cannot right every wrong or reverse each adversity—and . . . there cannot be an American solution to every world problem." [4]

The post-Cold War period taught the United States that at the very time that there were fewer restraints on U.S. intervention, its leaders must pay attention to the interests at stake in any conflict—as well as the cost, the time required, and the likelihood of success of an intervention. And, where its interests were not deemed sufficiently vital to act unilaterally, the nation must seek partners in either regional organizations such as the North Atlantic Treaty Organization (NATO) or the United Nations. As American troops in Somalia came increasingly under attack and congressional pressure to withdraw intensified, Clinton reflected national anxiety when he told the United Nations that if "the American people are to say yes to the U.N. peacekeeping, the United Nations must know when to say no." In justifying U.S. intervention in Haiti several months later, Clinton diminished the humanitarian concerns and instead framed the country's unrest as a threat to U.S. national interests.

Whether Clinton would adhere to this more limited and pragmatic American role or would on occasion surrender to the temptation of humanitarian intervention remained unclear in the mid-1990s. Seriously shaken by the 1994 congressional elections that brought the Republican Party control of both houses, the president's capacity to pursue his own agenda was further constrained because the post-Cold War Republican orientation tended to be more nationalistic and less assertive internationally. In any event, the tension between American national interests and the promotion of its code of politi-

4. Arthur Schlesinger, Jr., "How to Think about Bosnia," *Wall Street Journal,* May 3, 1993.

cal morality—a thread running through its two centuries of foreign relations—remained palpable.

COMPETING TRENDS IN WORLD POLITICS

While the debate on the guidelines for U.S. foreign policy beyond the Cold
War was under way, forces at work in world politics—fragmentation and integration—were reshaping the context of world politics and the opportunities for American involvement. Some trends were visible before the Cold War
ended; indeed, they were extensions of long-term advances in technology and
economic development. Others were more closely related to the collapse of
the Soviet Union, to the end of the bipolar balance of power, and to the revival of old antagonisms that had been suppressed by the superpowers. In fact,
world politics in the mid-1990s was schizophrenic in this regard, resulting in a
relentless cascade of events (both constructive and destructive) and further
complicating efforts by the United States to define for itself a coherent foreign
policy and world role.

THE PULL OF FRAGMENTATION

Bipolarity was, in a sense, relatively stable because of its very simplicity. It
was a system of challenge and response that virtually maintained itself. Like
any other zero-sum game, any gain for one side was a loss for the other. Thus
any effort by the Soviet Union to expand its power and improve its position
provoked the United States to react. The principal task was to mobilize the
necessary resources. Watching each other constantly, then, the superpowers
maintained the balance, always aware of the danger of nuclear war and its suicidal potential. As a result, there was no third world war; indeed, after the
1962 Cuban missile crisis there were no comparable crises between the superpowers. In Europe, the scene of the two earlier world wars and the principal
arena of American and Soviet confrontation, the curtain between the two
spheres of power remained safely closed for forty-five years. Despite the constant tensions that existed, the continent experienced the longest period of
peace in this century and one of the longest periods of stability in modern
times.[5] The wars that were fought occurred in the Third World and never escalated into global conflict.

The breakdown of bipolarity and fragmentation of state power that accompanied the end of the Cold War resulted in a considerably less stable and
peaceful world than was expected in the moments of euphoria attending the
war's end. Specifically, the uncertain balance of power wrought instability in

5. John L. Gaddis, "The Long Peace: Elements of Stability in the Postwar International System," *International Security* (Spring 1986): 99-142.

four ways. First, as noted in Chapter 11, the retreat of the Soviet empire from Eastern Europe revived the nationalistic, ethnic, and religious tensions that had accompanied the breakup of the Austro-Hungarian, Russian, and Ottoman (Turkish) empires after World War I and that had kept Eastern Europe in turmoil throughout the interwar period. Soviet hegemony after World War II prevented these conflicts from erupting—and maintained international stability—by suppressing, often ruthlessly, national aspirations and claims. The major events produced by the withdrawal of Soviet power from the area ranged from the peaceful disintegration of Czechoslovakia to the violent breakup of Yugoslavia.

A second result was the decomposition of the Soviet Union into constituent republics. But in its aftermath came tension among such successor states as Russia and Ukraine, war between Armenia and Azerbaijan, the attempted secession and crackdown in Chechnya, civil wars in Tajikistan and other states, and the prospect of renewed Russian imperialism within the old Soviet frontiers as Russian leaders used the alleged dangers to Russian minorities in these states as a pretext for military action. Furthermore, the uncertain future of Russia itself—whether the Kremlin would revert to traditional authoritarianism or move toward democracy and private enterprise—remained a critical concern for the region. Because Russia inherited the Soviet Union's huge nuclear arsenal, its future was of grave concern to the rest of the world as well.

A third consequence of the end of the superpower rivalry was the clear field left for aspirants to regional hegemony to pursue their aggressive designs. It was no longer the case that each superpower, dominant in its own sphere, could restrain its respective clients and prevent local conflicts. Middle powers were now free to act; expansionist rulers were encouraged to fill the power vacuums left by the superpowers. It is doubtful, as already noted, that Iraq's Saddam Hussein would have been able to invade Kuwait had the Soviet Union still been a key regional player who wanted to avoid a confrontation with the United States. Also, in many parts of the Arab world, including Algeria and Egypt, Islamic fundamentalists were becoming increasingly assertive, and often violent, in seeking political representation. Meanwhile, the People's Republic of China was converting much of its rapid economic growth into a military buildup that averaged 10 percent a year in the early 1990s. As a result, China's relations with the United States became more contentious during this period, and its intentions in such areas as the South China Sea stirred anxiety among its neighbors in East Asia, where the intentions of Japan, the two Koreas, the Philippines, and other countries became less and less clear. More generally, the post-Cold War system, no longer dominated by the superpowers with their common interest in avoiding the spread of weapons of mass destruction, witnessed the increasing proliferation of modern weapons technology—from chemical, biological, and nuclear weapons to short- and middle-range ballistic missiles. North Korea's challenge in 1994 to the Nuclear Non-Proliferation Treaty (NPT) and the enormous price paid by the United States to keep it within the NPT symbolized this pattern.

Fourth, the end of the Cold War strongly affected the American alliances across the Atlantic and Pacific. Organized to counter the power of the Soviet Union and China, these alliances gave priority to common interests in collective security. With the Cold War over, the rationale for the "Atlantic partnership" blurred. Not only had NATO's raison d'être vanished, but the disintegration of the Soviet Union had given priority to economic objectives—and competition between the emerging European Union and the North American trading bloc. As NATO's foundation slipped into history, its staying power was being sorely tested in such "out-of-area" trouble spots as Bosnia-Herzegovina.

The same was true for the bilateral alliances between the United States and Japan. While security aims were preeminent, the United States was willing to sacrifice its own economic objectives in the region. Indeed, to promote Japan's recovery after World War II the United States accepted Japanese imports while allowing the Japanese to protect their home markets by restricting American imports. But with the end of the Cold War, national economic aims were no longer subordinated to shared security aims, and the United States exerted constant pressure to end what it called Japan's unfair trading practices. Meanwhile, Japan's model of economic development—based on the promotion of exports and close cooperation between government and private industry—was emulated by other industrializing states, often with similarly lucrative results. As a result, arguments over trade protectionism became a central aspect of world politics in the 1990s, with the antagonistic parties being the United States and its former Cold War allies in the industrialized world.[6]

Not all the effects produced by the end of the Cold War were disruptive. It was Soviet support in the United Nations, for example, that allowed the United States to organize the multinational coalition against Iraq. Moreover, the Cold War's demise left Syria, a militant anti-Israeli Arab state and former Soviet client, with little choice but to support Washington unless it wished to be isolated with little control over its destiny. It also permitted the United States after its victory over Iraq to push for general Arab-Israeli peace negotiations, which led to governance of Gaza and the city of Jericho on the West Bank by the Palestine Liberation Organization (PLO) and to the accord between Israel and Jordan. Thus the end of the Cold War revealed the potential for greater

6. Robert Gilpin, *The Political Economy of International Relations* (Princeton: Princeton University Press, 1987).

1. SLOVENIA
2. CROATIA
3. BOSNIA
4. YUGOSLAVIA
5. MACEDONIA
6. ALBANIA

■ European Union members

▨ Members as of January 1, 1995

▦ Probable members by the year 2000

THE EUROPEAN UNION

301

cooperation in the late 1990s, which was propelled in other respects by the long-term trend toward transnational integration.

THE PUSH OF INTEGRATION

Alongside the process of fragmentation, which stemmed largely from the collapse of the Cold War and the end of bipolarity, a longer-term pattern of integration was reshaping international relations—and American foreign policy—in the 1990s. Reflecting technological advances in global communications and transportation, as well as the amalgamation of the world economy into a single marketplace, this process encouraged greater cooperation among states, rewarding order and stability within the international system.

New computer technologies and satellite network systems played a critical role in this process of integration. They in fact produced a global "information revolution," propelled by satellite telecommunications and interactive computer systems, which made it possible for people in almost any country to know within seconds what was happening elsewhere in the world. As a result, when atrocities occurring in remote countries were brought to the attention of a world audience, such acts produced strong reactions and often led to political and military interventions that would have been unthinkable in earlier periods. Televised images of earthquakes, floods, famines, and other natural disasters also were beamed around the world, leading to large-scale international relief efforts. The most prominent example of this occurred in the summer of 1986 after graphic pictures of starving Ethiopians were televised around the world. Under the banner of "Live Aid," well-known rock bands performed simultaneous benefit concerts in England and the United States, which were simulcast on television and radio stations worldwide. While the relief effort succeeded in raising millions of dollars for the famine victims, it also illustrated how global media could be used both to raise public awareness of human catastrophes and to rally collective efforts to respond to them. The diffusion of knowledge was further facilitated by new computer technology, which permitted users to gain easy access to the latest reports from overseas news wire services and government agencies.

On the economic front, the emergence of regional trading blocs may have represented a potential threat to global economic cooperation, but the integration of Western Europe into a more cohesive European Union (EU) brought its members closer together and gave them the opportunity to resolve their long-standing political differences. In the early 1990s EU members approved the Maastricht treaty, designed to move the regional organization beyond economic integration, including a single monetary system, toward closer collaboration in the areas of defense and foreign policy. The North American Free Trade Agreement (NAFTA) accords encouraged leaders in Canada, Mexico, and the United States to combine their efforts to resolve the social and political problems that often crossed their national borders. NAFTA, likely to be expanded to other Latin American countries in the next decade (as noted in Chapter 11, Chile was scheduled to open talks on its future membership early in 1995), further ensured that the connection between political stability and economic development would be recognized by its members. And in the Pacific, the steps taken by the fifteen member countries of Asia-Pacific Economic Cooperation (APEC) suggested that the process of economic integration had become a truly global phenomenon. This process may have increased the degree of competition among trading blocs, but it also elicited greater *political* coordination among states that was without precedent. As all states agreed, a stable international order was an essential prerequisite to the new world of geoeconomics. But beyond that consensus a wide range of disputes over the "rules of the game" appeared in rapid succession.

Perhaps the most important example of the emerging global economy is the 115-member General Agreement on Tariffs and Trade (GATT), which was to be replaced by the World Trade Organization (WTO) after the results of the Uruguay Round were implemented in 1995. Previous GATT agreements (in 1967 and 1979) had greatly increased world trade; the total value of imports and exports soared after 1979 from about $3 trillion to nearly $8 trillion. Moreover, even though global trade cooperation was being threatened frequently by the neomercantilist practices of many states, all countries, including the United States and Japan, at least had agreed to negotiate their differences through international organizations. The annual meetings of the Group of Seven (G-7), comprising the United States, Japan, Britain, Canada, France, Germany, and Italy, which together produced 70 percent of global wealth, further testified to the interdependence of these countries and to their recognition that no longer does any single country fully control its economic destiny.

Global integration also encouraged collective efforts among world leaders to solve such transnational problems as environmental pollution and population growth. At the 1992 Earth Summit in Brazil, world leaders demonstrated growing recognition of the dangers of air and water pollution, global warming, deforestation, and desertification to their long-term national security. The summit, which featured the largest assembly of national leaders in history, touched on other issues as well: the spread of disease such as the AIDS virus, the proliferation of weapons of mass destruction, the trafficking of illegal narcotics, and the social effects of poverty and famine. The assembled leaders pledged to cooperate more closely on these matters in the future and to direct flows of foreign aid toward the "sustainable development" of Third World countries. Their plan of action for the next century, *Agenda 21*, may not have included the specific measures and obligations that were sought by many in the United Nations, but it reflected an unusual convergence of national interests and established a basis for further agreements at the 1994 UN Conference on Population and Development in Cairo.

As noted in previous chapters, the United Nations itself was largely hamstrung during the Cold War by the rivalry between the Soviet Union and the United States. UN proposals to undertake peace-keeping efforts were often rejected because of the superpowers' veto in the Security Council. But this deadlock was eliminated with the end of the Cold War, allowing the United Nations to undertake a growing number of military interventions, including the liberation of Kuwait after Iraq's invasion. But these UN missions, as the Iraqi case demonstrated, depended on U.S. leadership. When it was lacking, the likelihood of a successful mission was undermined by disagreements among the most powerful states about how, or indeed whether, these conflicts should be resolved. The failures in Bosnia, Somalia, and Rwanda revealed the difficulties of organizing a multilateral peace-keeping effort when the great powers lacked a common purpose. But in other areas the United Nations succeeded in negotiating the conclusion of civil wars and in establishing order—in Angola, Cambodia, and El Salvador, for example—which provided some basis for hope for future peace-making and peace-keeping efforts.

Finally, for all of its difficulties in being transplanted to such places as Russia and Eastern Europe, democratic government became the basis of rule in an increasing number of countries. By the mid-1990s most Latin American countries had established at least nominally democratic systems. In Africa, South Africa also was becoming democratic, experiencing its first free election for the black majority and white minority, permitting multiple political parties to operate, and protecting a growing range of political and civil rights. Since most of the developing countries had little or no previous experience with democracy, their efforts in that direction were often plagued by civil unrest and their long-term prospects were uncertain. But the fact that so many states had at least professed a desire to establish political freedoms was encouraging, particularly because democratic states historically have not tended to fight other democratic states.

The tension between global fragmentation and integration will likely define the relations among states not only in the 1990s but well into the twenty-first century. Among their other effects, these equal and opposite forces are likely to complicate the task of defining the guidelines for the conduct of American foreign policy. In Washington, where the Republican Party assumed control of Congress in 1995 and vowed to pursue a foreign policy very different than that undertaken by the Democratic President Bill Clinton, internal struggles were likely to make a coherent response to these trends even more difficult.

But whether the United States will play an active role in the world or a more limited one, one critical prerequisite for any kind of influence is a stronger U.S. economy. The rapid expansion of the world economy in the 1980s and early 1990s was built largely on trade, overseas investment, and the active role of governments in promoting private industry. For the United States, adapting to the transformed global economy will be as important—and in many ways as difficult—as completing its transition to the post-Cold War era. Its success in the economic realm will be essential if the United States is to maintain its current level of global political and military commitments.

THE ECONOMIC BASIS OF POLITICAL POWER

America's twentieth-century predominance was based on a vigorous economy that had helped to win both world wars and to create the highest standard of living in the world. It was a mass-production economy that built high-quality goods for an ever-expanding market. In fact, any product labeled "Made in America" was sought all over the world. But the United States did not depend primarily on overseas markets to sustain its economic growth. Rich in resources, the nation's industry could provide the American consumer with abundant goods and create what in the 1950s was called the "affluent society." At the same time, the United States could sustain a massive, far-flung military, a burgeoning federal bureaucracy, and ever-growing entitlement programs.

But even before the first shock of higher oil prices in 1973, the U.S. economy was showing signs of weakness (see Chapter 11). By the late 1970s the rise in energy prices had demonstrated brutally and swiftly not only that the U.S. economy was vulnerable to external events but also that America's lethargic manufacturers were unprepared to compete in the rapidly changing global economy. Consumers, too, were a factor in these economic changes because, ultimately, the flood of imports that was required to satisfy consumer demand had to be paid for. In the 1980s imports rose even more as American consumers went on another binge of spending, this time with credit cards that often charged interest rates in excess of 20 percent. Meanwhile, unfair trading practices by other countries could not account for the general weaknesses of American firms, which continued to seek out short-term profits at the cost of long-term research and development. And American farmers, who long had been a mainstay in paying the nation's trade bills, found that their overseas markets were disappearing as the developing countries learned how to produce more food.

In some respects the relative decline of the United States as a global economic power, which many observers traced to the early 1970s and the first energy crisis, was comparable to that of Great Britain in the late nineteenth cen-

tury. The decline of British industry—in absolute terms as well as relative to
the world economy—was neither inevitable nor unavoidable. Having done so
well for so long, British manufacturers saw no need to change traditional attitudes toward business management, production, labor relations, and sales-
manship. These attitudes resulted in a lack of research and technological in-
novation; a low level of investment in new machinery, which was considered
too expensive; an educational system that deemphasized science, technology,
and business management; and cultural values that increasingly frowned on
commerce and business, the very activities that had energized Britain earlier
in the nineteenth century. British power declined as a consequence, a major
reason that the United States was forced out of its long isolationist stance during World War I.

By the 1980s some of the symptoms of Britain's economic decay were visible in the U.S. economy. Was American power therefore destined to decline
like Britain's? A pessimistic outlook was warranted, particularly when three
scions of American industrial leadership and prowess—General Motors,
IBM, and Pan-American Airlines (which actually went under)—foundered.
The Chrysler Corporation, too, would have declared bankruptcy in the late
1970s, idling millions of workers, had not the federal government stepped in
with an economic bailout.

But by the mid-1990s a considerably different picture had emerged: the
U.S. economy had rebounded strongly while the Japanese and European
economies had gone into a slump. What happened? The United States had
become part of the world market. Foreign corporations began to sell and produce their goods in the United States, competing with American companies
for a share of a market that previously had been dominated by U.S. corporations. In turn, the United States, previously self-sufficient, became increasingly dependent for its economic growth and employment on exports. It was, in
short, U.S. global competitiveness that turned its economy around. Like a
tennis player who improves his game by playing better players, U.S. corporations conditioned themselves by engaging in global competition. Along the
way they became "meaner and leaner" by laying off thousands of employees,
both executives and assembly line workers. As a result, full-time workers, often retrained and reeducated, worked overtime; any new employees often
were only part-time workers who were not given pensions, medical insur-
ance, or paid holidays; and job insecurity spread throughout the economy.
The bottom line, however, was that such U.S. corporations as Intel, Micro-
soft, and Motorola became world-class companies and leaders in their fields.

Even the automobile industry rebounded strongly, closing much of the
quality gap between itself and the Japanese. Moreover, as the United States
became the world's low-cost provider of many sophisticated goods and services, from plastics to software to financial services, foreign companies

moved to the United States in growing numbers. Japanese manufacturers, in particular, did so to overcome tariff barriers and the high cost of producing in Japan, which made their cars less competitive. The German automobile companies BMW and Mercedes built large factories in South Carolina and Alabama, respectively, and planned to export many of the new vehicles back to Europe. American workers became more productive as this process continued, but they were paid for fewer vacations and at a lower scale than their German counterparts. To those who complained about the growing penetration of overseas investment in the United States, prominent economists countered that such investments depended on long-term growth and improved productivity where the investments were made, both of which directly benefited workers, their families and communities, and the pace of national economic output.[7]

The Clinton administration's dogged support for NAFTA, APEC, and GATT, its pragmatic approach to trade with China and Vietnam, and its successful efforts to curb the federal deficit and prevent the resurgence of inflation, sustained hopes for a revived economy that could hold its own at home and compete successfully in the global economy. Most encouraging was Clinton's recognition that the United States could not play the role of major power in the absence of a strong economic base. Thus his foreign policy was in many ways reducible to foreign *economic* policy, a fact that became evident when he sacrificed other goals in order to preserve support in Washington for his economic initiatives.

Because Clinton was generally successful in these areas, during his first two years in office the U.S. economy grew steadily with low inflation and unemployment levels—and a lower federal deficit. Interest rates crept upward, however, but they did not cripple the economic recovery as many feared. Yet despite his achievements, Clinton remained generally unpopular among the American people, better known for his failure to reform health care than for his success in strengthening the U.S. economy. His political enemies hammered away at his character flaws, his dubious managerial skills, and his inability to rein in the federal bureaucracy as he had promised on the campaign trail. In foreign policy they ridiculed Clinton's flip-flops on Somalia, Yugoslavia, and especially in Haiti, where the U.S. occupation continued into 1995 amid strong domestic opposition. Leaders of the new Republican majority in Congress vowed to end this mission and others that were not clearly linked to U.S. national interests, and they advocated more defense spending for more conventional tasks—such as deterring a renewal of Russian expansionism in Europe and Asia. Thus the country's future direction was again cast into

7. Robert Reich, *The Work of Nations* (New York: Knopf, 1991). Also see Lester Thurow, *Head to Head* (New York: William Morrow, 1992).

doubt as domestic politics—and the early stages of the 1996 presidential campaign—further clouded the already muddy waters of American foreign policy.

BETWEEN COLD WAR AND MILLENNIUM

The Cold War between the United States and the Soviet Union defined world politics for nearly half a century after World War II, casting its shadow over every corner of the world. Security alliances were built on a global scale, while regional conflicts were complicated and often inflamed by the superpower struggle. A costly nuclear arms race ensued, which produced weapons stockpiles of incomprehensible destructive power. And for the first time in history, the prospect that two great powers would exterminate not just each other but much of humankind was widely recognized. In fact, this prospect became the central reality of superpower tensions and a driving force behind the eventual cooperation between Washington and Moscow.

For the United States, the onset of the Cold War coincided with its arrival as a great power—not just in wartime, when a threat to European order was thought to jeopardize American security, but on a permanent basis. It was a propitious time for the United States to assume this role, given its economic and military preponderance in the wake of World War II and the strength and popularity of its political system. For most American leaders of this period, a retreat into the isolation of the interwar period was unthinkable, both because of the obvious failures of this strategy during the 1930s and because of the perceived threat posed by the Soviet Union and, after its civil war ended in 1949, the People's Republic of China.

Despite its nuclear tensions and frequent crises, the Cold War provided a clarity to U.S. foreign policy that has been conspicuously absent in its aftermath. The task of communist containment was shared by every postwar American president, who otherwise disagreed sharply over the means of pursing the country's foreign policy. The ideological roots of the Soviet challenge and the repressive behavior of Soviet leaders aroused America's moralistic sentiments. Meanwhile, the threat of Soviet expansion into Western Europe, coupled with the Soviet Union's capability to strike American cities with long-range missiles, provoked American realists who perceived a threat to the European and global balance of power. Although this nationwide consensus was seriously weakened by the Vietnam War, the global rivalry between the superpowers remained the defining feature of world politics through the 1980s.

Under Presidents George Bush and Bill Clinton, the United States has taken the first halting steps toward redefining its world role in the post-Cold War era. Foreign economic policy has emerged as a major preoccupation in the mid-1990s, while the continued cohesion of NATO remains the basis of Atlantic security and an aggressive effort continues to prevent the spread of nuclear weapons. These priorities are still disconnected, however, and are being pursued in the absence of an overriding strategy for the country's foreign policy. It is likely, therefore, that this process of self-appraisal will continue indefinitely as power struggles in Washington unfold daily and as conflicts overseas—in Baghdad, Belgrade, Pyongyang, Jerusalem, Mogadishu, Port-au-Prince, and other yet unknown capitals and countries—demand the attention of the United States. The potential failure of the Mexican economy, the fate of China after the death of Deng Xiaoping, and the uncertain prospects for Boris Yeltsin's Russia, further mitigate against simple solutions.

Under such circumstances the American people can be expected to maintain their ambivalent relationship with the "outside world." The twin strains that have historically made up the American style of foreign policy—the urge to remain aloof from the vagaries of power politics and the urge to redeem the world through global crusading—will continue to compete for preeminence. Which view prevails, and whether some middle ground can be struck between these two extremes, will likely determine the course and the success of American foreign policy into the next century.

U.S. Administrations since World War II

Dates	President	Secretary of State	Secretary of Defense	National Security Adviser
1945-1953	Harry Truman	Edward Stettinius James Byrnes George Marshall Dean Acheson	James Forrestal Louis Johnson Robert Lovett George Marshall	
1953-1961	Dwight Eisenhower	John Dulles Christian Herter	Charles Wilson Neil McElroy Thomas Gates	
1961-1963	John Kennedy	Dean Rusk	Robert McNamara	McGeorge Bundy
1963-1969	Lyndon Johnson	Dean Rusk	Robert McNamara Clark Clifford	McGeorge Bundy W. W. Rostow
1969-1974	Richard Nixon	William Rogers Henry Kissinger	Melvin Laird Elliot Richardson James Schlesinger	Henry Kissinger
1974-1977	Gerald Ford	Henry Kissinger	James Schlesinger Donald Rumsfeld	Henry Kissinger Brent Scowcroft
1977-1981	Jimmy Carter	Cyrus Vance Edmund Muskie	Harold Brown	Zbigniew Brzezinski
1981-1989	Ronald Reagan	Alexander Haig George Shultz	Caspar Weinberger Frank Carlucci	Richard Allen William Clark Robert McFarlane John Poindexter Frank Carlucci Colin Powell
1989-1993	George Bush	James Baker Lawrence Eagleburger	Richard Cheney	Brent Scowcroft
1993-	Bill Clinton	Warren Christopher	Les Aspin William Perry	Anthony Lake

APPENDIX B

Chronology of Significant Events

1945	Yalta Conference seeks to organize postwar world. World War II with Germany ends. World War II with Japan ends after two atomic bombs are dropped. President Franklin Roosevelt dies, and Vice President Harry Truman succeeds him. United Nations is established. Soviet military forces occupy Poland, Romania, Bulgaria, Hungary, and Czechoslovakia.
1946	United States confronts the Soviet Union over Iran, and Moscow withdraws its troops. Winston Churchill, Britain's wartime prime minister, delivers "iron curtain" speech at Fulton, Missouri, warning of Soviet threat.
1947	Truman Doctrine commits the United States to assist Greece and Turkey. Plan for the economic recovery of Western Europe is devised by Secretary of State George Marshall, formerly U.S. chief of staff and architect of victory during World War II. George Kennan, a Foreign Service officer, provides the government with the analysis that becomes the basis of the containment policy of Soviet Russia. India becomes independent.
1948	Soviet coup d'état takes place in Czechoslovakia. Soviets blockade all ground traffic from West Germany to West Berlin and the Western airlift starts. Vandenberg resolution of U.S. Senate commits American support for the Brussels Pact of self-defense. Marshall Plan is passed by Congress. North and South Korea are established. The state of Israel is established and receives immediate U.S. recognition. Truman wins upset election. Stalin expels Yugoslavia's Tito from communist bloc.
1949	North Atlantic Treaty Organization (NATO) is formed. Soviet Union ends Berlin blockade. East and West Germany are established. Soviet Union explodes atomic bomb. Nationalist China collapses and People's Republic of China (PRC) is established. U.S. troops are withdrawn from South Korea. Truman announces Point Four foreign aid program for developing countries.
1950	Soviet Union and communist China sign thirty-year treaty of mutual assistance.

North Korea attacks South Korea by crossing the thirty-eighth parallel.
United States intervenes in behalf of South Korea.
Communist China intervenes after U.S. forces advance into North Korea toward China's frontier.
Sen. Joseph McCarthy begins his attacks on government for treason and "coddling communism."

1951   Gen. Dwight Eisenhower is appointed Supreme Allied Commander in Europe and Truman sends U.S. forces to Europe.
U.S.-Japanese mutual security pact is signed.
Truman fires Gen. Douglas MacArthur in Korea for proposing that the United States attack communist China.
European Coal and Steel Community (ECSC) is formed.

1952   Eisenhower is elected president.
Greece and Turkey join NATO.
Britain tests its first atomic weapon.

1953   Joseph Stalin dies.
Armistice negotiated along thirty-eighth parallel in Korea.
Soviet Union intervenes in East Germany to quell revolt.

1954   United States explodes first hydrogen bomb.
France is defeated at Dienbienphu in Indochina.
United States threatens to intervene in Indochina.
Vietnam is partitioned at the seventeenth parallel at the Geneva Conference.
Southeast Asia Treaty Organization (SEATO) is formed.
U.S.-Korean pact is signed to prevent a renewal of the war.
U.S.-Nationalist China defense treaty is signed.
Central Intelligence Agency overthrows Guatemala's left-wing government.

1955   Communist China shells the Nationalist Chinese (Taiwanese) islands of Quemoy and Matsu.
Formosa resolution authorizes Eisenhower to use force, if necessary, to protect Taiwan against a possible communist Chinese invasion.
Middle East Treaty Organization (Baghdad Pact) is formed.
West Germany joins NATO, and Soviets establish "their NATO," called the Warsaw Treaty Organization.

1956   United States withdraws offer to help finance Egypt's Aswan High Dam.
Egypt nationalizes the Suez Canal.
Suez War breaks out after Israel attacks Egypt, and France and Britain intervene.
UN forces are sent to Egypt to keep the peace between Israel and Egypt.
Soviets suppress Hungarian revolt and almost intervene in Poland.
Soviet leader Nikita Khrushchev attacks Stalin at twentieth Communist Party Congress.

1957   Soviet Union tests intercontinental ballistic missile (ICBM).
Soviets launch two *Sputniks,* or satellites, into space.

British test hydrogen bomb.

Eisenhower Doctrine commits the United States to assist Middle East countries that resist communist aggression or states closely tied to the Soviet Union, such as Egypt.

1958 United States lands marines in Lebanon, and Britain lands paratroopers in Jordan after Iraqi revolution.

Soviet Union declares it would end the four-power occupation of Berlin and turn West Berlin into a "free city."

European Economic Community (Common Market) is established.

First of several Berlin crises erupts.

Communist China shells Quemoy and Matsu again.

1959 Khrushchev visits Eisenhower for Camp David meeting over Berlin issue.

Fidel Castro seizes power in Cuba.

Central Treaty Organization (CENTO) replaces the Baghdad Pact.

1960 Soviets shoot down U.S. U-2 spy plane over the Soviet Union.

Paris summit conference collapses over U-2 incident.

The Congo becomes independent from Belgium, causing the first super-power crisis in sub-Saharan Africa.

UN forces sent to the Congo to help resolve the crisis.

France becomes an atomic power.

John Kennedy wins presidential election.

1961 Kennedy launches abortive Bay of Pigs invasion of Cuba.

Kennedy proposes Alliance for Progress for Latin America.

Soviets send Yuri Gagarin into orbital spaceflight.

Kennedy holds summit conference with Khrushchev in Vienna.

Kennedy sends first military advisers to South Vietnam.

Soviets build Berlin Wall.

1962 U.S. sends John Glenn into orbital spaceflight.

In Cuban missile crisis, the United States blockades Cuba to compel the Soviets to withdraw their missiles.

Chinese-Indian frontier conflict erupts.

1963 French president Charles de Gaulle vetoes Britain's entry into the Common Market.

"Hot line" established between the White House and the Kremlin for direct emergency communications.

Atomic test-ban treaty is signed.

President Kennedy is assassinated, and Vice President Lyndon Johnson succeeds him.

1964 Congress passes Gulf of Tonkin resolution, raising the U.S. commitment to the defense of South Vietnam.

Khrushchev falls from power and is replaced by Prime Minister Aleksei Kosygin and Communist Party Secretary Leonid Brezhnev.

1965 United States starts bombing North Vietnam and sends American land forces into South Vietnam.

Protests against the war start.
United States intervenes in the Dominican Republic.
War erupts between Pakistan and India.

1966   People's Republic of China becomes a nuclear power.
France withdraws its forces from NATO's integrated command structure but remains a member of the alliance.

1967   Six-day War between Israel and its Arab neighbors takes place.
Greek colonels seize power in Greece.

1968   Tet offensive in South Vietnam escalates demand for U.S. withdrawal from Vietnam.
Johnson withdraws from presidential race.
Richard Nixon elected president.
Vietnamese peace talks begin in Paris.
Nuclear Non-Proliferation Treaty is made.
Soviet Union intervenes in Czechoslovakia to quell revolt.

1969   Brezhnev Doctrine is proclaimed, asserting the right of Soviet Union to intervene in Soviet sphere to suppress "counterrevolution."
Antiballistic Missile (ABM) deployment is narrowly approved by Senate.
United States tests multiple independently targeted reentry vehicle (MIRV).
Negotiations on Strategic Arms Limitation Treaty (SALT) begin.
"Vietnamization" program starts. South Vietnamese are to do more of the fighting while the United States begins troop withdrawal.
Ho Chi Minh dies.
United States lands men on moon.
Lt. William Calley, Jr., stands trial for My Lai massacre of civilians in South Vietnam by U.S. troops.
First of several Sino-Soviet border clashes occurs.

1970   West Germany, East Germany, the Soviet Union, and Poland conclude treaties recognizing Poland's western border and acknowledging Germany's division into East and West Germany.
Senate repeals Gulf of Tonkin resolution.
U.S. invasion of Cambodia causes widespread student protests, which escalate after National Guard kills four students at Kent State University.
Chile elects a Marxist, Salvador Allende, president.

1971   India and Pakistan go to war over the Bangladesh (East Pakistan) secession effort.
People's Republic of China joins the United Nations.
Four-power Berlin settlement is reached, ensuring Western access to Berlin.

1972   Nixon visits communist China, beginning a process of normalizing relations after two decades of hostility.
North Vietnam invades South Vietnam.

Nixon retaliates by expanding air war against North Vietnam and blockading the harbor of Haiphong.

Nixon visits Moscow for summit conference with Soviet leaders; signs SALT I and ABM treaty.

Watergate affair starts when police arrest five men who had broken into Democratic Party headquarters.

Soviets buy enormous quantities of U.S. grains, raising U.S. domestic prices.

Paris peace talks, close to success, break down, and the United States bombs North Vietnam heavily during Christmas season.

Nixon reelected president in a landslide that carried every state but Massachusetts.

1973 Henry Kissinger is appointed secretary of state while remaining the president's national security adviser.

Vietnamese peace agreement is signed.

United States and China establish liaison offices, or informal embassies, in Washington and Beijing.

Yom Kippur War breaks out in Middle East.

Arab members of the Organization of Petroleum Exporting Countries (OPEC) embargo oil to the United States because of U.S. support for Israel.

Britain, Denmark, and Republic of Ireland join Common Market, increasing membership to nine countries.

OPEC quadruples oil prices.

U.S.-Soviet Mutual and Balanced Force Reductions talks in Europe start.

West and East Germany exchange recognition and ambassadors, acknowledging Germany's division into two countries.

Congress passes the War Powers Resolution over Nixon's veto.

Vice President Spiro Agnew resigns and Gerald Ford succeeds him.

Allende is overthrown by military in Chile.

1974 India explodes "peaceful" nuclear device.

Congress asserts right to veto large arms sales to other nations.

Annual Nixon-Brezhnev summit conference further reduces small numbers of ABMs the United States and Soviet Union are allowed by SALT I.

Kissinger negotiates first agreements between Israel and Egypt and Syria as part of his "step-by-step" diplomacy intended to achieve a comprehensive regional peace.

Nixon visits Egypt, Syria, and Israel.

Nixon resigns and Ford becomes unelected president; New York governor Nelson Rockefeller becomes vice president.

Ford and Brezhnev set Vladivostok guidelines for SALT II negotiations.

1975 Soviet Union rejects American-Soviet trade agreement because of the Jackson-Vanik amendment.

South Vietnam collapses and a unified communist Vietnam is established.

Cambodia falls to Cambodian communists.

Cambodians seize U.S. merchant ship *Mayaguez,* and the United States reacts forcefully to free crew and ship.

SEATO dissolves itself.

Helsinki agreements, including Western recognition of Europe's division (and Soviet domination in Eastern Europe), arrived at by Western and Eastern states.

Congress passes arms embargo against Turkey.

Lebanese civil war erupts.

Francisco Franco dies and King Juan Carlos starts to lead Spain to democracy.

In Angola three major factions struggle for control as Portugal grants independence.

1976   Soviet-Cuban forces in Angola win victory for Marxist-led faction over pro-Western factions.

Syrian forces intervene in Lebanon.

Mao Zedong dies.

Jimmy Carter elected president.

1977   Carter announces U.S. withdrawal from South Korea (to be reversed later).

Carter sends letter to leading Soviet dissident, and another dissident visits the White House.

Soviets denounce Carter's human rights campaign as violation of Soviet sovereignty.

Carter submits new SALT II plan to Soviet Union, which quickly rejects it because it is not based on Vladivostok guidelines.

Carter halts plans to produce B-1 bomber and instead chooses to deploy air-launched cruise missiles on B-52 bombers.

United States and Panama sign Panama Canal treaties.

Somalia expels Soviet advisers and denounces friendship treaty with Soviet Union.

Soviet-Cuban military help for Ethiopia grows.

Menachem Begin is elected prime minister in Israel.

Egyptian president Anwar Sadat pays historic visit to Israel, offering peace and friendship. Other Arab states denounce him.

1978   Soviet-Cuban military intervention in Ethiopia's war against Somalia forces latter out of Ogaden.

Soviet-inspired coup occurs in Afghanistan.

Camp David meeting of the United States, Israel, and Egypt arrives at "framework for peace" between two former enemies. Other Arab states denounce framework because it did not provide for a Palestine solution.

Senate approves sale of jet fighters to Israel, Egypt, and Saudi Arabia.

Panama Canal treaties approved by Senate.

Carter postpones neutron bomb (tactical warhead) production.

United States ends arms embargo on Turkey.

Rhodesian prime minister Ian Smith announces "internal solution" to the race problem—the formation of a black-led government.

1979   Shah Mohammad Reza Pahlavi leaves Iran.

United States officially recognizes the People's Republic of China. United States suspends formal relations with Taiwan government and ends mutual defense treaty.

China invades Vietnam to punish it for the invasion of Cambodia.

Shah's regime in Iran replaced by Islamic republic led by Ayatollah

Ruhollah Khomeini.

U.S. embassy in Tehran seized and employees held hostage by militant Islamic students after shah is hospitalized in United States for cancer treatment.

United States freezes Iran's financial assets in United States and boycotts Iranian oil.

Oil prices shoot upward as Iranian oil production drops and world supplies tighten.

SALT II treaty signed by Brezhnev and Carter at Vienna summit conference.

Soviets send 80,000 troops into Afghanistan to ensure survival of pro-Soviet regime.

NATO decides to deploy 572 theater nuclear weapons to counter Soviet "Eurostrategic" missile buildup.

1980   U.S. mission to rescue hostages in Tehran ends in disaster before it reaches embassy.

SALT II "temporarily" withdrawn from Senate by Carter after Soviet invasion of Afghanistan.

Carter embargoes shipments of feed grain and high technology to Soviet Union and declares United States will boycott summer Olympic games in Moscow.

Carter Doctrine commits United States to security of Persian Gulf oil-producing states if they are externally threatened.

United States organizes rapid deployment force to back up the Carter Doctrine.

Iraq attacks Iran.

Ronald Reagan elected president.

1981   U.S. hostages released moments after Reagan assumes presidency.

Reagan declares United States will not allow Saudi Arabia to become "another Iran."

Begin reelected in Israel.

Sadat assassinated in Egypt.

Reagan decides on large program to rebuild U.S. military power, including 100 MX missiles and 100 B-1 bombers.

Polish government imposes martial law.

United States imposes economic sanctions on Poland and on Soviet Union, believed to be behind Polish crackdown.

1982   Reagan announces economic assistance plan for Caribbean Basin (the Caribbean and Central America) as he supports El Salvador's government against rebel forces and attempts to isolate the Sandinistas in Nicaragua despite congressional criticism.

Israel invades Lebanon, attempting to destroy the Palestine Liberation Organization (PLO).

U.S. marines are sent into Beirut as part of a multinational peacekeeping force to supervise the PLO's leaving.

China and the United States sign agreement on the reduction of U.S. arms sales to Taiwan.

Brezhnev dies and is succeeded by Yuri Andropov, former head of the Soviet secret police.

Argentina invades the British Falkland Islands, long claimed by Argentina. Britain reconquers the islands.

United States imposes—and later, lifts—sanctions on U.S. and European companies selling equipment to the Soviets for building of a natural gas pipeline to Western Europe.

Secretary of State Alexander Haig resigns.

1983   Reagan denounces the Soviet Union as an "evil empire."

Bipartisan Scowcroft Commission recommends deployment of 100 MX missiles and eventual replacement of missiles equipped with MIRVs with mobile, smaller missiles with single warheads. Congress accepts these recommendations.

Catholic bishops in pastoral letter deplore nuclear deterrence for its immorality. French bishops endorse deterrence as "service to peace."

Two hundred forty-one marines killed in suicide truck-bomb attack on their barracks in Beirut.

Soviet Union shoots down Korean 747 jetliner with 269 passengers aboard after it strays into Soviet airspace.

U.S. forces, together with troops from six Caribbean states, invade the island of Grenada. They depose the Marxist government, return Cuban worker-soldiers to Cuba, and withdraw.

United States begins deployment of Pershing II and ground-launched cruise missiles in Europe. Soviet Union responds by breaking off all arms control talks.

1984   Bipartisan Kissinger Commission recommends extensive economic and military assistance to Central America to combat domestic poverty and Soviet-Cuban intervention. Congress critical of administration policy.

Andropov dies and Brezhnev's confidant, Konstantin Chernenko, succeeds him.

Reagan is reelected.

United States pulls marines out of Lebanon.

Napoleón Duarte wins Salvadoran presidency, defeating right-wing candidate.

Congress cuts off all military assistance to the contras in Nicaragua.

Latin American debtor countries meet at Cartagena to discuss the debt problem and repayment.

United States declares Iran a supporter of international terrorism.

1985   Chernenko dies and is succeeded by Mikhail Gorbachev.

Africa, especially Ethiopia, which is engaged in a civil war, suffers from widespread starvation.

Christian Democratic Party, led by Duarte, wins majority in Salvadoran National Assembly.

Various terrorist groups hijack a TWA plane flying from Athens to Rome, seize an Italian cruise ship, and attack Israel's El Al passengers at the Vienna and Rome airports.

Reagan orders limited economic sanctions against South Africa; Congress imposes harsher sanctions in 1986.

Reagan and Gorbachev hold their first summit conference in Geneva, Switzerland.

1986   Ferdinand Marcos in the Philippines and Jean-Claude Duvalier in Haiti are forced to flee their respective countries, and the Reagan administration proclaims its new human rights policy, opposing dictatorships of the left and right.

Congress approves $100 million for the Nicaraguan contras.

The United States attacks Libya for terrorist acts. Syria is shown to be involved in terrorism, and Britain breaks diplomatic relations with Syria after abortive attempt to blow up Israeli airliner.

World's worst nuclear accident takes place at Chernobyl in the Ukraine. Sweden breaks news of radioactivity coming from the Soviet Union.

Reagan and Gorbachev meet in Iceland, and Reagan refuses to trade limitations in Strategic Defense Initiative (SDI) research for deep cuts of Soviet strategic missiles and a mutual elimination of all intermediate-range missiles in Europe.

United States exceeds SALT II limits and declares that the unratified 1979 treaty is no longer "operational."

Iran-contra scandal breaks.

OPEC's oil price falls to $9-$10 a barrel, but then stabilizes at $18 a barrel.

Spain and Portugal join the European Economic Community.

U.S. dollar is allowed to drop substantially against Japanese yen and West German mark to improve U.S. exports and reduce huge trade deficit, but action proves ineffective.

1987	Congressional hearings into Iran-contra scandal raise doubts about Reagan's effectiveness for the remainder of his term.

The United States and the Soviet Union agree to a worldwide ban on short- and intermediate-range missiles, the so-called double zero option, ending years of tension over Soviet SS-20 missile deployment.

The United States reflags Kuwaiti oil tankers in the Persian Gulf and escorts them with U.S. warships to protect them from possible Iranian attacks.

Five Central American presidents devise a plan for peace in their area. The contras and Sandinistas are to negotiate an end to the civil war, and the Sandinista government commits itself to hold general election by spring 1990.

Palestinians in December begin the *intifada*, or uprising, protesting both the continued Israeli occupation of the West Bank and opposition to a Palestinian state, and, more indirectly, the PLO failure to seek a diplomatic solution.

Gorbachev at the seventieth anniversary celebration of Bolshevik Revolution denounces Stalin's historical legacy and defends his program of *perestroika*.

1988	George Bush elected president.

Gorbachev, at first national party conference since 1941, proposes to restructure Soviet government with strong presidency, selected by a more popularly responsive Supreme Soviet.

U.S. Navy shoots down Iranian commercial jetliner with 290 people aboard over Persian Gulf.

Iran and Iraq agree to a cease-fire in their eight-year-long war.

Panama's strongman, Gen. Manuel Noriega, is indicted for drug running by two Florida grand juries.

The right-wing Arena Party wins majority in Salvadoran Legislative Assembly.

PLO and Yasir Arafat declare the right of all states in the region to live in peace with secure boundaries; proclaim a Palestinian state in the West Bank and the Gaza Strip; recognize Israel; and reject terrorism.

The Soviet Baltic republics assert their desire for autonomy, if not independence; ethnic clashes in the southern Soviet Union between Azerbaijanis and Armenians lead to increasing violence.

Gorbachev makes dramatic announcement at UN of unilateral military reductions, including sizable cuts in troop levels and tanks (50,000 and 1,000 respectively), and other offensive weapons of the forces facing NATO.

1989   Gorbachev elected president of the Soviet Union, an alternative base of power to the Communist Party.

Free elections in Poland result in repudiation of the Polish Communist Party. Solidarity forms first noncommunist government in Eastern Europe.

Hungary allows emigration to the West. Mass demonstrations in East Germany protest regime celebrating its fortieth year; cabinet resigns. Hard-line Communist Party leaders are replaced.

Czechoslovakia and Bulgaria follow the reformist path of Poland, Hungary, and East Germany. Only in Romania does government resist and use force, but its leader Nicolae Ceausescu is nevertheless overthrown and executed.

Soviet Union withdraws its troops from Afghanistan.

Gorbachev in neutral Finland states that the Soviet Union has no moral or political right to interfere in the affairs of its neighbors. Statement effectively repudiates Brezhnev Doctrine.

The Ayatollah Khomeini dies in Iran.

Huge pro-democracy demonstrations in Beijing are violently suppressed by the communist leadership.

Berlin Wall is opened, beginning process of German reunification.

Panamanian general Noriega voids result of national election. Coup led by Panamanian officers fails. Noriega declares Panama to be in a state of war with the United States, which then invades Panama, overthrows Noriega, and brings him to the United States for trial.

Cuban troops begin withdrawal from Angola based on multilateral agreement under which Namibia achieves its independence.

1990   Lithuanian Communist Party breaks from the Soviet party and speaks for independent Lithuania.

Armenians and Azerbaijanis continue feud while local Communist Party loses control to the Azerbaijani popular front. Gorbachev sends in the Soviet army to restore order and keep the party in power.

Gorbachev, in a revolutionary statement to a plenum of the Communist Party, renounces the constitutionally guaranteed communist monopoly of power and declares his support for an eventual multiparty system as well as private enterprise.

Eastern European free elections in the spring produce noncommunist governments, except in Romania and Bulgaria, where the communists, under a new name, win by large majorities.

Iraqi troops invade neighboring Kuwait, provoking condemnation and economic sanctions by the United Nations.

After East German election in March, East and West Germany begin negotiating reunification. On July 1 they create a financial and economic union. Two weeks later Gorbachev agrees that a reunited Germany can choose to join NATO. On October 3 the two Germanies unify. In November the Conference on Security and Cooperation in Europe endorses Germany's unity. On December 2 elections in both Germanies produce the first postwar all-German parliament.

Soviet Union's two largest republics, Russia and the Ukraine, declare their sovereignty and assert that their laws are superior to those of the Soviet Union. Other republics follow.

Nicaraguan government agrees to free election and loses to rival coalition. The contras disband.

1991   All-German parliament and government are sworn in.

Iraq, refusing to withdraw from Kuwait, is forced out in forty-three days by the U.S.-led UN coalition.

United States and Soviet Union sign a Strategic Arms Reduction Talks (START) agreement, reducing strategic weapons by 30 percent.

Warsaw Treaty Organization formally dissolved. Soviet troops leave Hungary and Czechoslovakia.

Boris Yeltsin, Gorbachev's rival, becomes the first elected leader of the thousand-year-old Russian republic.

Coup against Gorbachev is launched by political opponents. Yeltsin defies the coup attempt and it fails. Gorbachev survives, but his authority declines further as Yeltsin establishes his primacy versus Soviet leaders.

Estonia, Latvia, and Lithuania are granted independence. After efforts to establish a confederation founder, Russia, Belarus, and Ukraine declare the Soviet Union dead and form the Commonwealth of Independent States. Other republics are invited to join.

European Free Trade Association, consisting of Austria, Switzerland, Sweden, Finland, Liechtenstein (neutrals during the Cold War), and Norway and Iceland (NATO members), establishes a common free trade area with the European Community (EC).

Soviet Union dissolves. Gorbachev resigns and cedes Kremlin to Yeltsin.

Slovenia and Croatia secede from Yugoslavia. Serb-dominated Yugoslav army resists secessions by force.

1992   Government of El Salvador reaches accord with Farabundo Marti Liberation Front (FMLN), ending decade of civil war.

U.S. government begins forcible repatriation of Haitian refugees. Establishment of joint military force for Commonwealth of Independent States.

UN peace-keeping troops intervene in Balkans. Voters in Bosnia-Herzegovina approve independence by referendum. European Community and United States recognize Bosnia-Herzegovina along with independent Croatia and Slovenia. United Nations offers membership to all three countries; Yugoslavia expelled by General Assembly.

Nineteen European states approve European Economic Area (EEA) to create free-trade zone beyond the borders of the EC.

U.S. Senate and Russian Supreme Soviet ratify START agreement.

France and Germany create 35,000-member joint defense force to serve as nucleus of regional security system for Western European Union.

U.S. and German governments announce G-7 plan to provide Russia with $24 billion in economic assistance upon Russia's entry into the International Monetary Fund.

NATO announces final removal of all ground-based tactical nuclear weapons from Europe.

Asia-Pacific Economic Cooperation (APEC) group announces program of liberalized and expanded trade within region.

Philippine government gains control of Subic Bay Naval Base from United States, ending century of American presence in country.

Bill Clinton elected president on platform of domestic reform.

1993   European Community initiates single market.

United States and Russia approve new START treaty calling for deeper cuts in strategic arsenals; they also sign military cooperation agreement providing for joint exercises and greater consultation in crises.

Terrorist bomb damages World Trade Center, killing six people and forcing the evacuation of 50,000.

North Korean government announces withdrawal from Nuclear Non-Proliferation Treaty (NPT).

United States pledges to accelerate efforts to restore deposed Haitian leader Jean-Bertrand Aristide to power. UN Security Council imposes economic sanctions against military regime.

United States endorses Vance-Owen plan to partition the former Yugoslavia along ethnic lines. United States airdrops relief supplies to besieged Bosnian Muslims. United Nations declares Sarajevo and other cities in Bosnia-Herzegovina to be "safe areas."

Twelve American soldiers are killed in Mogadishu, Somalia. Clinton orders reinforcements and sets timetable for U.S. withdrawal from Somalia.

Israel and Palestinian Liberation Organization sign peace treaty.

U.S. Congress ratifies North American Free Trade Agreement (NAFTA).

South African government approves new constitution, abolishing apartheid and setting agenda for national elections.

1994   United States and Japan reach agreement on future bilateral trade. For China, United States suspends linkage between bilateral trade and that country's behavior in human rights. Trade ties with Vietnam renewed as well.

Assassination of Rwandan president sparks civil war between Hutu and Tutsi tribes, resulting in more than 500,000 casualties.

North Korean government rejects U.S. and UN demands that it allow foreign inspection of its nuclear facilities. Kim Il Sung dies and is replaced by his son, Kim Jong Il. After protracted talks, North Korean government agrees to freeze nuclear program in exchange for U.S. economic and technological assistance.

GATT's Uruguay Round concludes. Multilateral trade agreement passed by member states.

Cuban refugees launch new boatlift to Florida coast. U.S. and Cuban governments reach agreement on future emigration levels.

Scandinavian states (except Norway) agree to join European Union.

United States begins "semi-permissive" occupation of Haiti. Military regime yields power to American troops and parliament disbands. Gen. Raul Cédras, leader of the military junta, is exiled to Panama; Aristide resumes leadership.

Iraqi armed forces mass along Kuwait border. U.S. forces are deployed to Persian Gulf to deter invasion.

Israel and Jordan sign peace agreement.

United Nations announces plans to withdraw from Somalia by March 1995; cites continuing clan warfare as reason for suspension of efforts.

Midterm elections bring collapse of Democratic majority in U.S. Congress.

1995

Russian troops reclaim control over Chechen capital of Grozny after secession attempt. Chechen rebels retreat to surrounding hillsides and vow to continue fight for independence.

Mexican economy badly damaged by devaluation of peso. Fiscal crisis results in massive loan guarantees from foreign countries to prevent further weakening of Mexican economy.

Massacre of Israeli citizens by Islamic terrorists threatens to undermine peace accord between Israel and PLO.

Serbian leaders reject peace plan for Croatia and Bosnia-Herzegovina, signaling continuation of struggle.

NATO officials place Poland and Hungary on fast track for membership, despite threats of "Cold Peace" by Russia's Boris Yeltsin.

United States and China threaten trade war over the latter's alleged violations of international copyright laws.

U.S. Marines deployed to Somalia to oversee evacuation of UN peacekeeping forces.

Republican majority in U.S. Congress promotes "National Security Restoration Act" calling for increased defense spending, cutbacks in foreign aid, and reduced support for UN peace-keeping efforts. Clinton administration resists most Republican measures.

Control over peace-keeping mission in Haiti transferred from United States to United Nations.

Select Bibliography

All of the entries in this bibliography are books. Readers who wish to keep up with the journal literature on American foreign policy will find the articles in *Foreign Affairs, Foreign Policy,* and *International Security* useful and relevant.

AMERICAN SOCIETY AND STYLE IN FOREIGN POLICY

Almond, Gabriel A. *The American People and Foreign Policy.* New York: Praeger, 1960.

Boorstin, Daniel J. *The Genius of American Politics.* Chicago: Phoenix Books, 1953.

Dallek, Robert. *The American Style of Foreign Policy.* New York: Knopf, 1983.

Hartz, Louis. *The Liberal Tradition in America.* New York: Harvest Books, 1955.

Herberg, Will. *Protestant, Catholic, and Jew.* Rev. ed. New York: Anchor Books, 1960.

Hofstadter, Richard. *The Paranoid Style in American Politics.* New York: Vintage Books, 1967.

Hunt, Michael H. *Ideology and U.S. Foreign Policy.* New Haven: Yale University Press, 1987.

Kennan, George F. *American Diplomacy, 1900-1950.* Chicago: University of Chicago Press, 1951.

Lippmann, Walter. *U.S. Foreign Policy: Shield of the Republic.* Boston: Little, Brown, 1943.

McElroy, Robert W. *Morality and American Foreign Policy.* Princeton: Princeton University Press, 1992.

Morgenthau, Hans J. *In Defense of the National Interest.* New York: Knopf, 1951.

Nichols, Bruce, and Gil Loescher, eds. *The Moral Nation.* South Bend, Ind.: University of Notre Dame Press, 1989.

Osgood, Robert. *Ideals and Self-Interest in America's Foreign Relations.* Chicago: University of Chicago Press, 1953.

Potter, David M. *The People of Plenty.* Chicago: Phoenix Books, 1954.

Stoessinger, John G. *Crusaders and Pragmatists.* 2d ed. New York: Norton, 1985.

Thompson, Kenneth W. *Traditions and Values in Politics and Diplomacy.* Baton Rouge: Louisiana State University Press, 1992.

von Vorys, Karl. *American National Interest.* New York: Praeger, 1990.

Weigel, George. *American Interests, American Purpose.* New York: Praeger, 1989.

AMERICAN FOREIGN POLICY DURING THE COLD WAR

Aron, Raymond. *The Imperial Republic.* Cambridge: Winthrop, 1974.

Bell, Coral. *The Diplomacy of Détente.* New York: St. Martin's, 1977.

Bowker, Mike, and Phil Williams. *Superpower Détente.* Newbury Park, Calif.: Sage Publications, 1988.

Brzezinski, Zbigniew. *Game Plan.* Boston: Atlantic Monthly Press, 1986.

Cingranelli, David Louis. *Ethics, American Foreign Policy, and the Third World.* New York: St. Martin's, 1993.

Dukes, Paul. *The Last Great Game.* New York: St. Martin's, 1989.

Fulbright, J. William. *The Arrogance of Power.* New York: Vintage Books, 1967.

———. *The Crippled Giant.* New York: Vintage Books, 1972.

———. *Old Myths and New Realities.* New York: Vintage Books, 1964.

Gaddis, John L. *The Long Peace.* New York: Oxford University Press, 1987.

————. *Russia, the Soviet Union and the United States.* New York: Wiley, 1978.

————. *Strategies of Containment.* New York: Oxford University Press, 1982.

————. *The United States and the Origins of the Cold War, 1941-1947.* New York: Columbia University Press, 1972.

Halle, Louis J. *The Cold War as History.* New York: Harper and Row, 1967.

Hoffmann, Stanley. *Gulliver's Troubles, or the Setting of American Foreign Policy.* New York: McGraw-Hill, 1968.

————. *Primacy or World Order.* New York: McGraw-Hill, 1978.

Larson, Deborah Welch. *Origins of Containment.* Princeton: Princeton University Press, 1985.

Leffler, Melvyn P. *A Preponderance of Power.* Stanford: Stanford University Press, 1992.

Leffler, Melvyn P., and David Painter, eds. *The Origins of the Cold War.* New York: Routledge, 1994.

McNamara, Robert S. *Out of the Cold.* New York: Simon and Schuster, 1989.

Mandelbaum, Richard, and Strobe Talbott. *Reagan and Gorbachev.* New York: Vintage Books, 1987.

Moens, Alexander. *Foreign Policy under Carter.* Boulder, Colo.: Westview Press, 1990.

Muravchik, Joshua. *The Uncertain Crusade.* New York: Hamilton Press, 1985.

Osgood, Robert, et al. *America and the World.* Baltimore: Johns Hopkins University Press, 1970.

————. *Retreat from Empire?* Baltimore: Johns Hopkins University Press, 1973.

Sanders, Jerry W. *Peddlers of Crisis.* Boston: South End Press, 1983.

Schlesinger, Arthur, Jr. *The Imperial Presidency.* Boston: Houghton Mifflin, 1973.

Schulzinger, Robert D. *The Wise Men of Foreign Affairs.* New York: Columbia University Press, 1985.

Smith, Gaddis. *Morality, Reason, and Power.* New York: Hill and Wang, 1986.

Steel, Ronald. *Pax Americana.* New York: Viking Press, 1967.

Tillema, Herbert K. *Appeal to Force.* New York: Crowell, 1973.

Tucker, Robert W. *The Purposes of American Power.* New York: Praeger, 1981.

Wilmot, Chester. *The Struggle for Europe.* New York: Hayes and Brothers, 1952.

Yergin, Daniel. *Shattered Peace.* Boston: Houghton Mifflin, 1977.

American Foreign Policy after the Cold War

Art, Robert J., and Seyom Brown, eds. *U.S. Foreign Policy: The Search for a New Role.* New York: Macmillan, 1993.

Brzezinski, Zbigniew. *Out of Control.* New York: Scribner's, 1993.

Chace, James. *The Consequences of the Peace.* New York: Oxford University Press, 1992.

Fry, Earl H. *America the Vincible.* Englewood Cliffs, N.J.: Prentice Hall, 1994.

Gaddis, John Lewis. *The United States and the End of the Cold War.* New York: Oxford University Press, 1992.

Garten, Jeffrey E. *A Cold Peace.* New York: Times Books, 1992.

Garthoff, Raymond. *The Great Transition.* Washington, D.C.: Brookings, 1994.

Huntington, Samuel P. *The Third Wave.* Norman: University of Oklahoma Press, 1991.

Hyland, William G. *The Cold War Is Over.* New York: Times Books, 1990.

Kapstein, Ethan B., ed. *Downsizing Defense.* Washington, D.C.: CQ Press, 1990.

Kegley, Charles W., Jr., and Gregory A. Raymond. *A Multipolar Peace?* New York: St. Martin's, 1994.

Kennedy, Paul. *Preparing for the Twenty-First Century.* New York: Random House, 1993.

Kissinger, Henry. *Diplomacy.* New York: Simon and Schuster, 1994.

Mueller, John. *Retreat From Doomsday.* New York: Basic Books, 1989.

Muller, Steven, and Gebhard Schweigler, eds. *From Occupation to Cooperation.* New York: Norton, 1992.

Nau, Richard. *The Myth of America's Decline.* New York: Oxford University Press, 1990.

Nye, Joseph S., Jr. *Bound to Lead.* New York: Basic Books, 1990.

Oye, Kenneth A., Robert J. Lieber, and Donald Rothchild. *Eagle in a New World.* New York: HarperCollins, 1992.

Payne, Richard J. *The Western European Allies, the Third World, and U.S. Foreign Policy.* New York: Greenwood, 1991.

Rubenstein, Alvin Z., ed. *America's National Interests in a Post-Cold War World.* New York: McGraw-Hill, 1994.

Russett, Bruce M. *Grasping the Democratic Peace.* Princeton: Princeton University Press, 1993.

Treverton, Gregory F. *America, Germany, and the Future of Europe.* Princeton: Princeton University Press, 1992.

Tucker, Robert W., and David C. Hendrickson. *The Imperial Temptation.* New York: Council on Foreign Relations, 1992.

DIPLOMATIC HISTORIES

Bailey, Thomas. *A Diplomatic History of the American People.* 10th ed. Englewood Cliffs, N.J.: Prentice Hall, 1980.

Bemis, Samuel. *A Diplomatic History of the United States.* 4th ed. New York: Holt, 1955.

Clarfield, Gerard. *U.S. Diplomatic History.* 2 vols. Englewood Cliffs, N.J.: Prentice Hall, 1992.

Combs, Jerald A. *The History of American Foreign Policy.* New York: Macmillan, 1975.

DeConde, Alexander. *A History of American Foreign Policy.* 3d ed. 2 vols. New York: Scribner's, 1978.

Ferrell, Robert H. *American Diplomacy.* 4th ed. New York: Norton, 1988.

Fleming, D. F. *The Cold War and Its Origins, 1917-1960.* 2 vols. Garden City, N.Y.: Doubleday, 1961.

Jones, Howard. *The Course of American Diplomacy.* 2d ed. Chicago: Dorsey Press, 1988.

Pratt, Julius W. *A History of United States Foreign Policy.* New York: Prentice Hall, 1955.

Rappaport, Armin. *A History of American Diplomacy.* New York: Macmillan, 1975.

Schulzinger, Robert D. *American Diplomacy in the Twentieth Century.* 3d ed. New York: Oxford University Press, 1994.

REVISIONIST INTERPRETATIONS AND DEBATES

Alperovitz, Gar. *Atomic Diplomacy.* New York: Vintage Books, 1967.

Barnet, Richard. *Roots of War.* New York: Atheneum, 1972.

Kolko, Gabriel. *The Roots of American Foreign Policy.* Boston: Beacon Press, 1969.

Kolko, Gabriel, and Joyce Kolko. *The Limits of Power.* New York: Harper and Row, 1972.

Kwitny, Jonathan. *Endless Enemies.* New York: Penguin, 1984.

LaFeber, Walter. *America, Russia, and the Cold War, 1945-1980.* New York: Wiley, 1981.

———. *The New Empire.* Ithaca: Cornell University Press, 1963.

Lebow, Richard Ned, and Janice Gross Stein. *We All Lost the Cold War.* Princeton: Princeton University Press, 1994.

Lens, Sidney. *The Forging of the American Empire.* New York: Crowell, 1971.

Maddox, Robert J. *The New Left and the Origins of the Cold War.* Princeton: Princeton University Press, 1973.

Melanson, Richard A. *Writing History and Making Policy.* Lanham, Md.: University Press of America, 1983.

Parenti, Michael. *The Sword and the Dollar*. New York: St. Martin's, 1989.

Paterson, Thomas G. *On Every Front*. New York: Norton, 1979.

———. *Soviet-American Confrontation*. Baltimore: Johns Hopkins University Press, 1973.

Tucker, Robert W. *The Radical Left and American Foreign Policy*. Baltimore: Johns Hopkins University Press, 1971.

Williams, William Appleman. *The Tragedy of American Diplomacy*. New York: Norton, 1988.

AMERICAN MILITARY STRATEGY

Blechman, Barry M., and Stephen S. Kaplan. *Force without War*. Washington, D.C.: Brookings, 1978.

Blight, James G., and David A. Welch. *On the Brink*. New York: Hill and Wang, 1989.

Brown, Harold. *The Strategic Defense Initiative*. Boulder, Colo.: Westview Press, 1987.

Dinerstein, Herbert. *The Making of a Missile Crisis*. Baltimore: Johns Hopkins University Press, 1976.

Emerson, Steven. *Secret Warriors*. New York: Putnam, 1988.

Flournoy, Michele A. *Nuclear Weapons after the Cold War*. New York: HarperCollins, 1993.

Freedman, Lawrence. *The Evolution of Nuclear Strategy*. 2d ed. New York: St. Martin's, 1989.

George, Alexander L., and Richard Smoke. *Deterrence in American Foreign Policy*. New York: Columbia University Press, 1974.

Gertcher, Frank L., and William Weide. *Beyond Deterrence*. Boulder, Colo.: Westview Press, 1990.

Glynn, Patrick. *Closing Pandora's Box*. New York: Basic Books, 1992.

Gray, Colin. *Nuclear Strategy and Nuclear Planning*. Philadelphia: Foreign Policy Research Institute, 1985.

———. *The Soviet-American Arms Race*. Lexington, Mass.: Lexington Books, 1976.

Herken, Gregg. *Counsels of War*. New York: Oxford University Press, 1987.

Hermann, Charles P., ed. *American Defense Annual*. 9th ed. New York: Lexington Books, 1994.

Jervis, Robert. *The Illogic of American National Strategy*. Ithaca: Cornell University Press, 1984.

Kissinger, Henry A. *The Necessity for Choice*. New York: Anchor Books, 1961.

———. *Nuclear Weapons and Foreign Policy*. New York: Harper and Brothers, 1957.

———. *The Troubled Partnership*. New York: Anchor Books, 1966.

Krepon, Michael. *Arms Control in the Reagan Administration*. Lanham, Md.: University Press of America, 1989.

Landau, Saul. *The Dangerous Doctrine*. Boulder, Colo.: Westview Press, 1988.

Levine, Robert A. *Still the Arms Debate*. Brookfield, Vt.: Dartmouth Publishing, 1990.

Luttwak, Edward N. *The Pentagon and the Art of War*. New York: Simon and Schuster, 1985.

McNamara, Robert S. *Blundering into Disaster*. New York: Parthenon Books, 1987.

Nolan, Janne E. *Guardians of the Arsenal*. New York: Basic Books, 1989.

Payne, Keith P. *Strategic Defense*. Lanham, Md.: Hamilton Press, 1986.

Powell, Robert. *Nuclear Deterrence Theory*. New York: Cambridge University Press, 1990.

Schwartz, William A., and Charles Derber. *The Nuclear Seduction*. Berkeley: University of California Press, 1990.

Smoke, Richard. *National Security and the Nuclear Dilemma*. 3d ed. New York: Random House, 1992.

Talbott, Strobe. *Deadly Gambits*. New York: Knopf, 1984.

————. *End Game.* New York: Harper and Row, 1980.

Tucker, Robert W. *The Nuclear Debate.* New York: Holmes and Meier, 1985.

Wolfe, Thomas W. *The SALT Experience.* Cambridge, Mass.: Ballinger, 1979.

AMERICAN POLICY IN EUROPE AND THE FORMER SOVIET UNION

Bialer, Seweryn, and Michael Mandelbaum. *The Global Rivals.* New York: Knopf, 1988.

————. *Gorbachev's Russia and American Foreign Policy.* Boulder, Colo.: Westview Press, 1988.

Blaney, John W., ed. *The Successor States to the USSR.* Washington, D.C.: CQ Press, 1995.

Cook, Don. *Forging the Alliance.* New York: Arbor House, 1989.

DePorte, A. W. *Europe between the Superpowers.* New Haven: Yale University Press, 1985.

Flanagan, Stephen J., and Fen O. Hampton, eds. *Securing Europe's Future.* Dover, Mass.: Auburn House, 1986.

Freedman, Lawrence, ed. *Europe Transformed.* New York: St. Martin's, 1990.

Grosser, Alfred. *The Western Alliance.* New York: Vintage Books, 1982.

Harrison, Glennon J. *Europe and the United States.* Armonk, N.Y.: M. E. Sharpe, 1994.

Holborn, Hajo. *The Political Collapse of Europe.* New York: Knopf, 1951.

Joffe, Josef. *The Limited Partnership.* Cambridge, Mass.: Ballinger, 1987.

Jones, Joseph. *The Fifteen Weeks.* New York: Viking Press, 1955.

Kapstein, Ethan B. *The Insecure Alliance.* New York: Oxford University Press, 1990.

Kleiman, Robert. *Atlantic Crisis.* New York: Norton, 1964.

Krauss, Melvyn. *How NATO Weakens the West.* New York: Simon and Schuster, 1986.

Laquer, Walter. *The Dream that Failed.* New York: Oxford University Press, 1994.

Midlarsky, Manus I., John A. Vasquez, and Peter V. Gladkov. *From Rivalry to Cooperation.* New York: HarperCollins, 1994.

Osgood, Robert E. *NATO.* Chicago: University of Chicago Press, 1962.

Sherwood, Elizabeth. *Allies in Crisis.* New Haven: Yale University Press, 1990.

Stokes, Gale. *The Walls Came Tumbling Down.* New York: Oxford University Press, 1993.

Tow, William T. *The Limits of Alliance.* Baltimore: Johns Hopkins University Press, 1990.

Treverton, Gregory F. *America, Germany, and the Future of Europe.* Princeton: Princeton University Press, 1990.

————. *Making the Alliance Work.* Ithaca: Cornell University Press, 1986.

Tucker, Robert W., and Linda Wrigley. *The Atlantic Alliance and Its Critics.* New York: Praeger, 1983.

Ullman, Richard H. *Securing Europe.* Princeton: Princeton University Press, 1991.

AMERICAN POLICY IN EAST ASIA

Balassa, Bela, and Marcus Noland. *Japan and the World Economy.* Washington, D.C.: Institute for International Economics, 1988.

Baritz, Loren. *Backfire.* New York: Morrow, 1985.

Barnett, A. Doak. *China Policy.* Washington, D.C.: Brookings, 1977.

Berman, Larry. *Lyndon Johnson's War.* New York: Norton, 1989.

Buckley, Roger. *U.S.-Japan Alliance Diplomacy, 1945-1990.* New York: Cambridge University Press, 1992.

Carter, K. Holly Maze. *The Asian Dilemma in U.S. Foreign Policy.* Armonk, N.Y.: M. E. Sharpe, 1989.

Cohen, Warren I. *America's Response to China.* 3d ed. New York: Columbia University Press, 1989.

Cumings, Bruce. *The Origins of the Korean War.* Princeton: Princeton University Press, 1981.

DiLeo, David L. *George Ball, Vietnam, and the Rethinking of Containment.* Chapel Hill: University of North Carolina Press, 1991.

Dulles, Foster R. *American Foreign Policy toward Communist China.* New York: Crowell, 1972.

Feis, Herbert. *China Tangle.* Princeton: Princeton University Press, 1953.

Gelb, Leslie, and Richard K. Betts. *The Irony of Vietnam.* Washington, D.C.: Brookings, 1979.

Gelb, Leslie, et al. *The Pentagon Papers.* New York: Bantam Books, 1971.

Halberstam, David. *The Best and the Brightest.* New York: Random House, 1969.

Herring, George C. *America's Longest War.* 2d ed. New York: Wiley, 1988.

———. *LBJ and Vietnam.* Austin: University of Texas Press, 1994.

Karnow, Stanley C. *Vietnam.* New York: Viking Press, 1983.

Kattenburg, Paul. *The Vietnam Trauma in American Foreign Policy, 1945-1975.* New Brunswick: Transaction Books, 1980.

Meisner, Maurice. *Mao's China.* New York: Free Press, 1977.

Merrill, John. *Korea.* Newark: University of Delaware Press, 1989.

Sheehan, Neil. *A Bright Shining Lie.* New York: Random House, 1988.

Spanier, John W. *The Truman-MacArthur Controversy and the Korean War.* Rev. ed. New York: Norton, 1965.

Tow, William T. *Encountering the Dominant Player.* New York: Columbia University Press, 1991.

Tsou, Tang. *America's Failure in China, 1941-1950.* 2 vols. Chicago: Phoenix Books, 1963.

AMERICAN POLICY IN THE MIDDLE EAST

Bill, James A. *The Eagle and the Lion.* New Haven: Yale University Press, 1988.

Cohen, Roger, and Claudio Gati. *In The Eyes of the Storm.* New York: Farrar, Straus and Giroux, 1991.

Cottam, Richard W. *Iran and the United States.* Pittsburgh: University of Pittsburgh Press, 1988.

Doran, Charles, *Myth, Oil and Politics.* New York: Free Press, 1977.

Gasiorowski, Mark J. *U.S. Foreign Policy and the Shah.* Ithaca: Cornell University Press, 1991.

Golan, Galia. *Yom Kippur and After.* New York: Cambridge University Press, 1977.

Lenczowski, George. *American Presidents and the Middle East.* Durham, N.C.: Duke University Press, 1990.

Miller, Judith, and Lauria Mylroie. *Saddam Hussein and the Crisis in the Gulf.* New York: Times Books, 1990.

Quandt, William. *Camp David.* Washington, D.C.: Brookings, 1986.

———. *Peace Process.* Washington, D.C.: Brookings, 1994.

Renshon, Stanley A., ed. *The Political Psychology of the Gulf War.* Pittsburgh: University of Pittsburgh Press, 1993.

Roger, Louis, and Owen Roger, eds. *Suez 1956.* New York: Oxford, 1989.

Sadat, Anwar. *In Search of Identity.* New York: Harper and Row, 1978.

Safran, Nadav. *Intifada.* New York: Simon and Schuster, 1989.

———. *Israel: The Embattled Ally.* Cambridge: Harvard University Press, 1978.

———. *Saudi Arabia: The Ceaseless Quest for Security.* Cambridge: Harvard University Press, 1985.

Sick, Gary. *All Fall Down.* New York: Penguin Books, 1986.

Spiegel, Steven L. *The Other Arab-Israeli Conflict*. Chicago: University of Chicago Press, 1985.

Woodward, Bob. *The Commanders*. New York: Simon and Schuster, 1991.

AMERICAN POLICY IN AFRICA

Alinghaus, Bruce E., ed. *Arms for Africa*. Lexington, Mass.: Lexington Books, 1983.

Bender, Gerald, James Coleman, and Richard Sklar, eds. *African Crisis Areas and U.S. Foreign Policy*. Berkeley: University of California Press, 1985.

Chester, Edward W. *Clash of Titans*. Maryknoll, N.Y.: Orbis, 1974.

Dickson, David A. *United States Foreign Policy toward Sub-Saharan Africa*. Lanham, Md.: University Press of America, 1985.

Feinberg, Richard E. *The Intemperate Zone*. New York: Norton, 1983.

Giliomee, Hermann, and Lawrence Schlemmer. *From Apartheid to Nation Building*. New York: Oxford University Press, 1990.

Jackson, Henry F. *From the Congo to Soweto: U.S. Foreign Policy toward Africa since 1960*. New York: Morrow, 1982.

Layachi, Azzedine. *The United States and North Africa*. New York: Praeger, 1990.

Lemarchand, René, ed. *American Policy in Southern Africa*. Washington, D.C.: University Press of America, 1978.

Packenham, Robert A. *Liberal America and the Third World*. Princeton: Princeton University Press, 1973.

Price, Robert M. *U.S. Foreign Policy in Sub-Saharan Africa*. Berkeley: Institute of International Studies, University of California, 1978.

Schraeder, Peter J. *United States Foreign Policy toward Africa*. New York: Cambridge University Press, 1994.

Skinner, Elliott P. *Beyond Constructive Engagement*. New York: Paragon Press, 1986.

AMERICAN POLICY IN LATIN AMERICA

Blasier, Cole. *The Hovering Giant*. Rev. ed. Pittsburgh: University of Pittsburgh Press, 1985.

Dinges, John. *Our Man in Panama*. New York: Random House, 1990.

Domínguez, Jorge I. *To Make a World Safe for Revolution*. Cambridge: Harvard University Press, 1989.

Draper, Theodore. *The Dominican Revolt*. New York: Commentary, 1968.

Duncan, W. Raymond. *The Soviet Union and Cuba*. New York: Praeger, 1985.

Erisman, H. Michael. *Cuba's International Relations*. Boulder, Colo.: Westview Press, 1985.

Gutman, Roy. *Banana Diplomacy*. New York: Simon and Schuster, 1988.

LaFeber, Walter. *Inevitable Revolutions*. New York: Norton, 1983.

Lake, Anthony. *Somoza Falling*. Boston: Houghton Mifflin, 1989.

———. *The "Tar Baby" Option*. New York: Columbia University Press, 1976.

Lowenthal, Abraham F. *Partners in Conflict*. Baltimore: Johns Hopkins University Press, 1987.

Pastor, Robert A. *Condemned to Repetition*. Princeton: Princeton University Press, 1987.

———. *Whirlpool*. Princeton: Princeton University Press, 1993.

Rabe, Stephen G. *Eisenhower and Latin America*. Chapel Hill: University of North Carolina Press, 1988.

Schlesinger, Stephen, and Stephen Kinzer. *Bitter Fruit*. Garden City, N.Y.: Anchor Books, 1982.

Shafer, Michael D. *Deadly Paradigms*. Princeton: Princeton University Press, 1988.

Sigmund, Paul. *The Overthrow of Allende and the Politics of Chile.* Pittsburgh: University of Pittsburgh Press, 1977.

Suchliki, Jaime. *Cuba.* New York: Brassey's, 1990.

AMERICA AND THE INTERNATIONAL POLITICAL ECONOMY

Baldwin, David A. *Economic Statecraft.* Princeton: Princeton University Press, 1985.

Bergsten, C. Fred. *America in the World Economy.* Washington, D.C.: Institute for International Economics, 1988.

Bhagwati, Jagdish. *The World Trading System at Risk.* Princeton: Princeton University Press, 1991.

Bhagwati, Jagdish, and Hugh T. Patrick, eds. *Aggressive Unilateralism.* Ann Arbor: University of Michigan Press, 1990.

Brown, Harrison. *The Human Future Revisited.* New York: Norton, 1978.

Cohen, Benjamin J. *In Whose Interest?* New Haven: Yale University Press, 1986.

Destler, I. M. *American Trade Politics.* 2d ed. Washington, D.C.: Twentieth Century Fund, 1992.

———. *Making Foreign Economic Policy.* Washington, D.C.: Brookings, 1980.

Friedberg, Aaron L. *The Weary Titan.* Princeton: Princeton University Press, 1988.

Gertcher, Frank L., and William Weide. *The Political Economy of National Defense.* Boulder, Colo.: Westview Press, 1987.

Gilpin, Robert. *The Political Economy of International Relations.* Princeton: Princeton University Press, 1987.

Hook, Steven W. *National Interest and Foreign Aid.* Boulder, Colo.: Lynne Rienner, 1995.

Kapstein, Ethan B. *The Political Economy of National Security.* New York: McGraw-Hill, 1992.

Krasner, Stephen D. *Structural Conflict.* Berkeley: University of California Press, 1985.

Lewis, Arthur. *The Evolution of the International Economic Order.* Princeton: Princeton University Press, 1978.

Prestowitz, Clyde. *Trading Places.* New York: Basic Books, 1988.

Reich, Robert. *The Work of Nations.* New York: Vintage, 1992.

Rosecrance, Richard. *America's Economic Resurgence.* New York: Harper and Row, 1990.

Rothstein, Robert. *The Weak in the World of the Strong.* New York: Columbia University Press, 1977.

Spero, Joan. *The Politics of International Economic Relations.* 4th ed. New York: St. Martin's, 1990.

Thurow, Lester C. *The Zero-Sum Solution.* New York: Simon and Schuster, 1985.

Tucker, Robert. *Inequality of Nations.* New York: Basic Books, 1977.

Tulchin, Martin, and Susan Tulchin. *Buying into America.* New York: Times Books, 1988.

Vogel, Ezra. *Japan as Number One.* New York: Harper and Row, 1979.

DOMESTIC POLITICS AND AMERICAN FOREIGN POLICY

Allison, Graham T. *Essence of Decision.* Boston: Little, Brown, 1971.

Barnet, Richard. *The Rockets Red Glare.* New York: Touchstone, 1990.

Blechman, Barry. *The Politics of National Security.* New York: Oxford University Press, 1990.

Caldwell, Daniel. *The Dynamics of Domestic Politics and Arms Control.* Columbia: University of South Carolina Press, 1991.

Charles-Philippe, David. *Foreign Policy Failure in the White House.* Lanham, Md.: University Press of America, 1994.

Crabb, Cecil V., Jr., and Pat M. Holt. *Invitation to Struggle.* 4th ed. Washington, D.C.: CQ Press, 1992.

Crabb, Cecil V., Jr., and Kevin V. Mulcahy. *Presidents and Foreign Policy Making.* Baton Rouge: Louisiana State University Press, 1986.

Darling, Arthur B. *The Central Intelligence Agency.* University Park: Pennsylvania State University Press, 1990.

Destler, I. M., Leslie H. Gelb, and Anthony Lake. *Our Own Worst Enemy.* New York: Simon and Schuster, 1984.

Dumbrell, John. *The Making of U.S. Foreign Policy.* New York: Manchester University Press, 1990.

Franck, Thomas M., and Edward Weisband. *Foreign Policy by Congress.* New York: Oxford University Press, 1979.

Halperin, Morton H. *Bureaucratic Politics and Foreign Policy.* Washington, D.C.: Brookings, 1974.

Henkin, Louis. *Foreign Affairs and the Constitution.* New York: Norton, 1972.

Hughes, Barry B. *The Domestic Context of American Foreign Policy.* San Francisco: W. H. Freeman, 1978.

Johnson, Loch K. *America's Secret Power.* New York: Oxford University Press, 1989.

Lord, Carnes. *The Presidency and the Management of National Security.* New York: Free Press, 1988.

McNaugher, Thomas L. *New Weapons, Old Politics.* Washington, D.C.: Brookings, 1989.

Mann, Thomas E., ed. *A Question of Balance.* Washington, D.C.: Brookings, 1990.

May, Christopher. *In the Name of War.* Cambridge: Harvard University Press, 1989.

Nathan, James A., and James K. Oliver. *Foreign Policy Making and the American Political System.* 2d ed. Boston: Little, Brown, 1987.

Pastor, Robert A. *Congress and the Politics of U.S. Foreign Economic Policy.* Berkeley: University of California Press, 1980.

Richelson, Jeffrey T. *The U.S. Intelligence Community.* Cambridge, Mass.: Ballinger, 1985.

Ripley, Randall B., and James Lindsay. *Congress Resurgent.* Ann Arbor: University of Michigan Press, 1993.

Rosati, Jerel A. *The Carter Administration's Quest for Global Community.* Columbia: University of South Carolina Press, 1987.

———. *The Politics of U.S. Foreign Policy.* Fort Worth: Harcourt Brace Jovanovich, 1993.

Rosenau, James N., and Ole R. Holsti. *American Leadership in World Affairs.* Boston: Allen and Unwin, 1984.

Rubin, Barry. *Secrets of State.* New York: Oxford University Press, 1985.

Shuman, Howard E., and Walter R. Thomas. *The Constitution and National Security.* Washington, D.C.: National Defense University Press, 1990.

Sobel, Richard, ed. *Public Opinion in U.S. Foreign Policy.* Lanham, Md.: Rowman and Littlefield, 1993.

Tivnan, Edward. *The Lobby.* New York: Simon and Schuster, 1987.

Tucker, Robert H., Charles B. Keely, and Linda Wrigley, eds. *Immigration and U.S. Foreign Policy.* Boulder, Colo.: Westview Press, 1990.

Warburg, Gerald. *Conflict and Consensus.* Cambridge, Mass.: Ballinger, 1989.

Wittkopf, Eugene R. *Faces of Internationalism.* Durham, N.C.: Duke University Press, 1990.

Yankelovich, Daniel, and I. M. Destler, eds. *Beyond the Beltway.* New York: Norton, 1994.

MEMOIRS AND BIOGRAPHIES OF AMERICAN LEADERS

Acheson, Dean. *Present at the Creation.* New York: Norton, 1969.

Ambrose, Stephen E. *Eisenhower.* 2 vols. New York: Simon and Schuster, 1983 and 1984.

———. *Nixon.* New York: Simon and Schuster, 1992.

Andrianopoulos, Gerry A. *Kissinger and Brzezinski.* New York: St. Martin's, 1991.

Brands, H. W. *The Wages of Globalism.* New York: Oxford University Press, 1994.

Brinkley, Douglas, ed. *Dean Acheson and the Making of U.S. Foreign Policy.* New York: St. Martin's, 1993.

Brown, Harold. *Thinking About National Security.* Boulder, Colo.: Westview Press, 1983.

Brzezinski, Zbigniew. *Power and Principle.* New York: Farrar, Straus and Giroux, 1983.

Bullock, Alan. *Hitler and Stalin.* New York: Knopf, 1992.

Bundy, McGeorge. *Danger and Survival.* New York: Random House, 1988.

Byrnes, James F. *Speaking Frankly.* New York: Harper and Brothers, 1947.

Cannon, Lou. *Reagan.* New York: Random House, 1981.

Carter, Jimmy. *Keeping Faith.* New York: Bantam Books, 1982.

Clifford, Clark M. *Counsel to the President.* New York: Random House, 1991.

Conquest, Richard. *Stalin.* New York: Viking, 1991.

Dallek, Robert. *Franklin D. Roosevelt and American Foreign Policy, 1932-1945.* New York: Oxford University Press, 1979.

Eisenhower, David. *Eisenhower at War.* New York: Random House, 1986.

Eisenhower, Dwight D. *Mandate for Change.* New York: New American Library, 1965.

———. *Waging Peace.* New York: Doubleday, 1965.

Feis, Herbert. *Churchill, Roosevelt, Stalin.* Princeton: Princeton University Press, 1957.

Ferrell, Robert H. *George C. Marshall.* New York: Cooper Square Publishers, 1966.

Guhin, Michael. *John Foster Dulles.* New York: Columbia University Press, 1972.

Hoopes, Townsend. *The Devil and John Foster Dulles.* Boston: Atlantic/Little, Brown, 1975.

Immerman, Richard H. *John Foster Dulles and the Diplomacy of the Cold War.* Princeton: Princeton University Press, 1990.

Isaacson, Walter. *Kissinger.* New York: Simon and Schuster, 1992.

Isaacson, Walter, and Evan Thomas. *The Wise Men.* New York: Simon and Schuster, 1986.

Johnson, Lyndon B. *The Vantage Point.* New York: Popular Library, 1971.

Kalb, Marvin, and Bernard Kalb. *Kissinger.* Boston: Little, Brown, 1974.

Kearns, Doris. *Lyndon Johnson and the American Dream.* New York: Harper and Row, 1976.

Kennan, George F. *Memoirs.* Boston: Little, Brown, 1967.

Kennedy, Robert S. *Thirteen Days.* New York: Norton, 1971.

Kissinger, Henry A. *The White House Years.* Boston: Little, Brown, 1979.

———. *Years of Upheaval.* Boston: Little, Brown, 1982.

McCullough, David. *Truman.* New York: Simon and Schuster, 1992.

McFarlane, Robert C., with Zofia Smardz. *Special Trust.* New York: Cadell and Davies, 1994.

McLellan, David S. *Cyrus Vance.* Totowa, N.J.: Rowman and Allanheld, 1985.

Manchester, William. *American Caesar.* Boston: Little, Brown, 1978.

Miscamble, Wilson D. *George F. Kennan and the Making of American Foreign Policy, 1947-1950.* Princeton: Princeton University Press, 1992.

Nixon, Richard. *RN.* New York: Grosset and Dunlap, 1978.

———. *Seize the Moment.* New York: Simon and Schuster, 1992.

Parmet, Herbert S. *Eisenhower and the American Crusades.* New York: Macmillan, 1972.

Pogue, Forrest C. *George C. Marshall.* New York: Viking Press, 1987.

Rusk, Dean, as told to Richard Rusk. *As I Saw It.* New York: Norton, 1990.

Schlesinger, Arthur M., Jr. *A Thousand Days.* New York: Crest Books, 1967.

Schulzinger, Robert D. *Henry Kissinger.* New York: Columbia University Press, 1989.

Sherwood, Robert E. *Roosevelt and Hopkins.* New York: Harper, 1948.

Smith, Gaddis. *Dean Acheson.* New York: Cooper Square Publishers, 1972.

Sorensen, Theodore C. *Kennedy.* New York: Bantam Books, 1966.

Starr, Harvey. *Henry Kissinger: Perception of International Politics.* Lexington: University Press of Kentucky, 1984.

Stoessinger, John. *Henry Kissinger.* New York: Norton, 1976.

Truman, Harry S. *Memoirs.* 2 vols. New York: New American Library, 1965.

Vance, Cyrus. *Hard Choices.* New York: Simon and Schuster, 1982.

Weinberger, Caspar W. *Fighting for Peace.* New York: Warner, 1990.

Index